OTHER DIPLOMA(

Cuba and Canada in the Shadow of the US

Other Diplomacies, Other Ties explores Cuba-Canada relations following the Revolution of 1959 and the major geopolitical and economic transformations that have occurred in recent years.

Through the conceptual lens of "other diplomacies," which emphasizes interactions among non-state actors, the contributors challenge the conventional wisdom regarding the actions of diplomats, politicians, journalists, spies, and émigrés. Featuring both Cuban and Canadian contributors, the volume offers a diverse range of research methodologies, including ethnography, archival work, and policy analysis, to encourage critical examination about the problems, possibilities, and promise of the long-standing relationship between Canada and Cuba. All decades of the post-1959 relationship – from the dramatic early years during which the diplomatic and political relationship was negotiated to contemporary education exchanges and the gradual formation of Cuban-Canadian diasporas – are critically reappraised.

Other Diplomacies, Other Ties is a nuanced and unique volume that also crucially gives voice to Cuban scholars' perspectives on the Cuba-Canada relationship.

LUIS RENÉ FERNÁNDEZ TABÍO is a senior professor and researcher at the University of Havana.

CYNTHIA WRIGHT is an assistant professor in the School of Gender, Sexuality, and Women's Studies at York University.

LANA WYLIE is an associate professor in the Department of Political Science at McMaster University.

Other Diplomacies, Other Ties

Cuba and Canada in the Shadow of the US

EDITED BY LUIS RENÉ FERNÁNDEZ TABÍO, CYNTHIA WRIGHT, AND LANA WYLIE

UNIVERSITY OF TORONTO PRESS
Toronto Buffalo London

© University of Toronto Press 2018
Toronto Buffalo London
www.utorontopress.com
Printed in Canada

ISBN 978-1-4426-5022-0 (cloth)   ISBN 978-1-4426-2831-1 (paper)

♾ Printed on acid-free, 100% post-consumer recycled paper
with vegetable-based inks.

Library and Archives Canada Cataloguing in Publication

Other diplomacies, other ties : Cuba and Canada in the shadow of the
US / edited by Luis René Fernández Tabío, Cynthia Wright, and Lana Wylie.

Includes bibliographical references and index.
ISBN 978-1-4426-5022-0 (cloth). – ISBN 978-1-4426-2831-1 (paper)

1. Canada – Relations – Cuba.   2. Cuba – Relations – Canada.
I. Fernández Tabío, Luis René, editor   II. Wright, Cynthia, 1957–, editor
III. Wylie, Lana, 1968–, editor

FC251.C82O84 2018   327.7107291   C2017-906092-9

This book has been published with the help of a grant from the Federation
for the Humanities and Social Sciences, through the Awards to Scholarly
Publications Program, using funds provided by the Social Sciences and
Humanities Research Council of Canada.

University of Toronto Press acknowledges the financial assistance to its
publishing program of the Canada Council for the Arts and the Ontario
Arts Council, an agency of the Government of Ontario.

Canada Council   Conseil des Arts
for the Arts   du Canada

ONTARIO ARTS COUNCIL
CONSEIL DES ARTS DE L'ONTARIO
an Ontario government agency
un organisme du gouvernement de l'Ontario

Funded by the   Financé par le
Government   gouvernement
of Canada   du Canada

Contents

Acknowledgments

The preparation of this volume has been a long process over a number of years, and the editors have accumulated a long list of people and institutions to whom we owe a large debt of gratitude. We mention below some of the key colleagues, students, organizations, research assistants, friends, and family who have helped us along the way, but we also know that many more people have had a broad impact on this project through conversations about the book's themes in the hallways, seminar rooms, and lecture theatres of our various universities and in the convention centres and coffee shops at our academic conferences. Likewise, conversations about "Cuba" or "Canada" with family members and friends also sparked ideas that appear in the following pages. We are grateful for the continued interest in our research and the various ways all to whom we owe so much have inspired our thinking and writing. Sincere apologies to anyone we may have missed here.

Our first acknowledgment must go to Daniel Quinlan, Acquisitions Editor in Political Science and Law at the University of Toronto Press, and our editor throughout the process of preparing this manuscript. Daniel's support for our project and his guidance, solid counsel, patience, and good humour throughout are deeply appreciated.

This volume would not have been possible without the work of all our contributors. Their insight, advice, and friendship along the way helped to shape the overall direction of the volume. They must also be thanked for the tremendous patience with which they met the numerous requests for revisions from us, the University of Toronto Press, and the reviewers. Additionally, dramatic oscillations in the

US-Cuba relationship in recent years necessitated numerous updates and rethinking. We greatly appreciate the collegial and professional way they met our deadlines and responded to our various requests.

We would also very much like to acknowledge and thank Joanne C. Elvy, who originally conceived of the idea for this volume, and who was crucially involved in the initial planning stages.

We particularly thank the many people who read drafts of the volume, including the three anonymous reviewers at the University of Toronto Press; discussants and chairs of conference panels; and our various colleagues and friends. We thank them for taking the time to read the manuscript, whether in part or as a whole, and for offering constructive and insightful commentary.

Many people assisted us in the preparation of the manuscript. Their fine work was absolutely invaluable to the book project and also saved our sanity on numerous occasions. We appreciate the excellent work of Wayne Herrington, Associate Managing Editor at the University of Toronto Press. Barry Norris, our meticulous freelance copy editor, was a pleasure to work with and improved the manuscript in countless ways. Peter Gellert did an excellent job of translating one of the chapters from Spanish to English, and we are deeply appreciative of his work. The following research assistants did crucial work often on tight timelines: Riva Gewarges, Angela Licata, Calum McNeil, and Eva Salinas. Thanks very much to all of you.

We would also like to thank the staff and our colleagues at the three academic units that the editors call their academic homes: Political Science, McMaster University, Hamilton (Lana); Gender, Sexuality, and Women's Studies, York University, Toronto (Cynthia); and Centro de Estudios Hemisféricos y sobre Estados Unidos (Centre for Hemispheric and United States Studies, CEHSEU), Universidad de La Habana (Luis René). We appreciate the support and encouragement each institution provided. We would especially like to thank the former director of CEHSEU, Dr. Jorge Hernández, for his support. His willingness to allow CEHSEU-based Cuban contributors to dedicate time to this volume is much appreciated.

Staff at the Canadian Embassy in Havana must also be gratefully acknowledged. Thanks to Mateo Barney and Anna Lise Domanski, both second secretary at the embassy, for their invaluable assistance and advice to the editors and to many of the volume's contributors. Special thanks to Ambassador Matthew Levin, who served as Canada's ambassador to Cuba from 2010 to 2013, for his time, advice, and encouragement. Also, thank you to former ambassador Mark Entwistle for his continued support of our scholarship.

We would also like to acknowledge the assistance of the Ministerio de Relaciones Exteriores de la República de Cuba (MINREX), as well as its support for workshops and seminars on topics relevant to this volume. Many of the authors presented papers on Cuba-Canada relations at these events. We would also like to thank Professor Isabel Allende, President of the Instituto Superior de Relaciones Internacionales, and Dr. Adalberto Ronda, Director of the Centro de Investigaciones sobre Politica Internacional, Havana. These individuals and their institutions provided additional opportunities for some of the contributors to present ideas that would later appear in their chapters. We would especially like to thank Dra. Beatriz Díaz and the Cátedra de Estudios sobre Canada for providing an annual seminar on Canada. Many of the authors and editors of this text have participated in these seminars, and the broader conversations and debates in all these forums spurred many of the ideas within the volume.

The editors would like to acknowledge the Social Sciences and Humanities Research Council of Canada (SSHRC) for supporting the research of numerous contributors. This book has been published with the help of a grant from the Federation for the Humanities and Social Sciences, through the Awards to Scholarly Publications Program, using funds provided by the SSHRC. We also appreciate the permission given to us by *Canadian Foreign Policy Journal* and Taylor and Francis to include an updated version of one of their articles in this volume.

Each of us also has specific people and institutions we need to thank. Lana is grateful to her co-editors for their time, hard work, and collegiality. Lana would like to thank Natasha Hritzuk and Grant McCarthy for their hospitality in their lovely home in the Berkshire mountains of western Massachusetts. She would also like to thank her parents, Lloyd and Ferne Wylie, her partner, Duane Hewitt, and her children, Chloe Hewitt and Duncan Wylie, for their support and patience.

Cynthia thanks Lana for asking her to co-edit this volume and for taking a risk on someone who at that time did not have a permanent academic home. Thanks also to Luis René for his invaluable work enabling a co-edited volume that includes Cuban scholarship and standpoints on the Cuba-Canada relationship. Many friends, family, and colleagues – too numerous to name here – have provided deeply appreciated support of all kinds over the years; Cynthia plans to thank each of you personally. In the meantime, she acknowledges Karen Dubinsky,

x   Acknowledgments

Catherine Krull, and Nathan Rao, whose assistance and support in the book's production were invaluable.

Luis René would like to personally acknowledge CEHSEU and the Department of International Relations, both at the Universidad de La Habana, for their assistance in organizing academic exchanges with Canada. He would also like to thank his wife Mercedes González and son Luis Carlos Fernández.

OTHER DIPLOMACIES, OTHER TIES

Cuba and Canada in the Shadow of the US

Introduction
Diplomacies: Constructing Canada and Cuba

LUIS RENÉ FERNÁNDEZ TABÍO, CYNTHIA WRIGHT, AND LANA WYLIE

This is a book about Cuba-Canada relations in the post-1959 context and "in the shadow of the United States." It focuses on the activities of a range of actors – including diplomats and politicians; students, activists, and Quebec nationalists; émigrés and journalists; spies and Cuban counterrevolutionaries in Canada – while remaining mindful of the ever-shifting social, economic, and geopolitical context for those encounters. The book engages the theme "other diplomacies, other ties" in all decades of the post-1959 relationship – from the dramatic early years in which the diplomatic and political relationship was negotiated through to contemporary education exchanges and the gradual formation of the Cuban-Canadian diaspora. At the same time, it acknowledges the crucial pre-1959 history – especially the period after 1898 – when the modalities of the Cuba-Canada encounter were forged through trade and capital investment, banking and railways, missionaries, and early diplomacy. In brief, the book examines other diplomacies, other ties by looking at the nature of those relationships, how they were represented, and the structural context that made them possible. Finally, and importantly, it does so through acknowledging the active role of Cuban actors in the negotiation of those ties.

The Cuban state has not been a passive victim of US hegemony. Particularly since the crisis of the 1990s, it has sought to reposition itself in the global context through skilful political diplomacy, solidarity, and humanitarian projects – including, for example, through medical internationalism.[1] For its part, Canada – a "bedrock partner" of the United States and a state with its own imperial aspirations[2] – nonetheless has maintained a political and economic relationship with Cuba throughout all these transitions, even as the US continued to internationalize its blockade[3] of the island. Moreover, on-the-ground, people-to-people contacts have intensified through mass Canadian tourism, educational exchanges, diverse solidarity projects, migration, music, sports, and more. Such developments and realignments call for new research agendas and appraisals of how they will affect the Cuba-Canada relationship.

This volume is the first devoted wholly to the theme of Cuba-Canada relations to include both Cuban and Canadian contributions and perspectives.[4] As such, it has evolved from ongoing interdisciplinary collaborations and discussions – in both Cuba and Canada – among many of the authors and editors, as well as from the scholarly work of a broader network of colleagues who have developed a rich scholarship on Cuba's foreign policy and internationalism.[5] In the Cuban context, numerous scholars have written on the Cuba-US relationship; in more recent years a cohort of scholars has begun to examine systematically both the history and contemporary dynamics of the Cuba-Canada relationship within a hemispheric perspective and to present their work at North American congresses. The book, then, captures ongoing conversations, but also extends them by fostering exchanges among and across the various disciplines represented by the contributors.[6]

This introduction begins with an account of the 17 December 2014 moment, highlighting what it might reveal about the Cuba-Canada-US relationship, (other) diplomacies, and the politics of people-to-people contacts. From there, we briefly consider more recent developments, including the election of Donald Trump as president of the United States and his efforts to reverse, at least partially, the process of normalization that began under Obama. We then develop our conceptual framework by looking at both the formal political/diplomatic level and what has recently been called "other diplomacies"[7] and the interaction between the two. Along the way we provide a brief account of the history of the Cuba-Canada relationship – including Prime Minister Justin Trudeau's 2016 visit to Havana on the eve of Fidel Castro's passing – and highlight some of the key themes that have characterized the connection between the two countries. Although the book introduces a broad conceptual terrain through multiple empirical points of entry, its emphasis is on encouraging critical thought about the problems, possibilities, and promise of the historical and contemporary relationship between Canada and Cuba since 1959.

Diplomacies, Secret Meetings, and the Making of 17 December 2014

On 17 December 2014 US president Barak Obama and Cuban president Raúl Castro stunned many, including long-term Cuba watchers, by announcing that they were officially starting a process to normalize relations between Cuba and the United States. The televised event was the culmination of a year and a half of secret high-level meetings – the majority conducted in Canada – between representatives of the two states. The two leaders also announced that their states had negotiated the mutual release of prisoners. Cuba released a US national, Alan Gross, who was arrested by Cuban authorities in 2009 and convicted for subversion in March 2011, and a CIA spy, later identified as Rolando "Rollie" Sarraff Trujillo, who had been held for two decades in Cuba after being caught handing over secrets to the US. Also freed were the three remaining members of the Cuban Five – Gerardo Hernández, Ramón Labariño, and Antonio Guerrero – who had been serving punishing sentences in the US and who had been the focus of a major international solidarity campaign. The freeing of prisoners by both parties was framed as a goodwill gesture carried out for humanitarian reasons.[8]

Most of the terms of the announcement are well known by now. As one commentator wrote of them, "[i]n a world accustomed to the usual sorts of modest diplomatic tinkering, the December 17 announcement between the United States and Cuba was stunning."[9] As part of the "normalization"[10] process, the presidents revealed that the "interest sections" in both capitals would be transitioned into embassies and led by ambassadors. The United States also agreed to remove Cuba from its list of "state sponsors of terrorism" – a designation that dated back to the Reagan years – and Raúl Castro said he would release fifty-three political prisoners identified by the US. Although Obama was unable to dismantle the blockade completely without the support of the US Congress, he did agree to use his executive power to ease some restrictions on US companies that wanted to conduct business in Cuba.[11] The decisions taken by the US president with respect to the communications industry, which even included the possibility of investment, revealed the real capacity of the executive in relation to Congress. The restraints on his action were more political – and defined in terms of the election cycle – than practical. Similarly Obama gave US citizens greater freedom to visit Cuba, and made it legal for them to use their credit cards and spend money while on the island.[12] He also told them they could now bring up to $400 in goods (including $100 in cigars and rum) back with them to the United States, and he raised the limit on remittances from $500 to $2,000 per quarter. US telecom and related technology companies would now be permitted to do business in Cuba.[13] Perhaps most strikingly, however, Obama bluntly admitted that the US approach to Cuba had been a failure.

Along with the secret meetings that led up to the 17 December announcement, the two states engaged in trust-building activities. As Calum McNeil discusses in Chapter 6, the historic lack of trust between the two sides was a major contributor to, as well as a consequence of, the long-standing conflict. Most interestingly, as part of these early feelers towards trust, the two sides negotiated a deal – widely referred to as "sperm diplomacy" in media accounts – in which the Cubans agreed to improve Alan Gross's prison conditions if the US enabled Cuban Five member Gerardo Hernández, then serving a double-life term, to inseminate his wife, Adriana Pérez, who lived in Cuba. (The United States does not permit conjugal visits, but does allow arranged insemination.) Some accounts positioned this "sperm diplomacy" as a non-political and purely humanitarian gesture, but *The Nation* more accurately called it "one of the more unusual confidence-builders in the annals of international diplomacy."[14] Indeed, it was especially important given the initial refusal of the US to release the Cuban Five.[15] Yet, as Philip Brenner explains in his analysis of the events, "[t]rust will be more difficult to build than reducing fears," and, as we discuss below, several significant outstanding issues remain.[16]

Canada played an important role in facilitating the secret meetings between Cuban and US officials by providing space for them to happen. One expert on Cuba-US affairs, Peter Kornbluh, revealed shortly after the 17 December announcement that, "[s]tarting in June 2013, the Canadian government, which since 1960 has quietly pressed Washington to pursue better relations with Havana, hosted seven secret meetings between Cuban and US officials."[17] Indeed, Canada's facilitating such secret meetings has been a feature of the long history of "back-channel diplomacy" between Cuba and the US.[18] Precisely because of the lack of formal diplomatic channels between the two countries and because of the involvement of right-wing Cubans in government positions in the US, "other diplomacies" of various types have been necessary, and often have involved third-party mediators.

Canadian prime minister Stephen Harper studiously downplayed Canada's involvement, stating, "I don't want to exaggerate Canada's role ... We facilitated places where the two countries could have a dialogue and explore ways of normalizing the relationship ... That's what we did and we think it's a good development, probably an overdue development."[19] Others, by contrast, have given Canada more credit. Raúl Castro thanked the Canadian government "for helping realize the high-level dialogue between the two countries."[20] Obama also offered his thanks, and senior US officials, including the president, characterized Canada's role as "indispensable."[21] In his June 2016 speech to Canada's Parliament, Obama reiterated, "I thank Canada for its indispensable role in hosting our negotiations with the Cuban government, and supporting our efforts to set aside half a century of failed policies to begin a new chapter with the Cuban people."[22]

Although New Democratic Party foreign affairs critic Paul Dewar waxed celebratory, observing, "this is what diplomacy looks like – and Canada is very good at it,"[23] in fact the 17 December moment underlined some long-term realities in the US-Canada-Cuba relationship, a number of which have their origins in the early post-59 period (see Raúl Rodríguez Rodríguez, in this volume). First, Canada has always been a close, if junior, ally of the United States. At the same time, however, Canada, along with Britain, another key US ally, always had certain doubts about US policies towards Cuba, perhaps especially the blockade. Indeed, the fact that both of these key US allies had certain reservations about the blockade suggests one reason it has substantially failed to have any impact on the policies of the Cuban state.[24] While not disagreeing with many US objectives in relation to Cuba, Canada has historically disagreed with some approaches to achieving them. And depending on the historical and geopolitical conjuncture, this fact has opened up interesting spaces for Canada-Cuba negotiations, (other) diplomacies, and on-the-ground ties – as this volume explores.

Still, as John M. Kirk and Peter McKenna (in this volume) illustrate, the Harper government consistently criticized Cuba's approach to democracy and human rights in terms that did not depart from those of the US. Harper's statement on normalization was no different: "Canada supports a future for Cuba that fully embraces the fundamental values of freedom, democracy, human rights, and the rule of law."[25] In an interview with the CBC, Harper again reiterated these views, and asserted that Cuba is "an economy and a society just overdue for entering into the twenty-first century." He also said he hoped Cuba would adopt democratic elections: "Although we have some tainted democracies in the hemisphere, this is really the only place where there are elections that are completely non-competitive."[26]

Indeed, despite the "normalization" under way – a re-establishment of diplomatic relations and a complex and contradictory process that is only beginning – the United States remains convinced that a fundamental goal of its relationship with the island nation should involve changing Cuba's political and economic systems through other means. The US still sees Cuba as in its backyard, and thus within its legitimate sphere of influence. Even after beginning this process of normalization, the Obama administration continued to reiterate rhetoric centred on so-called Western-style liberal democracy and human rights.[27] In his 17 December speech Obama said the United States "will continue to [raise] issues related to democracy and human rights in Cuba. But I believe that we can do more to support the Cuban people and promote our values through engagement."[28]

Likewise, although Obama's March 2016 speech in Havana – in which he equated the Cuban Revolution of 1959 with the American Revolution of 1776 and complimented the Cuban people and government for their many successes – has been correctly praised as groundbreaking in the history of US-Cuba relations, Obama also urged change on the island, and issued veiled critiques of Cuba's economic and political systems. He stated: "It should be easier to open a business here in Cuba. A worker should be able to get a job directly with companies who invest here in Cuba. Two currencies shouldn't separate the type of salaries that Cubans can earn." He also argued more pointedly that Cubans should be able "to organize and to criticize their government and to protest peacefully, and that the rule of law should not include arbitrary detentions of people who exercise those rights." "And," he asserted, "yes, I believe voters should be able to choose their governments in free and democratic elections."[29] Thus the means might have changed under Obama, but the goal of US policy towards Cuba remained largely the same: free markets and political regime change on the island, which surely would impede progress towards a full and productive normalization.

Moreover, and from the perspective of this volume's themes, the means are especially interesting. As Louis A. Perez noted of the Obama's administration's approach, "[t]he 'bold new policy' contemplates normal diplomatic relations with the Cuban government as a means to obtain wider access to the Cuban people, to enable the United States to 'empower' the Cuban people as agents of change." As he elaborated, the "new policy" in fact builds on an old idea: to use people-to-people contacts for so-called democracy promotion and the creation of a market economy. "The policy is designed to drive a wedge between the Cuban people and the Cuban government, to wean the Cuban people off their 'dependence' on the State as a means to promote the development of a civil society and market economy, whereupon the Cuban people thus 'empowered' would be motivated to act in behalf of their own economic interests as agents of political change."[30] President Trump's 16 June 2017 announcement in Miami both reversed some of the changes initiated by presidents Obama and Castro and signalled, through its reactionary Cold War rhetoric, a far more aggressive approach to the Cuban state than that of Obama. Yet, for all the differences, the Obama and Trump administrations share similar policy aims.

Thus, even before Trump's election, there were grounds for caution in relation to the process that began on 17 December; at the same time, it also needs to be said that the announcement constituted a victory for Cuban diplomacy, and was made possible through a confluence of forces. Various factors need to be considered, including Obama's support for normalization; opposition to the blockade within the hemisphere (as well as globally); pressure from Latin American and Caribbean states at the Summit of the Americas as well as within bodies such as the Community of Latin American and Caribbean States (CELAC); changing demographics and politics in the Cuban-American community; successful Cuban foreign policy and diplomacy that has engaged many states on its side; and, last but not least, an internal update of the Cuban socialist system that was beginning to show results and produce a positive change in perceptions about the future of Cuba. We survey many of these briefly in what follows before turning to a discussion of "other diplomacies, other ties."

Even before he was elected president, Barack Obama indicated support for the normalization of relations between the United States and Cuba. In 2004, for example, he announced that "it is time for us to end the embargo."[31] During his election campaign, however, he dropped talk of ending the blockade, but promised that his administration would "grant Cuban Americans unrestricted rights to visit family and send remittances to the island."[32] And although he did follow through on easing restrictions somewhat, most Cuba-watchers were disappointed, but not surprised, by his administration's Cuba policy, regarding it as merely a return to what travel policy looked like under the Bill Clinton administration. Moreover, other aspects of US policy – notably the economic sanctions – often made travel difficult.[33] The Obama administration also continued the George W. Bush era's "Cuba Program," and allocated approximately US$20 million a year for "building civil society" in Cuba, now renamed by Obama as "empowering the Cuban people." In July 2009, in another return to a Clinton policy, Obama reopened the migration talks with the Cuban government that had been suspended since 2004.[34] As Carlos Alzugaray has observed, migration talks have been politically central because of the long history of US-Cuban circulations of people and also, of course, for reasons of geographical proximity and geopolitics, not to speak of the post-59 history of US deployment of migration policy to undermine the Revolution.[35]

Obama also drew on older Clinton policy by quietly allowing more contact between US nationals and Cubans than had existed under the George W. Bush administration. For instance, under Obama, popular US and Cuban artists performed in each other's countries, sports teams travelled back and forth for games, and Cuban-Americans were allowed to take more trips to visit their relatives. Academic exchanges were revitalized despite ongoing difficulties. These small openings and less hostile rhetoric helped to create trust between the two sides that set some of the groundwork for the secret talks. At the same time, ongoing "democracy promotion" efforts inside Cuba by the United States Agency for International Development (USAID) consistently undermined the possibilities. While Obama focused on larger, key initiatives such as health care reform, which used most of his political capital, the normalization of relations between Havana and Washington remained on his to-do list. With the end of his term in sight, Obama knew he needed to move on this issue if he wanted to include ending five decades of hostility in his legacy.

The evolving views of the Cuban-American community in Florida and New Jersey, as well as new migration practices, also helped to spur the normalization initiative. The older and largely middle-class immigrants that left Cuba in droves following the triumph of the Revolution remain, in many cases, strident opponents of normalization. However, their children and grandchildren are more likely to support a lifting of the blockade, and younger Cuban-Americans were more likely to be Obama voters. Recent arrivals from the island who, generally speaking, left for economic, rather than political, reasons remain largely sympathetic to many of the achievements of the Revolution. They are also less white and less well off than were the early post-59 immigrants; indeed, the period since the Mariel boatlift of 1980 has marked a change in the composition and motives of Cuban immigrants. Perhaps most interestingly, new migration developments and travelling practices of

Cuban-Americans have also changed political outlooks, an outcome of the fact that "[n]early five hundred thousand Cubans from Florida and New Jersey travel to and from the island every year."[36] As Ricardo Alarcón, a senior Cuban statesman, has commented, "Pay attention to this. [Senator Marco] Rubio and others strongly oppose normalization for a simple reason that Obama's policy plus our policy of eliminating travel restrictions may lead to their biggest nightmare. You have a growing segment of Cuban-Americans who left Cuba or who will want to leave in the future but who want to return to Cuba any time they wish. It's different from the old antagonism of the sixties."[37] Although family visits by Cuban-Americans might deepen Cuban understandings of the US, the reverse is also true: Cuban-Americans also might come away changed – and not in ways the Republican right imagines.

Finally, 17 December and subsequent changes begun that day need to be understood in a more global context. The United States has been concerned with worldwide public opinion, especially in the wake of the disastrous Bush years, and is apprehensive about Cuba's stature in the western hemisphere. Cuba not only has normal diplomatic relations with every other state in the hemisphere; it is a popular player in the region for a variety of reasons, including its extensive medical diplomacy. Moreover, as Tom Hayden comments, "[m]any of the Cuban-supported guerrillas of the sixties had become political leaders in the new Latin America."[38] Support for Cuba has intensified over the past few years. In June 2009 the Organization of American States voted to lift Cuba's nearly five-decades-long suspension from the oldest international political organization in the hemisphere.

But the degree to which the states of the region support Cuba is best illustrated by the creation of organizations such as CELAC, and its declaration that Latin America and the Caribbean is a Zone of Peace, which advocates non-intervention into the internal affairs of the countries in the region. Support for Cuba is also demonstrated by the region's stance on the country's presence at Summit of the Americas meetings. Cuba had been excluded from these meetings since 2001, ostensibly because it was not a proper liberal democracy. Over the years, opposition to Cuba's exclusion had been growing such that it was a point of contention during the 2009 Summit of the Americas in Port of Spain, Trinidad, at which the region's leaders called for an end to this practice. Obama recognized that, because Cuba sends "thousands of doctors" throughout the hemisphere, the other states in the region were advocating for Havana.[39]

In 2012, at the summit in Cartagena, Colombia, the other states of the region made it clear that they were unwilling to continue to participate if Cuba were not invited to the 2015 summit in Panama. The fact that its neighbours are so willing to support Cuba in international forums by voting in favour of it and by criticizing the blockade in the UN General Assembly is evidence that Cuba's strategy to improve its international reputation by providing much-needed medical and disaster assistance is working.[40] It is also, of course, the result of changes in the Latin American political context – namely, the so-called Pink Tide, initiated with the election of Hugo Chávez in Venezuela in 1998. Obama alluded to Cuba's medical internationalism in his speech on 17 December, noting that "Cuba has sent hundreds of health care workers to Africa to fight Ebola."[41] In short, "[w]hat began as an effort in 1960 by the United States to isolate Cuba was ending in 2014 with a complete reversal, an America isolated in the world when it came to Cuba."[42]

Yet even before the ascendancy of Trump, the serious difficulties in the US-Cuba relationship were by no means over. The blockade was, and still is, in place. These punishing economic sanctions against Cuba, codified in the Helms–Burton Act of 1996, remain intact, and it will take an act of Congress to dismantle the blockade completely. Resistance in Congress is significant, and not just among the Cuban-American hardliners. For instance, upon hearing of the 17 December talks, Republican senator Lindsay Graham tweeted, "This is an incredibly bad idea."[43] The fiercest opposition, however, has come from Cuban-American senators Robert Menendez and Marco Rubio, both powerful figures – Rubio was a leading contender for the 2016 Republican presidential nomination. In fact, many of the Republican presidential front-runners that year indicated they would reverse normalization if elected.[44] Rubio and other Republican Cuban-American hardliners, including Mario Díaz-Balart, were also key figures behind Trump's decision to reverse some of the progress towards normalization. Apart from the all-important question of the blockade, as well as Trump's policy reversals, other outstanding issues remain, among them Guantánamo; reparations for the blockade; US funding for so-called democracy promotion in Cuba; and attempts by the US to undermine the Cuba-Venezuela alliance by introducing sanctions against Venezuela.

Even at the moment of the December 2014 opening between Cuba and the US, astute observers warned it might be years before the remaining key issues were resolved and that any progress might be undone. With the election of Donald Trump, these cautions have proved prescient.

Before he was elected, Trump suggested he was open to a relationship with Cuba; he also indicated he wanted a "better deal." To begin with, there is no single deal between the US and Cuba, but rather a series of bilateral agreements and various commercial arrangements and exchanges. These were essentially left untouched in President Trump's 16 June 2017 announcement in Miami.

Indeed, for all the Cold War pandering to a dwindling layer of far-right Cuban-American hardliners, the reality is that Trump left untouched key aspects of Obama's "deal." For example, there continues to be a US diplomatic presence in Cuba, and US residents may send remittances to family members on the island. US flights and cruises to Cuba are still permitted. Travel to Cuba by US citizens for the purposes of tourism remains prohibited by US statute, as it was under Obama and indeed has been for decades. Travel may be permitted so long as it falls within one of twelve authorized categories (such as education, religious, and journalism). So what has changed with Trump? In essence, two things. First, individual travel, within the permitted categories – always difficult for US visitors, though easier under Obama-era regulations – will now officially end. US travellers to the island will need to travel in groups with a licensed provider. Second, Trump's measures aim to prevent US money from going to Cuba's military, a central player in Cuba's crucial tourism sector as well as other enterprises. In practice, this will mean US businesses will be restricted from signing commercial deals with a host of Cuban entities, and US tourist groups will not be allowed to deal with companies and enterprises affiliated with the Cuban armed forces. Exactly how this will be audited and enforced remains unclear and, as always, Cubans and US citizens in favour of normalization will negotiate regulatory ambiguities, and loopholes.

What is clear is that Trump's measures are unpopular in the US, and numerous civil society organizations and business interests have spoken out strongly against them. There continue to be those in the US Congress who advocate for normalization. Even before the 16 June announcement, a group of former US military leaders wrote the Trump administration to make it clear that Cuba presents absolutely no national security threat to the United States and that it is in the US interest to continue working with Cuba on areas of mutual concern. Many US commentators have argued that Trump's policies are unlikely to succeed. As William LeoGrande succinctly warned, "if President Trump's negotiators pound the table demanding political concessions from Cuba, it won't get them far."[45] Whatever future policy directions and negotiating strategies emerge from the US administration, it seems clear that the end of the blockade is destined to remain a pressing political priority for Cuba for some time to come.

At the same time, there is the fact that "hundreds of thousands of Americans have visited Cuba, legally and illegally, as tourists, most of them bringing back deep sympathy for the island."[46] Together with US solidarity activists, including the thousands who have travelled to Cuba with the Venceremos Brigade, and the US civil society organizations and commercial interests that have opposed Trump's Cuba policies, they are potentially poised to be an important counterweight to the political power of the right-wing Cuban-American lobby. As Tom Hayden observes, "[m]any of those *brigadistas* later became mayors, members of Congress, and influential Americans in many fields. They are an invisible backbone of support for normalized relations today."[47] In the following section, we take a closer look at "other diplomacies," other ties, and some of the dynamics of various kinds of people-to-people relationships.

Diplomacy and Other Diplomacies

Scholarship that addresses global or international relationships traditionally focuses on state-to-state interactions. Diplomats, hired by their respective governments and charged with representing official state interests abroad, are normally considered the primary vehicle through which these interactions take place. Even in this age of inexpensive video conferencing, texting, and other means of instantaneous communication, diplomats remain tasked with much of the day-to-day management of the relationship between the peoples of different states and with the negotiation of identities, differences, and nationalisms within the international nation-state system and the global field of power.

Although certain strands of the International Relations literature recognize or even value the importance of non-state actors, the functions of these groups are generally viewed as operating very differently from the functions of their respective governments – as having vastly different tasks and employing distinct means. Andrew Cooper and Brian Hocking assert that, in International Relations scholarship, "[s]tate and non-state actors are viewed as inhabiting different environments, working to different rule-books and occupying very different positions on the scale of importance in world politics. They exist, therefore, in two solitudes with little or no interaction between their worlds."[48]

Furthermore, these non-state actors are not normally considered to be engaging in diplomacy, although this view has been challenged by scholars such as Costas Constantinou. In *On the Way to Diplomacy*, he argues that the 1961 Vienna Convention on Diplomatic Relations defined diplomacy narrowly and that its conception of diplomacy is "neither exclusive nor exhaustive of the functions, actors, processes of communication, agents or objectives of diplomacy."[49]

Conventional understandings of diplomacy are evolving and broadening, however, a process that has its roots, in part, in the end of the Cold War and resulting in what some scholars assert is a "renaissance in diplomacy studies."[50] Thomas Princen argues that, "although the work of foreign ministries remains essential for conducting the affairs of state, a much more complex picture of diplomacy emerges when one considers the expansion and complexity of issues, global communications, and the involvement of non-state and intergovernmental organizations."[51] Stuart Murray claims that "[s]uch views range from the traditional (where the state endures as the only diplomatic actor of significance) to the nontraditional (where diplomacy transcends the state and is practiced by nongovernmental organizations … , multinational corporations … , or even two individuals meeting from different countries, for example)."[52]

One new approach to understanding the constitution of foreign relations, broadly understood, has been developed through the concept of "other diplomacies." As a concept, other diplomacies "aims to capture analytically the everyday activities of societal non-state actors that have a diplomatic character."[53] As a number of scholars have noted, although not new, "other diplomatic" practices have greatly expanded in recent years because of communications technologies, expansion of travel and global markets, transformations in territoriality, and more.[54] As a term, "other diplomacies" was first used in 2010 in *Canadian Foreign Policy in Critical Perspective*, edited by Marshall Beier and Lana Wylie. More recently, Mary Young and Susan Henders' award-winning article, "'Other Diplomacies' and the Making of Canada-Asia Relations," greatly advanced the concept. As they elaborate, "[o]ther diplomacies refers to a range of things that non-state actors do as they interact with each other, including across political, legal and normative borders and differences of culture, language and other identities. As with state diplomacy, other diplomacies are centrally about negotiation and communication, which involve several practices, whether consciously or unconsciously."[55] That negotiation occurs in a field of power, one marked by many asymmetries, and depending on the context, these practices and interchanges might "help reproduce or alternatively challenge established power relations."[56] In other words, one way Young and Henders advance the conversation about non-state actors is by drawing our attention to the processes of "class, gender, race and ethnicity, nation and other distinctions within these relationships and how these are reproduced in everyday interactions"[57] (see also Karen Dubinsky, in this volume).

Representative practices, as Young and Henders observe, are central to both official and other diplomacies. Although conventional readings assume a prior constitution of identities in the diplomatic relationship, their approach calls attention to assumed boundaries and borders, the "everyday discursive and material practices" that produce identity and difference in complex ways.[58] Maurice Demers and Michel Nareau (in this volume) offer one way to think about this in the Cuba-Quebec context. Migration practices between Cuba and Canada are an`other important site for investigation of these processes (see Catherine Krull and Jean Stubbs, in this volume). In what follows, we briefly survey some others with reference to the Cuba-Canada relationship

Other Diplomacies in the Cuba-Canada Relationship

Young and Henders use this conceptual framework to better comprehend Canada-Asia relations, but we think it is well suited to advancing our understanding of Cuba-Canada relations. Thus this volume conceptualizes the relationship at the political/formal diplomatic level and through "other diplomacies."[59] State-led diplomacy and other diplomacies are often hard to disentangle. A fascinating example of official public diplomacy, Cuba's Expo 67 pavilion in Montreal (see Asa McKercher, in this volume), was also bound up with "other diplomacies," including those of the Cuba solidarity movement of the period. In addition, as Don Munton (in this volume) reminds us, diplomacy often includes spying: spies and diplomats might occupy the same embassy or, as was the case in the Canadian embassy in Havana, diplomats also might work as spies. Finally, "other diplomacies" as a concept embodies certain tensions for, as Young and Henders acknowledge, "it attempts to move away from the state and state-bound identities, while at the same time framing non-state diplomacy in statist and 'national' ways."[60]

The following chapters reveal the many ways official and other diplomacies interact, often in complimentary ways – but not always, as other diplomatic representations and messages sometimes conflict with official communications or goals. In particular the practices of diverse non-state actors in arenas such as economics, tourism, education, and solidarity are particularly relevant to the Cuba-Canada story. Through these and other practices and activities, non-state actors engage in diplomacies. They communicate, gather, and disseminate information, compromise, negotiate, engage in dialogue, and represent their societies and polities – or sometimes break with them. McNeil (in this volume) highlights the importance of the links between the two societies, and explains that "the sustained policy of engagement, and the routinized interpersonal interactions which it facilitates, has structured a social context in which trust and mutually beneficial learning have taken place setting an important example pertinent to any discussion of US-Cuba normalization."

Economic Connections

The role of economic actors and processes has been central in the Cuba-Canada relationship. Historically, economics not only predated, but has since led the political relationship (Rodríguez, in this volume). Cuba's importance for several empires in the Caribbean has been central to this history. John Kirk and Peter McKenna describe the importance of the very early economic relationship, when Cuban sugar and rum were traded for Canadian cod and lumber.[61] The immediate post-1898 moment and the end of Spanish colonial rule in Cuba witnessed a scramble among the United Kingdom, United States, and Canada for Cuba and the wider Caribbean. After 1898 the most significant Canadian economic participation in Cuba, as well as the wider Caribbean, was in banking – an important example is the activities of the Royal Bank of Canada.[62] (In part, this is because, before 1913, the United States did not allow US banks to establish in foreign countries.) Furthermore, Canadian capital took "collateral advantage" of the US economic domination of Cuba to make investments in railways and the insurance industry, and well before Canada and Cuba exchanged ambassadors in 1945, numerous Canadian farmers moved to Cuba to make their living in the sugar industry.

Although they focus primarily on official relations in their chapter, Kirk and McKenna also provide an update of the two countries' economic connections, and note that the Canadian company Sherritt International remains the largest single foreign investor on the island.

Cuba is Canada's largest market in the region, and trade between the two exceeds $1 billion annually. Although Canada's placement among Cuba's top trading partners has declined a bit over the years, Canada remains an important partner to Cuba. Furthermore, as Cuban economist Luis René Fernández Tabío explains in his chapter, the political and economic connections are facilitated by people-to-people connections. He reflects that "Canadians and Cubans appear to be comfortable with each other at a basic human level that allows them to bypass obstacles persistently set in place by the United States." At the same time, as Young and Henders note, it is in economic relationships that asymmetries in power relationships might be most telling.[63] This arena, historically and in the present, represents a prime site for future research. There is also a relationship to be traced between the historical formation of Canadian "public opinion" on Cuba and the evolution of the trade relationship between the two countries, including the attitude of Canadian capital to the US blockade.

Tourism

Canada has been, and remains, the top source of tourists to the island, so the diverse connections fostered through tourism are a major site for research. Cuba has had a complicated relationship with tourism, since US tourists seeking illicit sex and gambling were considered a source of the island's problems in the pre-revolutionary period.[64] Although international tourism gradually increased in the 1960s and 1970s, tourism did not become a major source of earnings on the island until the late 1980s, and it was not until 1997 that the Cuban revolutionary government first widely encouraged tourist visits.[65] Throughout the revolutionary period, some Cuban laws further complicated potential interactions between tourists and Cuban residents. In an effort to keep the two populations segregated, until 2008 Cubans not employed in tourist hotels were banned from the premises; Cubans were also banned from certain popular beach resort areas and other attractions marketed to foreigners.[66]

Tourism is now among Cuba's top sources of revenue. Indeed, Cuba ranks third, after the United States and Mexico, as a destination for Canadian travellers; approximately 1.2 million Canadians visited Cuba in 2014. In 2012 alone, Canadian tourists brought nearly $748 million into Cuba's economy.[67] In her chapter, Olga Rosa González Martin points out that Cuba as a tourist destination was the third most popular focus of newspaper articles that concentrated on the island. John Kirk has similarly underlined the point, from another angle, arguing that, "[u]ndoubtedly, these people-to-people contacts are far, far ahead of any bilateral government ties, which means that Ottawa has to bear in mind the potential displeasure of over a million people that any negative turn in the official relationship would have."[68] Although criss-crossed with complex relations of power – including those linked to the production of income inequalities and racial hierarchies – tourism is a prime site for the negotiation of other diplomacies.

Educational Opportunities, Sports, and Cultural Connections

Formal and informal academic ties between Canada and Cuba and the practice of what has been called "academic diplomacy"[69] are among the most vital sites of exchange in the Cuba-Canada relationship. As the Canadian government acknowledges, "[a]cademic coopera-tion represents one of the most important aspects of the relationship between Canada and Cuba, with expanding networks of academics and researchers from both countries working together in a wide range of disciplines."[70] Indeed, for all the enormous problems Cuba negoti-ated throughout the 1990s, that decade also saw the growth and devel-opment of academic ties. Scientists from the two countries, to take one example, have collaborated on new treatments for disease – most nota-bly on cancer vaccines.[71] And this volume, co-edited and authored by Cuban and Canadian academics from a variety of disciplines, is yet another example of the other diplomacies of academic networks. For-mal institutional linkages between Canadian and Cuban universities have enabled post-secondary students, as well as researchers and aca-demics, to connect via educational exchanges and visits. In her chapter, Dubinsky reflects on several years of organizing a senior undergradu-ate course in Havana for students from a Canadian university.

Dubinsky's chapter is especially valuable given that relatively little scholarly and critical reflective work has been done to document the long history and contemporary dynamics of Cuba-Canada academic collaboration and knowledge production – or to think through areas of future development. Here we briefly touch on two points. One is that Cuban institutions have long been interested in academic exchanges with North American counterparts, including, for example, in the area of Canadian studies. Annual events organized by the Cátedra de Estu-dios Canadienses at the University of Havana, under the direction of Professor Beatriz Díaz, are developing Canadian studies, not only in Havana, but also in the rest of the country. As well, the Centro de Estudios Hemisféricos y sobre Estados Unidos (CEHSEU, Centre for Hemispheric and US Studies), also at the University of Havana, has established, with official Canadian support, the Seminario Interuniversitario de Estudios Canadienses en América Latina (SEMINECAL, Inter-university Seminar on Canadian Studies in Latin America), a forum to encourage the participation of young scholars from Cuba and Latin America, and in which volume contributor Raúl Rodríguez plays an important role.

Second, given the restrictions imposed by the United States, conferences in Canada have become vital sites for building relationships between Cuban scholars and those from elsewhere. For example, although the congresses of the US-based Latin American Studies Association (LASA) historically have been welcoming to Cuban scholars, Cuban scholars have also regularly faced denial of visas by the US. The decision, therefore, by LASA organizers to hold congresses in Montreal and Toronto was important for enabling Cuban participation. There has also been enthusiastic support for Cuban-Canadian academic exchanges from the Canadian institutional side, including for the major international conference, "The Measure of a Revolution: Cuba, 1959–2009," held at Queen's University, in Kingston, Ontario, and attended by numerous Cuban scholars at a time when US policy towards Cuba did not allow an environment for free academic exchanges for Cuban scholars.

Likewise, various forms of cultural and sports diplomacy, such as through the Pan-American games, have been important in negotiating Cuba-Canada relations and, arguably, are even less researched and theorized than are the academic exchanges. Art and music have frequently facilitated official diplomatic relations.[72] The Canadian embassy in Cuba has showcased Canadian art, and has used art and music to commemorate the bilateral relationship. For instance, in June 2015, the embassy sponsored a concert in Havana, featuring one of Cuba's most popular musicians, Carlos Varela, celebrating 70 years of Cuba-Canada diplomatic relations.[73] Other events include "¡Cuba!: Art and History from 1868 to Today," a four-hundred-piece exhibit held in Montreal in 2008 that focused on the history of Cuban art, and an exhibition held at the Royal York Hotel in Toronto in December 2013 that showcased, for the first time outside Cuba, the work of seven of Cuba's leading artists.[74] The Cuban national ballet regularly performs in Canada, and musicians from the two countries often meet and play together.

States have long acknowledged the role of other diplomacies, such as cultural connections, in relationship building; indeed, the history of US Cold War cultural diplomacy is now well known. Consider also the emphasis in US Cuba policy on people-to-people ties that was put in place under Bill Clinton and then re-emphasized by Barack Obama. For its part, the Canadian government recognizes that "cultural and interpersonal ties contribute to strengthening people-to-people relations between Canadians and Cubans."[75] Here it is important to note that, although Canada's rhetoric historically has been less hostile than that of the United States, the Canadian government's underlying hope is that these contacts will foster an evolution of Cuban society that more closely resembles a free market model. In this respect, its position is similar to the motivation behind the people-to-people elements of US policy towards Cuba.

The Solidarity Movement

Cubans have a long history of travelling to both the US and Canada in search of political and material support for revolutionary projects. In the nineteenth century, a small number of individuals from Canada responded by fighting in Cuba's revolutionary wars against Spain. In the twentieth century, Fidel Castro's 1959 trip to Montreal, a few short months after the Cuban Revolution, was very popular – as was the Revolution itself.[76] Fair Play for Cuba, formed shortly after the Revolution, was among the most significant solidarity groups; the group's early delegations to Cuba remain an important example of people-to-people contacts.[77] Although the diverse solidarity projects and practices that have existed in Canada since the revolutionary triumph are in many ways an important example of "other diplomacies," they also rely on formal diplomacies in at least two basic ways. First, without the context of a formal diplomatic relationship, particular kinds of solidarity practices are much more difficult to sustain, as US solidarity workers can attest. Second, from the very beginning, Cuban diplomatic and consular figures have played an interesting role in relation to solidarity formations, with many developing close personal relationships with Cuban solidarity activists in Canada.[78]

The political meaning of post-revolutionary Cuba for diverse actors in the Canadian context has varied decade by decade, depending on the social and political orientation of the actors involved, Canadian regional politics, the direction of Cuban foreign policy, and the challenges facing the revolutionary project. In the 1960s, for example, as David Austin has shown, the political significance of Cuba for black and Caribbean activists in Montreal was connected to how they saw the political challenges facing the Anglo Caribbean.[79] Sean Mills has looked at how Cuba was located in international anti-colonial politics in Montreal for a similar period.[80] Indeed, Montreal has a long history of Cuba-Canada connections, as several contributors to this volume make clear (see the chapters by Keith Bolender, Demers and Nareau, Krull and Stubbs, and McKercher). By the 1980s Cuba was linked to struggles in the Central American context (Guatemala, El Salvador, Nicaragua), as well as to that of the Caribbean (notably with the invasion of Grenada). By the 1990s there was a deepening of solidarity projects in the face of serious new challenges as the US tightened the screws on the blockade. Recent years have seen the campaign to free the Cuban Five and a renewed emphasis on ending the blockade. Today there are solidarity organizations in most major Canadian cities, as well as a host of ties organized through labour unions, farmer-to-farmer projects, cooperatives, the Che Guevara Brigade, and more. Indeed, the range and depth of diverse people-to-people ties between Cuba and Canada are more extensive now than at any point in Cuba's post-revolutionary history.

Canada and Cuba: Conclusions and Trajectories

Although Canada's relationship with Cuba has remained broadly the same regardless of the party or leader in power in Ottawa, changes of government do have an impact on the overall tenor and degree of closeness between the two states and the spaces opened for "other diplomacies." Under Prime Minister Harper, trade and other types of connections were sustained, but the relationship cooled significantly (see John M. Kirk and Peter McKenna, in this volume). After the 2015 election of Justin Trudeau, most Cuba-watchers expected the relationship to flourish, given the historic friendship between his father, Pierre, and Fidel Castro. In the initial period following the election of the Liberal Party, however, some criticized the new government for its lack of attention to the bilateral Cuba-Canada relationship, arguing that Ottawa was failing to seize a crucial moment of opportunity on the island.[81]

In November 2016, over a year into his mandate, Trudeau did make an official short visit to Havana, where he met with Raúl Castro to discuss areas of common interest between the two states, including trade, development assistance, food security, climate change, gender equality, and regional security. He also met with civil society groups and students from the University of Havana. The brief visit, largely regarded as a success, was overshadowed ten days later, on 25 November, by the death of Cuba's historic revolutionary leader, Fidel Castro, and by the uproar in the Canadian media about the prime minister's statement of condolence. On learning of Castro's death, Trudeau observed: "Fidel Castro was a larger than life leader who served his people for almost half a century. A legendary revolutionary and orator, Mr. Castro made significant improvements to the education and healthcare of his island nation." He continued: "While a controversial figure, both Mr. Castro's supporters and detractors recognized his tremendous dedication and love for the Cuban people who had a deep and lasting affection for 'el Comandante.'"[82]

Although Trudeau's statement was similar to those made by many other world leaders, including Obama, some members of the US and Canadian right wing, aptly dubbed "anti-Communists posing as human rights warriors" by *Toronto Star* columnist Thomas Walkom, went on the offensive.[83] Emboldened by the election of Donald Trump just weeks earlier, they attacked Trudeau in Parliament, social media, and the press; indeed, much (though by no means all) of the mainstream Canadian media recycled Cold War narratives. Some right-wing politicians in the US and Canada decried Trudeau as an international embarrassment, but their assessments of Castro's legacy were in stark contrast to those articulated by independent commentators in the African American, South African, Latin American, and Caribbean contexts. Moreover, the fact remains that strident conservative commentaries will have no real effect on the basic parameters of Cuba-Canada relations. In the United States, by contrast, the precise direction of Cuba-US relations remains unclear in the context of a new presidency and an ascendant far right.

The next decade will be a crucial period for Cuba. Cubans have lived with almost six decades of hostility by the United States – including terrorism (see Bolender, in this volume) and a punishing economic blockade – and governed by a leadership that, not unreasonably, felt that Cuba's social, economic, and political way of life was under constant attack from the world's most powerful state. Cubans who are asked about their future answer carefully. On the one hand, they are relieved to see a possible end to some of the political and economic struggles that have their origins in the conflict with the US; on the other, they realize that the United States still has a vision of what it wants Cuba to become, and for many Cubans this vision is far too familiar. Older Cubans remember a Cuba that was essentially run from Washington and New York with little regard for the welfare of most people on the island. As a result of this US domination, as well as earlier Spanish colonial rule, anti-imperial sentiment runs deep in Cuban history. The 1959 Revolution was the culmination of more than a century of failed attempts to create an autonomous Cuba.

The Revolution led from the Sierra Maestra in the 1950s was an unquestionable success in ending US imperial presence on the island and creating the preconditions for a form of independence for the first time. The Revolution challenged deep race, gender, and class hierarchies, and utterly transformed life for the poorest Cubans who, before 1959, were often illiterate and uneducated, poor in health, and without enough food. In the early years of the Revolution, brigades of teachers were sent into the far reaches of the country to teach everyone, from children to grandparents, how to read and write. Seemingly overnight both rural and urban Cubans now had access to free and increasingly higher quality health care, and no longer had periods of hunger as they could rely on state-supplied rations of basic foodstuffs. Children of once illiterate farmers could now attend school from the earliest age through to high-quality and free post-secondary education, and become the new state's engineers, doctors, scientists, and teachers.

At the same time Cubans are no strangers to hardship, as they have endured difficult periods, most specifically during the early 1990s, when the country was abruptly cut off from its major source of support after the collapse of the Soviet Union and new forms of inequality made their appearance. These conditions were aggravated still more as the US sought to make Cuba collapse by further tightening the blockade. During this "special period," Cuba lost nearly 80 per cent of its imports and exports, dropping its gross domestic product by 33 per cent.[84] In a very short time the country could no longer obtain gas, food, and medicine from its typical sources, and normal life almost ground to a halt as people struggled to survive.[85] Yet Cuba has rebounded from this period to become one of the most successful economic and social leaders in the region. Today Cuba remains one of the healthiest and best-educated societies in the hemisphere – Cuban health statistics for life expectancy remain equal or superior to those of the US.[86] As recent scholarship has shown, Cuba's socialist system has delivered better results than the former European socialist states that have "transitioned" to capitalism.[87] Thus, although life in Cuba undoubtedly will change as a contradictory normalization process slowly unfolds, the Cuba-US relationship is unlikely to return to anything close to what it was in the 1950s.

Meanwhile, Cuba is undergoing the most dramatic internal shift since the triumph of the Revolution. Since officially assuming leadership in 2008, Raúl Castro has instituted major changes on the island. These have included, beginning in 2011, a comprehensive update of Cuban socialism that implies social and political, as well as economic, changes. He has also instituted term limits for Cuban presidents, stating that he himself will retire in 2018.[88] This formalizes what demographic change is beginning to necessitate: most of the first generation of revolutionary leadership is now well into their seventies and eighties, and as Cuba's leadership ages and passes on, the newer generation is instituting its own ideas and ways of governing the island. Moreover, the changes in everyday life occasioned by the further growth and development of tourism, the non-state sector, consumption, international investment and trade deals, internal and external migration, and new communications and media technologies have occasioned new debates and challenges within Cuba. One such challenge – an important theme in recent Cuban music, film, and political forums – is that of addressing the emergent forms of material inequality, including those along the lines of race and gender, that have come with these openings.

Thus the triple challenges of internal change, demographic and generational shifts, and negotiating the relationship with the US, will continue to transform everyday life for Cubans and Cuba's relationships with other countries. Canadians with official responsibility for managing the bilateral relationship, as well as those engaged in "other diplomacies," will face new realities and complexities. It is important to recognize that "normalization" is, and will be, a long and complex process that might again go into reverse; as we have seen, it was partially reversed by Trump's directives. At the very least, given that many have raised concerns that US policy shifts amount to soft power regime change, the road ahead will need to be carefully negotiated. The Cuban government has pointed to a long list of issues that should be resolved, including the blockade, Guantánamo, compensation for damages and losses to Cubans for the blockade and other hostile US policies towards Cuba, subversive radio and TV broadcasts aimed at Cuba, the financing of regime change forces inside Cuba and the building of "civil society" programs, and the Cuban Adjustment Act of 1966. Merely listing the issues involved is evidence of the complexity of "normalization."

The following chapters invite the reader to consider the ways in which teachers, students, business people, activists, researchers, spies, church people, artists, cultural workers, and athletes, as well as many others, are active in the spaces between Cuba and Canada, how they are engaged in diplomacies, and how the relationship between Canada and Cuba today would be different if these groups and individuals had not been significant actors. Along with the negotiations of power, border-making, and relationship of official state representatives, the practices of these figures need to be understood as fundamental to the historical and contemporary relationship between Canada and Cuba.

The Organization of the Book

The book is divided into three parts. The first, "Histories and (Other) Diplomacies," examines some of the key diplomatic and "other diplomatic" moments in the early post-59 period. Drawing on both Canadian and Cuban archives, Rodríguez's comprehensive chapter opens this part by reviewing the political and diplomatic history of the Cuba-Canada relationship, offering along the way some interesting insights into how the Cuban revolutionary state negotiated the early relationship with Canada. Don Munton's exploration of how Canadian diplomats gathered intelligence in Cuba after the US ended diplomatic relations raises some interesting questions about the porous boundaries between diplomacies and spying. The next three chapters are equally original, and all offer new insights into the long and important relationship between Quebec – especially Montreal – and Cuba. They examine the considerable influence of the Cuban Revolution on Quebec's liberation movement (Demers and Nareau), the long-reaching impact of Cuba's public diplomacy at Expo 67 (McKercher), and the forgotten story of terrorist attacks on Cuban targets in Canada during this period (Bolender). Drawing on a diverse range of sources, the chapters in this part highlight both formal diplomacies and various on-the-ground "other diplomacies," as well as their intertwined character. They reveal how a variety of long-lasting ties – and tensions – between Canada, Quebec, and Cuba were forged in the aftermath of the decision by the Diefenbaker government not to break diplomatic ties with revolutionary Cuba.

The second part, "Canada and Cuba in the Shadow of the US: Structures and Economies," broadly picks up chronologically where the first part ends. It explores the Cuba-Canada relationship from the latter part of the Cold War through to the beginning of Justin Trudeau's government. The chapters in this part focus on the structures that both contain and produce the relationship and associated diplomacies. Primary among these is, of course, the US-Canada-Cuba triangle. McNeil most explicitly conceptualizes this as a trilateral relationship, demonstrating how the United States has structured the Cuba-Canada relationship, and showing how the level of trust among the three different states has been a key influence on the trajectory of each relationship. The following two chapters, by long-time scholars of the Cuba-Canada relationship, anatomize recent developments in the economic (Fernández Tabío) and political (Kirk and McKenna) domains, with an eye to some of their structural characteristics. The last contribution in this part, by Rosa López-Oceguera, is a critical reminder that the post-59 Cuba-Canada relationship is also situated within the broader inter-American context and within the hemispheric institutions from which the US has sought to exclude Cuba. As Latin American states form regional blocs and seek to restructure the inter-American system to challenge US hegemony, crucial questions are raised about the future trajectory of the US-Canada-Cuba triangle.

The final part of the volume, "Constructing Canada and Cuba," draws on case studies to approach new and emerging themes in Cuba-Canada studies. It explores how representations of "Canada" and "Cuba" shape both perceptions and the movement of people (whether as students, visitors, tourists, or immigrants) between the two spaces. Although a small number of Canadian scholars have examined how Cuba is represented in the mainstream Canadian media, González Martin offers a Cuban perspective through a case study of one national newspaper, the *Globe and Mail*. Scholarly literature on Cuba-US academic exchanges reveals that they have been a vital site for "other diplomacies," but no parallel scholarship has examined such academic exchanges for the Cuba-Canada relationship. Drawing on her own extensive work in student and academic exchanges between Canada and Cuba, Dubinsky reflects on the undergraduate study experience in Havana as a contradictory and productive location for negotiating, constructing, and representing the Cuba-Canada encounter. Although small numbers of Cubans have always lived in Canada in the post-59 period, it is only in recent years that larger flows have come to Canada as visitors, students, workers, and permanent residents. Drawing on their major research project exploring the Cuban diaspora in sites "not Miami," Krull and Stubbs examine the making of the diaspora in Canada's two largest cities, Toronto and Montreal. Indeed, the ongoing circulation of Cubans between Canada and Cuba provides an immensely important and rich site for the further investigation of "other diplomacies, other ties" as Cubans resident in Canada increasingly play an active role in shaping and negotiating the encounter.

NOTES

1 Julie M. Feinsilver, "Fifty Years of Cuba's Medical Diplomacy: From Idealism to Pragmatism," *Cuban Studies* 41 (2010): 85–104.
2 For discussion, see Jerome Klassen, *Joining Empire: The Political Economy of the New Canadian Foreign Policy* (Toronto: University of Toronto Press, 2014).
3 This introduction in most cases follows Cuban usage and uses the word "blockade," rather than "embargo." This usage reflects the fact that the US embargo is also applied extraterritorially, and affects Cuba's trade with other states besides the United States. Any foreign company may also be penalized by the US for dealings with Cuba. In the context of a global economy, the blockade's extraterritorial character has major consequences for Cuba.
4 Recent collections not specifically about the Cuba-Canada relationship, but that contain both Cuban and Canadian contributors, include Maria Caridad Cumaná, Karen Dubinsky, and Xenia Reloba de la Cruz, *My Havana: The Musical City of Carlos Varela* (Toronto: University of Toronto Press, 2014); Catherine Krull, ed., *Cuba in Global Context: International Relations, Internationalism, and Transnationalism* (Gainesville: University Press of Florida, 2014); Phil Brenner et al., eds., *A Contemporary Cuba Reader: Reinventing the Revolution* (Lanham, MD: Rowman and Littlefield, 2007); Jorge Domínguez, Rafael Hernández, and Lorena G. Barberia, eds., *Debating US-Cuban Relations: Shall We Play Ball?* (New York: Routledge, 2012); and Soraya Castro Mariño and Ronald W. Pruessen, eds., *Fifty Years of Revolution: Perspectives on Cuba, the United States, and the World* (Gainesville: University Press of Florida, 2012).
5 The literature on Cuba's foreign policy is extensive, but see Carlos Alzugaray Treto, "Cuba: definiendo estrategias de política exterior en un mundo cambiante (2001–2011)," in *Cuba Futures: Cuba and the World*, ed. Mauricio

Font (New York: Bildner Center for Western Hemispheric Studies, 2011), 1–46; idem, "Cuba y el sistema internacional en la década de los '90," in *Problemas actuales de teoría sociopolitical*, ed. Emilio Duharte (Havana: Editorial Félix Varela, 2000); Joseph Tulchin, Andrés Serbín, and Rafael Hernández, eds., *Cuba and the Caribbean: Regional Issues and Trends in the Post-Cold War Era* (Lanham MD: Rowman and Littlefield, 1997); Piero Gleijeses, *Conflicting Missions: Havana, Washington, and Africa, 1959–1976* (Chapel Hill: University of North Carolina Press, 2002); Wayne Smith and Esteban Morales Domínguez, *Subject to Solution: Problems in Cuban-U.S. Relations* (Boulder, CO: Lynne Rienner, 1988); Raúl Rodríguez Rodríguez, "Canada, Cuba, and the United States as Seen in Cuban Diplomatic History, 1959–1962" (Cambridge, MA: Harvard University, David Rockefeller Center for Latin American Studies, 2010); and Marifeli Pérez-Stable, *The United States and Cuba: Intimate Enemies* (New York: Routledge, 2011).

6 One earlier example of this collaboration was a special issue of *Canadian Foreign Policy Journal* 16, no. 1 (2010). In Cuba there have been various studies on the relationship between Cuba and Canada and on Cuban foreign policy, many done inside the Centro de Estudios Hemisféricos y sobre Estados Unidos (CEHSEU, Centre for Hemispheric and US Studies) at the University of Havana by scholars including Raúl Rodríguez, Laneydi Martínez, Rosa López, and Luis René Fernández Tabío. Former members of CEHSEU staff, including Carlos Alzugaray Treto and Jorge Mario Sánchez Egozcue, have also published widely. The results of CEHSEU's research activities have been presented in articles and papers at international academic conferences. It is important to recognize the support of fellowships granted by the Canadian government to various professors and researchers from CEHSEU that have helped develop the academic assets that have contributed to the realization of this book.

7 J. Marshall Beier and Lana Wylie, *Canadian Foreign Policy in Critical Perspective* (Toronto: University of Toronto Press, 2010); Mary Young and Susan Henders, "'Other Diplomacies' and the Making of Canada-Asia Relations," *Canadian Foreign Policy Journal* 18, no. 3 (2012): 375–88.

8 For more on the Cuban 5, see Tom Hayden, *Listen Yankee! Why Cuba Still Matters* (New York: Seven Stories, 2015); and Stephen Kimber, *What Lies Across the Water: The Real Story of the Cuban Five* (Halifax; Winnipeg: Fernwood Publishing, 2013).

9 Hayden, *Listen Yankee!* xiv.

10 Of course, as Brenner points out, Cuba and the US have never had a "normal" relationship and, as the discussion below points out, much of the normalization process itself was and is "abnormal." See Philip Brenner,

"Establishing, Not Restoring, Normal Relations between the United States and Cuba," *AU-SSRC Implications of Normalization: Scholarly Perspectives on U.S.-Cuban Relations* (Washington, DC: American University, Center for Latin American & Latino Studies, April 2015), available online at http://www.american.edu/clals/Implications-of-Normalization-with-SSRC-Brenner.cfm, accessed 12 August 2015.

11 The fact is that the US president does have considerable executive power to weaken the effects of the embargo. For discussion, see Robert Muse, "US Presidential Action on Cuba: The New Normalization?" *Americas Quarterly* (Fall 2014), available online at http://www.americasquarterly.org/charticles/the-new-normalization/, accessed 13 August 2015.

12 In practical terms, credit card usage is limited in Cuba, as only a small number of US banks issue cards with this possibility.

13 United States, White House, "Charting a New Course on Cuba" (Washington, DC, [2016]), available online at https://obamawhitehouse.archives.gov/issues/foreign-policy/cuba, accessed 24 February 2017.

14 Peter Kornbluh, "A New Deal with Cuba: Caribbean Détente, After a Half-Century of Conflict," *Nation*, 23 December 2014, available online at https://www.thenation.com/article/new-deal-cuba/, accessed 13 August 2015.

15 The move also has significance given that the political campaign around the Cuban 5 has stressed, among other things, their roles as family men. For more on children and their role in Cuba-US affairs, see Karen Dubinsky, *Babies without Borders: Adoption and Migration across the Americas* (Toronto: University of Toronto Press, 2010).

16 Brenner, "Establishing, Not Restoring, Normal Relations."

17 Kornbluh, "New Deal with Cuba." A further meeting took place at the Vatican. See also William M. LeoGrande and Peter Kornbluh, *Back Channel to Cuba: The Hidden History of Negotiations between Washington and Havana* (Chapel Hill: University of North Carolina Press, 2014).

18 For a brief mention of this, see Ricardo Alarcon's comment in Hayden, *Listen Yankee!* 6.

19 Les Whittington and Bruce Campion-Smith, "Canada 'facilitated' Cuba-U.S. talks, Stephen Harper says," *Toronto Star*, 17 December 2014, available online at http://www.thestar.com/news/canada/2014/12/17/canada_facilitated_cubaus_talks_stephen_harper_says.html, accessed 13 August 2015.

20 "Barack Obama thanks Canada for hosting Cuba-U.S. meetings," *CBC News*, 17 December 2014, available online at http://www.cbc.ca/news/politics/barack-obama-thanks-canada-for-hosting-cuba-u-s-meetings-1.2876173, accessed 13 August 2015.

21 Mike Blanchfield, "White House thanks Canada for hosting meetings between U.S., Cuba," *Huffington Post*, 17 December 2014, available online at http://www.huffingtonpost.ca/2014/12/17/white-house-canada-cuba_n_6342342.html, accessed 13 August 2015.

22 "Full text of Barack Obama's speech to the Canadian House of Commons," *National Post*, 29 June 2016, available online at http://news.nationalpost.com/news/canada/full-text-of-barack-obamas-speech-to-the-canadian-house-of-commons, accessed 5 July 2016.

23 "Barack Obama thanks Canada for hosting Cuba-U.S. meetings."

24 Stephen Wilkinson, "Just How Special Is 'Special': Britain, Cuba, and US Relations 1958–2008, an Overview," *Diplomacy and Statecraft* 20, no. 2 (2009): 291–308.

25 "Barack Obama thanks Canada for hosting Cuba-U.S. meetings."

26 Whittington and Campion-Smith, "Canada 'facilitated' Cuba-U.S. talks, Stephen Harper says."

27 For a critique of "democracy promotion" by the United States, see William I. Robinson, *Promoting Polyarchy: Globalization, US Intervention, and Hegemony* (Cambridge: Cambridge University Press, 1996). See also Alessandro Badella, "American Hybris: US Democracy Promotion in Cuba after the Cold War – Part 1," *International Journal of Cuban Studies* 6, no. 2 (2014): 157–88.

28 Barack Obama, "Statement by the president on Cuba policy changes," press release, 17 December 2014 (Washington, DC: White House, Office of the Press Secretary), available online at https://www.whitehouse.gov/the-press-office/2014/12/17/statement-president-cuba-policy-changes, accessed 13 August 2015.

29 Barack Obama, "President Obama Speech in Cuba," *C-SPAN*, 22 March 2016, available online at https://www.youtube.com/watch?v=wEw3H0C-Lj8, accessed 1 June 2016.

30 Louis A. Pérez, Jr, "The United States Reengages Cuba: The Habit of Power," *AU-SSRC Implications of Normalization: Scholarly Perspectives on U.S.-Cuban Relations* (Washington, DC: American University, Center for Latin American & Latino Studies, April 2015), 4, 6, available online at http://www.american.edu/clals/Implications-of-Normalization-with-SSRC-Perez.cfm, accessed 13 August 2015.

31 Barack Obama. "Barack Obama on the Cuban Embargo," *YouTube*, 20 January 2004, available online at https://www.youtube.com/watch?v=I1FoZyRIDFE.

32 Barack Obama, "Our main goal: Freedom in Cuba," *Miami Herald*, 21 August 2007. Cooperation on Haiti included a US offer to provide

supplies to Cuban doctors working in that country and the Cuban decision
to open its airspace to US planes engaged in the relief effort.

33 For details and discussion, see Alessandro Badella, "Between Carter and
Clinton: Obama's Policy towards Cuba," *Caribbean Journal of International
Relations & Diplomacy* 2, no. 2 (2014): 29–59.

34 For more, see Ruth Ellen Wasem, "Cuban Migration to the United States:
Policy and Trends" (Washington, DC: Congressional Research Service,
2 June 2009), 18, available online at https://fas.org/sgp/crs/row/R40566.
pdf, accessed 13 August 2015.

35 Carlos Alzugaray Treto, "Cuba's National Security vis-à-vis the United
States: Conflict or Cooperation?" in Domínguez, Hernández, and Barberia,
Debating US-Cuban Relations, 59–60.

36 Hayden, *Listen Yankee!* 9.

37 Ibid., 236.

38 Ibid., xvi.

39 "Obama: Summit of the Americas 'productive,'" *CNN*, 19 April 2009, available online at http://www.cnn.com/2009/POLITICS/04/19/obama.latin.
america/index.html, accessed 13 August 2015.

40 See United Nations, General Assembly, "Election of the Human Rights Council" (New York, 2012), available online at http://www.un.org/en/ga/67/
meetings/elections/hrc.shtml, accessed 13 August 2015. It is interesting to
note that Cuba's election to the UNHRC in 2006 was supported by 135 states,
while Canada's election to the same body garnered five fewer votes. See
United Nations, General Assembly, "General Assembly elects 47 members of
new Human Rights Council; marks 'new beginning' for human rights promotion, protection," press release, 9 May 2006, available online at http://www.
un.org/press/en/2006/ga10459.doc.htm, accessed 13 August 2015.

41 Obama, "Statement by the president on Cuba policy changes."

42 Hayden, *Listen Yankee!* 210.

43 Amy Davidson, "Barack Obama's Cuba Surprise," *New Yorker*, 17 December 2014, available online at http://www.newyorker.com/news/amy-
davidson/obama-administrations-cuba-surprise, accessed 13 August 2015.

44 For more information on the Republican reaction, see Stephen Collinson,
"2016 Republicans slam Cuba announcement," *CNN*, 19 December 2014,
available online at http://www.cnn.com/2014/12/17/politics/us-cuba-
2016-reax/index.html, accessed 22 August 2015.

45 William M. LeoGrande, "What Trump misses about Cuba," *New York
Times*, 1 December 2016, available online at http://www.nytimes.
com/2016/12/01/opinion/what-trump-misses-about-cuba.html, accessed
15 December 2016.

46 Hayden, *Listen Yankee!* 8.
47 Ibid., 7–8.
48 Andrew F. Cooper and Brian Hocking, "Governments, Non-governmental Organisations and the Re-calibration of Diplomacy," *Global Society* 14, no. 3 (2007): 361–76.
49 Costas M. Constantinou, *On the Way to Diplomacy* (Minneapolis: University of Minnesota Press, 1996), xv.
50 Stuart Murray, "Consolidating the Gains Made in Diplomacy Studies: A Taxonomy 1," *International Studies Perspectives* 9, no. 1 (2008): 22–39.
51 Thomas Princen, "NGOs: Creating a Niche in Environmental Diplomacy," in *Environmental NGOs in World Politics: Linking the Local and the Global*, ed. Thomas Princen and Matthias Finger (London: Routledge, 1994), 31.
52 Murray, "Consolidating the Gains."
53 Young and Henders, "'Other Diplomacies.'"
54 Ibid., 379.
55 Ibid., 378.
56 Ibid., 376.
57 Ibid., 379.
58 Ibid.
59 Ibid.; Beier and Wylie, *Canadian Foreign Policy*.
60 Young and Henders, "'Other Diplomacies,'" 377.
61 John M. Kirk and Peter McKenna, *Canada-Cuba Relations: The Other Good Neighbor Policy* (Gainesville: University Press of Florida, 1997).
62 Peter James Hudson, "Imperial Designs: The Royal Bank of Canada in the Caribbean," *Race & Class* 52, no. 1 (2015): 33–48.
63 Young and Henders, "'Other Diplomacies,'" 383.
64 Thomas D. Hinch, "Cuban Tourism Industry – Its Re-emergence and Future," *Tourism Management* 11, no. 3 (1990): 214–26; and Amalia L. Cabezas, *Economies of Desire: Sex and Tourism in Cuba and the Dominican Republic* (Philadelphia: Temple University Press, 2009).
65 The Cuban government established the Instituto Nacional de Turismo in 1976 with the aim of making tourism a major industry on the island.
66 Manuel Roig-Franzia, "Cuba repeals ban on its citizens staying in hotels on island," *Washington Post*, 31 March 2008, available online at http://www.washingtonpost.com/wp-dyn/content/article/2008/03/31/AR2008033100703.html, accessed 13 August 2015.
67 Michelle McQuigge, "End of golden era for Canadian tourists in Cuba? Affordable vacations will be hard come by, experts say," *MoneySense*, 18 December 2014, available online at http://www.moneysense.ca/spend/travel/end-of-golden-era-for-canadian-tourists-in-cuba/, accessed 13 August 2015.

68 John M. Kirk, "Foreword," in *Cuba Solidarity in Canada: Five Decades of People-to-People Foreign Relations*, ed. Nino Pagliccia (Victoria, BC: Friesen Press, 2014), xvii.

69 Milagros Martínez, "Cuba and the United States: New Opportunities for Academic Diplomacy," *LASAFORUM* 42, no. 2 (2011): 4–6.

70 Canada, Embassy of Canada to Cuba, "Canada-Cuba Relations" (Havana, February 2013), available online at http://www.canadainternational.gc.ca/cuba/bilateral_relations_bilaterales/canada_cuba.aspx?lang=eng, accessed 13 August 2015.

71 Lana Wylie, "Ambassador MD: The Role of Health and Biotechnology in Cuban Foreign Policy," in *Our Place in the Sun: Canada and Cuba in the Castro Era*, ed. Robert Wright and Lana Wylie (Toronto: University of Toronto Press, 2009), 223–45.

72 For information on early Cuban cinema, see Sarah Larsen and Susan Lord, "Cinema in Search of the Public in Cuba: A Translation of 'En Cuba el cine busca al publico' published in *Cine Cubano* 13 (1963)," *Public* 40 (2009), available online at http://public.journals.yorku.ca/index.php/public/article/view/31977/29238, accessed 13 August 2015.

73 Redacción Digital, "Carlos Varela y Sam Roberts Band comparten escenario para celebrar amistad Cuba-Canadá," *Granma*, 26 June 2015, available online at http://www.granma.cu/ciencia/2015-06-26/carlos-varela-y-sam-roberts-band-comparten-escenario-para-celebrar-amistad-cuba-canada, accessed 15 August 2015. See also Caridad Cumaná, Dubinsky, and Reloba de la Cruz, *My Havana*.

74 "See It: '¡Cuba!' in Montreal," *Canadian Art*, 31 January 2008, available online at http://canadianart.ca/must-sees/cuba/, accessed 13 August 2015; and Cuba Tourist Board in Canada, "Seven leading Cuban contemporary artists' works on display at new Toronto gallery," press release, [December 2013], available online at http://gocuba.ca/client/news/show.php?news_id=49, accessed 13 August 2015.

75 Canada, Embassy of Canada to Cuba, "Canada-Cuba Relations."

76 Robert Wright, *Three Nights in Havana: Pierre Trudeau, Fidel Castro and the Cold War World* (Toronto: HarperCollins Canada, 2007).

77 Cynthia Wright, "Between Nation and Empire: The Fair Play for Cuba Committees and the Making of Canada-Cuba Solidarity in the Early 1960s," in Wright and Wylie, *Our Place in the Sun*, 96–120.

78 See, for example, the discussion in Felipe Stuart Courneyeur, "Cuban Palm Trees under Vancouver's Lions Gate: A Memoir of the 1960s Fair

Play for Cuba Committees in Western Canada" (n.p.: Felipe Stuart Courneyeur, 2014), available online at https://johnriddell.files.wordpress.
com/2014/09/cuban-palm-trees-under-vancouvers-lions-gate.pdf,
accessed 7 August 2015.

79 David Austin, *Fear of a Black Nation: Race, Sex, and Security and Sixties Montreal* (Toronto: Between the Lines, 2013).

80 Sean Mills, *The Empire Within: Postcolonial Thought and Political Activism in
Sixties Montreal* (Montreal; Kingston, ON: McGill-Queen's University Press,
2010).

81 Gregory Biniowsky, "The Cuba moment is finally ripe, and Ottawa isn't
seizing it Havana," *Globe and Mail*, 22 March 2016, available online
at http://www.theglobeandmail.com/report-on-business/rob-
commentary/the-cuba-moment-is-finally-ripe-and-ottawa-isnt-seizing-it/
article29315672/, accessed 9 December 2016.

82 Justin Trudeau, "Statement by the Prime Minister of Canada on the death
of former Cuban President Fidel Castro," press release, 26 November 2016,
available online at http://pm.gc.ca/eng/news/2016/11/26/statement-
prime-minister-canada-death-former-cuban-president-fidel-castro,
accessed 9 December 2016.

83 Thomas Walkom, "Justin Trudeau loses his nerve, skips Fidel Castro's
funeral: Walkom," *Toronto Star*, 30 November 2016, available online at
https://www.thestar.com/opinion/commentary/2016/11/30/justin-
trudeau-loses-his-nerve-skips-fidel-castros-funeral-walkom.html, accessed
15 December 2016.

84 Jorge Pérez-López and Carmelo Mesa-Lago, "Cuban GDP Statistics under
the Special Period: Discontinuities, Obfuscation, and Puzzles," *Cuba in
Transition* 19 (2009): 153–67.

85 For a good review of some of the major works addressing this period in
Cuban history, see Archibald R.M. Ritter, "Shifting Realities in Special
Period Cuba," *Latin American Research Review* 45, no. 3 (2010): 229–38.

86 See World Health Organization, "Cuba" (Geneva, 2015), available online at
http://www.who.int/countries/cub/en/, accessed 13 August 2015.

87 Emily Morris, "Unexpected Cuba," *New Left Review* 88 (July–August 2014):
5–45.

88 Arnold August, "Democracy Still in Motion: The 2013 Election Results in
Cuba," *International Journal of Cuban Studies* 6, no. 1 (2014): 87–94.

PART ONE

Histories and (Other) Diplomacies

1 Canada and Cuba: Historical Overview of Their Political and Diplomatic Relations

RAÚL RODRÍGUEZ RODRÍGUEZ

The first eventful years of the post-1959 Cuban-Canadian relationship were critical in shaping the future of Canadian policy towards Cuba. Although Canada's Progressive Conservative government was willing to continue trade and diplomatic relations with the revolutionary Cuban state, it was neither prepared to challenge US hegemony in Latin America and the Caribbean in the context of the Cold War nor willing to strain a multifaceted bilateral relation with Canada's southern neighbour. Nevertheless, Canada's export-oriented economy was poised to benefit from new opportunities opening up in Cuba. Post-1959 Cuba also provided an opportunity for Canada to craft an independent foreign policy based on its own national interest.

An extensive review of regular despatches from the Canadian embassy in Havana from 1959 to 1962 reveals that successive ambassadors, from their own individual perspectives, viewed as their primary goals the assessment of the popular support for, and long-term viability of, the new government in Havana and its relationship with domestic and international left-leaning movements. The Canadian embassy also observed the deterioration of relations between Cuba and the United States, and made suggestions on how Canada could act and react within that context.

The Cuban documents, especially the despatches from the Cuban embassy in Ottawa, show how the new state's young diplomacy was able to understand Canada's position and craft its own strategy with its national interest in mind. The documents stress the potential for Cuba-Canada trade relations and the importance of safeguarding and strengthening the political and diplomatic relationship as a way to minimize the impact of the economic and political actions of the United States.

Despite some minor fluctuations and temporary irritants, mostly due to ideological differences in terms of foreign policy, the eventful early years of the bilateral relationship set the tone and framework for the evolution of post-1959 Cuba-Canada bilateral political and diplomatic relations to the present.

The Post-1959 International and Regional Context and the Character of the Cuban Revolution

A basic feature of Canada's economic structure is its dependency on foreign trade, accounted for by its small domestic market and rich natural resources. Not surprisingly, Cuba-Canadian relations have been based primarily on trade since the mid-eighteenth century.[1] In that context, British North America sought to diversify trade and compete with the United States for the markets of the Spanish West Indies, and Cuba was an important part of that strategy. This was the first of several subsequent attempts to secure markets for Canadian exports that included Cuba.

A short inter-imperialist conflict in 1898 resulted in the transfer of colonial hegemony of Cuba from Spain to the United States. The US occupation government promulgated a series of decrees that allowed for the chartering of foreign banks,[2] and Canadian banks and insurance companies[3] were quick to establish solid operations in Cuba. In fact Canadian chartered banks pioneered the finance of international trade between the United States and the Caribbean, of which Cuba was to become a centrepiece. Subsequently the Royal Bank of Canada[4] and the Bank of Nova Scotia[5] were to have an important presence in Cuba's financial sector prior to 1959.[6]

The triumph of the Cuban Revolution in January 1959 was the result of genuine social upheaval that occurred in the framework of a bipolar order of international relations that emerged from the Second World War and, later, the Cold War. This was a turning point in the history of the Cuban republic, as it marked the beginning of a process of profound socio-economic and political transformation on the island. This transformation translated into a clean break with the prevailing socio-economic and political pattern in the rest of the western hemisphere, and thus necessitated a reorientation of Cuba's foreign policy priorities.

It is also in this Cold War context that Canadian foreign policy sought its place in the world, and started to come to grips with the new reality of having to reorient the centre of its foreign relations from the declining Britain to the United States.[7] This was also the time of the rise of national liberation movements against colonialism in Africa and Asia and the institutionalization of US control in Latin America after the creation of the Organization of American States (OAS) as a pillar of its Monroe Doctrine–inspired hegemonic domination of the western hemisphere.

At this time, Canada's political and diplomatic projection in the hemisphere was limited due to a combination of two main factors. First, Canada's national and economic interests were best served by its connections across the Atlantic, mainly with Britain and the Commonwealth, especially prior to 1945. Second, the United States was opposed to Canada's involvement in the region's institutions until 1961,[8] when the Kennedy administration urged Canada to join the OAS. The Diefenbaker government initiated a few diplomatic actions in the region, especially in Mexico and Brazil, and maintained Canada's trade and diplomatic relations with Cuba, but ultimately decided not to become a member of the OAS.[9]

In the few months after taking power in 1959, the new Cuban government began to implement the Moncada program, the platform of the 26th of July Movement (M-26-7). (The program was named after the military garrison attacked on 26 July 1953 by a group led by Fidel Castro.) Soon, the 1940 Constitution was reinstated and amended, the telephone company was nationalized as early as March, and on 17 May the Agrarian Reform law was enacted.[10] These changes pointed to the beginning of a strong and swift structural transformation that incorporated new property and class relations and, in a search for economic sovereignty and social justice, limited the possibilities of private capital accumulation.

By the end of 1959 the Eisenhower administration began to articulate a policy based mainly, but not solely, on economic sanctions against Cuba. The deterioration of the relationship between Cuba and the United States soon after the triumph of the Cuban Revolution provided Canada and Cuba, whose international trade depended heavily on the US market, with a unique opportunity to improve their bilateral relationship. As US-Cuba political and economic relations escalated into a spiral of conflict, the Cuban government tried to strengthen bilateral relations with other states. Canada was among those Western states that potentially could become an alternative trading partner; it is geographically closer to Cuba than are western European states, and Canadian financial institutions had operated successfully in Cuba since the advent of the twentieth century. Canada was in the best position to become an important trading partner for Cuba. It is in this context that the Canadian government's response to the Cuban Revolution during its early years must be placed.

Canada, the End of the Batista Government, and the Triumph of the Cuban Revolution

An internal Canadian government memo dated 9 January 1959 reveals that "our rejection to sell weapons to Batista may have contributed to earn the good will of the new government."[11] Canada had not been a major source of military equipment for the government of Cuban dictator Fulgencio Batista; however, from 1953 to May 1958 several orders for de Havilland Beaver aircraft and parts to Cuba were fulfilled after being licensed for export there.[12] When the Eisenhower administration announced the suspension of arms sales to the Batista regime in March 1958, the Cuban embassy in Ottawa actively procured Canadian suppliers, but the Canadian government refused most of their requests.[13] This decision earned Canada some consideration once the rebels reached Havana and established a new government.

Also working in Canada's favour, and creating a positive perception of Canada's position with the new Cuban government, was the involvement of the US and UK governments in supplying weapons to the Batista government. In 1958, for example, the British government had sanctioned the export of military and related equipment, most significantly fifteen Comet tanks and seventeen Sea Fury fighter planes. After twelve planes had been delivered by December that year, the sale was suspended under public pressure. Other British military supplies reached Cuba during the year; originally sold to Israel, they were bought by Nicaragua's dictator Anastasio Somoza, a close ally of the United States, who later sold them to Batista.[14] The United States had tried politically and diplomatically to prevent the revolutionary movement from achieving power, and despite imposing a formal weapons embargo, kept a military mission in Cuba and supplied weapons through its military base at Guantánamo.[15]

On the diplomatic and political front, the *Toronto Daily Star* reported on 2 January 1959 that an External Affairs spokesman said that the Canadian government would "wait a decent interval" before recognizing the new government, implying that, although the government would make up its own mind, it would be guided by the attitude of the United States.[16] Canada formally announced recognition of the new Cuban revolutionary government on 8 January, one day after the United States. On the official recognition, Prime Minister John Diefenbaker wrote in his memoirs: "Our interaction is guided by the international rules that exist between two sovereign nations." He further elaborated that "it was Canada's duty to maintain with Cuba the cordial relations customary with the recognized government of another country."[17] Secretary of State for External Affairs Sidney Smith then instructed Canada's ambassador in Cuba to "confirm the desire of the Canadian government to maintain friendly relations with the Cuban Revolutionary government."[18]

A closer examination, with the benefit of hindsight and access to original documents, reveals the main elements that were taken into account at the time. According to an internal memo signed by Smith in relation to a Cuban government request for recognition, Canada doubted that the Cuban government "fulfills the usual conditions for recognition," yet Canada's main concern was "not to lag behind other governments who have already extended recognition." The postscript also reveals another element the Diefenbaker government considered: "As Canada has a large investment in Cuba it is highly desirable that Canada should not lag in recognizing the new government."[19] It is not clear, however, what the document meant by a "large investment," since Cuba-Canada bilateral trade in 1958 was not significant in terms of either products or value.[20]

In April 1959, in his first trip abroad as prime minister, Fidel Castro travelled to the United States and Canada. On 26 April he arrived in Montreal, where he met with the media and the business community, representatives of which, especially from the Royal Bank of Canada and Sun Life Insurance, requested that Cuba's prime minister be met with suitable honours.

The reaction of the Canadian government, however, was rather less enthusiastic. Moreover, Canadian officials explained their position in detail to the US government. On 13 April External Affairs official Marcel Cadeux wrote, in a memo to Assistant Under-Secretary of State for External Affairs John W. Holmes: "I then stressed that the visit of Fidel Castro was not entertained with any particular enthusiasm."[21] Three days later the Canadian embassy in Havana also expressed opposition to Castro's visit. Ambassador Hector Allard wrote on 16 March: "Castro is obviously doing his very best to squeeze an invitation somehow to get to Canada and I am only hopeful that the junior chamber of commerce in Montreal will not put into operation their reported intention to invite Castro to Canada."[22]

The issue of arms exports to Cuba resurfaced after January 1959 as the new Cuban government tried to reorganize its defence and security apparatus. In February the government requested, through the Canadian embassy in Havana, the services of ten Royal Canadian Mounted Police (RCMP) officers to help train Cuba's police and internal security forces.[23] This role was not a new one for the RCMP: instances of such cooperation had occurred in Latin America and the Caribbean since the Second World War. Despite some initial positive reporting about the feasibility of cooperation nothing came of it.[24] Furthermore, later that year the Canadian government refused to allow de Havilland Canada to fill Cuba's order for additional Beaver aircraft for civilian and agricultural use.

Cuba's Nationalization of Foreign Companies

Nationalization of foreign property was a key element of the new Cuban government's economic policy. The first action came as early as 3 March 1959, when the telephone company was nationalized. But the most important new law was the 17 May 1959 agrarian reform, a long-overdue action basically aimed at transforming the pattern of land tenure on the island.[25]

The decision to nationalize all US-owned property without quick compensation led to the first of several US proclamations directed against trade with the revolutionary government. From Cuba's perspective, the nationalizations were a sovereign act in the national interest.[26] Moreover, the Cuban state was literally unable to make compensation payments due in large measure to the lack of cooperation on the part of the US government.[27] In response, on 19 October 1960, the Eisenhower administration placed Cuba on the US Export Control List, cutting off all exports to Cuba except non-subsidized foodstuffs, medicines, and medical supplies.

In contrast, the revolutionary government treated Canadian companies and interests differently. The case of two Canadian banks serves as a good example of such exceptional treatment. On 13 and 14 October 1960, new decrees placed 382 Cuban- and foreign-owned businesses, with an estimated value of US$2 billion in total assets, under both state ownership and the state control for the first time.[28] The entire trade sector of the economy was nationalized, as well as all banking establishments except two: the twenty-three branches of the Royal Bank and the eight branches of the Bank of Nova Scotia.[29] Indeed, the two Canadian banks were·the only foreign banks permitted to operate in the country.[30]

Other Canadian interests were also protected. For instance, when the US-owned Nicaro nickel plant was closed in October 1960, the newspaper *Revolución* reported that Canada now held a "monopoly of nickel" in Cuba. The Canadian ambassador, Allan Anderson, was then contacted to ensure that he did not interpret the reporting as in any way hindering "Cuba's good relations with Canada."[31] On another occasion, Cuba's acting minister of foreign relations, Carlos Olivares Sánchez, met with the Canadian ambassador to inform him "privately" of "the value which the Cuban government sets on friendly relations with Canada" and its decision to appoint as ambassador to Canada Américo Cruz, a career diplomat then serving as Cuban ambassador to Argentina.[32]

Despite the positive signals from the Cuban Ministry of Foreign Affairs regarding the bilateral relationship, Ambassador Anderson was not optimistic that cordial relations would be sustained. In November 1960 he complained that the recent nationalization of "a couple of Canadian firms" had generated "so much telegraphic correspondence with Ottawa that I shudder to think what it may be like when the bell rings for the Canadian banks."[33] For the time being, however, his feeling was that the Cubans' "sole purpose is to get, while it is still possible, whatever goods can be got from Canada to fill the various needs which cannot be supplied from the Sino-Soviet group."[34] Although Cuba's intentions with regard to trade with Canada might have been broader, the embassy's concerns, as well as those of the Department of External Affairs, were generally limited to the dealings of the Royal Bank and the Bank of Nova Scotia.

The reasons Cuba's new government exempted the Canadian banks from the October decrees have been the subject of a good deal of speculation. One widely accepted thesis suggests that the government sought to keep open at least one banking channel to the free currency exchange market. Canadian banks, as in the case of the potential purchase of spare parts and manufactured goods, were in the best position because of their long-standing involvement in Cuban banking affairs and their financial connections with the United States and the United Kingdom.

The Canadian government was pleased with the exceptional treatment accorded to Canadian companies and nationals; it was one reason for maintaining a completely different approach than that of the United

States towards political and diplomatic relations with Cuba. Shortly before his departure in May 1960, Ambassador Anderson had a final interview with the Cuban foreign minister, Raúl Roa, who "admired Canada's habits adhering to basic principles in international affairs and voting according to her own light rather than meekly following UK or USA or anybody else."[35] This was a constant position of Cuban diplomats in their interactions with their Canadian counterparts, which suggests an understanding of Canadian sensitivity and national pride.

Cuba-Canada Trade and the US Embargo

Despite the growing tensions between Washington and Havana during 1959, US companies exported US$436 million in products and spare parts to Cuba, $26 million in automobile parts, $27 million in electrical equipment, and nearly $22 million in industrial machinery.[36] The following year, Cuba generated great interest in Canada. First there was the issue of the treatment accorded to Canadian businesses there. Second, as the US government ratcheted up the economic pressure, Canadian companies appeared poised to fill the large void left by US companies.

In that context the top leadership of the new revolutionary government tried to preserve and further expand Cuba's economic links with Canada. Canadian companies had the same technology and standards as US-based companies – indeed, in most cases, they were US subsidiaries. Cuba's ambassador in Ottawa, Américo Cruz,[37] noted in a report to his minister: "In terms of economic relations they [Canadians] have a situation similar to what we had previous to 1959,"[38] obviously referring to the fact that the international trade of both Canada and Cuba was heavily dependent on the US market.

On 8 December 1960 a ten-member Cuban delegation headed by Minister of the Economy Regino Boti and composed of high-ranking representatives of the Cuban banking, energy, and transportation sectors visited Ottawa to promote a significant increase in trade between the two countries.[39] In the initial response, Canada's minister for international trade, George Hees, stated: "Canada would be willing to sell the products that Cuba is unable to acquire as a result of the US embargo."[40]

Indeed, in a speech to the House of Commons on 12 December, Prime Minister Diefenbaker expressed the Canadian government's opposition to US commercial sanctions against Cuba: "We respect the other nation's opinions as to their relations with Cuba as much as we expect that our points of view be respected. Canada reserves the right to trade with any country, including Cuba, and any commodity it so pleases."[41] The Cuban trade mission and Canada's initial response elevated tensions in Canada-US relations.

Consideration of the US reaction, however, contributed to a clarification and redefinition of Canada's position regarding trade relations with Cuba. On 23 December Diefenbaker issued a statement that highlighted the Canadian government's desire to maintain commercial relations with Cuba, set Canada's position in relation to the US commercial embargo, and, most important, presented a brief summary of the main aspects of Canadian foreign policy towards the Cuban Revolution.[42] Henceforth the Canadian government sought to walk a fine line between "practical compliance" and "independent trading"[43] in its bilateral interactions with Cuba for years to come.

In another interesting development, before issuing the all-important 23 December statement the Diefenbaker government decided to apply export controls on trade with Cuba based on the Export and Imports Permit Act of 1954.[44] On 16 December Trade Minister Hees introduced an amendment to the act prohibiting licences to re-export goods to Cuba and defining a list of Canadian products that would not be allowed to be exported to Cuba or that would require a special licence.[45] On this occasion the minister was clear: "As the Prime Minister has said, we do not intend to allow what would be in effect smuggling US-origin goods to Cuba."[46]

Canada was also concerned that the US embargo might drive Cuba into the Soviet camp. Thus it was up to countries such as Canada and the United Kingdom[47] to do what they could to maintain links with Havana. As Diefenbaker remarked, "[w]e do not minimize American concern, but it is the Government's view that to maintain mutually beneficial economic relations with Cuba may help and contribute to the restoration of traditional relationships between Cuba and the Western world."[48] It was widely believed that isolating the island from Western trade and diplomatic contact would instead drive it to rely further on less desirable associations.[49]

Another important element that provided economic benefit and helped deflect US criticism was the fact that Canada maintained a trade surplus with Cuba from 1959 to 1964. Canadian officials were quick to point out that, rather than helping a communist nation, "trade with Cuba in non-strategic goods runs heavily in favour of Canada." And when told that Canada's trade was helping Cuba promote communist subversion, they would reply, "on the contrary, Cuban trade with Canada is absorbing dollars secured from other sources."[50]

Finally, Diefenbaker expressed his opinion about Canada's trade with Cuba and Canada's position towards embargoes in general by pointing out that "[e]mbargoes and trade controls are powerful and sometimes double-edged weapons. If we use them towards Cuba we may be under pressure to use them elsewhere and unnecessary damage will be done to Canadian trade."[51]

The Cuban Perspective on Early Political and Diplomatic Ties with Canada

A detailed dispatch by Cuba's ambassador in Ottawa dated 16 January 1961 contains important references to the impact of the high-level Cuban trade delegation's visit to Ottawa the month before and the embassy's overall impression of the effect of the United States on the Cuba-Canada bilateral relationship. The dispatch is a summary of the ambassador's meeting with Howard Green, Canada's secretary of state for external affairs. Green, according to the dispatch, underlined how important it was for Canada "to maintain cordial relations with the United States," while assuring that "the overall policy of Canada was that of maintaining an independent foreign (?) and commercial policy and that they would maintain friendly relation with Cuba."[52] Once again, Ambassador Cruz was reminded of Canada's sensitivity and vulnerability to US reaction.

In his long report, Cruz stated that Green "went on to tell me that they are receiving great pressure from the United States because of the cordial welcome that was accorded to the Cuban commercial delegation that recently visited Ottawa, which led to some rectification from Canadian officials as to their intention towards the revolutionary government of Cuba."[53] Evidently Cruz "got the message" from Green, as the ambassador recommended continuing to promote trade with a low profile and discretion: "It is my opinion that we must conduct ourselves more quietly because we are generating problems for them and they could be forced to change their policy towards Cuba, they know that and they tell us."[54]

The rather nuanced three-page dispatch shows, in short, that both Canadian and Cuban officials were aware of the impact of the United States on the bilateral relationship. A week later, on 24 January, Cruz conveyed the same impression in another dispatch to Havana: "[T]o show off our good relations with them a bit too much has brought about serious problems with the United States for them, therefore it is my opinion that we must not speak too much about this."[55]

That the Cuban revolutionary government understood the Canadian government's position and the potential impact of the US response is reflected in a letter from the Cuban Ministry of Foreign Affairs to Ambassador Cruz in Ottawa: "We call your attention to the fact that the resistance provided by the government of Canada, up to now, to the United States' continuing pressures, aimed at forcing Canada to join the blockade of Cuba, must not be underestimated."[56] In this message and in subsequent communications between the ambassador and the Cuban Foreign Ministry, Cruz was clearly instructed to work hard in confidence-building actions and to use "the tools of the diplomatic arsenal to safeguard the interests of maintaining relations with Canada, despite the fundamental ideological differences that separate both governments."[57]

The Cuban embassy in Ottawa would follow these instructions and work hard to promote the bilateral relationship, even overlooking potential irritants. For instance, Canadian Customs and the RCMP strictly enforced all regulations to the point of searching Cuban ships in Canadian ports. One very public case was the search and confiscation of part of the cargo aboard the Cuban vessel *Bahía de Siguanea* at the port of Montreal.[58] At this point the Cuban government's reaction was guided by the intention of preserving its commercial relations, as the following instruction to Ambassador Cruz reveals: "[I]f they search our shipments, it could be because they want to do something that pleases the United States, [so] the best position is to overlook these actions and continue to work hard in confidence-building measures between Canada and Cuba."[59]

Canadian Diplomatic Reaction to the Cuba-US Conflict

An important aspect of Cuba-Canada relations was the Canadian reaction to the conflict between the United States and Cuba. Canadian officials were keenly aware that their policies towards Cuba could affect Canada-US relations. It was obvious to the Canadian government that the deterioration of Cuba-US relations and the consequent increase of the triangular tension were not desirable. In a personal letter to British prime minister Harold Macmillan dated 19 July 1960, Diefenbaker wrote: "[T]he evolution of events in Cuba is potentially dangerous. I would like to see some things done that lead to a better relation between Cuba and the United States."[60] An instance of the role Canada could play had been provided three days earlier. On 16 July, Mexican president Adolfo López Mateos wrote to Diefenbaker asking that Canada join Mexico and Brazil in an effort to mediate the crisis between the United States and Cuba.[61]

Despite Diefenbaker's belief that Canada could become involved, he decided to turn down the Mexican president's offer, realizing that, with the US position so deeply entrenched, joint mediation with Brazil and Mexico would be unsuccessful. He also believed it would anger the United States, which was, after all, Canada's closest ally. A dispatch from the US embassy in Ottawa clarified the Canadian position: "I was summoned to call on External Affairs Minister Green this morning. He asked me to convey a personal message from the Prime Minister to the President to the effect that the President of Mexico recently suggested to the Prime Minister that they together with the President of Brazil should offer the United States and Cuba their good offices in finding ways to ameliorate the present situation … the Prime Minister is anxious to make clear that he is not contemplating action on the part of Canada unless this would be agreeable to the United States."[62] The Mexican initiative thus was aborted in its early stages, but only after top-level communications involving the leaders of the three countries.

From the Cuban side, the position was clarified in the early part of 1960: "We hereby instruct you to respond and explain that the Cuban government appreciates that friendly gesture of the government of Canada, but Cuba will deal with its differences with the United States in a bilateral way and through direct talks."[63]

Another moment for Canada came in May 1961, during Minister Howard Green's trip to Europe to participate in a NATO ministerial conference in Oslo, Norway. Speaking to the press in Geneva, he stated that Canada was ready to mediate in the Cuba-US dispute.[64] The Kennedy administration reacted with displeasure, however, and instructed Secretary of State Dean Rusk, who was on his way to Oslo, to meet with Green and explain to him the reality of what was happening in Cuba.[65] After the meeting, the *Washington Post* reported on 11 May, Green asserted that Canada was ready to play a larger role in the hemisphere, and criticized the US position on Cuba by expressing quite a different perception of the events there than that held by the United States.[66]

At the NATO meeting the day before, Green had stated that the Cuban revolutionaries were nationalists, rather than communists, and urged the United States to accept the principle of letting the Cubans choose their own form of government without outside interference.[67] Rusk's take was radically different. He placed the Cuban process squarely in the context of the Cold War, and urged the NATO foreign ministers to consider what steps could be taken to check the spread of Sino-Soviet penetration in Latin America.[68] For his part, Diefenbaker, as he did a year earlier when he considered the Mexican request, distanced himself from his external affairs minister's statement. At this point, it became obvious that, despite divergent perceptions about events in Cuba and the nature and the scope of the Cuban process, the Canadian government was not ready to confront the United States over Cuba.

From the Bay of Pigs to the Missile Crisis: The Defence and Security Dimensions

Canada remained firm in its position to continue trade and formal diplomatic relations with Cuba, despite pressure from the United States. However, the Canadian political, ideological, and diplomatic response to the US-sponsored Bay of Pigs invasion in April 1961 illustrates a different Canadian position towards Cuba. Canada's official response to the invasion organized by the US Central Intelligence Agency confirmed Canada's position as unequivocally on the side of the United States and the Western powers in the context of the Cold War. In a statement in the House of Commons, Diefenbaker clearly accused Cuba of providing international communism with a bridgehead from which the penetration of the whole of Latin America could be launched.[69]

Following a long meeting with Canada's under-secretary of state for external affairs and other officials from the Latin America desk, Ambassador Cruz wrote an extensive report to his ministry in Havana, noting that, although Canadian officials acknowledged that the invasion had been organized and financed by the United States, Canada did not, and would not, condemn its southern neighbour for its role in the invasion. Canadian officials went on to explain that Canada considered that Cuba had not done enough to improve its relations with the United States, and that it was only to Cuba's advantage to try to reach an agreement with the United States to save the Revolution or otherwise face destruction. Cruz nonetheless regarded the meeting as fruitful in that "we have been able to find out the real thoughts of this government and the their policy in relation to our struggle against imperialism ... [T]he meeting has allowed us to know that we cannot expect much of this county and it shows that their position is right on the side of the United States."[70] Indeed, the Canadian government's reaction would negatively surpass Cruz's low expectations by denying a Cuban request for humanitarian aid.[71] He reported: "I conveyed my dismay for not receiving cooperation from the Canadian government for a humanitarian action consisting in transporting medicines for the wounded with urgent need." The ambassador went on to warn: "[T]his episode in my opinion will be one of many to come in the future against Cuba."[72]

The Canadian reaction to the Bay of Pigs invasion and its aftermath[73] was a watershed moment for the Cuban ambassador, as he finally understood the nuances of Canadian policy. It showed that, despite Ottawa's rejection of US pressure in terms of trade and diplomacy towards Cuba and the prevalence of the "liberal" strain in the Canadian's approach to Cuba that favoured dialogue and engagement, Canada was firmly on the side of its NATO partners.[74]

The pattern of framing the Cuba-US conflict within the bipolar logic of the Cold War is even clearer in a Canadian statement on hemispheric and global problems on 3 July 1961: "The Canadian Government is as concerned as any government over the Communistic trends of the Cuban Government."[75]

Nineteen sixty-two would prove to be a more complex period for the Cuba-Canada bilateral relationship as issues other than trade came into play in the context of the Cold War. An increased US effort to bring about regime change in Cuba combined economic isolation with diplomatic, military, and subversive components. This US pressure, along with Cuba's worsening economic situation, led to the decline of Cuba's foreign-exchange resources, thus limiting Cuba's ability to increase its trade with Canada.

Soon after the Bay of Pigs fiasco, the US government started to put together Operation Mongoose,[76] the largest subversion operation the United States had ever organized against any foreign state. The thoroughness of the plan and the diversity of threats to Cuba's national security were among the factors that led the Cuban government to accept the installation of Soviet nuclear missiles in Cuban territory.[77]

The ensuing Cuban missile crisis – or October Crisis, as it is widely referred to in Cuba – was the most dramatic event of the Cold War, with the United States and the Soviet Union coming to the brink of nuclear war. Canada's role in the crisis, however, generally tends to be minimized in the numerous international conferences, books, and even films about the event, with the notable exception of Peter Haydon's important contribution.[78]

Apart from the much-publicized Kennedy-Diefenbaker fallout and the obvious rift in Canadian civil and military relations with the United States, the Canadian prime minister paid a high political price, and was heavily criticized for being hesitant and unable to make tough decisions.[79] Nonetheless, as Canada's navy was closely integrated with US forces under NATO maritime command, it became an important part of the submarine barrier permitting units of the US navy to move south into the blockade zone.[80] Thus, despite its initial reticence, basically in reaction to its not being consulted beforehand, given the Canada-US partnership in North American air defence, Canada opted to meet its commitment to the United States.

As Don Munton further explains in his chapter in this volume, during the early years of the Revolution, the Canadian embassy in Havana also provided intelligence on Cuba to the US and other allies on a regular basis. Since Canada lacked a spy agency at that time, Canadian diplomats would be sent out to collect intelligence on military installations and other information, including the initial preparations for the installation of Soviet missiles. Information from high-level meetings between Canadian and Cuban officials were also made available to US intelligence.[81] The reports would be sent from the Canadian embassy in Havana by diplomatic pouch to External Affairs in Ottawa, which would then forward them to the Canadian embassy in Washington. An official there would then gather the reports in an envelope and "walk them over to the State Department."[82]

In Havana, Canadian embassy officials helped verify *in situ*, without authorization from the Cuban government, the dismantling and removal of Soviet missiles already in Cuba in the days following the end of the crisis. The dispatches of Ambassador George Kidd during the crisis included comments on the positions of Soviet missiles and, once the crisis ended, the ambassador reported on the withdrawal of weapons and Soviet military personnel.[83] In addition, at the request of the US State Department, the Canadian embassy monitored the strength of the signal of Voice of America radio broadcasts in Cuban territory.

After the crisis of 1962, obviously due to the volume of information generated by these activities, the Canadian government dedicated an official with the specific task of collecting and classifying information.

For eleven years, from 1961 to 1972, Canadian diplomats assigned to the embassy in Havana made efforts to collect military and socio-economic information, including monitoring Soviet facilities, handling Cuban agents on behalf of the US government, and even reporting on the tensions between Cuba and the Soviet Union after the end of the Missile Crisis.[84] Although these activities originated from a request from the US government, the Canadian authorities cooperated regularly, demonstrating a high degree of convergence with the US. Indeed, an internal memo from External Affairs on the feasibility and importance of maintaining the embassy in Cuba lists among the pros the collection of general and specific information that the United States would seek.[85]

Conclusion

Cuba-Canada political and diplomatic relations have been driven by two basic factors. One is the need for the Canadian export economy to find every viable way to promote trade. The other, especially after the Second World War, is the need for Canada to define an independent foreign policy based on its national interests in the context of the western hemisphere and beyond. This latter factor has been a recurrent theme in Canadian political culture, and enjoys high levels of public approval domestically.

No other period illustrates the combination of these two factors like the years 1959 to 1962 and from the standpoint of Cuba-Canada bilateral relations. For Canada's Progressive Conservative government in this period, an option for an independent Cuba policy was based on a national sovereignty position consistent with its tradition in favour of multilateral over unilateral action. A made-in-Canada foreign policy towards Cuba also distinguished Canada from the United States. The aforementioned considerations were relatively more important than the trade benefits that Canada could obtain from maintaining an economic relationship with Cuba. This has been a permanent element in favour of the two countries' diplomatic and political ties over the past fifty years.

Canadian documents and dispatches show a predominant liberal strain in Canadian political culture as Canadian officials genuinely believed that embargo and isolation would push Cuba to the east side of the Cold War divide. The Diefenbaker government walked a thin line in terms of Canada's Cuba policy by stressing engagement, trade, and political dialogue despite ideological disagreement. This Canadian position has endured the test of time in the post–Cold War period and well into the twenty-first century.

As the documents indicate, early Cuban revolutionary diplomacy endeavoured to maintain and promote ties with Canada. Cuba's leaders valued and understood Canada's position, while they tried to construct a new model of economic and social development. The Canadian trade and political relationship was a much-needed short-term open door to the West in the early years. However, maintaining political and diplomatic relations with Canada was also seen as part of Cuba's national interest and within the objectives of Cuban foreign policy, as it represented a way to construct a different kind of relationship with the West, rather than one of subordination and dependent capitalism. In this sense, Cuban relations with Canada might be seen as a model of diplomatic engagement.

Cuba-Canada political and diplomatic ties have shown remarkable continuity over the past 50 years despite highs and lows and minor irritants derived from basic ideological divergence. Scholars and commentators have come up with different phrases to characterize Canada's policy towards Cuba over the past few decades, from Lester Pearson's "coldly correct" in the 1960s and Brian Mulroney's "disinterest and neglect" in the 1980s, from Pierre Trudeau's famous "Viva Cuba" to the post–Cold War "constructive engagement" of Jean Chrétien. We have also seen episodes of "northern ice" and a Cuban reference to Canada as "enemy territory."

But as a matter of fact, both Liberal and Conservative Canadian governments have refrained from questioning the legitimacy of the Cuban government that emerged after 1959, and have not imposed any conditionality on the maintenance of trade, political, or diplomatic relations. The Cuban government has valued these Canadian positions as an important diplomatic asset to keep engagement and channels of communication open.

At the end of 2014 the governments of Cuba and the United States agreed to re-establish diplomatic relations and start a process to normalize bilateral interactions. Canada did not participate in the substance of the discussions, but the Canadian government was indispensable in providing a venue and support for these efforts. Its good offices, and the hosting of the talks between Cuba and the United States, led to the most significant diplomatic breakthrough in more than fifty years in the western hemisphere.

Canadian prime minister Stephen Harper was quick to state that the role of Canada in the US-Cuba talks was limited. He claimed Canada only provided the space for the negotiators to meet and agreed to keep the existence of the talks secret. The Cuban government accepted Canadian involvement and publicly acknowledged it. This is the result of confidence built over the years and a positive perception of Canada's willingness to maintain open diplomatic and trade relations with Cuba despite their ideological differences. After all, looking back, this is generally consistent with the positions espoused by Diefenbaker and especially Green in the early post-1959 period.

NOTES

1 A museum in Lunenburg, Nova Scotia, holds labels from Havana and Santiago de Cuba companies that imported salted cod; see John M. Kirk and Peter McKenna, *Canada-Cuba Relations: The Other Good Neighbor* (Gainesville: University of Florida Press, 1995), 7. In an address to the University of Havana in 1995 marking the fiftieth anniversary of the establishment of diplomatic relations between Canada and Cuba, the speaker of the House of Commons, Gilbert Parent, noted: "When we established our official relationship in 1945 ... commerce was at the centre of our interest in Cuba. While many years have passed, trade and investment remain a major focus of our partnership"; Gilbert Parent, "Canada and Cuba Mark 50 Years of Dialogue," *Canadian Speeches: Issues of the Day* 9, no. 7 (1995): 36–9.

2 Rolando Rodríguez García, *Cuba: las máscaras y las sombras: la primera ocupación* (Havana: Editorial Ciencias Sociales, 2007).

3 During the first decade of the republic, two banks and two insurance companies were incorporated in Cuba. The Royal Bank arrived in 1899 and the Bank of Nova Scotia in 1906. Both banks would be largely involved in financing Cuba-US trade. In 1907 Sun life Assurance was followed by Confederation Life.

4 The Royal Bank was the most successful. By 1923 the Canadian bank had come into possession of at least 16 sugar mills and 120 hectares of fertile sugar cane land. According to a report on Cuba by the World Bank, the Royal Bank was listed number one among all commercial banks in total deposits; see Francis Adam Truslow, *Report on Cuba* (Washington, DC: International Bank for Reconstruction and Development, 1951).

5 Neil C. Quigley, "The Bank of Nova Scotia in the Caribbean," *Business History Review* 63 (1989): 797–838.

6 Truslow, *Report on Cuba*.

7   From 1940 to 1957 Canada's ruling class was radically reshaped. In 1939
    the United Kingdom still seemed a powerful force, and the men who ruled
    Canada turned as much to Britain as to the United States, economically,
    culturally, and politically. After 1940 the ruling class found its centre of
    gravity in the United States. See George P. Grant, *Lament for a Nation* (Mon-
    treal; Kingston, ON: McGill-Queen's University Press, 2005).

8   This assertion is widely supported in the existing literature on Canada's
    Latin American relations. See J.C.M. Ogelsby, *Gringos from the Far North:
    Essays in the History of Canadian-Latin American Relations, 1866–1968*
    (Toronto: Macmillan of Canada, 1976); Peter McKenna, *Canada and the OAS:
    From Dilettante to Full Partner* (Montreal; Kingston, ON: McGill-Queen's
    University Press, 1995); and James Rochlin, *Discovering the Americas: The
    Evolution of Canadian Foreign Policy towards Latin America* (Vancouver:
    UBC Press, 1993). On the US opposition to Canadian participation in the
    institutions of the Inter-American System, see Douglas G. Anglin, "United
    States Opposition to Canadian Membership in the Pan American Union: A
    Canadian View," *International Organization* 15, no. 1 (1961): 1–20.

9   Asa McKercher, "Southern Exposure: Diefenbaker, Latin America and
    the Organization of American States," *Canadian Historical Review* 93, no. 1
    (2012): 57–80.

10 For an excellent compilation of the text of the new laws and their impact,
    see José Bell, Delia Luisa López, and Tania Caram, eds., *Documentos de la
    Revolución cubana 1959* (Havana: Editorial Ciencias Sociales, 2008).

11 Memorandum for the Minister, Library and Archives Canada (hereafter
    cited as LAC), RG 25, vol. 7584, file 10, 44-AK-40.

12 A recent article sheds some light on Canadian involvement in arms sales
    to the Batista army, mainly citing the sales of Beaver aircraft. See Dennis
    Molinaro, "'Calculated Diplomacy': John Diefenbaker and the Origins of
    Canada's Cuba Policy," in *Our Place in the Sun: Canada and Cuba in the Cas-
    tro Era*, ed. Robert Wright and Lana Wylie (Toronto: University of Toronto
    Press, 2009), 75–95. The Batista regime's air force, however, was equipped
    mostly with US and UK aircraft. The Canadian-made Beavers were not
    sold for military purposes and, as documents show, the Canadians did not
    know they would be modified to fight the guerrillas.

13 Canadian documents reveal that the Cuban diplomatic mission tried
    very hard, well into November 1958, to obtain weapons from Canada. A
    Canadian internal document dated 21 November 1958 details the efforts of
    the Cuban diplomats in that regard; see "Export of Arms to Cuba," Interim
    Report, LAC, RG 25, vol. 7584, file 10, AK 11044, part 2.1. The only licensed
    Canadian export of military-related equipment was an order of spare parts

for Staghound armoured vehicles on 8 October 1958. Requests for thirty-three Sea Fury aircraft and spares, Browning rifles, pistols, and clips were refused; see "Export of 33 Sea Fury Aircraft to Cuba," LAC, RG 25, vol. 7584, file 10, AK 11044, part 2.1.

14 Chris Hull, "Our Arms in Havana: British Military Sales to Batista and Castro 1958–59," *Diplomacy and Statecraft* 18, no. 3 (2007): 593–616.

15 Carlos Alzugaray Treto, *Crónica de un fracaso imperial: la administración Eisenhower y el derrocamiento de la dictadura de Batista* (Havana: Editorial Ciencias Sociales, 2000).

16 "Wait decent interval to recognize Castro," *Toronto Daily Star*, 2 January 1959.

17 John G. Diefenbaker, *One Canada: Memoirs of the Right Honourable John G. Diefenbaker* (Toronto: Macmillan, 1976), 169.

18 "New Cuban Govt. Recognized," *Canadian Weekly Bulletin* 14, no. 2 (14 January 1959), 6.

19 Sidney Smith, "Recognition of the New Cuban Government," Memorandum to Prime Minister, 8 January 1959, LAC, RG 25, vol. 7257, file 10224-40, part 5.1.

20 For more on Cuba-Canada trade at that time, see Archibald R.M. Ritter, "Canadian-Cuban Economic Relations: Past, Present, and Prospective," in Wright and Wylie, *Our Place in the Sun*, table 1.

21 Marcel Cadieux, Memorandum from Assistant Under Secretary of State for American Division, "Fidel Castro's Visit to Canada," 13 April 1959, DEA/11562-116-40, Documents on Canadian External Relations, vol. 26, 1959, Department of Foreign Affairs and International Trade.

22 FM Havana Mar16/59 Restd, To TT External 45 Priority FM WASHDC Ref YourTel X47 Mar12, Fidel Castro, YourTeL Crossed My TeL 44 Mar13.

23 Harold Boyer, "Canada and the Cuban Revolution: A Study in International Relations" (PhD diss., Simon Fraser University, 1972).

24 "RCMP may help Castro plan police," *Toronto Daily Star*, 4 February 1959.

25 The Cuban Constitution of 1940 proscribed latifundia; however, up to 1959 no law had been enacted to enforce that provision. Article 24 of the document provided the legal framework for expropriation in the name of the national interest.

26 Miguel A. D'Estéfano Pisani, *La política exterior de la Revolución cubana* (Havana: Editorial Ciencias Sociales, 2002).

27 Batista government officials took more than US$470 million from the Cuban National Bank to the United States and never returned, even though the US government had recognized the Cuban government.

28 José Bell, Delia Luisa López, and Tania Caram, eds., *Documentos de la Revolución cubana 1960* (Havana: Editorial Ciencias Sociales, 2008).
29 The Royal Bank closed its operations in Cuba in 1961. It had a satisfactory agreement with the Cuban National Bank and maintained an office in Cuba until 1965. The Royal Bank was allowed to send out its capital stock in US bonds; the National Bank of Cuba assumed responsibility for all savings and current accounts of the Canadian bank's twenty-three branches, as well as its liabilities.
30 United Kingdom, Foreign Office, "Cuba," telegram to Canadian Department of External Affairs, 10 November 1960, LAC, RG 25, vol. 5351, file 10224-40, part 10.
31 Canadian Embassy, Havana, "Castro Reaction to US Decision to Close Nicaro Nickel Plant," numbered letter L-690, 3 October 1960, LAC, RG 25, vol. 5048, file 2444-40, part 4.
32 Anderson added, "I was to keep this to myself, as advance information … Therefore please assume that I have *not* told you this, at least not officially." Canadian Embassy, Havana, "Conversation with Acting Minister," numbered letter L-708, 6 October 1960, LAC, RG 25, vol. 5074, file 4568-40, part 2.
33 Canadian Embassy, Havana, "Havana Chancery: Mixed Impressions," dispatch D-811, 4 November 1960, LAC, RG 25, vol. 5074, file 4568-40, part 2.
34 Canadian Embassy, Havana, "Canadian Position in Cuba," numbered letter L-837, 14 November 1960, LAC, RG 25, vol. 5074, file 4568-40, part 2.
35 Canadian Embassy, Havana, "Interview with Cuban Foreign Minister," telegram, 19 May 1961, LAC, RG 25, vol. 5075, file 4568-40, part 6.
36 Thus, trade was to become the most important issue in Cuba-Canada relations in the following year; see Norton Anderson, "Can we do business with Castro's Cuba?" *Financial Post*, 29 October 1960.
37 Cruz was highly regarded by the Cuban government as a man of revolutionary prestige; he was appointed Cuban ambassador to Ottawa after the defection of the previous ambassador, Luis Baralt.
38 Américo Cruz, Ambassador to Canada, to Raúl Roa, Minister of External Relations, 16 January 1961, Ministerio de Relaciones Exteriores (henceforth MINREX) Archives.
39 Press reports speak of Cuba's offer to purchase $150 million worth of Canadian goods, which would have represented a tenfold increase in bilateral trade. See "Opposing Foreign Trade, Trade by Countries," Right Honourable John G. Diefenbaker Centre for the Study of Canada (hereafter Diefenbaker Canada Centre), Diefenbaker Papers, MG01/VI/722/C962.

40 "Minister says Canada welcomes Cuba trade," *Sacramento Bee*, 10 December 1960, Diefenbaker Canada Centre, Diefenbaker Papers.
41 John G. Diefenbaker, Prime Minister's speech to the House of Commons, 4th Session, 24th Parliament, 12 December 1960.
42 John G. Diefenbaker, "Trade with Cuba," press release, Ottawa, 23 December 1960, Diefenbaker Canada Centre, Diefenbaker Papers.
43 Morris Morley, "The United States and the Global Economic Blockade of Cuba: A Study in Political Pressures on America's Allies," *Canadian Journal of Political Science* 7, no. 1 (1984): 37.
44 Norman Robertson, Memorandum for the Minister, Canadian Export Controls, 20 September 1960, LAC, RG 25, vol. 5425, file 11044-AK-40, part 4.
45 On 16 December 1960 the Canadian government applied export and import controls on trade with Cuba that were similar to those applied to the socialist countries. They were, in fact, the same as those of NATO's Coordinating Committee for Multilateral Export Controls (COCOM); see ibid. It is significant that no other NATO member country applied COCOM restrictions to Cuba even when, in February 1962, the US government formally made that request to the North Atlantic Council, the political structure of the military alliance. See Asa McKercher, "The Most Serious Problem? Canada-US Relations and Cuba, 1962," *Cold War History* 12, no. 1 (2012): 69–88.
46 Canada, Parliament, House of Commons, *Debates*, 4th Session, 24th Parliament, vol. 107, 16 December 1960, 867.
47 British prime minister Harold Macmillan had openly supported this position – that is, that isolating Cuba would only drive the island nation closer to the Soviet Union.
48 Diefenbaker, "Trade with Cuba."
49 These differences in views and the pressures brought to bear against Canada by US officials were evident, for example, at the July 1960 closed-door meeting of the Canada-United States Ministerial Committee on Joint Defense. See H. Basil Robinson, *Diefenbaker's World* (Toronto: University of Toronto Press, 1989), 146.
50 Diefenbaker Papers, Diefenbaker Canada Centre.
51 Ibid.
52 Cruz to Roa, 16 January 1961.
53 Ibid.
54 Ibid.
55 Américo Cruz, Ambassador to Canada, to Carlos Olivarez Sánchez, Deputy Minister of Foreign Affairs, 24 January 1961, MINREX Archives.

56 Carlos Olivares Sanchez, Political Under-Secretary, Ministry of External Relations, to Américo Cruz, Ambassador to Canada, 11 April 1962, MINREX Archives.
57 Ibid.
58 The Canadian customs authorities confiscated an unspecified number of pistons for car engines and 1,685 bags of chemicals that had "Made in Canada" pasted over the original "Made in USA" label; see Morley, "United States," 194. The search of the *Bahía de Siguanea* also showed the strictness of the Canadian authorities towards Cuba. In this case, once they had removed and confiscated part of the cargo of US origin, Ambassador Cruz asked the Canadian authorities to allow the ship to set sail for Cuba, but his request was denied. See "Seizure of Shipment for Cuba," 31 May 1961, LAC, RG 25, vol. 5425, file 1,1044-AK-40, part 1.
59 Sánchez to Cruz, 11 April 1962.
60 John G. Diefenbaker to Harold Macmillan, Diefenbaker Canada Centre, Diefenbaker Papers, Correspondence (VIP) 1960–1963, MG01/XII/AI282.4.
61 Adolfo López Mateos to John G. Diefenbaker, 6 July 1960, Diefenbaker Canada Centre, series XII, Personal and Confidential, vol. 9, file 845, Cuba, 425019-20.
62 Harvard University, Lamont Library, Confidential US State Department Central Files, Cuba 1960, January 1963, file A.575.8, reel 4.
63 Carlos Olivares Sánchez, Political Deputy Minister, to Luis Baralt, Ambassador to Canada, 17 March 1960, MINREX Archives.
64 "How Green almost got hit in the U.S. Cuba Fight," *Maclean's*, 17 June 1961.
65 "The Cuban Situation," Briefing Paper, 12 May 1961, President's Office files, Countries, Canada Security, John F. Kennedy Papers, John F. Kennedy Library, Boston.
66 Arthur Gavshon, "Canada set to mediate in the Cuba U.S Dispute," *Washington Post*, 11 May 1961.
67 Ibid.
68 Marquis Child, "What Rusk told our NATO allies," *Washington Post*, 10 May 1961.
69 "PM attacks Castro regime," *Gazette* (Montreal), 20 April 1961.
70 Américo Cruz, Ambassador to Canada, to Carlos Olivarez Sánchez, Deputy Minister of Foreign Affairs, 27 April 1961, MINREX Archives.
71 The Canadian government refused to provide a plane to fly much-needed medical supplies that Cuba had purchased in Canada to take care of those wounded as a result of combat actions during the Bay of Pigs invasion.
72 Cruz to Sánchez, 27 April 1961.

73 Canadian government officials played a role in "private" negotiations in
1962 to secure the release of the Bay of Pigs prisoners. The $60 million in
compensation money sent to Cuba was funnelled through the Royal Bank;
see Duncan McDowall, *Quick to the Frontier: Canada's Royal Bank* (Toronto:
McClelland & Stewart, 1993).

74 Kirk and McKenna, *Canada-Cuba Relations*, 56.

75 John G. Diefenbaker, Address to the Kiwanis International Convention,
Toronto, 3 July 1961, Diefenbaker Canada Centre, Diefenbaker Papers.

76 In early November 1961, barely six months after the Bay of Pigs, the US
government embarked on an all-out plan to overthrow the government of
Cuba. This included all possible forms of aggression, economic embargo,
political and diplomatic isolation, sabotage, support of terrorist activities,
psychological warfare, and media campaigns.

77 For a Cuban perspective, see Rubén Jiménez Gómez, *Octubre de 1962: la
mayor crisis de la era nuclear* (Havana: Editorial Ciencias Sociales, 2003); and
Tómas Diez Acosta, *Octubre de 1962: a un paso del holocausto* (Havana: Editorial Política, 2008).

78 Peter T. Haydon, *The 1962 Cuban Missile Crisis: Canadian Involvement Reconsidered* (Toronto: Canadian Institute of Strategic Studies, 1993).

79 The initial appraisal of the attitude of Prime Minister Diefenbaker was
Peter C. Newman's *Renegade in Power*, published in 1963 shortly after
Diefenbaker's defeat in the elections of that year. In the chapter devoted
to the Cuban missile crisis, Newman criticizes Diefenbaker's indecision and lack of political leadership, and considers this to be one of the
main causes of Diefenbaker's electoral defeat; see Newman, *Renegade
in Power: The Diefenbaker Years* (Toronto: McClelland & Stewart, 1963),
333–40. Another journalistic volume published on the Diefenbaker government was Patrick Nicholson's *Vision and Indecision*. He notes that the
Canadian response to the request of the US administration was influenced by several factors, including differences of opinion among the
members of the cabinet, distrust and antipathy toward Kennedy on the
part of Diefenbaker, not wanting to set a precedent under NORAD, and
Diefenbaker's reluctance to deploy nuclear weapons on Canadian soil;
Nicholson, *Vision and Indecision* (Don Mills, ON: Longmans Canada,
1968), 386–7.

80 Don Munton, "Ottawa and the great missile showdown," *Globe and Mail*,
22 October 1992.

81 Don Munton, "Intelligence Cooperation Meets International Studies
Theory: Explaining Canadian Operations in Castro's Cuba," *Intelligence and
National Security* 24, no. 1 (2009): 120.

82 "Charade in Havana: Documents show Canadian diplomats gathered intelligence about Cuba for the US," *National Post*, 25 January 2003.

83 Asa McKercher, "A Half-hearted Response? Canada and the Cuban Missile Crisis, 1962," *International History Review* 33, no. 2 (2011): 335–52.

84 Munton, "Intelligence Cooperation," 120–3.

85 "Canada's Relations with Cuba," memorandum, 15 April 1963, LAC, RG 25, vol. 10044, file 207-2, part 1.

2 Canadian Intelligence and Diplomacy in Cuba

DON MUNTON

Diplomacy and intelligence have gone hand in hand for centuries. In the real world the connections between diplomacy and intelligence are deep and intimate. In the world of scholarly discourse, on the other hand, the two are frequently dissociated and treated quite separately. Here, as elsewhere, an academic fondness for stark, often false, dichotomies, such as intelligence versus diplomacy, does us a great disservice.

This chapter aims to show that intelligence was for a decade a significant part of Canadian diplomacy towards Fidel Castro's Cuba. From the early 1960s onward, diplomats in Canada's embassy in Havana collected intelligence throughout Cuba at the behest of the United States. External Affairs officials in Ottawa and Washington were also deeply involved. The intelligence effort targeted the Castro government as well as the Soviet military presence in Cuba. The focus in this chapter is on *how* the Canadian diplomat-spies gathered their intelligence, rather than on *what* they ascertained.[1]

This was not for Canada a sort of pilot project or one-off. The Department of External Affairs, as it was known then, had begun intelligence collection and international liaison in the early post–Second World War era, working closely and sharing intelligence with Washington and London.[2] But, for Canada, connections between diplomacy and intelligence drew particularly close following the 1959 Cuban Revolution.

Ottawa never publicly disclosed Canada's intelligence operations in Cuba, or elsewhere for that matter. External Affairs and its political masters kept a tight lid on information about its forays into the sometimes murky world of international espionage. Partly as a result, the literature on Canadian foreign policy has largely missed or ignored these activities[3] – connections between intelligence and diplomacy remain largely unexplored in the Canadian context.[4]

This chapter also aims to probe another largely uncharted area: the interactions between intelligence and non-governmental groups and civil society. Canadian diplomats' intelligence activities not only involved, but depended on, civil society in Cuba. At the same time, the actions of some non-governmental groups complicated Canadian diplomacy. I raise these matters towards the end of the chapter.

Before exploring Canada's Cuba intelligence operations, we need to address some background questions. How are diplomacy and intelligence linked, in general terms? Can we, and how are we, to distinguish between the two? And how do we define intelligence?

Distinguishing between Diplomacy and Intelligence

Some observers suggest intelligence is distinguished – even defined – by an innate secretiveness. To be sure, secrecy is an endemic and pervasive aspect of intelligence matters, and part of the organizational culture of intelligence agencies. Intelligence processes, however, are not uniquely secretive. Most government agencies have secrets, and foreign ministries abound in them. Diplomacy is not normally carried out in public, to say the least. And diplomats can be as reluctant to divulge secrets as their intelligence counterparts. As well, not all intelligence material is secret – indeed, authoritative estimates suggest that the vast bulk of the information intelligence agencies process comes from open, public sources.[5]

Other observers draw a functional distinction between intelligence agencies and foreign ministries. Basically, the former gather information; the latter use that information to shape policy. Or, in other words, spies produce and diplomats consume. There is more than a grain of truth here: although information from intelligence agencies supports the policy-making process, those agencies do not themselves generally formulate national policy. Once again, however, the real world is more complicated than these dichotomies suggest. There is, in fact, much similarity between the "diplomatic reporting" carried out by embassies for foreign ministries and the "intelligence" collection provided by intelligence agencies. Indeed, I argue that diplomatic reporting and intelligence gathering overlap considerably, and can do so to the point they are virtually indistinguishable with respect to general content and purpose.

Serious discussions in the foreign policy literature on the distinction between intelligence and diplomacy are curiously rare. One of the few extended conceptual treatments is provided by Michael Herman, a former senior British intelligence official turned academic and author. Herman begins his essay, "Diplomacy and Intelligence," by emphasizing the broad commonalities of the two.[6] Governments do both; they collect intelligence and conduct diplomacy, and have long done so. Both intelligence and diplomacy inform governments about other countries and global developments. Intelligence and diplomacy interact and complement each other, but, as Herman notes, they also compete.

Commonalities aside, Herman concludes that there is a "reasonably clear" distinction between them. His own arguments, however, raise questions about that conclusion in terms of providing a clear dichotomy. The core of Herman's case is differences between intelligence and diplomatic institutions *qua* institutions. That is to say, he essentially argues that intelligence officers and intelligence agencies mostly do intelligence work, while diplomats and foreign ministries mostly do diplomacy. That is fair enough, as far as it goes. Diplomacy is a unique institution. Without question it involves much more than the collection and analysis of information that is the heart of intelligence work. The problem here is that differentiating broad agency mandates does not provide a hard and fast or clear distinction between intelligence and diplomacy with respect to the actual activities involved in collecting information or the nature of the information collected. Generalizing about agencies, as Herman does, focuses more on who is doing the work than on the kind of work they are doing or how they are doing it.

Herman also asserts that diplomats and intelligence officers generally employ different methods. The latter operate in a clandestine, even illegal, fashion, or at least are more likely to do so, he notes. Diplomats do not use clandestine sources – or at least not generally. For Herman, diplomats are "front door people," while "intelligence officers of all kinds go figuratively (and sometimes actually) up the backstairs." Both seek information, but diplomats "usually avoid infringing their host countries' laws" – or "at least think seriously before so doing."

Telling here are Herman's caution-ridden adverbial phrases: "*more likely*" to operate covertly, "*generally*" do not use clandestine sources, "*usually*" avoid breaking laws. These qualifiers reveal an awareness that distinctions between intelligence and diplomacy based on *modus operandi* are much less than absolute. Indeed, on the matter of collecting information through clandestine means, Herman himself allows that "some diplomats, in some countries, do still indulge in covert collection."[7] Thus, even operating covertly is not a characteristic unique to intelligence. In short, Herman's operational distinctions between diplomacy and intelligence seem decidedly grey, and somewhat less than "reasonably clear."

There is arguably much similarity between the diplomatic reporting carried out by embassies for foreign ministries and the intelligence collection provided by intelligence agencies. With respect to general content and purpose, diplomatic reporting and intelligence gathering can be virtually indistinguishable.[8] It is not a matter of a thin line; there is often no line at all. The two functional areas are not one and the same, but they blend together. As British historian and theorist Martin Wight noted, reporting is "a function that the ambassador shares with the spy."[9] And, as we shall see, Canadian diplomats in Cuba fully understood intelligence collection to be part of their mandate.

To acknowledge similarities and overlaps between diplomacy and intelligence, however, is not to suggest that all diplomats collect intelligence all of the time. Many do not collect intelligence at all. But some diplomats do collect genuine intelligence, if not much of the time then at least some of the time. To be clear, this claim does not rest on certain well-known juxtapositions in the worlds of intelligence and diplomacy. It does not, in short, rely on a sort of guilt by association. The assertion that diplomats engage in intelligence work is not mere presumption from the fact that embassies serve as bases for intelligence gathering, including signals intelligence, or eavesdropping. Nor does it rest on the fact that foreign service officers often share their embassies with designated military attachés whose job it is to collect military intelligence, nor from the widespread practice of posting intelligence officers to embassies posing as diplomats under what is known as "official cover." And the claim definitely does not depend on a few historical cases where diplomats turn and spy on their own governments, such as Donald McLean of the infamous Cambridge Four. My focus here is not on those working alongside diplomats or masquerading as diplomats, but rather on the gathering and analysing of intelligence by diplomats.

Canadian Diplomacy and Intelligence

Making the general case that diplomats engage in intelligence does not by itself prove that Canadian diplomats do so, let alone that they did so in Castro's Cuba. Indeed, there is a common notion that Canada does not collect foreign intelligence, that it has never done so, and that it has no capability to do so, or ever had such. All of these notions about

Canada are demonstrably incorrect, but they nonetheless remain current, and their popularity is reason enough to afford them some attention here.

Observers often note Canada lacks an intelligence agency in the shape of the United States Central Intelligence Agency (CIA) or the British Secret Intelligence Service (SIS, or MI6). Some of these observers acknowledge that Canada has long had a signals intelligence organization (the Communications Security Establishment, CSE) and a security intelligence organization (the Canadian Security Intelligence Service, CSIS, and before that the RCMP Security Service). Both of these bodies collect intelligence abroad. The former, however, collects only electronic and other signals, while the latter collects information related to threats to domestic Canadian security, such as potential terrorist attacks, and is thus mostly internal in focus. Thus, neither agency has *general foreign intelligence* responsibilities.[10] Some commentators assume – mistakenly – that, without a designated foreign intelligence agency, Canada therefore must lack a foreign intelligence capability, and thus cannot engage in gathering foreign intelligence.[11] In fact Canada does have such a foreign intelligence capability, and has used it for decades. The Canadian government gathers foreign intelligence in a fairly common way: by employing its foreign ministry and its diplomats.

The Department of External Affairs quietly established an intelligence and security unit in the early post-war era. It was officially if euphemistically entitled Defence Liaison II Division, but known as DL2. Within a few years DL2 was one of the largest divisions in the entire department. It was reorganized and renamed several times over succeeding decades, but never abolished.[12] External Affairs began significant foreign intelligence collection activities in the 1950s (the forerunner of the CSE had begun collecting signals intelligence during the Second World War). Officers from DL2 chaired both Canada's Joint Intelligence Committee and the policy committee directing the work of the CSE, making clear the department held a central position in coordinating Canada's international intelligence relationships.[13]

Evidence of Canadian foreign intelligence collection (or field operations) has long been in the public realm. In the 1980s Dalhousie University scholar James Eayrs revealed that Canada's participation during the 1950s in the International Commissions for Security and Cooperation (ICSC) in Indochina (Vietnam, Laos, and Cambodia) included extensive collection of political and military intelligence.[14] For almost two decades External Affairs provided this intelligence to the United

States, United Kingdom, and other Western allies – as it did with intelligence from Cuba. A few years later Canadian diplomats were again called on to provide intelligence for their allies, this time from Tehran in 1979, after the US embassy there was occupied and hostages taken.[15]

This intelligence capability and activity occasionally has been acknowledged unofficially. A former Canadian diplomat and prominent intelligence practitioner noted in 1990 that Canada has "a first-class capability" to collect foreign intelligence" and uses it. External Affairs, he said, "engages in wide-ranging and professional ... collection efforts."[16] The intelligence work continued through the Cold War era and into recent decades – a fact confirmed by two retired Canadian foreign service officers, Daniel Livermore and Kurt Jensen,[17] by an auditor general's report in the mid-1990s that outlined the department's intelligence mandate,[18] and by a recent public inquiry commission, which noted that most geographic branches in the department collect and analyse intelligence from open sources.[19] Finally, the Canadian foreign service has for some years included officers assigned to the semi-secretive Global Security Reporting Program (GSRP),[20] specifically tasked with intelligence collection.

Defining Intelligence

To answer conclusively whether Canadian diplomats in Cuba engaged in "intelligence," one needs a formal definition of the term. Intelligence has been defined conservatively as "information relevant to a government's formulation and implementation of policy to further its national security interests and to deal with threats from actual or potential adversaries."[21] In accordance with this definition, information about a neighbouring state's military buildup or a terrorist group's plans to explode bombs would qualify as intelligence, but information on a country's education policies or health care programs would not. If one accepts this definition, then, did Canada's activities in Cuba produce intelligence?

Canada did not fully share the view of many Americans that communist Cuba itself was a national security threat. At the same time, Ottawa did view both the Soviet military presence in Cuba and the possibility of Cuban or communist subversion in Latin America as threats to the Western world. Canada also had a general security interest in furthering intelligence cooperation among members of the Western alliance through its activities in Cuba. The products of Canada's Cuba efforts arguably meet the test of being information relevant to government policies designed to serve national security interests and to respond to threats from adversaries. They thus differ from the sort of diplomatic reporting that comprises much of the day-to-day operations of any foreign ministry. Missions abroad, from Tokyo to Kabul to Bogotá, provide information on events and developments in host countries and elsewhere, from the latest Japanese economic trends to the plight of refugees from war-torn countries to the growing presence of Canadian corporations in Colombia. To be sure, headquarters staff digest these reports, compile analyses, and advise ministers, but only some of this sort of information relates to national security or threats thereto.[22]

Formal definitions aside, those involved in or aware of Canada's operations in Cuba perceived and treated the information obtained as intelligence. The diplomats in Havana certainly thought of themselves as engaged in intelligence work, and often used covert or semi-covert methods to gather information.[23] Official External Affairs documents from the 1960s use that term for the material coming from the Havana embassy. The special procedures External Affairs adopted for handling information from Cuba were those reserved for intelligence matters. Canadian officials and their British and US counterparts regarded the information as intelligence, and prime ministers and presidents discussed the work in those terms.[24] In Cuba, commonplace diplomatic reporting evolved into the provision of genuine human intelligence, or "Humint" for short.

Canadian Intelligence in Cuba: The Historical Background

Prior to 1961 the Canadian embassy had provided traditional diplomatic reporting from Havana – in particular, covering the turmoil and decline of the repressive regime of Fulgencio Batista.[25] Canadian foreign intelligence operations in Cuba began as a result of a direct request from the US State Department in April 1961. Deteriorating relations with Cuba after the coming to power in 1959 of Fidel Castro's 26th of July Movement had led the United States to break off relations in early 1961. To fill the intelligence void left by the closure of its Havana embassy, Washington turned to Britain and Canada for assistance in collecting on-the-ground Humint, especially of a political and military nature. Since Canada lacked a foreign intelligence agency, the task fell to diplomats at the Canadian embassy, who frequently undertook "tasked" operations, responding to specific requests from the CIA and other US intelligence bodies. External Affairs shared raw information and analyses with the Americans as well as with Canada's Department of National Defence and with the British. External Affairs also collaborated operationally in Cuba with UK personnel, including field officers from MI6.[26]

Following Cuba's decisive defeat of the 1961 CIA-organized Bay of Pigs invasion, the Cuban government, with some justification, continued to perceive the United States as a serious threat,[27] and Castro and his colleagues turned to Moscow for assistance. Soviet leader Nikita Khrushchev responded initially by sending Soviet defensive weaponry to Cuba, including the latest anti-aircraft, surface-to-air missiles (SAMs). By mid-1962 Khrushchev was secretly sending Soviet combat troops, and by September of that year missiles with nuclear warheads, some of which could reach US territory, were arriving – the deployment that led to the Cuban missile crisis.[28] In the aftermath of the crisis, and at the request of President John F. Kennedy, Canada upgraded its intelligence work in Cuba in 1963 with the addition of an embassy officer specially assigned to collect intelligence. The Havana operations continued until the early 1970s.

This chapter is not the place for an in-depth discussion of Canada's diplomacy towards Cuba in first decade of the Castro government and the Revolution.[29] Suffice it to say there were yet more connections between diplomacy and intelligence. The Canadian government took some steps in the early 1960s to limit trade with Cuba, but never fully subscribed to the US attempt to isolate Cuba economically and politically. Although Washington would have preferred even less Canada-Cuba trade than there was, it never pushed Canada to break diplomatic relations with the Castro government. US officials fully realized that an end to diplomatic relations would end the flow of intelligence from the Canadian embassy in Havana.

Collecting Intelligence in Cuba: The Operations

How did Canadian diplomats collect intelligence? That is, what types of intelligence did they compile?

Some of the information flowing from Havana was open source intelligence originating from public, non-covert sources such as Cuban government announcements and media coverage. The Canadian embassy, for example, often translated stories from *Revolución*, the daily newspaper of the 26th of July Movement, as well as speeches by Cuban government figures, and forwarded these to Ottawa. Obtaining such information would have been the sort of task carried out routinely by the US embassy before it closed. A continuing stream of requests for public material from Washington reflected the US intelligence community's interest in the conditions and inner workings of the close-by but increasingly closed Cuban polity. Ottawa forwarded US requests to its ambassador in Havana with a "personal and secret" classification – even though the requested material was publicly available.[30] What was sensitive for Ottawa was not the material involved, but the specific requests from Washington and the existence of the Canada-US intelligence liaison arrangement.

The diplomat-spies also regularly observed and reported on public events such the annual January military parade in Havana. The 1962 parade stood out by providing the first hard evidence that the Soviet Union was placing modern defensive missiles in Cuba.[31] On one occasion, Washington even requested photographs of the television coverage of a particular military display. (Recall that these days long predated even commercial video tape recorders.) The Canadians also directly observed events and developments, and reported on what they saw, not only in the capital area, but also in the more distant provinces. Some examples may suffice.

In the early summer of 1961, Canadian *chargé d'affaires* Malcolm Bow toured through eastern Cuba – an underreported region at the far end of the island from Havana. Bow's trip received the active support of the Castro government, including both a car and guide. It was therefore decidedly not covert. His confidential assessments for Ottawa of the impact of government reforms and centralization in the rural areas, however, were none too favourable, and were not shared with the Cubans.[32] Canada's Washington embassy passed Bow's reports to the CIA, where senior agency officials read them with interest.[33]

In August 1962 the Canadian ambassador in Havana, George Kidd, advised Ottawa – and thus Washington – that Soviet military forces were being spotted in Cuba, the tip of the iceberg of what was becoming an enormous Soviet buildup. He concluded that these forces appeared to be mostly advisers – an incorrect conclusion, but one shared at this point by Washington. Neither the British and Canadian embassies nor the American intelligence community observed the first instalments of Soviet medium-range ballistic missiles that began arriving in Cuba in September. The first hard evidence of Soviet missile sites came only a month later, on 14 October 1962, from photographs taken by a high-altitude American U-2 spy plane. The crisis began nine days later, when President Kennedy demanded removal of the missiles. A few days after that, a Canadian, on-the-ground "scouting mission" reported ominous news: Soviet forces appeared to be making almost frantic efforts to continue missile site construction, with numerous trucks carrying what appeared to be camouflage material to the sites.[34] Then, on 28 October, Khrushchev suddenly announced he was ceasing construction of the sites and removing the missiles. The British and Canadians subsequently reported on the withdrawal of both missiles and troops.

Washington, however, maintained a strong interest in military intelligence on Cuba, with U-2 flights over the island continuing into 1963 and beyond. One US concern was Soviet SAMs – a US spy plane had been shot down by one in October 1962 – with Cuba insisting it would shoot down US planes, and Washington threatening to retaliate for any attacks on their spy planes. A second US concern was the extent of the remaining presence in Cuba of Soviet troops and short-range defensive missiles. The Canadian diplomat-spies thus mounted an intensive program beginning in 1963 to identify and locate SAM sites and Soviet military bases in Cuba. They drove around the Cuban countryside in search of Soviet installations, often using locational information supplied by Washington. From April through June 1963 alone they found and observed about a dozen SAM sites, near Bahía Honda, Blanquizal, Canímar, Deleite, La Coloma, the La Maya-Guantánamo area, Malas Aguas, Mariel, Manatí, and Santa Lucía. The nature of some of the information requested – such as the precise coordinates of individual sites – strongly suggests that Washington was seeking, at least in part, information for potential tactical military purposes.

In addition to SAM locations, the Canadians searched for, found, and reported on facilities for Soviet-supplied Komar patrol boats, coastal defence missiles and cruise missiles (all of them short-range, defensive weapons), and major Soviet military camps. The Canadians and British also monitored Cuban shipping activity, ports, and airfields. They closely observed radar and communications equipment, and frequently reported on activity at major Soviet bases such as at Remedios in central Cuba and on the rapidly growing installation at Torrens (Lourdes), southwest of Havana, which ultimately became the largest Soviet signals intelligence interception facility in the world.

In 1970 Washington developed concerns anew over possible missile installations in Cuba. The Soviets appeared to be constructing a port facility near Cienfuegos, on Cuba's southern coast, possibly for use by Soviet nuclear ballistic missile submarines. Such a facility, in Washington's view, would comprise a significant violation of US-USSR understandings reached during the Cuban missile crisis. In addition to employing its satellite reconnaissance capabilities, the US intelligence community again turned to Britain and Canada for on-site intelligence. A joint Anglo-Canadian operation was mounted to do on-the-ground surveillance of Cienfuegos developments.[35] US national security adviser Henry Kissinger confronted the Soviets about the facility. Moscow eventually ceased the construction work near Cienfuegos, all the while insisting no submarine base had ever been planned.[36]

On these and other intelligence forays, the Canadian diplomats used covert as well as overt means to make their observations. They were generally cautious and discrete, approaching Cuban or Soviet military bases when sentries were not evident, otherwise observing as best they could from a safe distance, but they made no attempt to enter secured areas. Their task was made easier by the lack of restrictions on foreign diplomats' movements around Cuba, in contrast to the Soviet Union, where such movements were tightly controlled, leading to the imposition of reciprocal restrictions by some Western countries.

Occasional sources of information for the Havana embassy were Canadians living or travelling in Cuba. The visitors included, for example, tourists, church representatives, and business people.[37] Some travellers apparently approached embassy personnel themselves and voluntarily shared their observations, usually on a one-time basis.[38] Their information was normally forwarded to Ottawa (likely without their knowledge). A long-standing program run out of Ottawa interviewing Canadian visitors returning particularly from communist countries included after 1962 those returning from Cuba.[39] The sources resident in Cuba included other diplomats, largely, but not exclusively, from Western countries, and missionaries, especially Catholic priests and nuns. The latter were understandably well-informed about government actions affecting the Catholic Church in Cuba, but they could also provide general perspectives on Cuban developments.

As with most Humint operations, the Canadians also regularly gathered information from a wide range of local people, who provided general insights into life in revolutionary Cuba and specific knowledge of their area. That is, they used Cuban "sources" or "agents." Support for Castro and the Revolution among Cubans in general typically was strong, but never universal: some Cubans opposed the Revolution or the authoritarian nature of the Castro government or both. Among the dissenters were many who were willing to talk frankly to foreign diplomats and able to provide useful first- or second-hand information. Most of these sources were eager to share what information they could, and the regular agents were generally judged as reliable. None apparently was paid. A few of these informants later defected to the United States or Canada. Some sources seem to have been "drop-ins": people who voluntarily approach foreigners with information. Others were almost certainly recruited by the Canadians. Some were unwitting informants, including a multitude of hitchhikers picked up by Canadian diplomat-spies out on regular forays. Indeed, poverty and an inadequate transportation system ensured an unending supply of hitchhikers. Typical was the case of one embassy officer who assisted, and gently queried, dozens of hitchhikers on a single driving trip through the eastern Cuban countryside.[40] The hitchhikers were often Cuban soldiers on leave, many of whom were able to offer information on and directions to out-of-the-way military bases. Hitchhikers often mistook the fair-skinned foreigners speaking poor Spanish for Russians, which likely facilitated some conversations.

Canada's regular agents in Cuba included officials and former officials in Cuban government agencies, shipping company employees, former prisoners, a civil engineer, a senior Cuban pilot who had flown for the Canadian air force during the Second World War, and a worker at the putative Soviet submarine base at Cienfuegos. The worker, recruited as an agent by the British and Canadians, offered inside information on the construction project. The pilot supplied detailed information on the state of Cuba's civilian airline fleet.[41] The embassy also reported information from additional sources whose names and particulars it chose not to reveal to Ottawa, presumably for security reasons. Local residents also provided general insights into life in revolutionary Cuba and specific knowledge of their local area.

Although the Canadians, generally speaking, did not themselves break Cuban laws in their information gathering, their sources and agents were not in the same position. Many of these individuals could easily have run afoul of Cuban authorities if caught providing sensitive information or were merely suspected of doing so.

Intelligence and Civil Society

It might be assumed that the state-centric, secretive world of intelligence is generally indifferent, if not unfriendly, towards civil society,
groups, or individuals, whatever their inclinations and influence. At the
very least it would seem less so engaged than the world of diplomacy.
That assumption, while eminently plausible, might well be incorrect,
at least in one respect. Diplomacy necessarily emphasizes a myriad of
official government-to-government interactions, such as formal representations and negotiations. The day-to-day collection of intelligence,
on the other hand, relies often heavily on non-official contacts with
individuals and non-governmental organizations (NGOs). A key job of
intelligence personnel in the field is to find sources of information. The
Canadians in Cuba did that.

As should be clear from the discussion so far, intelligence gathering
in Cuba did not rely solely on government sources and direct observation by diplomats. Indeed, the intelligence efforts of the Canadian
embassy involved much contact with individual citizens and groups.
Individuals, particularly the disaffected, are thus also a key part of the
world of intelligence. What information the Canadians did obtain, for
example, on Soviet troop arrivals in Cuba in mid-1962 mostly came
from Cubans who themselves were regular sources for the Canadians
or who informed those who were. They told the Canadians about sur-
reptitious nighttime operations to unload Soviet ships and about unusual military convoys on highways. Some reports referred to vehicles
with Russian drivers on roads leading from Cuban ports and to Soviet-
manned tanks engaged in military manoeuvres in central Cuba – a level
of detail that suggests very well placed informants.

The anti-Castro groups inside and outside Cuba in the 1960s were
frequent sources of information and rumours, and sometimes of misin-
formation. Some were, as well, global actors in their own right.[42] Committed dissidents and members of the anti-Castro movements had a
vested interest in stoking US concerns about the Castro government.
Experience taught the Canadian diplomats they should discount at
least some of what they heard from opposition groups in Cuba, just as
the US intelligence community learned to discount much information
it received from exiles in the United States and anti-regime sources in
Cuba. Their reports nevertheless usually had to be checked out.

In the late fall of 1962, for example, the US State Department urgently
sought the help of the Canadian ambassador in Cuba. Could he

evaluate a sensational intelligence report from the French ambassador in Havana suggesting that post–missile crisis tensions had caused a major breach in the Castro government? According to this information, likely gained from an anti-Castro source, certain senior Cuban figures were reportedly preparing to leave Cuba. Ambassador Kidd quickly, if gently, disputed the report. He was correct: no serious internal split had emerged. In another case, again at the request of Washington, the embassy checked out a report in the US press, attributed to a Cuban exile, that the Soviets were covertly building a submarine base, this time in Oriente province. The Canadians investigated thoroughly, but could find no evidence to support the report. They spoke to numerous local inhabitants, but none had seen anything like a submarine base under construction in the area. Moreover, the Canadian report noted, the purported site was an open and heavily populated bay, a most unlikely location for a secret military facility.

In short, these examples suggest that the prominent and growing role of NGOs and civil society organizations in global affairs is not restricted to the world of diplomacy, as conventionally conceived.[43] Civil society plays a part in the intelligence world as well as in diplomacy, and although space does not permit the matter to be pursued here, it beckons as a fruitful area of future inquiry.

Conclusion: Intelligence and Diplomacy

Diplomats interact and work with colleagues in the intelligence community, but also do intelligence work themselves. Diplomatic reporting is not only similar to intelligence reporting but often indistinguishable from it.

Collecting intelligence for the United States was a significant and essential aspect of Canadian diplomacy towards Fidel Castro's Cuba. Canada's embassy in Havana, previously a small post dominated by commercial issues, was the base from which the diplomats conducted their intelligence operations. The Canadian mission's official mandate was to maintain cordial relations with the government of Cuba and to foster trade – without being, or appearing, crassly opportunistic. Its other job was to conduct espionage. Although only a relatively few officials in Canada and the United States were aware of this role, it allowed Canada to provide Washington valued support while appearing publicly to challenge US policy.

The intelligence Canadian diplomats gathered added useful background for foreign policy decisions, as intelligence is intended to do.

Some of it also, on occasion, gave the US intelligence community a view of developments in Cuba that differed from its own. The intelligence effort, however, went well beyond collecting bits of information. In all respects, and from the outset, the decade-long Cuba collection and sharing program fostered the intelligence liaison relationship among Canada, the United States, and the United Kingdom, and was a critical if secret reality of Canada's Cuba diplomacy.

Cuba, however, was not a unique case. At the same time as the diplomat-spies in Havana were parsing Fidel Castro's speeches and combing rural Cuba for Soviet military forces, Canadians working under the auspices of the ICSC continued to provide intelligence on the unresolved conflict in Indochina. Contrary to the common assumption, Canada's lack of a dedicated intelligence agency did not mean it was either unable or unwilling to engage in foreign intelligence work during the latter part of the twentieth century. It meant, rather, that foreign service officers were called on to provide a critical capability: to collect and analyse human intelligence.

Canada's long-standing intelligence work raises both ethical and practical policy questions. In particular, is it *right* to spy? And do intelligence activities *harm* states and their reputations? These are important questions, but one can discuss them only briefly here. Some might – and might well – ask if Canada's human intelligence activities in Cuba were honourable or proper. Let me deconstruct the question before answering it. First, it is safe to note that such a question is seldom if ever asked, say, about the United Kingdom's intelligence efforts in Cuba, or elsewhere. Asking it in the Canadian context thus says something about Canadian conceptions as well as about intelligence. Second, the question also reflects a common notion, perhaps based on so-called spy films of the James Bond and Jason Bourne variety, that intelligence work is driven by deception and permeated by violence. Suffice it to say this view is simplistic and based on misconceptions. Intelligence is primarily about gathering information, not about murdering one's opponents.

Was Canada not only violating its diplomatic privileges by spying in Cuba in the 1960s, but also behaving deceptively and perhaps abusing Cuba's trust? It seems unlikely any trust was abused. One could ask: was Cuba disrespecting its diplomatic position in Canada or its relationship with Canada by using its Montreal trade office to collect information about the United States and to evade the US trade embargo? Canada and Cuba not only made use of their respective posts for activities that went beyond the normal confines of diplomacy, but, it seems clear, they both were also well aware of the other's activities. Indeed, both allowed these to continue, and were thus fully complicit. Cuba's interests compelled it to conduct the activities it did. Canada had no illusions that Cuba would sacrifice its interests by eschewing those activities. In turn, Cuba did not expect Canada to refrain from assisting its US ally.

Do intelligence activities negatively affect a country's standing or its ability to achieve its foreign policy objectives? As always, there are both potential costs and benefits. Other countries might regard less favourably those believed to be collecting intelligence in unseemly ways. Certainly when governments discover offensive intelligence operations mounted against them, they often take actions against the perpetrators. Most diplomats, however, are well aware of intelligence activities in general. Among the states with which Canadians engage are the other four so-called Five Eyes countries (the United States, United Kingdom, Australia, and New Zealand), which know Canada's intelligence work well. Many other countries' representatives are undoubtedly aware of, if not well informed about, the intensive intelligence sharing among the Five Eyes. And some others, though less informed, probably have long assumed that two allies as close as Canada and the United States would cooperate in intelligence matters just as they do in many other areas. In short, Canada's intelligence activities are probably less newsworthy to others, friend and foe alike, than to many Canadians.

On the other hand, there are potential benefits to sharing intelligence – and these benefits are at the root of why states engage in it so often and so widely. Intelligence cooperation operates on a *quid pro quo* basis: the more information you have to share with others, and the more you share, the more they are inclined to share with you. If the information one receives in return is value added and improves policy-making, then intelligence liaison will facilitate, not undermine, foreign policy and potentially increase one's influence. For example, knowledge beforehand of, say, a leadership split within a foreign government, could recommend a particular approach to that government over other possible approaches, and might improve the chances of securing its support or influencing it. Intelligence enhances a country's capabilities and, when employed wisely, contributes to effective policy-making – and thereby adds more than it detracts.

The linkages between intelligence efforts and diplomacy in the various cases of Canadian foreign intelligence operations for which we now have evidence (in Indochina, Cuba, Tehran, and other places) need to be explored more fully. New cases will be unearthed, of that one can be sure. The Cuba case and other examples demonstrate that intelligence in all its aspects is part and parcel of Canada's foreign policy writ large, and reflect a seldom-explored and deeper complexity to Canadian activities abroad.

NOTES

This chapter is based on a forthcoming book, *Canadian Spies in Castro's Cuba*. Research for this project received funding support from the Social Sciences and Humanities Research Council of Canada and the Arthur Schlesinger Fellowship Program at the John F. Kennedy Presidential Library. The author is also grateful to Diana Ellis, to the editors of this volume, and to anonymous reviewers for their comments on the chapter.

1 On the major issues the Canadians covered in their reports, see Don Munton, "Our Men in Havana: Canadian Foreign Intelligence Operations in Castro's Cuba," *International Journal* 70, no. 1 (2015): 23–39. The term "diplomat-spies" is intended to be an accurate portrayal of the tasks involved, not a pejorative. Some of the Canadians so engaged have themselves begun to use the term "spy" with a degree of pride; see John Graham, "Bill Warden, 1934–2011: Diplomat, Bus Driver, Sailor, Spy," *Bout de Papier* 26, no. 1 (2011): 31–2.
2 Kurt F. Jensen, *Cautious Beginnings: Canadian Foreign Intelligence, 1939–51* (Vancouver: UBC Press, 2008).
3 Although the first-ever textbook on Canadian foreign policy – James Eayrs, *The Art of the Possible: Government and Foreign Policy in Canada* (Toronto: University of Toronto Press, 1961) – contained a full chapter, no less, on intelligence, later texts tended to ignore the subject. See, for example, Andrew Cooper, *Canadian Foreign Policy: Old Habits and New Directions* (Scarborough, ON: Prentice-Hall, 1997); and Kim Richard Nossal, *The Politics of Canadian Foreign Policy* (Scarborough, ON: Prentice-Hall, 1985).
4 British scholars more often link intelligence and diplomacy – usefully so. See, among numerous other examples, Richard. J. Aldrich and Michael F. Hopkins, eds., *Intelligence, Defence and Diplomacy: British Policy in the Post-War World* (Ilford, UK: Frank Cass, 1994); and Nicholas Tamkin, *Britain, Turkey and the Soviet Union, 1940-45: Strategy,*

Diplomacy and Intelligence in the Eastern Mediterranean (Basingstoke, UK: Palgrave Macmillan, 2009).

5 Abram N. Shulsky and Gary J. Schmitt, *Silent Warfare: Understanding the World of Intelligence*, 3rd ed. (Dulles, VA: Potomac Books, 2002), 38.

6 Michael Herman, "Diplomacy and Intelligence," *Diplomacy & Statecraft* 9, no. 2 (1998): 1–22.

7 Ibid., 7, 2, 8.

8 Writers on intelligence commonly claim that diplomatic reporting is a form of foreign intelligence. See, for example, Mark Lowenthal, *Intelligence: From Secrets to Policy* (Washington, DC: CQ Press, 2006), 95; and Alistair Hensler, "Creating a Canadian Foreign Intelligence Service," *Canadian Foreign Policy* 3, no. 3 (1995): 21. Hensler is a former Canadian Security Intelligence Service official.

9 Martin Wight, *Power Politics* (Harmondsworth, UK: Penguin, 1978), 116.

10 The Canadian media commonly but wrongly refer to CSIS as "Canada's spy agency." It is, more correctly, Canada's counter-spy agency, but that responsibility represents only part of its "security intelligence" mandate.

11 This logic is the key premise of some who have joined an ongoing debate on whether or not Canada should "create" a foreign intelligence agency. See, for example, Barry Cooper, *CFIS: A Foreign Intelligence Service for Canada* (Calgary: Canadian Defence & Foreign Affairs Institute, 2007).

12 For an organizational history of External Affairs/Foreign Affairs intelligence units, see Harjit Virdee and Don Munton, "Missing Links: An Organizational Archaeology of Intelligence Structures in Canada's Foreign Ministry," unpublished.

13 Scott Anderson, "The Evolution of the Canadian Intelligence Establishment, 1945–1950," *Intelligence and National Security* 9, no. 3 (1993): 459–60, 462. Anderson describes Under-Secretary Norman Robertson as "the single most influential official in the government" on intelligence matters (460). The CSE was and remains Canada's foremost agency in the "UKUSA" signals intelligence alliance featured in the revelations of American Edward Snowden.

14 James Eayrs, *In Defence of Canada*, vol. 5, *Indochina: Roots of Complicity* (Toronto: University of Toronto Press, 1965), chap 8. Eayrs's disclosures are rarely noted by contemporary scholars, but have never been challenged.

15 The earliest account of Canadian intelligence operations in Tehran was Jean Pelletier and Claude Adams, *The Canadian Caper: The Inside Story of the*

Daring Rescue of Six American Diplomats Trapped in Tehran (Toronto: Macmillan, Toronto, 1981). It formed the basis of a later movie. A more recent book by Robert Wright, *Our Man in Tehran: Ken Taylor, the CIA and the Iran Hostage Crisis* (Toronto: HarperCollins Canada, 2010), oddly claims to be telling the story "for the first time" (xii), but adds only modestly to what was already known.

16 John Starnes, op-ed, *Ottawa Citizen*, 23 October 1990; see also Hensler, "Creating a Canadian Foreign Intelligence Service," 21.

17 Kurt F. Jensen, "Toward a Canadian Foreign Intelligence Service," *Bout de Papier* 22, no. 2 (2006): 21–3; idem, "Canada's Foreign Intelligence Interview Program, 1953–90," *Intelligence and National Security* 19, no. 1 (2004): 95–104; and Daniel Livermore, "Does Canada Need a Foreign Intelligence Agency?" CIPS Policy Brief 3 (Ottawa: Centre for International Policy Studies, 2009).

18 Canada, Auditor General of Canada, *Report* (Ottawa, 1996), chap. 27, available online at https://fas.org/irp/world/canada/docs/oag96/ch9627e.html.

19 Canada, Commission of Inquiry into the Actions of Canadian Officials in Relation to Maher Arar, *Report of the Events Relating to Maher Arar: Factual Background*, vol. 2 (Ottawa: Public Works and Government Services Canada, 2006), available online at http://epe.lac-bac.gc.ca/100/206/301/pco-bcp/commissions/maher_arar/07-09-13/www.ararcommission.ca/eng/Vol_II_English.pdf; I am indebted to Harjit Virdee for this reference.

20 Jensen, "Toward a Canadian Foreign Intelligence Service."

21 Shulsky and Schmitt, *Silent Warfare*, 1; there are broader and wider definitions than this one.

22 Kurt Jensen, as well as many others, argues that diplomatic reporting is for most countries one of their major sources of foreign intelligence; see Jensen, "Toward a Canadian Foreign Intelligence Service," 21.

23 Graham, "Bill Warden, 1934–2011"; Graham also uses "clandestine" as a synonym for "covert" to refer to collection that is in some sense disguised or secret from the intended target.

24 For examples, see Munton, "Our Men in Havana," passim.

25 Don Munton and David Vogt, "Inside Castro's Cuba: The Revolution and Canada's Embassy in Havana," in *Our Place in the Sun: Canada and Cuba in the Castro Era*, ed. Robert Wright and Lana Wylie (Toronto: University of Toronto Press, 2009), 44–74.

26 For details on the documentary evidence of Canada's Cuba operations, see Munton, "Our Men in Havana," passim.

27 On the infamous Operation Mongoose, the secret US campaign to subvert the Castro government, and its successors, see Aleksandr Fursenko and Timothy Naftali, *"One Hell of a Gamble": Khrushchev, Castro, and Kennedy, 1958–1964* (New York: W.W. Norton, 1997), chap. 7; and Lawrence Freedman, *Kennedy's Wars: Berlin, Cuba, Laos, and Vietnam* (New York: Oxford University Press, 2000), chap. 17.

28 For a short history of the missile crisis, see Don Munton and David Welch, *The Cuban Missile Crisis: A Concise History*, 2nd ed. (New York: Oxford University Press, 2012).

29 See the editors' introduction and the chapter by Rodríguez.

30 Letter ("personal and secret"), A.E. Ritchie, External Affairs, to George Kidd, Havana, 17 October 1961, Library and Archives Canada (hereafter LAC), RG 25, vol. 5076, AK 4568-40, part 7.

31 Military parades in Cuba were sometimes more than routine displays. The January 1962 Havana military parade provided US intelligence with proof the Soviets had begun supplying Cuba with a defensive cruise missile, the SS-N-2, or AS-1-"Kennel"; see United States, Central Intelligence Agency, "Cruise Missile Deployment in Cuba," CIA/RR CB 63-18, 20 February 1963, National Security Files, Countries, Cuba, box 50A, Intelligence Materials, 2/63), John F. Kennedy Library, Boston.

32 Despatch, D-378, 2 June 1961, LAC, RG 25, vol. 5352, AK 10244-40, part 2.

33 Letter, G.C. Cook, Canadian Embassy, Washington, to J.K. Starnes, DL2, 23 August 1961, LAC, RG 25, vol. 5352, AK 10224-40, part 2.

34 Telegram, "Russian Missile Sites," 27 October 1962, LAC, RG 24, vol. 231, AK S1400-65, part 1.

35 Author's interview with William Warden, former Canadian diplomat, 6 April 2007.

36 Henry Kissinger, *White House Years* (Boston: Little, Brown, 1979), chap. 16.

37 Telegram, 8 November 1960, LAC, RG 25, vol. 5074, AK 4568-40, part 2. A.C. Forrest, editor of the *Observer*, was on what might be described as a private intelligence mission; the US Presbyterian Church had asked him to assess the situation in Cuba (V.A.C. Forrest, "Catholic Church assesses Castro," *Ottawa Journal*, 18 January 1961).

38 It is unclear if these individuals knew or suspected their observations would be passed on to Ottawa, let alone to Washington, but it seems quite unlikely they all understood they were participating in intelligence collection.

39 Jensen, "Canada's Foreign Intelligence Interview Program." The program conducted voluntary post-visit interviews with Canadian travellers, and

was thus mostly "passive"; see Memorandum, DL2, "Information on travellers to Cuba," 11 July 1962, LAC, RG 25, vol. 5077, AK 4568-40, part 10.

40 D.W. Fulford, "Trip to Eastern Half of Cuba," 6 April 1962, LAC, RG 25, vol. 4036, AK 10448-C-40.

41 Letter, Canadian Embassy, Havana, L-481, 3 September 1963, LAC, RG 25, vol. 10044, 20-1-2-Cuba, part 1.

42 Certain exile groups, such as Alpha 666, engaged in paramilitary-style attacks against Cuban targets.

43 In 2005 Richard Langhorne declared "the end of the diplomatic primacy of states"; see Langhorne, "The Diplomacy of Non-State Actors," *Diplomacy & Statecraft* 16, no. 2 (2005): 332.

3 Lifting the Sugarcane Curtain: Security, Solidarity, and Cuba's Pavilion at Expo 67

ASA McKERCHER

From April to October 1967 more than fifty-three million visitors, including a cavalcade of presidents, prime ministers, movie stars, and royalty, travelled to the Universal and International Exposition in Montreal. Crowded onto a 365-hectare expanse across the St Lawrence River, pavilions from sixty-two nations and dozens of companies and charitable groups competed for attention under the slogan "Man and His World." "Suddenly you're there," wrote one reporter, "and it's a huge cauldron, throbbing with people, boiling with activity, overflowing with the assault of clashing ideas – a psychedelic trip without LSD into a world of the unknown."[1] Yet visitors well knew that this world was one wracked by conflict. As journalist Robertson Cochrane noted, "[t]he bustling mini-world of Expo 67 – much like the real, live world and its man – is something short of a showcase of altruism and universal brotherhood." Protests against both the Vietnam War and racial discrimination in the United States threatened to spill over into Expo; the Six-Day War that June cast a pall over the festivities; and there were controversies over the content of the Canadian Indian pavilion, the Christian pavilion, and the Israeli and West German pavilions. But, Cochrane reported, "[t]he Cuban trouble is by far the most serious. Ask a man on the street here about it and the answer typically is: 'You won't catch me setting foot in that pavilion.'"[2] And yet Cuba's pavilion was one of the most visited exhibits at Expo 67.

International events such as world's fairs are always intensely political: enemies are forced to confront one another and clashing ideologies are mixed together. During the Cold War, this ideological and geopolitical tension was palpable as national delegations pursued political agendas through cultural displays. "A world's fair in the 1960s," wrote one commentator, "is a place to display images rather than facts. No one building can tell you all about a society, but it can tell you how a people – or their leaders – want their society to appear."[3] The first international exposition in which revolutionary Cuba participated, Expo 67 allowed Cuban officials to display their country to millions of North Americans who would never get the chance to visit the island, a result of stringent travel bans and the restriction of air travel by the US and Canadian governments. A pariah in the West, Cuba used Expo to break out of its isolation and to practise public diplomacy – that is, "international relations beyond traditional diplomacy," involving "the cultivation by governments of public opinion in other countries" and "the process of intercultural communications."[4] In Montreal, Cuban public diplomacy focused on promoting both Cuban culture – food, drink, art, and music – and the Revolution

For Cuba this outward projection was of vital importance. As Antoni Kapcia has pointed out, since "the Revolution was always as much about achieving and defending real independence as about social change, its external projection was always integral to the whole process of transformation."[5] Furthermore, with Expo 67 occurring one year after Havana hosted the Tricontinental Conference – part of a Cuban effort to stake out, as Canadian diplomats recorded, a "leading role in the 'anti-imperialist' struggle" – the pavilion played up the Third World's challenge to the United States and to capitalism.[6] Cuba's emphasis on these themes, at Montreal and elsewhere, resonated deeply for student activists and radicals throughout the West, including in Canada.[7] Through their Expo pavilion, the Cubans fostered solidarity with political supporters in North America, many of whom, like Cuba itself, were seeking to challenge the status quo.

Occurring not just against the happy backdrop of celebrations of Canada's centenary, Expo 67 fell in the midst of growing political and social unrest. With Quebec separatists, student activists, and countercultural radicals looking to Cuba for inspiration, government officials hardly welcomed the Cuban presence in Montreal. Indeed, just as the Cuban pavilion's unabashed message was applauded by those on the left, it was looked upon with scepticism by other Canadians, whose sensibilities and points of view were challenged by the island nation's display. As a headline in an Ottawa newspaper blared: "The Cubans are coming!"[8] The Cuban pavilion was a cause of insecurity, then, not simply because it was the target of terrorist violence by counterrevolutionaries, but also because it stood as a revolutionary symbol. Canadian reactions to this symbol reflected the friendly unease of Cuba-Canada relations in the 1960s. Moreover, the reactions highlighted the successes, but also the limitations, of Cuban public diplomacy in the West during the Cold War.[9]

What follows is an examination of Cuba's involvement in Expo, the attendant tensions that were generated, and the reaction to the Cuban pavilion's revolutionary message in Canada as represented in the mainstream press.[10] Exploring Cuban public diplomacy as seen through Expo, this chapter also examines the relationship between Canada and Cuba, both official and unofficial, while adding to the growing historiography surrounding Havana's influence upon the New Left. At Montreal the pavilion was a success in that it cemented support among radicals and contributed to establishing Havana as a leading proponent of Third World causes. In terms of the Revolution's wider acceptance, however, Expo was a disappointment, as many Canadians, at least as reflected in the press, appeared to reject the pavilion's zealousness. Ignoring, downplaying, or criticizing the Cubans' revolutionary message, many Canadians instead focused on an older image of Cuba as a place for licentious abandon. In imagining Cuba in this way – by indulging in the "pleasures of imperialism" – these Canadians thereby mimicked many of the racial and gendered notions of the Cuban "other" common in US attitudes towards the island and its people, thus demonstrating similarities in *norteamericanos*' views of Cuba.[11] Even so, the pavilion served as a point of contact with Cuba for Canadian visitors who, despite their distaste for revolution, took away a positive image of the country.

Organizing for Expo

The very fact that Montreal served as the site of the 1967 exposition was important. Cuba had not participated in previous world's fairs held in Seattle in 1962 and New York in 1964–65, but, unlike the United States, Canada maintained diplomatic and trade relations with the island. Nonetheless Ottawa was hardly supportive of the revolutionary government, particularly given the direction of Havana's foreign policy. Canadian officials had also long sought to downplay their differences with Washington over Cuba. Since the Canadian authorities were well aware that Cuba was a "deeply emotional" issue for many in the United States, they worried that ostentatious displays of Canada's differing approach could damage the vital US relationship.[12]

Furthermore, although Canadian policy-makers disagreed with Washington's aggressive stance towards Castro, they had no desire to see their important ally and trading partner undermined. Meeting with President John Kennedy in May 1963, Prime Minister Lester Pearson had affirmed that his government would maintain its ties with Havana, "but would do nothing to indicate support or sympathy for the Castro regime."[13]

Cuba's participation in the Montreal fair seemed to fly in the face of this promise. So, as plans were made in January 1963 to invite countries to participate in Expo, the Canadian embassy in Havana noted that "Cuba's rather special situation" necessitated playing down the invitation to the Cuban government.[14] When an invitation was eventually extended, the Cubans accepted. The next issue involved Cuba's representative at official Expo events. Each participating country was allocated a national day, generally coinciding with a national holiday, on which visiting dignitaries would attend ceremonies held at that country's pavilion. Invitations were extended from Canada's governor general to heads of state abroad. As its national day at Expo, Cuba was allotted 26 July, the date symbolizing the beginning of the Revolution, and an invitation was extended to Osvaldo Dorticós Torrado, Cuba's president, in September 1966. For Ottawa, a problem soon arose. In January 1967 Cuban foreign minister Raúl Roa García hinted to the Canadian embassy in Havana that Fidel Castro, instead of Dorticós, might visit Montreal. Canadian authorities held mixed views on this possibility. In intra-governmental consultations, diplomats from the Department of External Affairs advised that security problems at Expo "would be enormously increased" by Castro's presence. Although admitting that there was "a good deal to be said for Castro breaking out of his isolation within the communist bloc by visiting Canada and EXPO," they felt it was important to recognize that they would have no control over the mercurial Cuban leader, whose "presence would almost certainly prove embarrassing politically." Conversely Expo officials indicated their enthusiasm for a Castro visit, which would be "advantageous" by boosting attendance, publicity, and interest.[15]

Arguments opposing Castro's participation won out. Citing his deep concern that a visit by the Cuban prime minister would result in demonstrations, as well as the likelihood of a terrorist attack or assassination attempt by Cuban exiles, Pearson told Paul Martin, Canada's secretary of state for external affairs, to discourage Castro's attendance. Canadian diplomats subsequently informed Cuban ambassador Américo

Cruz of their concerns for Castro's security. Replying that he would recommend to his government that Castro not attend, Cruz strongly emphasized his hope that the decision had nothing to do with pressure from the United States.[16] Examining this issue, two scholars have been critical of Ottawa's "insistent pressure ... on Havana to prevent Fidel Castro from attending the Expo celebrations," which Cuban officials "not unreasonably attributed to pressure from Washington."[17] The available evidence in Canadian and US archives contains little to indicate that there was any US pressure on Canada. True, the US embassy in Ottawa was pleased indeed when it learned that Castro would not be coming to Montreal,[18] but Washington does not seem to have pressed the matter. Certainly Canadian officials were themselves cognizant of the undesirability of giving the Cuban leader a public platform from which he might inveigh against the United States. As Leon Mayrand, Canada's ambassador in Havana, had confided to his British colleague, a visit by the Cuban leader "could hardly have done Canadian-American relations much good." Yet the overriding issue, Mayrand underlined, was that Castro or Dorticós might be attacked, a prospect that filled officials in Ottawa "with horror."[19]

In Canadian government documents, the emphasis was definitely placed on security, not on the US factor, which in fact goes largely unmentioned. "The paramount consideration with respect to a visit to Canada by Castro is security," noted one report.[20] In another memo advocating that Castro be dissuaded from attending Expo, Pearson was advised that, although relations with the United States were important, the only issue weighed by External Affairs was the "strictly relevant" issue of security. In this regard, "the principal threat arises from the possibility of a combined effort by several Cuban refugee organizations based in Miami and New York who seem to regard 'Cuba-at-EXPO' as a prime target and who, as matters stand, might well be tempted to try some sort of action on July 26." A further potential problem could be posed by "small but perhaps vociferous opposing demonstrations by pro- and anti-Castro elements" or, worst of all, a lone assassin who might attack on a whim. Given these factors, Pearson agreed it was necessary to discourage Castro from attending the fair. Although expecting that this move would have ill effects on Cuba-Canada relations, he judged that "the effect would be even worse, and perhaps more lasting, if Castro or any Cuban leader came to harm in Canada." The point, Pearson noted, was to avoid anything "tragic."[21]

Indeed, there was a genuine security risk from Cuban counterrevolutionaries, whose actions Keith Bolender analyses in his contribution to this volume. Beginning with the bombing of a Cuban cargo ship in Montreal harbour in 1964, the Miami-based Asociación Nacionalista Cubana (ANC) had waged a terrorist campaign throughout North America; targets included the United Nations in New York in 1965 and Cuba's embassy in Ottawa in September 1966. In a press interview, Felipe Rivero Díaz, the group's head, promised that the embassy bombing was "the official start of a reign of terror designed to break" Castro's hold on power, adding that Canadians should be worried.[22] Complaining to Canadian officials that Rivero, despite admitting guilt and promising further attacks, was living openly in the United States, Ambassador Cruz emphasized his hope that all necessary arrangements would be taken to protect Cuba's Expo pavilion.[23] Senior Canadian diplomats agreed that Cruz's complaints about "the impunity" with which counterrevolutionaries behaved were "completely justified." They pressed the Royal Canadian Mounted Police (RCMP) into stepping up security preparations.[24]

Yet, as Expo approached, fears of an attack grew. On 11 March 1967 the ANC bombed a Montreal auction house selling goods belonging to Cuban refugees that had been seized by the Cuban government. A month later, and just days before Expo opened, a bomb made from a bazooka shell – the ANC's preferred weapon – bearing the words "Washington No, Moscow No, Cuba Yes" was discovered near the Expo site, prompting police to descend on the Cuban pavilion.[25] These incidents generated deep concern, which continued even after the arrest of Rivero and other ANC members by US authorities in May. Throughout the year the US Federal Bureau of Investigation highlighted the threat to the Cuban pavilion, to Cuban diplomats in Canada, and to Cuban athletes at the Pan-American Games held in Winnipeg that summer.[26] In May a bomb was thrown at the Cuban pavilion from a passing boat; thankfully, it exploded harmlessly.[27]

Given these security issues, criticism that "the Canadians did everything they could to politely dissuade the Cuban leader from attending, bizarrely arguing that the RCMP could not ensure his safety"[28] seems slightly off the mark. True, Pearson had little affection for Castro, and had assured the Americans that he would show Cuba's prime minister little sympathy. But there was a genuine counterrevolutionary terrorist threat in Montreal, and during his previous visits to North America in 1959 and 1960, Castro had shown a propensity for throwing caution to the wind and ignoring the staid nature of diplomatic protocol by mixing with the public and wading out into crowds, often breaking free from his bodyguards.[29] Given the likelihood that Cuba's leader might display similar conduct in Montreal, Canadian diplomatic officials judged that, since the RCMP "will be heavily taxed during the EXPO period by threats from Czech, Ukrainian, Yugoslav and other exiles as well as Cubans," there was a real need to dissuade Castro's attendance. Moreover, Cuba's national day celebrations – and hence a likely trip by Castro – coincided with French president Charles de Gaulle's planned attendance at Expo, a visit posing its own headaches for Canadian authorities. Matters were made worse, Canadian diplomats felt, by the fact that the Mounties were not "fully aware of the dimensions" of the threat to Cuba's pavilion.[30] As opening day approached, Martin informed Pearson that, although it seemed unlikely that Castro would attend, the Cuban leader "has at least one trait in common with [US] President [Lyndon] Johnson – a fondness for deciding on trips on short notice."[31] Press speculation on this issue was widespread; the *Ottawa Citizen*, for instance, noted that the possibility of Castro's visiting Canada was causing "palpitations" for Canadian authorities. Perhaps in the interests of security, one reporter mused condescendingly, Castro could be persuaded "to adopt a suitable disguise – he could shave and wear a morning coat and striped trousers."[32]

Fearful of the Cuban pavilion's becoming the site of counterrevolutionary violence, on instructions from Pearson Canadian diplomats re-emphasized to Cruz that the prime minister held deep reservations about a visit by Castro, stemming "entirely" from an assessment about "a threat of unpredictable proportions," rather than from "political motivations" or "pressure of any sort from [the] USA."[33] Privately Pearson ordered the Canadian embassy in Havana to refuse a visit by Castro should the Cubans suggest it.[34] The prime minister even toyed with delaying or calling off Cuba's 26 July celebrations in Montreal, largely because of a sense that, with de Gaulle's visit, police and security officials would be taxed to the limit. Martin opposed this move. It was true, he noted, that "the imponderable nature of the threat to Castro" could "create a security problem of much greater potential magnitude than any we are at present accepting on account of EXPO." But arguing that Canada, as the host country, had invited Cuba and that cancelling its national day celebrations would look unfortunate, Martin advised that nothing should be done to damage bilateral relations.[35]

These efforts to deter Castro's attending caused some bruising of the Cuba-Canada relationship. Much to the relief of officials in Ottawa, Cruz confirmed that Dorticós, not Castro, would attend. His government, Cruz emphasized, did "not wish in any way to embarrass the Canadian government" or cause any "anxiety" in Ottawa. The issue was settled, although Dorticós subsequently cancelled and Marcelo Fernández Font, the foreign trade minister, travelled to Canada instead.[36] Perhaps a sign of Cuban displeasure, this move eliminated a source of bilateral tension. It also left Canadian officials elated, as it lessened the risk of an attack and put to rest fears that Castro might say something embarrassing. Having either recognized the security risks or judged that it was imprudent to alarm Ottawa, Havana's decision in no way meant that it was reticent about using Expo to promote Cuba and the Revolution.

Cuba's Pavilion

The contretemps over Castro's invitation aside, the Cubans were buoyant about participating in what *Granma*, the official newspaper of the Cuban Communist Party, called "[o]ne of the most important world events," at which Cuba would "have an original pavilion, with modern design, situated in a magnificent location."[37] In January 1966 Cuba's National Council of Culture launched a nationwide architectural contest for the pavilion's design. Twenty-five entries were received; the eventual winners, Sergio Baroni and Vittorio Garatti, were Italian architects who had designed a number of buildings in Havana, including elements of the National Art Schools. As Baroni stressed, the pavilion was designed to lift the "sugar-cane curtain" around Cuba because, "[a]fter all, it wasn't the Cubans who made the curtain."[38] *Exposicuba*, a government agency formed under the Ministry of Culture but soon transferred to the Ministry of the Interior, then carried out planning for the pavilion, which would circumvent US isolation policy by bringing a Cuban presence into North America. However, the link between *Exposicuba* and Cuban security officials raised eyebrows in Ottawa. Recognizing that some propaganda was "inevitable on such fertile ground as Expo," Canadian authorities concluded that a lot of propaganda would embarrass the United States, Expo, and Canada.[39] These fears were off the mark. In March 1967, as final preparations for Expo were being made, the Canadian embassy in Havana reported that the Cubans did not seem set on going "on the offensive" against the

United States in their displays, but rather seemed ready to showcase the Revolution's achievements and thereby leave implicit the "fatuity" of US policy towards Cuba. Although "the possibility of the Cubans making efforts to use Expo to carry on their propaganda war with the United States" could not be eliminated, the embassy contended that there was not yet any reason to complain about the exhibit.[40]

The pavilion, three storeys of stacked rectangular cuboid made of interlocking steel and aluminum squares coated with white vinyl, was later described by the designer of other pavilions as being one of Expo's several "smaller gems."[41] The building included a restaurant, seating a hundred, and a bar. Scattered across the Expo site, the Cubans also maintained several other buildings: a smaller restaurant, three small kiosks selling Cuban tobacco products, record albums, and other artistic goods, and a *Coppelia* ice cream parlour mimicking one that had recently opened in Vedado, Havana. Outside the main pavilion building, projectors displayed films of dance, sporting events, and the Cuban countryside onto three screens. Inside, the walls were lined with hundreds of photographs, blown-up newspaper articles, and more films.[42] Together the photographic and film exhibits were meant to "present to the millions of visitors images of the efforts and successes of a people who have won their own destiny." On display, were Cubans' "400 year tradition of rebellious struggle; first, against colonialism; then, against intervention; of late, against US imperialism," along with images showing the revolutions in literacy, housing, and public health, all areas where Cuba could serve as a model. Beyond showcasing the Revolution itself, the pavilion also played up the necessity of solidarity, which was "our people's concept about the relations that must exist between peoples of the world."[43] This mix of the external promotion of the Revolution with solidarity was – and remains – the essence of Cuban public diplomacy. At a ceremony in early April, Armando Hart Dávalos, secretary of the Central Committee of the Cuban Communist Party and among the Revolution's leading ideologues, praised the departing delegation of tour guides, chefs, and bartenders for being exemplary "ambassadors of our revolution."[44]

Leaving Havana by ship, the delegates arrived in Montreal in mid-April after a week at sea. Their unabashed arrival was reported on widely in the Canadian press, as their ship – bearing a giant image of revolutionary hero Ernesto "Che" Guevara alongside a giant banner on which was printed Che's famous aphorism, "*¡Hasta la victoria siempre!*" – was welcomed into port by a crowd of supporters waving Cuban flags, singing "The Internationale," and offering shouts of support.[45] This pageantry went over well with Canadians. One reporter applauded the "normality" of the Cubans aboard ship: the woman were "mostly young, mostly goodlooking," while the men "were well-dressed and clean-shaven." Displaying similar condescension, the *Toronto Star*'s correspondent was thankful that "only one Castro-style beard and one Castro-style beret could be seen in the whole shipload."[46] Beyond this clean-cut image, another journalist was enthusiastic about the almost "Hollywood-oriented publicity stunts" that preceded the delegation's arrival, including threats by émigré terrorists to blow up the pavilion and comments by Opposition leader John Diefenbaker, who had complained in the House of Commons about Cuba's use of secret police to guard its pavilion. Then, "the already electric atmosphere was recharged when the Cuban contingent, 200 strong, arrived via passenger freighter chanting 'Fidel, Fidel,' and waving flags of the Cuban revolution." Given this excitement it was "no wonder" that, during a preview for the press, the pavilion was packed "to capacity" by reporters.[47] In these accounts, Cuba's pavilion was treated as an exciting spectacle and as a site of danger and intrigue, where Cold War boundaries could be crossed.

Expectations among the press were high. Cultural affairs columnist Leslie Millin wrote in the *Globe and Mail* that, "with their obsession with security, their unusual pavilion design and their unique status as a Western Hemisphere Communist government, the Cubans have attracted curiosity and attention at the World's Fair far out of proportion to the size of their country."[48] With such attention focused upon them, the Cubans had an excellent opportunity to influence North American perceptions of Cuba. In doing so, they sought to cast their country, not as the debauched tourist destination of the pre-revolutionary period, but as the vanguard of revolution. Marking this dichotomy between pre- and post-1959 Cuba was important. In an advertisement printed in the official guidebook and other Expo publications, the Cubans asked: "What does the name CUBA suggest to you? Sunny beaches ... Afro-Cuban rhythm ... the world's best rum and tobacco? Or a revolutionary people who sacrifice and struggle for a better life?" The ad went on to note that, through films, photographs, and slides, the pavilion presented the history of the Revolution and its achievements, adding only briefly that visitors could enjoy seafood and rum at the restaurant. "Cuba," it concluded boldly, "the first socialist country of the Western Hemisphere, invites you to visit its pavilion at EXPO 67."[49]

Presenting the Revolution to the North American audience, not feeding and refreshing them, was *Exposicuba*'s central task. "'I think a lot of Americans will come to see us,'" José Fernández de Cossío, the pavilion's commissioner general, remarked to the press, "'anyway I hope they do.'"[50] Hence *Granma* reported that, "[a]mongst the many important tasks performed by our delegation [rank] the activities of the hosts and guides." The public face of the pavilion, the guides spent much of their time speaking with the more than 7,500 daily visitors, answering questions about Cuban history, and often debating "recalcitrant" members of the "bourgeoisie." According to this report, the guides could often be found explaining "the Revolution, guerrillas, Communism – all the words that form a spectre for curious capitalists." They even showed "courage in responding in certain cases to insults and provocations from agents of the [Central Intelligence Agency]."[51] Unsurprisingly, differences between Cuba and the United States were pronounced, both in the exhibits and in Cuban press reports. The US pavilion, reported *Verde Olivo*, an immense globe, was stuffed with photos and items of the rich and famous, while in the Cuban pavilion visitors encountered "a different reality" – namely, "the millions around the world suffering from hunger" and the "miserable life of millions of people on three continents who do not know how to read or write, who do not have shoes or medicine."[52] Furthermore, the photographs of Hollywood celebrities that filled the US pavilion masked "the inequality, violence and injustice that characterize North American life."[53] In contrast to US distortions stood the honesty of Cuba's pavilion. Cubans, *Bohemia* contended, could take pride in that they were displaying their history, from Columbus to the Revolution, "without sidestepping the sad stages of oppression and misery, the economic dependency and imperialist penetration." Such honesty "wakens the curiosity and admiration of the majority of humanity."[54]

The exhibition, however, did not simply focus on Cuba. Much of it dealt with wider issues, from US foreign policy to the tricontinental struggle. Not neutral, these films and displays left criticism of Washington implicit, with wording that fit Expo regulations requiring exhibits to be largely apolitical. As Pearson was informed, the pavilion was "somewhat militant," but not intolerable.[55] For instance, a small row occurred over one installation that contained a photograph with a banner in the background displaying the by-now-common slogan, "The Andes will be the Sierra Maestra of Ecuador." This comparison to the Cuban mountain range where Castro led the revolutionary forces

prompted Expo officials to lodge a complaint on behalf of the Ecua-
dorian embassy.[56] Far less contentious were large banners critical of
the United States blaring phrases such as "Atomic Blackmail" or those
praising Third World revolution bearing statements such as "The Turning Point of History Has Come" and "Man's Long Journey Through
Centuries of Exploitation and Murder Comes to an End." More contentious was a large panel listing the names of various countries – including
Cuba, Congo, Vietnam, Panama, Laos, and the Dominican Republic –
all surrounding the word "Aggression," which stood as shorthand for
the United States.[57] Witnessing this display, an American correspondent
reported home that, in Cuba's pavilion, the United States got "slapped
around pretty hard," and so "the best thing for an American to do"
afterwards was "to step into an adjacent Cuban bar" for "a first-rate
Cuban rum drink."[58]

Bold in its portrayal of Cuba, the Revolution, and Cuban views of
the world, the pavilion held back little. Yet, how were these messages
received? As the *Toronto Star* contended, although the "revolutionary
message in Cuba's Expo pavilion is sizzling hot … it doesn't always
get across to the visitors."[59] The bold messages on display did appeal
to visitors who hailed from the left. Despite being an intensely popular destination, however, the pavilion also seemed to repel many of
its visitors. Cuba's display, judged one reporter, was "divided evenly
between ideology and ice cream."[60] The Cuban pavilion presented a
serious image of a country in the midst of a profound social, political,
and economic revolution. But this image was obscured somewhat by
the lighter side of the pavilion on display in the restaurant and bar, a
view of Cuba deeply ingrained in North Americans' minds.

The Reception

Reactions to Cuba's exhibition were as mixed as the drinks in the pavilion's bar, but the interest in the pavilion was clear from the large lines
of visitors waiting to enter it. The reason for its popularity was clear:
the exhibition offered a view inside Cuba in an era when tourist travel
to the island was next to nil, the pavilion itself was stylistically unique,
and the Cubans provided an entertaining experience. Cuba's display,
the official Expo guidebook observed, "represents the youthful spirit of
the Cuban Revolution, openness, gaiety and rapid development … As
to the good things in life for which Cuba is famous, a restaurant and bar
serve fresh Cuban seafood specially brought to Montreal and Cuban

drinks such as Daiquiri and Cuba Libre prepared with Cuban rum."[61] In his bestselling unofficial guidebook, meanwhile, Montreal *Gazette* columnist Bill Bantey offered another anodyne description: "The revolutionary movement is presented as an open-ended phenomenon expanding in all directions, the elements of the exhibit leading to show how defence is integrated with production, production with education, education with health, health with social life, etc." What he chose to praise were the restaurant's lobster and shrimp and the bar's daiquiris and Centennial Punch, a rum drink, chosen via a competition among sixty-four Cuban cocktail-makers, to celebrate Canada's centennial.[62]

Other reporters offered more lively judgments. A writer for Montreal's *La Presse* highlighted the potent appeal both of the centennial cocktail and the "original way [the Cubans] were celebrating our Expo and their revolution."[63] The *Globe and Mail*'s Martin O'Malley characterized the pavilion as a "thrill ride": the threat of attack and the fact that the pavilion "could come down at any moment"; the "jaunty bravado" of the workers; and the "ominous-looking men straight out of a Dick Tracy comic strip." He also noted the presence of "dark-skinned" guards, a comment doubtless reflecting fears of the non-Western "Other" – a reminder that Canadians were not above viewing Cuba and Cubans through the same racial lenses as their American neighbours.[64] O'Malley added that there was "a fairly common half-quip among press types covering Expo: 'Have they bombed Cuba yet?'" His advice to those visitors concerned about an attack by counterrevolutionary terrorists was that they bolster their "courage with a shot of Cuban rum" or with an "*El Centenario*."[65] In a similar vein, columnist Georgina Hammond felt some disappointment upon visiting the Cuban pavilion, since "[n]othing much happened. The pavilion was not blown up." Still, she felt it "worth a visit," if only to see the photographic display, reminding readers that "one does not have to agree with its message in order to tour the pavilion."[66] There was general agreement in the mainstream press, then, that what the Cuban pavilion offered was a hint of revolution, even danger, mixed with rum. After touring the pavilion early on, a correspondent for the Canadian Press agency was underwhelmed: "Revolutionary victory is the main theme," and so there were "few surprises in the small pavilion." The correspondent predicted, then, that the "most popular part of the pavilion probably will be the terrace restaurant and bar."[67] Cuban alcohol was not only a draw, but was itself potentially dangerous. Commenting on a warning issued by the US government to its citizens that they would not be permitted to purchase goods from the Cuban pavilion, the *Toronto Star* noted that this included food and beverage purchases, meaning that "the law-abiding American" would miss the centennial cocktail.[68]

The emphasis placed on the entertainment offered at the Cuban pavilion over its revolutionary message doubtless reflected a bias against Cuba. Yet it also reflected the reality of Expo, where visitors came to be entertained as well as educated. Since the Cuban pavilion offered much more than mere entertainment, many visitors were put off by the displays. The *Gazette* complained about footage "of street and jungle fighting, complete with actual film of men being shot dead and tanks rolling over corpses," all while "a tape recorder boomed out the irregular chatter of a machine-gun."[69] Writing that a tour of the pavilion began "innocently enough" with a welcome from a "pretty hostess" and an array of blown-up newspaper stories and headlines, a *Globe and Mail* reporter bemoaned that one was then confronted by "violence – rats streaming out of sewers, rats streaming down staircases, men getting clubbed, shot, mutilated and murdered – all portrayed on a steadily churning black and white film on the second floor."[70] "This is not a pleasant pavilion," added another journalist. "It is not meant to be. It is meant to shock." Canadian visitors he interviewed were not impressed, with one stating: "'It's a waste of time. Their revolution doesn't interest us,'" while another argued, in comments reflecting a sense that international expos should focus on consumer comforts: "'They're crying their eyes out about loss of export sales ... Why don't they show us what products they have to offer, instead of all this propaganda.'"[71] Praising the Czechoslovaks, who were "eschewing the Communist hard-sell" in their pavilion, popular television personality Pierre Berton drew a comparison with the Cuban pavilion, which was "the only shrill thing about [Expo]." Along similar lines, author Mordecai Richler dubbed Cuba's display the "most truculent" in Montreal.[72] The consensus among mainstream reporters was that the Cuban message was too much.

That the Canadian press looked unfavourably upon the violence on display in the Cuban pavilion is unsurprising. In the wake of Castro's seizure of power in January 1959, the new government had carried out summary executions of members of the Batista regime. In part the trials had been political theatre on the part of revolutionaries eager to maintain order, establish their legitimacy, and respond to a popular sense of honourable justice, given "the dishonorable killings of honorable people [that] were at the core of the widespread abhorrence of

Batistiano violence."[73] The drumhead trials were greeted with unease in North America, sapping some of the early enthusiasm for the Revolution on the part of the Canadian and US press.[74] With the consolidation of communism on the island, Cuba's tilt towards the Sino-Soviet bloc, and Cuban foreign policy throughout the Third World, Canada's mainstream press – like the Canadian government – took an increasingly dim view of the Revolution, even as it offered little support for US policy, especially when Washington sought to infringe upon Canadian independence. The Cuban pavilion's display of violence as a fact in Cuba's history – the result of colonialism, imperial competition, centuries of slavery, and political instability – was startling for Canadian visitors who, elsewhere at Expo, encountered triumphant displays of modernity devoid of the harsh reality of life beyond the First World.[75] Moreover, the presentation of Batista's violent rule serving as a major justification of the revolutionary project was a point seemingly lost on Canadian reporters, who focused on and then dismissed the violence itself. Put off by "pictures of death in Havana streets, of the atrocities of the Batista regime, of the violence of the revolution," the *Montreal Star*'s reporter was glad to find himself in the bar, with its "exuberant music, the whiff of good cigars and the clatter of glasses on marble tables."[76]

Even among those commentators who disagreed with the pavilion's message there was agreement that the Cubans had at least put on a good show. In his best-selling retrospective, *This Was Expo*, cultural critic Robert Fulford praised the pavilion's "pleasant jumble of odd angles and box shapes, like a Cubist painting suddenly blown up in three dimensions." However, he detested the "heavy-handed and oppressive propaganda," which had been like "a typographic nightmare." Still, he admitted, "its anti-American message was hardly forgettable."[77] Agreeing on the aesthetic of the pavilion itself – "rather jolly, with its traffic-light windows" – one architectural critic felt that, inside, "the exhibit was one mewling shriek of protest and complaint. Even those sympathetic to the Cuban revolt must have been repelled by the noisy, sabre-rattling films and the reams of text dangling around like fly-paper. The best part of Cuba was the bar."[78] Instead of the revolutionary message, what resonated was an old view of Cuba as a place for licentious behaviour. This view was put most succinctly in a wider piece on Expo, which chose to focus on the fact that "the Cuban pavilion sells the revolution hard" by offering "ugly photographs of the Batista regime, movies of bloody battles, and references to 'the shiverings of death and the singing summer joy of VICTORY.'" Thankfully, the article noted, "the bar in the Cuban pavilion features rich, dark, polished wood, gleaming mirrors, suave bartenders and an atmosphere that speaks so clearly of the old days in Havana that the place is full of nostalgic Americans."[79] Nostalgia for a certain view of pre-revolutionary Cuba was much in evidence, as was a lack of appreciation for the dark side of that era.

The Cubans themselves helped to foster this emphasis by including a festive atmosphere that seemed to overshadow the revolutionary message. But the lighter side did draw visitors as well as favourable press coverage. Positive reports flooded in following the 26 July celebrations, the *Fiesta cubana*, which saw a large outdoor concert followed by a massive conga line that proceeded throughout the Expo site. "Cuba's day at Expo yesterday," a reporter wrote, "was an almost ludicrous contrast between tight-lipped maximum security and light-hearted conga dancers snaking through the crowds."[80] Another wrote of "startled Expo-goers" who gaped as "[w]omen dancers waved their shoes above their heads while shouts of 'Fidel' and 'Viva Fidel' punctuated a revolutionary song which features a repeated chorus of 'Long live Cuba and the revolution.'"[81] The dancers, the *Gazette*'s Sandra Donlan added, "picked up quite a following of young Canadians … The Cubans' gaiety was infectious and people seemed to converge from all over to clap and spur them on." In conclusion, she wrote that, although Castro had not come to Montreal, nevertheless "he cast a long shadow on the day's proceedings."[82] Castro's shadow, at least in these portrayals, was not that of a serious revolutionary bearing an important message. Instead, the Canadian media, not favourably disposed towards the Revolution, dismissed the Cuban pavilion's political message and slanted their coverage of Cuba's presence at Expo towards frivolity and fun.

To some extent the Cubans embraced the popularity generated by Cuban rum. A photographic montage in *Verde Olivo*, a journal of the Cuban military, contained an image of the bar, filled to capacity, with the caption: "In the bar, constantly filled with Canadians, *norteamericanos*, French, British and people from all parts of the world, who all speak a single language: Caney Rum." For the domestic audience, then, the popularity of the bar served as an indicator of support for Cuba. It also had another purpose: to show solidarity.

As the caption of another photo indicated, however, "[i]n the corner of the bar, two young *norteamericanos* have arrived in Montreal to protest in front of the US pavilion against aggression in Vietnam."[83] Thus, although many visitors were repulsed by, or at least unreceptive to, what they saw in the pavilion, others were drawn to Cuba's message. Unsurprisingly, Canadians on the left held far different views of the Cuban pavilion. Artist Barry Lord, who had been ejected from Expo for being among the few protestors who shouted at Lyndon Johnson during the president's brief stop in Montreal, recalled that, upon returning to the festival several days later, he was followed by a police officer. Defiantly he brought his police minder into the Cuban pavilion and, "[i]nside, I made certain that he could see the seditious nature of the books and records I bought. Together we studied the revolutionary slogans and history graphically presented by the Cubans. Near the exit we stood for some minutes in front of a sign which proclaimed that man was passing into a new age of freedom, cooperation, and human brotherhood."[84] For supporters of Cuba, entry into the pavilion could be a means of protest.

Cuba's presence in Montreal also served as a focal point of activity. Circulating advertisements welcoming supporters to "Join the Fiesta Cubana at Expo 67," the Toronto branch of the Fair Play for Cuba Committee (FPCC) – the central branch in Canada – ran a two-day excursion to the pavilion for members in July, complete with a guided tour of the pavilion and a private reception with Cuban diplomatic officials.[85] On 1 July, the FPCC also ran an anti–Vietnam War rally in Montreal. Due to restrictions on protests during Expo, the event was held well away from the festivities. Even so, it drew over fifteen hundred demonstrators, and allowed the FPCC to distribute hundreds of copies of speeches by Castro and Che. The theme of the rally, as FPCC chairman Hans Modlich explained to Jorge Enrique Mendoza, Granma's director, was "taking Vietnam to Expo '67." The war in Vietnam, he continued, "is of course completely forgotten at Expo, except in the Cuban Pavilion."[86] Believing their efforts to distribute Cuban publications, notably several thousand copies of Guevara's "Message to the Tri-Continental," had been successful in having "reached the most promising layers of radicalizing youth here in Canada," Modlich beseeched Isidoro Malmierca Peoli, Granma's editor, to send more literature, especially since "preparations in solidarity with the Cuban Revolution are nearing their peak here in Canada with the approaching of July 26 and especially in anticipation of the [Organization of Latin American Solidarity] congress," scheduled to meet in Havana in August. In this light, Modlich hoped to begin distributing Granma on a large scale among activists in Canada and the United States.[87]

For Modlich and other sympathizers, the Cuban pavilion also served as an inspiration. Writing Ambassador Cruz, the chairman of the Vancouver Fair Play For Cuba Committee, who had brought with him to Montreal a delegation of supporters from Canada and the United States, expressed how "very proud of Cuba" he had been upon viewing the *Fiesta cubana*.[88] In his annual report to FPCC members, Modlich praised the "fortunate" timing of Expo, which had come as anti–Vietnam War sentiments in Canada were renewing interest in Cuba. Paraphrasing Expo's theme of "Man and His World," Modlich contended that, in their "stimulating exhibit," the Cubans had been the only pavilion "dealing with man & real world."[89] There was a transformative process at play, too, for, in a letter to *Exposicuba*, Modlich praised the "magnificent Pavilion," which left him "completely transfixed as if back in Havana." Most visitors, he added, had been "sincerely impressed and engaged by what they saw despite their lack of political awareness." In sum, he wrote that the pavilion was "an inspiring victory ... right next door to New York City and the other large eastern metropoles of North America – no wonder the bourgeois press is up in arms."[90]

Nor were Canadian leftists the only ones inspired by the Cuban pavilion. The staff at the US Socialist Workers Party's *Militant Labor Forum* asked the Toronto FPCC – which had long served as a conduit through which Cuban publications reached the United States – to send copies of all the pamphlets, handouts, and books available at the Cuban pavilion, as these were unavailable in New York.[91] In fact, in the wake of Expo, these sorts of requests flooded into the FPCC offices in Toronto. For instance, captivated by the "high revolutionary consciousness" he had encountered at the Cuban pavilion, one Detroit-based activist, noting that mail service between Cuba and the United States was non-existent, asked whether he would be able to take up a correspondence with a member of the Cuban delegation by funnelling mail to and from Cuba through the FPCC.[92] Meanwhile representatives of wings of the Socialist Workers Party and the Young Socialist Alliance based in Berkeley, California, and Madison, Wisconsin, sought copies of the Cuban films and publications they had seen displayed in the pavilion.[93] Part library, part meeting ground, and part monument, the Cuban pavilion also served as a commemorative site. Only days before Expo ended, word was received that Che Guevara had been killed in Bolivia. This news led the pavilion to display a large version of the famous Alberto Korda photograph of the revolutionary leader, accompanied by some of his famous quotations. The vigil in Montreal was an initial step in the process of the "public and popular mythification of *Che*, the fallen hero"[94]

By giving voice to the concerns of the Third World and by appealing to leftists, the Cuban pavilion delivered an important message, one that found little traction more broadly, however, among Expo visitors. Advocacy of revolution even led to fears that Cuba was seeking to promote violence within Canada. Due to the threat posed by émigré terrorists, Pearson had agreed to allow Cuba to send a large delegation to Expo, so that, in addition to local and federal police, Cuban security personnel would guard the pavilion. Of the total Cuban delegation of 240, 50 were guards.[95] Attacked by his parliamentary opponents over why the Cubans had not been asked "to leave their armies of security personnel at home," Pearson soon sought a reduction in the size of the Cuban presence.[96] Clarifications were sought, and Expo officials and Canadian diplomats agreed that the number of Cuban guards was in line with other, similarly sized pavilions; moreover, extra security was needed at the several kiosks selling Cuban art, music, and other goods dotted across the Expo site as well as at a rented apartment building in Montreal where its delegation was housed.[97]

The Canadian government might have recognized the need for these guards, but their presence worried other Canadians. In July, just as Cuba prepared to celebrate the *Fiesta cubana*, there were reports that Cuban security officials at Expo were operating "two terrorist training camps" in the Laurentian Mountains north of Montreal.[98] In an editorial, the right-wing *Toronto Telegram* subsequently noted that in 1965 Quebec separatists had attended courses at the University of Havana, while "there have been overtones of association between small extremist French Canadian separatist groups and alleged guerrilla veterans among the bloated staff of the Cuban Expo Pavilion." Charging Cuba with fomenting race riots in the United States, the paper asked how soon Canada could expect something similar among French Canadians. After all, Cuba "is openly playing the oldest Communist game of all, violent international revolution."[99] Then, in the House of Commons in October, Robert Thompson, leader of the conservative Social Credit Party, charged that Radio Havana was broadcasting a daily French-language program giving "instructions in subversive activity and guerrilla warfare," as well as another program urging First Nations, Métis, and Inuit people "to rise in a 'red power' rebellion."[100] Repeating this charge in an open letter to Paul Martin, he also complained that the Cuban pavilion distributed *Granma* and other Cuban publications, and

he raised allegations that Cuban guards were training rebels, distributing copies of Che's *Guerrilla Warfare* to university students, and providing arms and ammunition to separatists.[101]

   Thompson's litany of charges left Cuban diplomats aghast. Reviewing Radio Havana broadcasts, senior Cuban officials, including Vice
President Carlos Rafael Rodríguez, concluded that the allegations were
baseless.[102] Officials in Ottawa had had some concerns about Cuba's
expanded presence in Montreal, and with good reason: the city was the
site of growing revolutionary agitation on the part of French-Canadian
nationalists, and, as in many places in the 1960s, radicals there "watched
events in Cuba with unprecedented interest."[103] Canadian authorities
were conscious of this appeal. With Expo a month away from opening,
Canadian diplomats had reminded organizers that, although security
was important, "we must also bear in mind our responsibility to ensure,
to the extent that we reasonably can, that Canada is not used as a base
by the Cubans for subversive activities."[104] As to Thompson's charges,
an investigation by Canadian authorities found little evidence to support them, leading Canada's undersecretary of state to advise Martin
that, even "if the Cuban were disposed to actively engage in activities of this nature in Canada, it is most doubtful that they would resort
to such an apparently crude and overt attempt to develop a guerrilla
movement in Quebec."[105] Ultimately the allegations of Thompson and
others represented fears generated by the image presented by Cuba and
by the Revolution's challenge to the First World. Moreover, as Maurice
Demers and Michel Nareau note in their contribution to this volume,
Cuba served as an inspiration to disaffected *Québécois* who sought
their own independent, socialist country.[106] Other links to Cubans and
Quebec separatists were more innocent. Exiled in Cuba after hijacking
an airplane in 1969, Pierre Charette, a member of the separatist terror
group Front de libération du Québec, made sure to visit Isidoro Arditi,
a chef at the Habana Libre hotel whom he had befriended at the Cuban
pavilion, where Arditi had been managing the pavilion's restaurant.[107]

   Cuba's revolutionary image and its challenge to the status quo were
both displayed at the Cuban pavilion. An analysis of the exhibit prepared for Canadian ministers highlighted the pavilion's "militant
revolutionary theme," which was objectionable from Ottawa's point
of view. Still, the report judged it to be "at least an honest reflection
of the Castro regime's attitude toward the outside world." On the
bright side, Cuba, the report concluded, "for a country of its size – has
made a major effort to contribute significantly to EXPO."[108] Its message

aside, Canadian authorities were pleased with Cuba's participation at Montreal. Paul Bridle, head of the Latin American Division at External Affairs, expressed to the US embassy his relief that the Cuban delegation visiting for the 26 July celebrations had "displayed model conduct throughout their tour, indulged in no propaganda … and neither faced nor provoked incidents of any kind."[109] Meeting with Pearson and government ministers in Ottawa, Marcelo Fernández Font, the delegation's head, stated, in his only public comments, that "Cuba, linked to Canada by tight commercial, cultural, social, and political bonds, could not be absent from the Exposition."[110] And Canada, because it maintained these links through its effort to maintain normal relations with Cuba, had not excluded the Cubans from Expo, even as the island nation's participation created anxiety. As for Canadians themselves, Pierre Dupuy, the fair's commissioner general, remarked to Font that the "long queues standing at the entrance of your pavilion" were "proof of the interest of Expo visitors in Cuba."[111] The Montreal Expo let Canadians peer behind the sugarcane curtain to see images of Cuba, its Revolution, and its people, and thus the fair represented an important place for interaction between Canadians and Cubans in a world divided by the Cold War.

Conclusions

Reflecting on Expo 67 in a commemorative book, Pierre Dupuy enthused that, "when the lights go out for the last time, when the crowds have left the pavilions and the avenues, a World Exhibition begins a new life. Less glittering but more profound, this new life is nourished in the souls of those who visited the Exhibition, and it will blossom into a legend for generations to come."[112] In writing these words, Dupuy certainly did not have in mind the views of student activists such as Todd Gitlin. Arriving in Montreal, Gitlin was soon "dazzled by the multimedia Canadian and Czech pavilions, which were influenced by Marshall McLuhan and other avant-garde wizards." What impressed him most, however, "was the modest Cuban exhibit, showing no industrial goods or technological wonders, only a modernist photo-essay juxtaposing photographic blow-ups of fragments of poetry exalting the continuity of the fight against Batista with the revolutionary present. After a short conversation with the Cuban guide I swapped a JOBS OR INCOME NOW button for her Cuban pin … I raved about the pavilion and [Castro's recent interview in *Le Nouvel Observateur*] for weeks, and wrote a poem pitying Americans who couldn't understand how glorious it would be to abolish money."[113] Inspired by what he had seen and heard at the Cuban display, Gitlin, a significant figure in the US New Left, subsequently journeyed to Cuba, bringing with him dozens of other students. Cuba's revolutionary message in Montreal had an attractive power, then – a testament to the power of public diplomacy and intercultural exchange. The pavilion itself was also appealing as a source of inspiration and as a place to congregate and protest. By giving voice to the concerns of the Third World, Cuba's exhibit delivered an important message for leftists, activists, and other radicals.

Unsurprisingly the political message at Cuba's pavilion found little traction more broadly. Advocacy of revolution led to fears that Cuba was seeking to promote violence in Canada. Even ignoring this sort of extreme opinion, it was evident from mainstream press coverage of the pavilion that Cuba's presence in Montreal generated a sense of insecurity. Images that Canadians encountered of life outside North America were jarring, and the favourable presentation of an anti-"imperialist" narrative and of an anti-capitalist society were off-putting. Still, while many Canadians might have scorned the pavilion's revolutionary proselytization, they at least enjoyed themselves at the Cuban bar, and perhaps came to better appreciate some aspects of the Revolution. Cuba might not, as *Granma* noted, have left "a wake of friendliness and popularity," but it did leave an imprinted message of a revolutionary society pushing against both foreign intervention and global inequality.[114] The pavilion reinforced certain negative images of Cuba even as it generated a positive reaction, in part thanks to the bar.

But in focusing so much on the frivolous aspects of Cuba's pavilion, Canadian observers harkened back to a pre-1959 view of the island as "exotic and very tropical, a place for fun, adventure, and abandon. It was a background for honeymoons, a playground for vacations, a brothel, a casino, a cabaret, a good liberty port – a place for flings, sprees, and binges."[115] At Expo, the Cubans sought to project the image of the new Cuba, but North Americans latched onto older imagery – replete with cultural constructions of a Cuban "other" – that, in effect, made Cuba seem less threatening. If public diplomacy is about using semi-official channels to bypass official barriers and speak directly to the people of another country, then Expo was a success for Havana. "I spent a lot of time visiting the 'exotic' pavilions," one Expo tourist noted years later, and "Cuba was a bit secretive – their tourism ventures were not yet established but it was fun to get to hear Cuban music which seemed less austere than their Government."[116] This fun side of Cuba is what today annually draws over a million Canadian tourists to Cuba. Indeed, for the vast majority of Canadians who visit the island, Cuba – to paraphrase a guidebook critical of this rum and sun tourism – "is only Varadero."[117] A similar process took place with regard to American views of Mexico, where an early twentieth-century sense of the country "as a land plagued by social upheaval and moral degeneracy" gave way decades later to a more positive appreciation, partly the result of tourism.[118] In the end, by providing visitors with a peek inside revolutionary Cuba, the Expo pavilion proved to be an important step towards both dispelling myths about the danger of Cuba and forging the close people-to-people relations with Canada that mark a contemporary Cuba-Canada relationship free of Cold War fears.

NOTES

My thanks to the Social Sciences and Humanities Research Council of Canada, which supported the research conducted for this chapter. As I had the good fortune to present a draft at the 2012 Annual Meeting of the Society for Historians of American Foreign Relations with the support of a SHAFR Global Scholars Conference Grant, my thanks also go to Tom Zeiler, as well as to Raúl Rodríguez Rodríguez. For their helpful comments and suggestions, I also thank Cynthia Wright, Lana Wylie, and Luis René Fernández Tabío.

1 Bill Bantey, *Bill Bantey's Expo 67* (Montreal: Gazette Publishing Company, 1967), 10.
2 Robertson Cochrane, "Controversy's rocking the Expo boat," *Toronto Star*, 18 April 1967. See also Rhona Richman Kenneally and Johanne Sloan, eds., *Expo 67: Not Just a Souvenir* (Toronto: University of Toronto Press, 2010); and Eva-Marie Kröller, "Expo 67: Canada's Camelot," *Canadian Literature* 152/153 (1997): 36–51.
3 Robert Fulford, *This Was Expo* (Toronto: McClelland & Stewart, 1968), 166. See, for example, György Péteri, "Sites of Convergence: The USSR and Communist Eastern Europe at International Fairs Abroad and at Home," *Journal of Contemporary History* 47, no. 1 (2012): 3–12; Jack Masey and Conway Lloyd Morgan, *Cold War Confrontations: US Exhibitions and Their Role in the Cultural Cold War* (Baden, Germany: Lars Müller Publishers, 2008); Marilyn S. Kushner, "Exhibiting Art at the American National Exhibition in Moscow, 1959: Domestic Politics and Cultural Diplomacy," *Journal of*

Cold War Studies 4, no. 1 (2002): 6–26; Tomas Tolvaisas, "Cold War 'Bridge-Building': U.S. Exchange Exhibits and Their Reception in the Soviet Union, 1959–1967," *Journal of Cold War Studies* 12, no. 4 (2010): 3–31; and Ellen Mickiewicz, "Efficacy and Evidence: Evaluating U.S. Goals at the American National Exhibition in Moscow, 1959," *Journal of Cold War Studies* 13, no. 4 (2011): 138–71.

4 Edward R. Murrow Center of Public Diplomacy brochure, quoted in Nicholas J. Cull, "'Public Diplomacy': The Evolution of a Phrase," in *Routledge Handbook of Public Diplomacy*, ed. Nancy Snow and Philip M. Taylor (Abingdon, UK: Routledge, 2008), 19; see also Nicholas J. Cull, "Public Diplomacy: Taxonomies and Histories," *Annals of the American Academy of Political and Social Sciences* 616 (2008): 31–54.

5 Antoni Kapcia, *Cuba in Revolution: A History since the Fifties* (London: Reaktion Books, 2008), 110.

6 Canadian Embassy, Havana, to Department of External Affairs, no. 89, 8 February 1966, Library and Archives Canada (hereafter LAC), RG 25, vol. 9083, file 20-4-26, part 1.

7 See Cynthia Wright, "Between Nation and Empire: The Fair Play for Cuba Committees and the Making of Canada-Cuba Solidarity in the Early 1960s," in *Our Place in the Sun: Canada and Cuba in the Castro Era*, ed. Robert Wright and Lana Wylie (Toronto: University of Toronto Press, 2009), 96–120; and Sean Mills, *The Empire Within: Postcolonial Thought and Political Activism in Sixties Montreal* (Montreal; Kingston, ON: McGill-Queen's University Press, 2010). See also John A. Gronbeck-Tedesco, "The Left in Transition: The Cuban Revolution in US Third World Politics," *Journal of Latin American Studies* 40, no. 4 (2008): 651–73.

8 "The Cubans are coming!" *Ottawa Citizen*, 20 April 1967.

9 On Castro's 1959 tour of North America as an exercise in "populist" diplomacy, see Alan McPherson, "The Limits of Populist Diplomacy: Fidel Castro's April 1959 Trip to North America," *Diplomacy & Statecraft* 18, no. 1 (2007): 237–68.

10 Admittedly this approach is useful, though not without its limitations; see, for instance, Robert Teigrob, *Warming Up to the Cold War: Canada and the United States' Coalition of the Willing, from Hiroshima to Korea* (Toronto: University of Toronto Press, 2009).

11 See the chapter on the pleasures of imperialism in Edward Said, *Culture and Imperialism* (New York: Vintage Books, 1993). On US views of Cuba, see Louis A. Pérez, Jr, *Cuba in the American Imagination: Metaphor and the Imperial Ethos* (Chapel Hill: University of North Carolina Press, 2008). For comparative Canadian and US views of Cuba, see Lana Wylie, *Perceptions*

of Cuba: Canadian and American Policies in Comparative Perspective
(Toronto: University of Toronto Press, 2010).

12 Canadian Embassy, Washington, to Department of External Affairs, tel.
627, 1 March 1962, LAC, RG 25, vol. 5030, file 1415-40, part 10. On Cuba-
Canada relations, see John M. Kirk and Peter McKenna, *Canada-Cuba
Relations: The Other Good Neighbor Policy* (Gainesville: University Press of
Florida, 1997).

13 Summary Record, "Hyannis Port Meetings 10–11 May 1963," 15 May 1963,
LAC, MG 32 B12, vol. 252, file 6.

14 Canadian Embassy, Havana, to Department of External Affairs, 16 January
1963, LAC, RG 25, vol. 5077, file 4568-40, part 11.

15 Marcel Cadieux to Paul Martin, "EXPO: Cuban State Visit," 17 January
1967, LAC, RG 25, vol. 10076, file 20-CUBA-9, part 1.

16 Department of External Affairs to Canadian Embassy, Havana, XL-102, 22
February 1967, LAC, RG 25, vol. 10044, file 20-1-2-CUBA, part 5.1.

17 Kirk and McKenna, *Canada-Cuba Relations*, 76.

18 US Embassy, Ottawa, to Department of State, tel. 869, 19 July 1967,
National Archives and Records Administration (hereafter NARA), RG 59,
CFP 1967–1969, box 2019, folder POL Cuba.

19 Henry Dudgeon to Thomas Barker, 18 July 1967, National Archives of the
United Kingdom, FCO 7/548.

20 Latin American Division to DL(2) Division, "EXPO – Possible Visits by
Cuban Leaders," 10 January 1967, LAC, RG 25, vol. 10502, file 55-7-3-MTL-
2-CUBA, part 1.

21 Marcel Cadieux to Paul Martin, "Cuba and EXPO," 27 June 1967, and Martin to Lester Pearson, "Question of Cuban Visit to Canada and
EXPO," 27 June 1967, LAC, RG 25, vol. 10045, file 20-1-2-CUBA,
part 5.2.

22 Quoted in Bill Trent, "They Fight Castro from Afar," *Ottawa Citizen
Weekend Magazine*, 9 November 1966.

23 Christopher Eberts to Marcel Cadieux, "Safety Arrangements for the
Cuban Chancery," 24 November 1966, LAC, RG 25, vol. 9404, file 20-22-3,
part 1.

24 Ted Rettie to RCMP commissioner, 21 March 1967, LAC, RG 25, vol. 10502,
file 55-7-3-MTL-2-CUBA, part 1.

25 Eddie Collister, "Cuba Expo pavilion guarded by police after shell found,"
Gazette (Montreal), 10 April 1967. A second bazooka shell with a launching
device was left at the Expo site during the visit of the UN secretary-general
in September; see "Bazooka bomb probe on," *Gazette* (Montreal),
26 September 1967.

26 See Marvin Watson to Lyndon Johnson, 21 July 1967, and Hoover to Watson, 9 March 1967, Lyndon Baines Johnson Presidential Library, Office Files of Mildred Stegall, box 64a, folder Cuba and Related Matters.

27 "Bomb misses Cuban exhibit," *Toronto Telegram*, 31 May 1967.

28 Peter McKenna and John M. Kirk, "Through Sun and Ice: Canada, Cuba, and Fifty Years of 'Normal' Relations," in *Canada Looks South: In Search of an Americas Policy*, ed. Peter McKenna (Toronto: University of Toronto Press, 2012), 150.

29 See McPherson, "Limits of Populist Diplomacy"; and Brenda Gayle Plummer, "Castro in Harlem: A Cold War Watershed," in *Rethinking the Cold War: Essays on Its Dynamics, Meaning, and Morality*, ed. Allen Hunter (Philadelphia: Temple University Press, 1997), 133–53.

30 John Graham to DL(2) Division, "Cuban Exile Threats and Safety Measures for Cuban Pavilion and Cuban Officials," 17 March 1967, LAC, RG 25, vol. 10502, file 55-7-3-MTL-2-CUBA, part 1.

31 Paul Martin to Lester Pearson, "Expo: Possible Visit to Canada by Castro," 17 April 1967, LAC, RG 25, vol. 10076, file 20-CUBA-9, part 1.

32 "Cubans are coming!" *Ottawa Citizen*, 20 April 1967; "Castro and Dorticos plan visit," *Montreal Star*, 17 April 1967; "No reply from Dorticos," *Gazette* (Montreal), 18 April 1967; "Fidel Castro va venir à l'Expo" [Fidel Castro is coming to Expo], *La Presse* (Montreal), 18 April 1967.

33 Department of External Affairs to Canadian Embassy, Havana, tel. XL-245, 22 April 1967, LAC, RG 25, vol. 10076, file 20-CUBA-9, part 1.

34 Lester Pearson to Canadian Embassy, Havana, tel. XL-355, 7 July 1967, LAC, RG 25, vol. 10502, file 55-7-3-MTL-2-CUBA, part 2.

35 Paul Martin to Lester Pearson, "Cuba and EXPO," 27 June 1967, LAC, RG 25, vol. 10502, file 55-7-3-MTL-2-CUBA, part 2.

36 Paul Martin to Lester Pearson, "Cuba and EXPO," 5 July 1967; and John Graham to Langley, "Cuban Visit to Ottawa," 13 July 1967, LAC, RG 25, vol. 10076, file 20-CUBA-9, part 1.

37 "Séran exhibidos numerosos productos cubanos en la Feria Universal que se céleberá en Canadá," *Granma*, 14 October 1966.

38 Quoted in Leslie Millin, "Cuba lifts sugar-cane curtain to tell of the continuing revolution," *Globe and Mail*, 11 April 1967.

39 Blair Seaborn to Pierre Asselin, 15 February 1967, LAC, RG 25, vol. 10502, file 55-7-3-MTL-2-CUBA, part 1.

40 Canadian Embassy, Havana, to Department of External Affairs, "EXPOSICUBA: Cuba and the World's Fair," 8 March 1967, LAC, RG 25, vol. 10502, file 55-7-3-MTL-2-CUBA, part 1.

41 Joseph Baker, "The Ambitious Expo," *Canadian Architect* 52, no. 8 (August 2007): 43–4.
42 "Listo pabellón Cuba para exposición de Canadá," *Granma*, 21 December 1966.
43 "Destino: Montreal," *Verde Olivo*, 16 April 1967.
44 "Clausura Hart curso ofrecido a delegación de Expo 67," *Granma*, 3 April 1967.
45 Alfredo Reyes Trejo, "Dos crónicas," *Verde Olivo*, 7 May 1967.
46 Robertson Cochrane, "Expo Cubans: Only one beard in a boatload," *Toronto Star*, 17 April 1967.
47 Georgina Hammond, "Everyone knows opening imminent as Expo pavilions shown to press," *Vancouver Sun*, 21 April 1967.
48 Millin, "Cuba lifts sugar-cane curtain."
49 "The Cuban Pavilion," *Expo 67: Official Guide/Guide Officiel* (Toronto: MacLean-Hunter, 1967), 125.
50 Quoted in Geoffrey James, "Pavilion contrasts show Cuba's two faces," *Montreal Star*, 17 April 1967.
51 "La guia frente, corazon y voz de Cuba en Canadá," *Granma*, 6 October 1967.
52 "Guia para turista," *Verde Olivo*, 18 June 1967.
53 "Expo a medio camino," *Verde Olivo*, 3 September 1967.
54 "Cuba: su verdad triunfu en Montreal," *Bohemia*, 12 May 1967.
55 Martin to Pearson, "Cuba and EXPO," 27 June 1967.
56 Department of External Affairs to Canadian Embassy, Quito, XL-502, 29 September 1967, LAC, RG 25, vol. 8859, file 20-CUBA-1-3 part 5.
57 See the images in Fulford, *This Was Expo*, 18.
58 E.J. Kahn, "Our Far-Flung Correspondents: Expo," *New Yorker*, 10 June 1967.
59 Robert McKenzie, "Visitors cool to Cuba's Expo pitch," *Toronto Star*, 2 May 1967.
60 James, "Pavilion contrasts show Cuba's two faces."
61 "Cuba," *Expo 67*, 129.
62 Bantey, *Bill Bantey's Expo 67*, 22–3.
63 Luc Perreault, "Cuba va célébrer chaudement notre Expo et son indépendance," *La Presse* (Montreal), 20 July 1967. As Maurice Demers and Michel Nareau note in their contribution to this collection, the mainstream Quebec press was sceptical of the Cuban Revolution and government.
64 See Pérez Jr, *Cuba in the American Imagination*. Many Canadians cling to an "ideology of racelessness," which posits that, unlike in the United States, racism does not exist in Canada; see Constance Backhouse, *Colour-Coded: A*

Legal History of Racism in Canada, 1900–1950 (Toronto: University of Toronto Press, 1998), 14. Yet this ideology is undermined by the sorts of cultural assumptions about Cuba and Cubans inherent in press coverage of the pavilion.

65 Martin O'Malley, "Lurking guards, rats and revolution add Tracy touch to Cuban Pavilion," *Globe and Mail*, 10 May 1967.

66 Hammond, "Everyone knows opening imminent."

67 "Cuban Expo pavilion offers few surprises," *Globe and Mail*, 17 April 1967.

68 "U.S. tourists warned," *Toronto Star*, 25 April 1967; "Cuban Goods Pose Expo 67 Problem," *New York Times*, 23 April 1967. Canadian officials investigated the US government's "farcical" restriction, but found that the US Treasury Department would not make any effort to police the Cuban pavilion. Instead it would enforce import restrictions at the Canada-US border; see Canadian Embassy, Washington, DC, to Department of External Affairs, tel. 1543, 24 April 1967, LAC, RG 25, vol. 10502, file 55-7-3-MTL-2-CUBA, part 1.

69 "Cuba Day ceremonies come off without hitch," *Gazette* (Montreal), 27 July 1967.

70 O'Malley, "Lurking guards, rats and revolution."

71 McKenzie, "Visitors cool to Cuba's Expo pitch."

72 Pierre Berton, "By God, we did it. And generally we did it well," *Maclean's*, June 1967; Mordecai Richler, "Notes on Expo," *New York Review of Books*, 14 September 1967.

73 Michelle Chase, "The Trials: Violence and Justice in the Aftermath of the Cuban Revolution," in *A Century of Revolution: Insurgent and Counterinsurgent Violence during Latin America's Long Cold War*, ed. Greg Grandin and Gilbert M. Joseph (Durham, NC: Duke University Press, 2010), 175.

74 Robert Wright, *Three Nights in Havana: Pierre Trudeau, Fidel Castro and the Cold War World* (Toronto: HarperCollins, 2007), 46–7.

75 Violence as a sad fact in Cuban history and as a resulting "entrenched tradition" in the island's culture is highlighted in Richard Gott, *Cuba: A New History* (New Haven, CT: Yale University Press, 2004), 10.

76 James, "Pavilion contrasts show Cuba's two faces."

77 Fulford, *This Was Expo*, 44, 148.

78 Audrey Stankiewicz, "The Last Word," *Canadian Architect* 12 (July–December 1967): 50.

79 "The Wondrous Fair," *Canadian Magazine*, 17 June 1967.

80 Bruce Lawson, "Cuba's day at Expo mixes air of fiesta with heavy security," *Globe and Mail*, 27 July 1967.

81 "Cubans swing at Expo," *North Bay Nugget*, 27 July 1967.

82 Sandra Donlan, "Cuba's day marked by joyous celebration," *Gazette* (Montreal), 27 July 1967.

83 "Cuba triunfa en Montreal," *Verde Olivo*, 21 May 1967.

84 Barry Lord, "A Visit to Expo '67," *Canadian Dimension* 4 (September–October 1967), 31.

85 Fair Play for Cuba Committee handbill, "Join the Fiesta Cubana at Expo 67," n.d., Fair Play for Cuba Committee to Hamilton Friends of the Latin American Peoples, 20 July 1967, LAC, Ross Dowson Papers, R10995, vol. 72, file F5 – 1961–69.

86 Hans Modlich to Jorge Enrique Mendoza, 23 July 1967, LAC, R10995, vol. 72, file F5 – 1967–69.

87 Hans Modlich to Isidoro Malmierca Peoli, 15 July 1967, LAC, R10995, vol. 72, file F5 – 1967–69.

88 Phil Courneyeur to Américo Cruz, 24 August 1967, LAC, R10995, vol. 72, file F5 – 1961–69.

89 Annual chairman's report, n.d., LAC, R10995, vol. 72, file F5 – 1961–69.

90 Hans Modlich to [?] Avelado, 13 May 1967, LAC, R10995, vol. 72, file F5 – 1961–69.

91 Militant Labor Forum to Fair Play for Cuba Committee, 25 September 1967, LAC, R10995, vol. 72, file F5 – 1967–68.

92 N.M. to Fair Play for Cuba Committee, 25 December 1967, LAC, R10995, vol. 72, file F5 – 1967–68.

93 T. Camejo to Fair Play for Cuba Committee, 16 July 1967; and W. Lippmann to Fair Play for Cuba Committee, 5 June 1967, LAC, R10995, vol. 71, file F5 – 1964–67.

94 Antoni Kapcia, *Cuba: Island of Dreams* (Oxford: Berg, 2000), 189; "Cuba at Expo shows picture of slain Che," *Toronto Star*, 23 October 1967.

95 H. Basil Robinson to [?] Hodgson, "Cuban Security Personnel at Expo '67," 19 April 1967, LAC, RG 25, vol. 10045, file 20-1-2-CUBA, part 5.2.

96 Canada, Parliament, House of Commons, *Debates*, 1st Session, 27th Parliament, vol. 14, 10 April 1967, 14. The comment was by John Diefenbaker, who, as prime minister, opted to continue diplomatic relations with Cuba and not to join the US embargo, despite intense US pressure.

97 Max Wershof to L.A.D. Stephens, "Cuban Security at EXPO," 15 April 1967; and Marcel Cadieux to Lester Pearson, "Cuban Security Personnel at Expo '67," 26 April 1967, LAC, RG 25, vol. 10502, file 55-7-3-MTL-2-CUBA, part 1.

98 "Castro's Expo guards training terrorists?" *Ottawa Citizen*, 26 July 1967.

99 "Reminder from Havana," *Toronto Telegram*, 31 July 1967.

100 Canada, Parliament, House of Commons, *Debates*, 2nd Session, 27th Parliament, vol. 3, 17 October 1967, 3170.

101 Robert Thompson to Paul Martin, 30 October 1967, LAC, RG 25, vol. 10045, file 20-1-2-CUBA, part 6.
102 Kirk and McKenna, *Canada-Cuba Relations*, 75.
103 Mills, *Empire Within*, 73.
104 Blair Seaborn to Pierre Asselin, 30 March 1967; and John Graham to DL(2) Division, "EXPO-Cuba," 28 March 1967, LAC, RG 25, vol. 10502, file 55-7-3-MTL-2-CUBA, part 1.
105 Marcel Cadieux to Paul Martin, "Alleged Cuban Subversive Activities directed at Canada," 22 November 1967, LAC, RG 25, vol. 10045, file 20-1-2-CUBA, part 6.
106 See also Mills, *Empire Within*.
107 Pierre Charette, *Mes dix années d'exil à Cuba* (Montreal: Stanké, 1979), 26.
108 "Visit of Marcelo Fernandez Font – Addendum," July 1967, LAC, RG 25, vol. 10076, file 20-CUBA-9 FP.
109 US Embassy, Ottawa, to Department of State, A-164, 10 August 1967, NARA, RG 59, CFP 1967-1969, box 890, folder FT CAN-A.
110 Quoted in "Cuba Day ceremonies come off without hitch," *Gazette* (Montreal), 27 July 1967.
111 Quoted in ibid.
112 Pierre Dupuy, *Expo 67: The Official Souvenir Album* (Toronto: Thomas Nelson, 1968), 7.
113 Todd Gitlin, *The Sixties: Years of Hope, Days of Rage* (New York: Bantam, 1993), 274.
114 "Cuba dejo en Expo 67 una estela de simpatia y popularidad," *Granma*, 31 October 1967.
115 Louis A. Pérez Jr, *On Becoming Cuban: Identity, Nationality, and Culture* (Chapel Hill: University of North Carolina Press, 1999), 490.
116 Michael Pilon, "Expo 67 was the centre piece for me in 1967," letter to the editor, *Ottawa Citizen*, 5 June 2007.
117 Jerzy Adamuszek, *Cuba Is Not Only Varadero* (Saint-Laurent, QC: Yunia Publications, 1997).
118 Eric Zolov, "Discovering a Land 'Mysterious and Obvious': The Renarrativizing of Postrevolutionary Mexico," in *Fragments of a Golden Age: The Political Culture in Mexico since 1940*, ed. Gilbert Joseph, Anne Rubenstein, and Eric Zolov (Durham, NC: Duke University Press, 2001), 234.

4 When Cuban-American Terrorism Came to Canada

KEITH BOLENDER

In a period spanning almost a decade starting from the mid-1960s, violent Cuban-American organizations dedicated to the overthrow of Fidel Castro and his socialist revolution brought their fight to Canada. The groups, with a long history of terrorist activities against their former homeland since the triumph of the Revolution in 1959, targeted Cuban government offices and trade operations in Montreal and Ottawa – in one incident exploding a bomb at the Cuban pavilion during the Expo 67 celebrations that threatened to disrupt Canada's most important one-hundredth-anniversary event.

The counterrevolutionary organizations, based mostly in the United States, that claimed responsibility for the more than one dozen attacks justified the violence as retribution for Canada's continued commercial and political engagement with the Castro government. Canada additionally was perceived to provide easy targets with little chance the perpetrators would be caught. Although Cuba had suffered from acts of terrorism since the early months after the triumph of the Revolution, the incidents in Canada that began in 1964 represented the first time that anti-Castro violence moved outside the Caribbean island or the United States. As the late Jean-Guy Allard, a former journalist based in Montreal at the time of the bombings, explained, "Canada was easy to get to, and it was known the Canadian government maintained relations with Cuba at a time few other countries in the Americas did. The anti-Castro Cubans were looking for anywhere to hurt the government, Canada was seen as a friend of Cuba, and any friend of Cuba was an enemy to these anti-Castro types."[1]

Although the bombings elicited a fair amount of local attention in their day, the events are all but forgotten now – as is much of the long and deadly history of terrorism against Cuba since Castro overthrew the Batista dictatorship more than half a century ago. In addition, the terrorist activity had only a minor impact on the uneven relationship between Cuba and Canada during the early years of the Revolution and even less determination on Canada's designation as the United States' closest ally. Although it was well established that the acts were carried out by Cuban-Americans residing in Florida, the Liberal governments under Lester Pearson and Pierre Trudeau took negligible action other than informal complaints to US officials.[2] The Pearson government, always hesitant towards the socialist Castro regime and its efforts to export revolution in the 1960s, did little to press the Americans to investigate or proceed against the alleged terrorists. Under the Trudeau government, relations with Cuba became extremely warm, the closest since the Revolution. Trudeau felt particular affinity for Fidel Castro, becoming the first Canadian prime minister to visit the communist island and connecting immediately on a personal level with the Cuban leader. The feeling was mutual, with Castro articulating personal kinship that lasted long after the historic meeting between the two in 1976,[3] and the final expression coming when the Cuban leader attended Trudeau's funeral in 2000. Even that friendship, sustained despite a variety of diplomatic differences, including Trudeau's public censure of Cuba's involvement in Angola in the mid-1970s, had no influence on resolving the problem of Cuban-American terrorism on Canadian soil. The difficulty of forcing an end to the violence could not be found in either of those two countries, but rather in the United States, where it originated – and there was scant indication that the Americans, maintaining a stance that had not altered since the Revolution's triumph, were inclined to do anything about it. This attitude is in sharp contrast to the United States' decade-long war against terrorism following the horrendous acts of 11 September 2001.

Canada's Policy of Engagement: At Odds with US Regime Change Strategy

The public display of warmth between Trudeau and Castro merely solidified the United States' long-held opinion that Canada was an unreliable partner in its Cold War strategy against Cuba, providing even less incentive to apply pressure against the Cuban-American groups suspected of committing violent acts in Canada. US policy-makers were continually piqued at their northern neighbour's independent foreign policy when it came to Cuba, a strategy that was well established under the Progressive Conservative government of John Diefenbaker in 1959. As a result, despite the evidence produced, no one was charged with terrorist activities against Cuban targets in Canada. Other than strenuous protests from Cuban officials, all others were content to keep the matter unresolved to avoid embarrassing political ramifications between the two North American allies.[4] The half-hearted Canadian protests did nothing to dissuade US officials from the strategy of isolation, economic embargo, and support for violent attacks against Cuban civilians and commercial targets. Canada's policy of engagement with the Castro government has led to a series of disagreements with the US strategy of isolation and regime change with respect to Cuba, putting the two allies in conflict over trade and diplomacy, a history well covered by Raúl Rodríguez Rodríguez (in this volume).

This conflict between the United States and Canada was highlighted by US legislation against Cuba in the mid-1990s that prohibited subsidiaries of US companies from doing business in Cuba,[5] leading to protests and counter-legislation from the Canadian side. American pressure dominated, however, and all US subsidiaries in Canada that were doing business in Cuba were forced to end such commercial relations. Canada continues to object to US extraterritorial aspects of its laws against Cuba, but to little affect.[6]

In a unique analysis of the incidents that occurred on Canadian soil, this chapter examines the historical aspects of anti-Castro activity in Canada, and the material and physical costs and political fallout that maintain resonance today as the United States and Canada continue to chart different paths when dealing with the socialist island. Drawing directly from media articles of the day that show how for the most part the anti-Castro groups were able to operate with impunity, I additionally rely on commentary from current Canadian experts on Cuba matters, some of whom lived through the violence and have attempted to bring it into higher public profile.

Canada's response to the terrorism was complicated by the various police authorities that often overlapped in the investigations. At the local level, Quebec police had the first opportunity to examine the incidents, but as the terrorism escalated, the Royal Canadian Mounted Police (RCMP) became more involved in consultation with the federal government. All investigations were made more challenging by the reluctance of Cuban diplomatic staff in Ottawa to cooperate fully with Canadian efforts to solve the crimes. Cuban officials were frustrated by the lack of arrests and convictions of those suspected of the terrorism, and as a result became hesitant to share intelligence information with the Canadians out of a sense of distrust and fear of compromising efforts to thwart further acts. It made for an uneasy and sometimes contentious relationship between the Cubans who were in physical danger from the terrorist bombings and the Canadian authorities trying to solve the crimes.

The inability of authorities in Canada and the United States to bring to justice those responsible for the acts of terrorism contributed in a small way to the development within the Castro government of a sense of isolation – leading to the establishment of a society overprotective of its citizens, resulting in certain civil rights restrictions, a hypersensitivity to criticism, and a strong reaction against nationals perceived to be actively pursuing anti-revolutionary regime change policies. Various sources are available to examine further the history of terrorism against Cuba, the government's national and international policies in response, and the effect it has had on the socialist society.[7]

Anti-Castro Groups Come to Canada

Canada's difficult experiences with anti-Castro organizations began a few years before the terrorist acts. In October 1960 a group of exiles meeting in Montreal garnered considerable media attention when their plots against the revolutionary government were discovered. Montreal was the largest centre for the Cuban government's commercial operations in Canada, and became a natural gathering point for those opposed to the regime. The anti-revolutionary Cubans met at the home of Major-General José Eleuterio Pedraza Cabrera, one-time commander-in-chief of Batista's army and later head of the Movimiento de Liberación Anti-comunista (Anti-Communist Liberation Movement). When the Diefenbaker government refused to follow the US decision to break diplomatic ties with Cuba in January 1961, the Canadian embassy in Havana and the Department of External Affairs in Ottawa received threats. A group calling itself the People's Revolutionary Alliance warned that Canadian economic interests in Cuba would be taken over once Castro was overthrown.[8] The threats turned to violence shortly after. In total more than a dozen incidents took place, the earliest occurring on 9 August 1964 with an attack on the Cuban ship *María Teresa* in the port of Montreal. Guillermo Novo Sampoll, leader of the Miami-based anti-Castro Movimiento Nacionalista Cubano (MNC, Cuban Nationalist Movement) was the prime suspect, although no arrests were made following a cursory investigation.[9]

Two years passed before the next incident, when the Cuban embassy in Ottawa was shaken by an explosion of a bazooka rocket on 22 September 1966. The early-morning blast made front-page news in the Montreal *Gazette*,[10] causing minor damage to the sidewalk in front of the embassy and scaring the four domestic staff inside. An extensive investigation by the Ottawa police pointed to the activities of two Cubans who had come to the city days previously. Felipe Rivero Díaz, a member of the MNC, claimed responsibility for the act. He boasted that the Ottawa embassy was targeted because of the Canadian government's "insulting and provocative" attitude to the position of Cubans "enslaved by international communism."[11] Prime Minister Pearson responded to Rivero's assertion with a call for US officials to investigate anti-Castro groups in Miami, although no official protest was made over the matter.[12]

A bizarre report on the incident in the *Ottawa Citizen* claimed that the police were suggesting the attack was some sort of publicity stunt, since in their original location the rockets – there were, in fact, two of them, but only one exploded – would have done no damage.[13] The rockets had been placed in a plaid suitcase sitting on the lawn of the embassy grounds, behind a large elm tree. A passerby noticed the suitcase and placed it on a white car parked in front of the embassy – the car was later suspected to have been rented by a Cuban residing in Miami. The second rocket was discovered unexploded on the street, with police speculating it was originally in the suitcase. Had it gone off, authorities commented, considerable injuries would have occurred. The newspaper article ended with the lively description of Cuban ambassador Américo Cruz, who arrived "within an hour of the blast puffing on a cigar."[14]

In October 1966 the office of the Cuban trade delegation in the nation's capital was bombed, fortunately causing no injuries. It was the final act of terrorism of the year, and the calm remained until a flurry of incidents took place a few months later that cast a dangerous pall over Canada's one-hundredth-birthday celebrations.

Bombing at the Expo 67 Cuban Pavilion

Canada's Centennial in 1967 saw a dramatic increase in terrorist activity. In March a Cuban freighter was bombed in the Montreal harbour.

Two months later, on 31 May, an explosion did significant damage to the Cuban pavilion at Expo 67, and on 15 October the Cuban trade delegation in Montreal was targeted. The Centennial year also saw a bomb go off at the warehouses of Fraser Brothers, a Montreal-based firm trading with Cuba. Quebec cabinetmaker Dieudonné Boudreau was injured in the explosion while attempting to diffuse the bomb. The company was targeted for allegedly selling furniture confiscated from Cuban exiles.[15]

The bombing at Expo 67 was attributed to members of a group called Acción Nacionalista Cubana (Cuban Nationalist Action); the MNC's Rivero was arrested in connection with the attack but never charged.[16] The explosion triggered significant consternation among organizers worried about negative publicity during Canada's premier celebration of its one-hundredth anniversary. The blast created additional political tension from an unexpected direction when the Cuban side publicly announced that Fidel Castro would be coming to visit Expo, as Asa McKercher explores in this volume. Canadian officials were aghast at the possibility, insisting it would be unsafe for the Cuban leader to attend for fear of further terrorist acts. Privately the Canadians complained that the real objection to the visit was that it would generate protests from the United States, adding unnecessary strain at a time when Washington felt Canada was altogether too cozy with the Castro government. Prime Minister Pearson was keen not to antagonize Canada's powerful neighbour, and was able to use the bombing as a convincing reason Castro should not visit Expo.[17] Journalist Jean-Guy Allard remembered the incident:

> I was working as a ticket taker at Expo – this was before becoming a journalist. I was then nineteen and I got this summer job at *La Ronde* newspaper. I even made friends with some young Cubans working at Cuban boutiques, there were a couple of them on the site. The bomb was put along a wall at the side of the pavilion and caused little damage but had the desired media impact wanted by the terrorists. There was a great deal of concern that there would be more bombings and it would have a real negative effect on Expo – obviously people wouldn't want to come if there were any security problems. These anti-Castro types were not concerned with who would be hurt or killed by the bombs; they just wanted to create problems for Canada and its relationship with Cuba.[18]

Police reports at the time indicated a number of Cuban workers at Expo regularly received death threats. Allard, who wrote extensively on the Cuban-Americans allegedly involved in the history of terrorism against Cuba, also researched the shadowy financial dealings of certain Cuban immigrants operating out of Canada. In a 2004 article, Allard wrote of Cuban-born Máximo Morales, who pleaded guilty to charges of conspiracy and importing 115 kilograms of cocaine in one of the most important seizures of the drug in Montreal's history. Morales, arrested in 1990, was considered the right-hand man of Ismael Sambra, former leader of the anti-Castro Cuban Canadian Foundation.[19]

Terrorism against Canadian targets continued with an attempted bombing at the Cuban consulate in Montreal on 29 May 1969, the device failing to go off. Toronto became a rare objective when, in December 1970, the Cuban consulate office was bombed just one day after members of the Front de Libération du Québec (FLQ) separatist group were flown to Havana after Castro agreed to a personal request from Prime Minister Trudeau.[20] The Cuban Trade Commission in Montreal was again bombed on 12 July 1971, this time causing widespread damage.

The next attack on the Trade Commission in Montreal turned deadly twenty minutes after midnight on 4 April 1972, when Sergio Pérez Castillo – described by Cuban authorities as a guard who lived with his wife and child in the thirteen-storey building that housed the Trade Commission offices – died when a blast destroyed much of the top floor of the building and sent hundreds of bricks showering down on the neighbourhood.[21] A second official was injured. When Montreal police arrived to investigate, they were confronted by a number of Cubans armed and unwilling to allow the authorities to pass. Identifying themselves as representatives of the Cuban government, six of the officials were arrested and taken into custody for questioning – and released shortly after. Police seized a collection of weapons from the mission, with Cuban officials explaining the need for protection from anti-revolutionaries. An article in the Cuba national newspaper *Granma* described the chaotic confrontation between police and Cuban officials:

> In the group was a woman with a child in her arms while a man lay on the floor with his leg severed. This young Cuban was Sergio Pérez Castillo, 25 years old, father of the boy, and asked to be helped. But the police did not understand a word of what they were told, and instead of offering their help, began firing orders, creating a dangerous situation with the Cubans who felt threatened and indicated clearly that they would not grant an untimely intrusion in their offices, which were considered diplomatic territory. The confrontation lasted more than two hours before Perez, pale

and unconscious, was put into an ambulance and transported to hospital Maisonneuve. It was too late. The young Cuban died an hour later without regaining consciousness.[22]

The confrontation between the Cuban mission staff and police continued, with police finally disarming the employees, who then frantically began destroying files in the belief that the law enforcement agents were after sensitive material. "They thought we were after their files, but the only thing we were interested in was the fact there had been a criminal act, and we had an investigation to carry out. They wouldn't cooperate with us at all, none would give their names," a detective commented.[23] Cuban officials later stated the misunderstanding was based on the number of attempts to destroy the mission and the confusion after the explosion, which was the third time the building had been targeted. The matter of diplomatic immunity and the obstruction of Cuban officials was criticized in an editorial in the *Ottawa Citizen* that took the officials to task for worrying more about protecting files than about those who might have been injured in the explosion.[24]

A subsequent investigation revealed that the bomb had been placed in the false ceiling in the hallway outside the mission offices.[25] An anti-revolutionary group known as Representación Cubana en el Exilio (RECE, Cuban Representation in Exile) claimed responsibility for the attack that killed Pérez Castillo. The head of RECE at the time, Antonio "Tony" Calatayud, was alleged to have been trained as a demolition expert by the US Central Intelligence Agency (CIA); he was never questioned, however, by either the RCMP or the US Federal Bureau of Investigation.[26]

The incident created a minor diplomatic storm, with Castro criticizing the Montreal police for their "brutal and Fascist" methods during the investigation.[27] Castro went on to claim that the police were in league with the CIA, and hinted at reprisals against Canadian staff at the Havana embassy.[28] Suspicions were heightened when Cuban politicians claimed its embassy in Ottawa was being bugged by Canadian law enforcement officials, hinting that the CIA was behind the illegal electronic surveillance. Despite the ill feelings, Castro tempered his anger with statements condemning the terrorists, and the Canadian government downplayed the hyperbole. The dispute was soon forgotten, and relations between the two nations continued to improve.

The Downing of Cubana Airlines Flight 455

Although the death of Pérez Castillo slowed down the bombings as the RCMP stepped up security and Cuban officials became more vigilant, it did not stop the attacks. On 21 January 1974 a bomb exploded at the Cuban embassy in Ottawa. This incident was attributed to Orlando Bosch, a Cuban exile infamous for his long history of violence. Bosch, a physician, left Cuba shortly after Castro came to power, turning his disillusionment with the Revolution into violent activity against it. Bosch became a CIA agent in 1962, then helped found the anti-revolutionary Coordinación de Organizaciones Revolucionarias Unidas (CORU, Coordination of United Revolutionary Organizations), defined at the time by the FBI as a "terrorist organization."[29]

In 1976 Bosch became implicated in the worst terrorist act against Cuba: the bombing of Cubana Airlines flight 455 off the coast of Barbados. All seventy-two on board were killed, mostly members of the Cuban national fencing team on their way home from a victorious tournament in Venezuela. Two Venezuelans who admitted to planting the bombs on the plane, Freddy Lugo and Hernán Ricardo, confessed it was Bosch and fellow Cuban exile Luis Posada Carriles who masterminded the act.[30] Subsequent documents released by the United States indicated American officials were aware of the attack and of the involvement of Bosch and Carriles, but did nothing to warn the Cubans.[31] All four were arrested and tried under a military court in Venezuela.

The bombing, which remains the second-worst act of air terrorism in the Americas after 9/11, resulted in both Lugo and Ricardo receiving long sentences, while Bosch was acquitted due to a technicality, as the evidence gathered in Barbados was not received in time and not translated into Spanish. Carriles escaped from jail while awaiting sentencing. Bosch, who returned to the United States illegally following his acquittal in 1987, was declared by the US Justice Department as one of the western hemisphere's most deadly terrorists. Requests for his deportation[32] were overridden by President George H.W. Bush, who issued Bosch a full pardon in 1990. Bosch died in Miami in 2011; Carriles continues to live in the city unfettered, having overcome some minor immigration charges in 2011. Both the Cuban and Venezuelan governments continue to request his extradition.

In the months prior to the Cubana Airlines bombing, a number of encouraging diplomatic signs had indicated movement towards ending Cuba's isolation among the Western democracies. US president

Jimmy Carter declared it was time to consider normalization of relations with the Castro regime, and looked somewhat favourably upon Pierre Trudeau's three-day visit to Cuba, which took place ten months prior to the bombing. The downing of the Cubana Airlines plane, however, contributed to ending this period of political thaw, and began a period of increased Cuban-American terrorism.[33]

Indeed, on 22 September 1976, a few weeks *before* the Cubana Airlines bombing, terror returned to Canada when an explosive device thrown from a car at the Cuban consulate in Montreal caused minor damage. Although no one was injured, the act brought forth a stream of demands to put an end to the terrorism. A strongly worded editorial in the *Ottawa Citizen* condemned the anti-Castro groups, calling the incident an attack not just on Cuba but also on Canada. The editorial echoed the Canadian government's position that, although it might not agree with Cuba's socio-economic system, it rejected the overthrow of any government based on economic embargoes or acts of terrorism. The editorial reiterated Canada's right to conduct trade and normal relations with anyone it chose without threats from "madmen, or of persons without the slightest degree of understanding of the spirit of democracy they claim to defend."[34]

Attempts by the authorities to resolve the attacks against Cuban targets in Quebec were complicated in the early stages, as resources were stretched as a result of violence by a certain segment of the province's separatist movement, coming to head during the FLQ crisis of October 1970. The Cuban-American terrorism added yet another strain to the demands on local and national police and intelligence agencies. A Cuban official who asked to remain anonymous commented: "We knew the Quebec police were putting a lot of attention on the FLQ bombings, which were more numerous during that time, and then the kidnappings of 1970s. So we understood they didn't have the time or resources to handle that and the Cuban-American terrorism. It was one of the reasons why the Cuban side took care of so much of their own security, and were always concerned with even the local police coming into the consul or embassy after the attacks."[35]

The terror in Canada finally came to a halt following one last act: a large explosion on 14 January 1980 that damaged the Cuban consulate in Montreal. No one was hurt, but the blast damaged windows and two neighbouring buildings, including a house recently bought by Pierre Trudeau. The crudely built bomb, consisting of two sticks of dynamite, a detonator, battery, and clock, exploded after being tossed over the consulate gate. Again a minor incident occurred between police officers and Cuban security staff, who held the police at bay for twenty minutes while the grounds were checked for additional devices. None was found.[36]

Although no other acts of violence took place against Cuban targets in Canada, attempts were uncovered in the early 1990s. Renaldo Hernández, a Cuban intelligence officer now living in Toronto, recalled an attempt in 1993 against a Cuban ship in the port of Montreal:

> A guy by the name of Chino Tang [Antonio "El Chino" Tang Baez] from Alpha 66, a terrorist organization in Miami, was based in Montreal with other members of this organization. He was planning to bomb a Cuban ship in the port of Montreal. I was monitoring him with an agent I handled in his own house. It was a dangerous operation for the agent and myself. I don't recall the name of the agent. He had been "defected"[37] in Halifax or another Canadian port. He was a worker in the Cuban merchant fleet, and he was defected with the purpose of infiltrating this group of Alpha 66 in Montreal. I don't remember the details, but Chino Tang was using the facilities of a foreign Consulate in Montreal. He was especially assisted with coded communications with Alpha 66 in Miami. The Cuban intelligence passed the information to [the] RCMP. Nobody was detained, but apparently they prevented the terrorist bombing. Chino Tang was a violent person with a long history of terrorist actions.[38]

Although attacking Cuban interests in Canada was a focus for anti-Castro groups, a number of internationally based Canadian entities with ties to the island were also targeted in the 1960s and '70s. In 1968 the Canada Tourism office on Fifth Avenue in New York City and offices of a Canadian airline in Miami were attacked, with authorities believing it was the work of anti-Castro groups in both cases. MNC members claimed responsibility for the bombings, and warned of possible reprisals against Canadian banks with branches in Cuba and against the Canadian embassy in Havana.[39] Throughout those decades, Canadian diplomats in New York, Washington, and other US cities were threatened with reprisals for Canada's policy of engagement with Cuba.

Targeting Canadian Tourists

Although the bombings in Montreal and Ottawa ended in the 1970s, a decade later Canadians were to find themselves again caught up in anti-revolutionary violence. Following the collapse of the Soviet Union in 1991, the Cuban economy fell into a great depression, known as the Special Period, during which the country's gross domestic product shrank by 35 per cent in less than two years and the island lost 80 per cent of its trade. In an effort to gain much needed foreign currency, the Cuban government decided to open up the island's tourist industry. Canadians, who had come in small numbers beforehand, now travelled to Cuban beaches and hotels by the thousands, the majority coming from Quebec. It did not take long for anti-revolutionary groups in Miami to respond. In late 1993 Canadian newspapers reported on Alpha 66 warnings that tourists travelling to Cuba would be attacked: "[T]he anti-Castro terrorist group Alpha 66 announced that it now considered tourists in Cuba as justifiable targets for kidnappings and assassinations. Since Canadian tourists make up the largest single group of tourists in Cuba ... it is clear that we constitute the largest probable target."[40] The Miami group specifically warned Canadians not to travel to Cuba if they valued their safety. Later, Alpha 66 announced in Florida that several of its commandos had attacked a Canadian-filled tourist hotel on the northern coast of Cuba on 11 March 1995, marking the start of a campaign against the tourist industry. "All the Cuban tourist centres are military objectives for Alpha 66," said Humberto Pérez, a spokesperson for the group. The attacks were coordinated in Miami, he added.[41]

Terrorism against Cuban tourism turned deadly during a six-month period starting in April 1997 when a series of bombs exploded at tourist facilities in Havana and Varadero. One device detonated in the lobby of the Hotel Copacabana on the north coast of Havana, killing Italian-Canadian businessman Fabio di Celmo. In a series of interviews with the *New York Times*, long-time anti-Castro foe Luis Posada Carriles admitted his involvement in coordinating the attacks, claiming he wanted to scare off tourists, and that di Celmo was simply "in the wrong place at the wrong time." The report also revealed Posada's allegation that the Cuban-American National Foundation, a Miami-based political organization suspected of violent anti-revolutionary activity, had financed the campaign – a claim the foundation denied.[42]

In response to the tourist bombings and the death of di Celmo, the Law Union of Ontario passed a resolution underscoring the responsibility of the Canadian government to ensure the safety of Canadians vacationing in Cuba. It urged Canada, "as a member of the Organization of American States (OAS), to demand that the United States government comply with the Inter-American Convention Against Terrorism and immediately cease harbouring, aiding and abetting organizations that plot and encourage terrorist activities against the people and government of Cuba."[43] To date, however, the US government has made no move against Posada Carriles or others whom the Cuban government claims are terrorists living in the United States.[44] The continued sheltering of Posada and the lack of any arrests in the United States for anti-Castro terrorist acts in Canada call attention to the inconsistencies of the US "campaign against terrorism."

Despite the threats and bombing campaign, tourism from Canada continued to increase – indeed, Canadians rank first among visitors to the island.[45] The largest number of Canadian tourists come from Quebec, and a steady stream of provincial officials and business leaders have travelled to the island to maintain and augment the strong commercial relationship between the province and the island.

The attacks on Cuban targets in Canada represented only a small segment of the terrorism directed against the revolutionary government and its supporters, and were far from the worst incidents. The various anti-revolutionary organizations have conducted much more serious attacks against fellow Cuban-Americans in New York and Miami who dared to express any level of sympathy for the Revolution. Explosions in these US cities were particularly devastating in the 1960s and '70s, injuring dozens of exiles who even hinted at favouring engagement with Castro. Well-known Miami media personality Emilio Milián, for example, had his legs blown off in 1975 by a bomb placed under this car following his denunciation of Cuban-American violence against those who objected to the terrorism. Months earlier, anti-Castro leader José Elías de la Torriente had been shot in the back for appearing to take a more conciliatory approach to the island government.[46] The cigar factory of a businessman in Miami's Little Havana district who offered a cigar to Fidel Castro was firebombed repeatedly. A local magazine publisher was attacked because of ideas allegedly contrary to the cause of a free Cuba. Miami's Mexican and Venezuelan consulates were bombed in reprisal for those governments' policies. Max Lesnick, an early critic of the Castro government who then used his popular Miami radio program to become a vocal supporter of normalization, has been the victim of dozens of threats and attempts on his life for his moderate position. In one of the few cases where the authorities moved against the alleged terrorists, Eduardo Arocena, of the anti-Castro group Omega 7, was convicted in 1985 for his terrorist activities in New York and Miami.[47]

Arocena was guilty of attempting to kill a foreign official and to use explosives to cause damage to personal property. Now seventy, Arocena remains in a federal prison facility despite requests for his release. With the passage of time the terrorism has largely abated, although incidents still occur. As late as 2012 a travel agency in Coral Gables, Florida, known for its promotion of trips to Cuba was destroyed in a bombing that local authorities suspected was arson. No arrests were ever made.[48]

Most of the deaths and destruction as a result of terrorism by anti-revolutionary groups, however, have occurred inside Cuba. An estimated six hundred acts have killed three thousand five hundred civilians, with thousands more injured. The Revolution, aimed most forcefully against US political hegemony and economic domination of the island, elicited an immediate violent response from the United States and those exiles who backed Washington's policy of regime change. President Dwight Eisenhower approved the elimination of the new government mere months after Castro's triumph, and the methods implemented included economic embargo, isolation among the other countries of the Americas – with only Mexico and Canada refusing to accede – unrelenting propaganda, and the development of a military solution that resulted in the disastrous invasion of Cuba in April 1961 at the Bay of Pigs. Prior to the invasion, a concentrated series of terrorist acts had been committed against Cuban civilian targets, including the bombing of sugar cane and tobacco fields, as well as sabotage against major industrial sites. In addition to US plots to overthrow Castro, a substantial anti-revolutionary movement conducted attacks on the island, notably between 1959 and the Cuban missile crisis of October 1962.

The most infamous terrorist strategy, Operation Mongoose, developed and supported by the US government, has been called one of the worst examples of state-sponsored terrorism of the twentieth century.[49] These attacks encompassed the capture, torture, and murder of a dozen teenaged Cubans sent to the countryside to help teach farmers to read and write during the Literacy Campaign. In 1960 the French ship *La Coubre*, carrying Belgium armaments, blew up in Havana harbour, killing more than one hundred. The freighter had docked in Miami three days earlier and its cargo was known to anti-Castro organizations and the CIA. A psy-op campaign known as Operation Peter Pan began in the early 1960s, resulting in thousands of Cuban children being sent out of the country based on the lie that the Cuban government would take all those under age seventeen from their parental homes and place them in communist indoctrination centres in Cuba and the Soviet Union. Cuban parents, mostly from the urban middle classes, sent their offspring to the United States in panicked reaction to the deceitful scheme. The operation was developed by the Cuban church with the support of the CIA.[50]

By the mid-1960s Cuban authorities had eliminated most of the counterrevolutionaries in country, either by direct neutralization or through the emigration of those opposing the government. Large numbers of anti-Castro individuals settled in south Florida, particularly Miami, where they began to organize into groups that would undertake violent activities from stateside. During the 1970s terror against Cuban civilians involved not just the bombing of the Cubana Airlines flight in 1976, but also the destruction of the small village of Boca de Sama, which killed two and injured eight. In the early 1980s Cuba was subjected to a series of biological attacks, including swine flu, anthrax, and tobacco rust. The worst of the biological terrorism was the introduction of dengue 2, until then unknown in Cuba. Approximately three hundred thousand cases were reported in a six-month period from one side of the island to the other, a condition international scientists concluded could not occur naturally. More than one hundred children died from the disease. Omega 7 leader Eduardo Arocena testified that he travelled to Cuba in 1980 to "introduce some germs" into the country to "start the chemical war," – as reported by the *New York Times*. One of them was dengue 2.[51]

The Case of the Cuban Five

The terrorism led the Cuban government to send intelligence officials to Florida in an attempt to infiltrate the violent anti-revolutionary organizations. Although the effort did help thwart various acts, it also led to the arrest of five agents in 1998 on charges of conspiracy to commit espionage. Nothing was done against the Cuban-Americans suspected of terrorist activities; instead the Cuban agents were sentenced to excessively long jail terms. Known as the Cuban Five, the release of the final three as part of US president Barack Obama's December 2014 decision to normalize relations with Cuba fulfilled a high priority for the Castro government. The campaign to free the Five had developed into an international campaign, resulting in greater attention to the little-known history of terrorism against Cuba, including the incidents in Canada.[52]

The terrorist acts against Cuba have resulted in the implementation of extensive security measures designed to protect Cuba's government and citizens, but they have also led to certain civil rights restrictions. These measures have been severely criticized by anti-Cuban political and media elements in the United States, which, in turn, has helped develop a siege mentality within the revolutionary leadership that is manifested in a sense of defensiveness, hypersensitivity to criticism, and defiance towards those who diminish, deny, or obscure the long history of terrorism against Cuba. Surveillance programs that the Cuban government found justified to institute for reasons of safety against further terrorist attacks now might be scrutinized in a limited context to the US response to 9/11 and revelations of the extent of information collection by the US National Security Agency.

Although terrorism has been the most obviously destructive facet of the hostile US policy towards Cuba, it represents just one element. Other aspects of the strategy of regime change include a comprehensive economic embargo that has denied Cuba the ability to trade with what should be its most important partner, non-stop propaganda that refuses to acknowledge that anything good has come from the Revolution, and extraterritorial aspects of embargo laws that prohibit companies with US ties, including many Canadian subsidiaries, from doing business in Cuba. It is a comprehensive, decades-long US effort to make things so bad for average Cubans that they will rise up against the government – a strategy admitted to by State Department officials in an April 1960 report: "Every possible means should be undertaken promptly to weaken the economic life of Cuba[,] ... a line of action which, while as adroit and inconspicuous as possible, makes the greatest inroads in denying money and supplies to Cuba, to decrease monetary and real wages, to bring about hunger, desperation and overthrow of the government."[53]

US hostility has additionally created a mini-industry in south Florida where anti-Castro politicians such as Ileana Ros-Lehtinen, David Rivera, and Marco Rubio maintain their hands on the steering wheel of policy. Millions of dollars have been spent through government programs such as USAID in the effort to maintain the siege against Cuba. The grip of the anti-Castro Cubans weakened considerably following President Obama's 17 December 2014 announcement to normalize relations with Cuba. Since then, there has been considerable movement towards normalization, including the opening of embassies in Washington and Havana and the expanding determination within US political and business communities to end the embargo and lift travel restrictions.

Despite Obama's apparent readiness to establish a new relationship with Cuba, however, some saw this as a new strategy aimed at regime change. In June 2017 President Donald Trump reversed a few of Obama's openings to Cuba. Many issues remain, including the continued diminishing of the substantial economic reforms taking place in Cuba, as well as the topic of the return of Guantánamo Bay and the complicated compensation claims of both sides. In addition, the US government continues to refuse requests to indict suspected terrorists such as Posada Carriles. Terrorism became indirectly connected with Obama's December announcement when the president included the release of the final three of the Cuban Five as part of the move towards normalization. Although the US side has consistently described the Five as spies, those who had been championing their release attempted to connect their incarceration with the history of terrorism against Cuba. It was one of the few times that the mainstream media and the general public in the United States were exposed – in however limited a way – to the narrative that Cuba had long been victimized by acts of terrorism and that the Cuban Five were in Florida to help prevent further incidents.

Terrorism, indeed, has had the most direct influence on the revolutionary government's attempt to create defences against the siege. This has been a particularly challenging endeavour, as so much of the history of terrorism against Cuba remains unknown, including those acts that occurred on Canadian soil decades ago. They are now little remembered when examining the complexities of Canada's determination to sustain a direct relationship with the Cuban revolutionary government. In retrospect the terrorist attacks in Canada had little, if any, negative bearing on the commitment by the governments in Ottawa and Havana to maintain their engagement. In the early years the Progressive Conservative Diefenbaker government showed surprising accommodation to the Revolution in Cuba, based in part on Diefenbaker's sympathy for this small nation's standing up to the US colossus. Diefenbaker was a solid anti-communist, and strongly criticized Trudeau for his visit to Cuba and his close relationship with Castro while in opposition. But as prime minister, Diefenbaker held just as tightly to his belief in self-determination when it came to foreign policy matters and the sovereignty of nations.

Personalities played a part in the period when Cuba-Canada relations were at their best. Following the arm's-length approach to Castro by the Pearson government, fellow Liberal prime minister Pierre Trudeau developed an immediate and deep personal connection with the Cuban leader. Although neither the Pearson nor the Trudeau government pressed the United States to move against the Cuban-Americans suspected in the terrorist attacks on Canadian soil during that time, Trudeau more readily criticized the US government for its inactivity against the alleged terrorists.[54] It was Trudeau's close association with Castro, however, that might have given US officials less inducement to pursue the violent members of anti-revolutionary organizations in Florida who were conducting operations in Canada – indeed, the United States rarely seemed much disposed to act against the terrorist groups wherever they struck. No arrests were made after the terrorist attacks in Canada, by either Canadian or US authorities, and little serious investigation was conducted. This failure to take action led to frustration and anger on the part of Cuban officials, but at no time was there any sense that it would seriously rupture Cuba-Canada relations.

Since the triumph of the Cuban Revolution in 1959, Canada has continued its policy of engagement with the island nation, despite the often difficult issues the two countries have faced. Neither political differences, nor economic disputes, nor the period when anti-revolutionary terrorism came to Canada have been able to break the ties between the two countries situated on either side of the world's greatest superpower.

NOTES

1 E-mail interview with author, 12 April 2013. Allard, an expert on the violence Cuban-Americans have inflicted on revolutionary supporters, wrote extensively on the subject, including for the Cuban national newspaper Granma and in his book Posada Carriles: Cuatro décadas de terror (Havana: Editora Política, 2006).
2 John Kirk and Peter McKenna, Canada-Cuba Relations: The Other Good Neighbor Policy (Gainesville: University Press of Florida, 1997), 80–90.
3 Robert Wright, Three Nights in Havana: Pierre Trudeau, Fidel Castro and the Cold War World (Toronto: HarperCollins Canada, 2007), 69–70.
4 Kirk and McKenna, Canada-Cuba Relations, 77.

5 See, in particular, the Cuban Democracy Act of 1994 (also known as the Torricelli Act) and the Cuban Liberty and Democratic Solidarity (Libertad) Act of 1996 (also known as the Helms–Burton Act).

6 Keith Bolender, *Cuba Under Siege: American Policy, the Revolution and Its People* (Basingstoke, UK: Palgrave Macmillan, 2012), 76–8.

7 For further reading, see Keith Bolender, *Voices from the Other Side; An Oral History of Terrorism Against Cuba* (London: Pluto Press, 2010); and idem, *Cuba Under Siege*. For the Cuban response against US-based anti-revolutionary organizations, see Stephen Kimber, *What Lies Across the Water: The Real Story of the Cuban Five* (Winnipeg: Fernwood Publishing, 2013). Also, the eminent Cuba scholar Louis A. Pérez Jr has written a variety of books on Cuban society and how it has been influenced by US hostility, including *The Structure of Cuban History: Meanings and Purpose of the Past* (Chapel Hill: University of North Carolina Press, 2013); and *Cuba in the American Imagination: Metaphor and the Imperial Ethos* (Chapel Hill: University of North Carolina Press, 2010).

8 Wright, *Three Nights in Havana*, 69–70.

9 Jean-Guy Allard, "The Miami Mafia in Canada," *Granma*, 16 April 2004, available online at http://www.latinamericanstudies.org/belligerence/canada.htm.

10 "Castro's foes set off rocket in Cuban embassy in Ottawa," *Gazette* (Montreal), 23 September 1966.

11 Ibid.

12 "PM protests 'boasting' by exiles," *Ottawa Citizen*, 23 September 1966.

13 Walt Lacosta, "Bomb a publicity stunt?" *Ottawa Citizen*, 23 September 1966.

14 Ibid.

15 Wright, *Three Nights in Havana*, 110.

16 Allard, "Miami Mafia."

17 Wright, *Three Nights in Havana*, 112.

18 E-mail interview with author, 12 April 2013.

19 Allard, "Miami Mafia."

20 Wright, *Three Nights in Havana*, 113.

21 Eddie Collister, "Cubans on arms, obstruction charges," *Gazette* (Montreal), 5 April 1972.

22 Quoted in Allard, "Miami Mafia"; the translation is Allard's.

23 Ibid.

24 "Protection refused," *Ottawa Citizen*, 5 April 1972.

25 Ibid.

26 Allard, "Miami Mafia."

27 "Livid Castro warns of reprisals," *Ottawa Citizen*, 5 April 1972.

28 Ibid.
29 Peter Kornbluh, "The Posada File: Part II," National Security Archive Electronic Briefing Book 157 (Washington, DC: George Washington University, National Security Archive, 9 June 2005), available online at http://nsarchive.gwu.edu/NSAEBB/NSAEBB157/.
30 Bolender, *Voices from the Other Side.*
31 Kornbluh, "Posada File."
32 "Bosch denounces US report on terrorist activities," *Miami Herald*, 5 August 1989.
33 Wright, *Three Nights in Havana*, 115.
34 "Terror on Chapel Street," *Ottawa Citizen*, 23 September 1976.
35 Interview with author, January 2013.
36 "Mystery blast rocks Cuban consulate," *Montreal Gazette*, 15 January 1980, 8.
37 In this case "defected" means the Cuban government set up an intelligence officer to leave Cuba in order in infiltrate anti-revolutionary organizations, using the cover story that he left Cuba illegally – "defected" – to gain the trust of the organizations' leadership.
38 Email interview with author, June 2013.
39 Wright, *Three Nights in Havana*, 113.
40 John Kirk, "Cuban-American groups threaten Canadian tourists," *Globe and Mail*, 11 October 1993.
41 Cited in Ruch Wayne Millar, "Terrorist Provocations against Cuba: A Selection of Items Retrieved from News Sources, 1992–96" (Saskatoon, SK, 18 April 1996), available online at http://www.hartford-hwp.com/archives/43b/142.html.
42 Ann Louise Bardach and Larry Rohter, "Key Cuban foe claims exile backing," *New York Times*, 12 July 1998.
43 "Anti-Cuba Terrorist Attacks – The Canadian Connection," Canadian Network on Cuba, available online at canadiannetworkoncuba.ca/tribunal/Media/The%20Canadian%20Connection.pdf, accessed 12 July 2013.
44 Jean-Guy Allard, "Promotor de una 'lista de patrocinadores del terror,' EEUU da asilo a decenas de terroristas y prófugos." *Contrainjerencia*, 21 August 2011. Available online at http://www.contrainjerencia.com/?p=24321, accessed 12 February 2013.
45 Cuban Embassy, Ottawa, "Cuba Diplomática." Available online at http://havanareporternews.com/tourism/cuba-increasingly-preferred-destination-for-canadian-tourists.html.
46 "Arocena and terror," *Miami Herald*, 15 February 1985.
47 Ibid.

48 Christine Amario, "Coral Gables travel agency fire was arson," *Huffington Post*, 13 May 2012.

49 Lars Schoultz, *That Infernal Little Cuban Republic* (Chapel Hill: University of North Carolina Press, 2011).

50 For the definitive work on Operation Peter Pan, see Ramón Torreira Crespo and José Buajasán Marrawi, *Operación Peter Pan: un caso de guerra psicológica contra Cuba* (Havana: Editoria Politica, 2000).

51 Jane Franklin, "Looking for Terrorists in Cuba's Health System," *Z Magazine*, June 2003, available online at http://andromeda.rutgers.edu/~hbf/j/health.htm, accessed 25 September 2015.

52 The most extensive coverage of the Cuban Five can be found in Kimber's *What Lies Across the Water*.

53 John P. Glennon, ed., *Foreign Relations of the United States, 1958–1960*, vol. 6, *Cuba* (Washington, DC: US Government Printing Office, 1991), 885.

54 Wright, *Three Nights in Havana*, 90.

5 From Damnation to Liberation: Representing Cuba in Quebec in the Second Half of the Twentieth Century

MAURICE DEMERS AND MICHEL NAREAU

When Fidel Castro came to Montreal in April 1959, Gérard Pelletier, a journalist working for *Le Devoir* and *La Presse* before becoming a successful politician and diplomat, wrote that the city had been visited by "the most romantic character in the news."[1] Many young Quebecers found that Castro's revolution was much more than an astounding achievement: it was a direct inspiration for their own liberation struggle. Of course, throughout the Western world the Cuban Revolution provided a stimulating model to people disenchanted by the political culture that emerged with the post-war economic boom; for them, the huge socio-economic discrepancies that plagued capitalist countries became a cause for concern requiring a complete overhaul of the system. Montreal was not different than Paris, New York, or Toronto, for that matter.

But Cuba did find a particular resonance in the writings of progressive groups and radical left-wing activists in Quebec in the 1960s, a time when the French-speaking province was experiencing a rapid transformation of its cultural and social arrangements. The Quiet Revolution, as this period of rapid modernization is known in Quebec, not only saw the provincial government expand its fields of action – largely recovering social services and education from religious groups; it also coincided with the new role Quebec intended to play on the world stage.[2] The emergence of a renewed form of Quebec nationalism that sought greater control over the province's destiny influenced this political stance. This new political context also inspired Jean Lesage to run in the 1962 provincial election under the political motto "*Maîtres chez nous*" [Masters in our own house], and it convinced his government of the need to finish the nationalization of electricity by 1963.

But many citizens also wanted to go beyond what Lesage was proposing, and political groups started to ask for complete political independence and a socialist model of society. The example of the Cuban Revolution inspired them to promote national self-determination for Quebec. Whether socialist leaning or simply inspired by Liberation Theology, various *Québécois* therefore saw the Cuban example as a model of emancipatory nationalism favouring greater social justice. They crafted an image of Cuba that influenced the relations of the French-speaking province with the Caribbean island. They were not the only one to discuss the political issues related to the Cuban Revolution – the mass media certainly covered events transforming the Caribbean island, too – but we consider their representation of Cuba and the significance of the Revolution for Quebec to be of particular interest not only because of its originality, but also because it was a representation that motivated some individuals to take action, often espousing the belief that revolutionary changes were necessary to emancipate Quebec.

This chapter traces the evolution of this discourse on Cuba by analysing the political writings of Adèle Lauzon, Gabriel Gagnon, and Pierre Vallières; the literary production of Hubert Aquin, Bernard Andrès, and Louise Desjardins, among others; and texts on Cuban subjects published in religious publications during the second half of the twentieth century. Clerics and nuns were the first to publish about the island because of the establishment in Cuba of the French-Canadian Catholic missions of Les Frères de la Charité (1905), Les Sœurs de Notre-Dame du Bon-Conseil (1944), La Société des Missions-Étrangères (1945), Les Sœurs Missionnaires de l'Immaculée-Conception (1948), and Les Servantes du Saint-Cœur de Marie (1950). As a result of this involvement, the Cuban Revolution had a direct impact on the 114 French-Canadian missionaries present on the island in 1959 who then relayed information about the socio-political situation of the island before and after Fidel Castro took power. The climate of opinion in Catholic publications evolved from a negative appreciation in the early 1960s of the socialist character of the Revolution to a positive reading of the economic alternative it represented when Liberation Theology seriously influenced missionary communities at the end of the decade. As for writers and intellectuals, they were more prone to embrace the ideals of the Revolution. The global transformation the Revolution launched, and its anti-imperialist nature, represented a model of national liberation that left-wing writers could hope for in Quebec. The monthly publications *Parti pris* and *Socialisme* constituted significant spaces where this pro-Cuban discourse could be articulated in Quebec. In this chapter, we show how these two types of representations can be intertwined to offer a broader interpretation of the symbolic meaning(s) Cuba acquired in Quebec's progressive and left-wing publications during the Quiet Revolution, and how it continued to shape a positive representation of the island in the following decades. Using the insights of the theory of cultural transfers to shed light on our analysis of the texts we examine, we are able to highlight what caught the attention of French-Canadian authors, and what was left out about the Cuban situation in their publications.[3] This, in turn, can inform us about the intent behind Quebec-Cuba connections during the second half of the twentieth century.

An Ambivalent Reception: The Cuban Revolution Portrayed by Catholic Clerics and Intellectual Magazines

Jean Ménard, a missionary from Quebec's Société des Missions-Étrangères, arrived in Cuba a few months after Fidel Castro took power. He was enthralled by the revolutionary changes taking place: "While walking in the streets, I saw people paint their house, repairing the streets and sidewalks. I noticed that many got involved in the government's immunization and literacy campaigns on a voluntary basis. Coming from the Quebec of Premier Duplessis, I could not believe what I was seeing! I had moved from a subjugated society to one full of creativity."[4] The French-Canadian cleric explains that he left his presbytery in a rural parish to get involved with this popular mobilization, "encouraging health brigades who went to vaccinate the poor against malaria, dengue and typhoid, and those who worked to teach people in the countryside how to read and write."[5] The Cuban experience left a lasting impression on Ménard as he continued his missionary work in Chile and Nicaragua in the following decades, seeking to create the conditions that would bring about social justice to his impoverished flock. Jacques Lacaille, a missionary who came to work in Santiago de Chile's slums during the Augusto Pinochet dictatorship, was also influenced by the example Cuba provided. He explains in his memoirs *En mission dans la tourmente des dictatures* that, during his summer vacation from the seminary, he listened admiringly to Castro's speeches on his shortwave radio.[6] The ideals defended by the *Líder máximo* inspired him for years to come.

Nevertheless, not everyone shared Ménard's and Lacaille's enthusiasm for the Cuban Revolution. Most missionaries, like the Sœurs de

Notre-Dame du Bon-Conseil, might have welcomed the liberation from Batista's dictatorship and seen Castro as a source of "hope responding to a desire for freedom" for the population.[7] But the rapid radicalization of the Revolution and the deteriorating relations with the Catholic Church had missionaries worry and "stay on their guard."[8] Some of them denounced the surveillance of their activities, and were either expelled from the country or called back to Canada. As a result of this evolution, the Catholic hierarchy became outspokenly opposed to the socialist orientation of the regime, fearing – much like Washington – that the Cuban example would "contaminate" other Latin American societies.

In order to analyse this eventuality, a workshop was organized in Montreal in 1961 that brought together leading French-Canadian clerics and intellectuals who had worked in Latin America or were specializing in Latin American studies. The papers presented at this workshop, entitled "Struggle for Latin America," showed a deep concern for Castro's rapprochement with the Soviet Union and the influence Cuba had on other left-wing movements in the region. Richard Pattee, a professor at Université Laval and former organizer for the *National Catholic Welfare Conference* in the United States, explained that this rapprochement and influence constituted a "particularly dangerous trend."[9] The *prêtre des missions étrangère* Marcel Gérin, who had worked for seventeen years in Cuba as a missionary and in 1961 was heading the recently created Canadian Catholic Office of Latin America, went further, saying that Castro had to be neutralized, "[o]therwise, the malignant tumor that has been declared in the Caribbean will soon spread to the whole body of our continent."[10] Other stakeholders, such as Paul Bouchard, Joseph Ledit, and Luigi d'Appolonia – who were either teaching Latin American history or writing about the region in francophone media – also shared their preoccupation with the situation, explaining that, if the anti-imperialist objectives of the Revolution were understandable, the socialist orientation of the government was unacceptable.

The Jesuit publication *Relations*, the magazine following Latin American events in Quebec most closely since the 1940s, well represented the ambivalent reception of the Cuban Revolution in Catholic circles.[11] Sympathetic at first to the idea of emancipation from the dictatorship and the corrupting influence of US capitalism, it quickly changed its editorial position when the conflict with the United States pushed the revolutionary government to seek assistance in the Soviet Union. From that point, *Relations* published texts that were highly critical of the decisions taken by the new government, voicing the reprobation of the Cuban hierarchy, interviewing Fidel Castro's sister Juana to broadcast her criticism of the regime, and even giving its moral support to the Bay of Pigs invasion.[12] Yet missionaries who had been advocating for years for radical socio-economic changes in Latin America started to express their solidarity with the Caribbean island from the middle of the 1960s onward in French-Canadian Catholic publications. Even the main focus of the articles published in *Relations* changed in the second half of the 1960s from the threat of communism to the danger that poverty represented for the region's stability. From then on the image of Cuba conveyed by Catholic publications became more in tune with what could be read in left-wing magazines, which had taken a positive image of the Revolution since the beginning of the decade. With the exception of the conservative publication *L'Action nationale*, which published a good number of texts critical of the Cuban Revolution during the 1960s, most intellectuals publishing in cultural journals were quite enthused by the revolutionary changes taking place in Cuba.[13] Mostly indifferent to the situation of Cuba in the 1950s, the likes of Raoul Roy, Judith Jasmin, Pierre Vadeboncoeur, and Adèle Lauzon developed a growing interest in the model the Cuban Revolution provided.

Articles by Adèle Lauzon illustrate the process well. In the early 1960s, she wrote many texts about Cuba for a variety of publications, from the widely distributed *Maclean's* magazine to the literary journal *Écrits du Canada français* to Quebec's most prominent intellectual publication of the time, *Cité libre*. Lauzon is one of the few who established significant linkages with Cuba at the beginning of the 1960s. Indeed, she went on assignment in Cuba, got close to the Castro government, and established important links with Ernesto Guevara. She recounts in her memoirs that she maintained a correspondence with the revolutionary leader.[14] She was able to interview Guevara for an hour and a half in 1961, and found him very gracious, provoking a real "spiritual revelation."[15] As a result of her connections, Lauzon played the role of a cultural mediator for the revolution in Quebec, forcing political actors (especially on the left) to position themselves according to this historic achievement. That is the main reason she became the target of denunciations in *L'Action nationale*, which accused her of displaying exaggerated fondness for the Cuban regime.[16]

Adèle Lauzon was already a well-known trade unionist when she became an international correspondent for *Maclean's*. She had covered the war in Algeria, among other things, for the magazine before being posted to Cuba. Thanks to her good contacts with Fernando García Gutiérrez and Max Figueroa, she was able to have access to revolutionary leaders, and wrote five articles for *Cité libre* in a year about the political situation on the island. Her first was a November 1960 article entitled *"Essayer de comprendre"* [try to understand], which criticized the US and Canadian postures towards Cuba, Latin America, and the Third World.[17] This was the first text published in *Cité libre* on the Cuban situation, which had been of little interest to the editors before her collaboration with the journal.[18]

At the beginning of the 1960s, *Cité libre* was at the peak of its influence in Quebec.[19] The journal was founded to bring together opponents of Maurice Duplessis and present liberal solutions to the problems of Quebec.[20] Its openness to the world was mostly centred on the United States and Europe. In this way, Lauzon's articles – along with other articles on decolonization – worked to strengthen Third World perspectives in the journal, and established why Cuba could not be overlooked in Quebec. In the other four articles she wrote for *Cité libre* in 1960, Lauzon attempted to build bridges between Cuba and Canada, explain the objectives of the Revolution, and reflect on the accomplishments of the revolutionary transformation of the country, putting particular emphasis on the social and political gains since Castro took power.

Lauzon's most substantial contribution, however, was published, not in *Cité libre*, but in *Les Écrits du Canada français*, which appeared after her one-month stay in Havana and its surroundings in May 1961.[21] The forty-nine-page article is a shortened travelogue that Lauzon first wanted to publish as a book. It presents a subjective point of view, written in a genre that implies, as Pierre Rajotte explains, the staging of oneself faced with the discovery of another.[22] In the article, this discovery is fundamentally positive, since the country is presented as a model; the epigraph taken from a text signed by Claude Faux says it all: "If Cuba wouldn't last, a certain form of hope would disappear from the face of the Earth."[23]

More than anything, Lauzon's article in *Les Écrits du Canada français* reflects her enthusiasm for the Revolution. She calls this accomplishment a "Cuban dream," and portrays it as a revolution of poets – to use the words of René Despestre,[24] a Haitian writer she met there. It is a subjective view: empathetic and characterized by sentiments of solidarity that were influenced by her readings of French intellectuals such as Claude Julien and Jean-Paul Sartre who were supportive of Castro. Lauzon pays particular attention to the new possibilities granted to the impoverished population and the spaces created in which to articulate a political discourse emanating from the masses. Her reportage attempts to present factual evidence demonstrating that the Revolution had achieved an alternative form of democratization. She credits Fidel Castro for that achievement, and describes him as a fundamentally independent individual seeking the self-determination of his nation – an image of the *Líder máximo* that found an echo in Quebec. She writes: "If we refuse to acknowledge Fidel's independence and that of his supporters, we would interpret erroneously their actions." The familiar tone of her article – referring to Castro by his first name – is partially the product of the personal contacts she had with him either in Montreal during Castro's visit in 1959 or in Cuba during her stay.

Lauzon narrates the events happening in Cuba, translating for a North American audience the excitement of a society that was reinventing itself. The reader feels Lauzon's delight for what's happening and her exhilaration for having been "on stage with Castro, and shaking his hand"[25] during an informal meeting at the Faculty of Education, which turned out to be "a session of real revolutionary euphoria which are so common in Cuba."[26] The only historical references in the first section of her text are made to valorize the Revolution, being based on the parallels she establishes between Fidel Castro and José Martí, emphasizing the common objectives of their national liberation struggles and their desire for political independence – themes that garnered much interest in Quebec in the 1960s. In the second part of her article, she presents a short biography of Castro by quoting him extensively, as if the common platform they shared made her his spokesperson in Quebec. Yet, in this way, Lauzon contributed significantly to the early mythical consecration of Castro and Guevara in Canada. She endorsed the heroic narrative of the Sierra Maestra, and embraced Guevara's *foco* theory, explaining it for a francophone audience and showing along the way how Cuba was a model for Latin America and Quebec. Her presentation of the events happening on the island makes abstraction of the past, of tensions between social classes, and of the conditions of Afro-Cubans and peasants. In this way, the representation of Cuba she articulates offers the idea of a united people consolidating national independence, an idea particularly meaningful in Latin America and Quebec – in other words, "our hemisphere," as she writes.[27] In her view and later that of Pierre Vallières and Gabriel Gagnon, among others, hemispheric solidarity became a significant leverage facilitating Quebec's national liberation struggle.

A New Transnational Solidarity Is Born

Cuba's revolutionary posture had a deep impact in left-wing circles in Quebec, especially from the middle of the 1960s onward. In those years, social pressures to accelerate and radicalize the socio-political changes of the Quiet Revolution increased dramatically, and new militant discourses were expressed forcefully in new cultural and political journals. Those social pressures also led to the formation of political groups, legal or not, that wanted to foster a transition towards socialism and political independence for Quebec, opposing in this way capitalism and the federal state. This conjuncture seriously antagonized the rising star of the Liberals in Ottawa, Pierre Elliott Trudeau, who claimed that the Cuban influence in Quebec – and that of decolonization, for that matter – was nonsensical. Sean Mills writes about the reaction in Montreal: "In response to Pierre Trudeau, who continually argued that Quebec was neither Cuba nor Algeria, and could therefore not draw on their examples, Montreal poets and theorist Paul Chamberlain argued that the authors of *Parti Pris* understood Quebec's particular nature better than anyone. What Trudeau refused to recognize, [Chamberlain] wrote was that "by applying them to our situation, we are transforming the very meaning of the terms 'colonization' and 'decolonization.'"[28]

It is in this context that the journals *Socialisme*, *Parti pris*, *Chroniques*, and *Liberté* were launched. This period of heightened activism also led to the formation of the Front de libération du Québec (FLQ) in 1963. Solidarity with Cuba became a priority for these groups because the Revolution represented an explicit model to duplicate in Quebec and legitimated new forms of expressing political claims. As Robert Major said, *Parti pris* "embodied the most radical wing of the left in Quebec in the 1960s. At a pivotal moment of Quebec's history, the journal not only forcefully expressed the demands of the left – and occasionally expressed them brilliantly – but also articulated them in an uncompromising manner, bringing them to their logical conclusion: revolution."[29] Founded in 1963 by André Major, Paul Chamberland, André Brochu, Pierre Maheu, and Jean-Marc Piotte, the journal transformed Quebec's discursive landscape. In fact, *Parti pris* reshaped the neonationalist project by matching literature and politics, using a militant prose that articulated the alienation of everyday life in Quebec, and by politicizing popular expressions, turning Quebec's vernacular – known as *joual* in reference to the way popular classes pronounced the word *cheval* – into a combative anti-imperialist language of self-determination linking it to a project in favour of political independence, socialism, and secularism.[30] With three thousand subscribers, *Parti pris* published a copy every month up until 1968, focusing on Quebec and its incapacity to control fully its national projects and act independently on the world stage. Although the journal was relatively short lived, its impact lasted longer as a publishing house established by the editors.

Ideologically, *Parti pris* was influenced by Marxism, existentialism, and decolonization, something that André J. Bélanger, Robert Major, and Lise Gauvin have studied.[31] These studies, however, do not take significantly into consideration the influence of Cuba on the journal's ideological orientation. A journal that advocated for a socialist, independent, and secular Quebec could only be struck by the Cuban experience. Even though, at first glance, this reference looks less important than we might think,[32] articles on Cuba became more numerous in the last two years of the journal.[33] Cuba was first mentioned in the journal as an example granting legitimacy to the independence struggle in Quebec and the promotion of socialism in this French-speaking nation. For example, Jacques Brault uses Cuban and Argentine examples to advocate for the establishment of an independent (and decolonized) literature,[34] while Jacques Poisson points to the Mexican and Cuban models to advocate for an independent French-Canadian press agency independent of foreign ones and capitalist influences.[35]

From the third volume of *Parti pris* onward, articles about Latin America – most of them touching on the influence in the region of the Cuban Revolution – became more numerous. This was the result of new writers joining the publication, collaborators who brought a fresh perspective considering that Quebec's liberation struggle had to be connected with pan-continental mobilization.[36] It then became crucial to understand the inner workings of other countries of the Americas. In a special edition of *Parti pris* entitled "Québec Si, Yankee No,"[37] in which Latin America is presented as a model of ways to mediate the French-speaking province's relations with the United States, Gilles Dostaler analyses the Andean revolutionary movements influenced by the Cuban Revolution.[38] In another article on land reform, the author attempts to understand what was achieved in Cuba and portray this as a revolutionary victory for a French-Canadian audience that did not necessarily understand the urgency of the problem in Latin America, as this was not a demand of left-wing movements in Quebec.[39]

With this opening, a new discourse emerged in *Parti pris* focusing on the "Lessons of Latin America" for Quebec, to use the title of Gabriel

Gagnon's article.[40] For the authors of *Parti pris*, the revolutionary actions in Latin America responded to a geopolitical logic encompassing the situation of Quebec. In this way, the region represented an inspiration: "With the exception of Cuba, the republics located south of the Rio Grande have not inspired our revolutionary culture as much as the European and Asian cases have, even though these republics are subjected to the same kind of US imperialism Canada and an eventually independent Quebec are. Yet, these countries offer instructive examples that could shed light on our strategies to tackle the alternative socialism and neo-capitalism, because their pre-revolutionary conditions are similar to ours."[41]

Even if the they did not have a deep understanding of the history and socio-economic conditions of the region, indifference towards the subcontinent was sharply criticized in the pages of *Parti pris*, and the necessity of establishing strategic linkages was exposed because, "with a few exceptions, mobilization and political actions are confronted with the same kind of problems in the poor neighbourhoods of Montreal than those of Latin American shantytowns."[42] To prove his point, Gagnon identifies three common areas of struggle: the rural world, urban spaces, and a transnational community. He pleads for a new Latin American-Quebec solidarity based upon collaboration among revolutionary groups inspired by Cuba, even though the *foco* theory might not be the best strategy to use: "First of all, we ought to be conscious of the impossibility of creating alone a free and socialist Quebec: more than the support of our national bourgeoisie or that of the American government, we need the help of revolutionary groups from Latin America and that of left-wing forces from the United States. That's the reason why we need to know better the situation south of the Rio Grande and get connected with decolonizing movements in those countries."[43]

Pierre Vallières' approach to the subject was also inspired by the reading of Latin America's geopolitical situation stemming from Guevara's anti-imperialist positions – and favoured by the translation of his writings in the journal in 1968[44] and that of his Bolivian Diary by the *Parti pris* publishing house.[45] In a certain way, these initiatives attempted to create multiple centres of anti-imperialist resistance as Guevara had called for by wishing for the multiplication of Vietnams in the world. For example, following the Tricontinental Conference in Havana, Vallières wrote an article celebrating the Cuban example in which he states: "One can only admire and try to emulate the revolutionary coherence of the Cuban people."[46] In this way, there is hope for Quebec and the world because Cuba defends "a continental strategy for the continuation of the revolution":[47] "Because the key is not to create revolutionary outbreaks: they already exist everywhere, from Quebec to Chile. The key is to get organize in order to reach the final victory ... Economically, politically, militarily, our struggle is the same one ... That is why our struggle is that of Cuba and Cuba's struggle ours. We cannot dissociate from each other without condemning ourselves to defeat ... Quebecers too are from a 'Latin' America and are part, much like the other peoples from South America, of the Third World."[48]

The reconfiguration of the discourse of a shared Latin identity linking French Canada and Latin America (and resisting Anglo-Protestant imperialism), displacing it from a right-wing perspective common in the 1930s and 1940s to a left-wing one, represented an attempt to cast Quebec's own liberation struggle in a broader frame of reference giving legitimacy to this course of action in Canada. Therefore, it is not surprising to see that the following edition of *Parti pris* was entitled "Hasta la victoria siempre!" As Roger Soublière notes, for an individual who went to the Caribbean island in 1968 for the cultural congress of Havana, "Cuba was an example."[49] Soublière uses as a pretext the regime's celebration of the year of the heroic *guerrillero* to reflect on the best revolutionary strategies and the question of imperialism. He ends the piece with a call for continental solidarity with Cuba and all the other revolutionary struggles – from that of the Black Panthers to the ones in the Andes – claiming in the final sentence: "Patria o muerte! Venceremos!"[50]

These examples demonstrate how Cuba became a model in the pages of *Parti pris* after the arrival of Gabriel Gagnon, Gaëtan Tremblay, and Luc Racine. The journal came to symbolize an alternative form of continental collaboration based upon resistance to capitalism and US imperialism. If *Parti pris*'s discourse on Cuba was enthusiastic – despite showing a somewhat superficial understanding of that model – the FLQ was deeply influenced by the Cuban Revolution, the strategies used on the island to gain power, and the turmoil in the rest of Latin America. The FLQ was a clandestine organization, structured around independent networks of a few militants who sought to liberate Quebec from Canada and capitalism through armed struggle. Georges Schoeters, one of three FLQ founders who had met with Guevara, began his own violent struggle (planting bombs) after two trips to Cuba, the first as a student in 1959 and the second in order to collaborate with the land reform on the island. Since the Canadian and Cuban governments had diplomatic ties, however, few direct connections between the FLQ and the revolutionaries in Havana resulted from these first exchanges, An exception was the Cuban consul in Montreal, Julia González, who was called back to the island after her friendship with FLQ members was discovered and the Royal Canadian Mounted Police raised complaints.[51]

The Vallières-Gagnon network was the one most influenced by Guevara's idea that violent actions in themselves could create the winning conditions for a successful revolution. Yet the group's most common references about its revolutionary strategy were to the Brazilian communist activist Carlos Marighela and his *Minimanual of the Urban Guerrilla* and to the Uruguayan Tupamaros for their strategic kidnappings and other urban actions. Cuba, therefore, was an entry point to gain access to revolutionary movements in Latin America, where socio-economic conditions were believed to be more similar to the situation in Quebec. For its part, the Geoffroy network – François Bachand, Jacques Larue-Langlois, Raymond Villeneuve, and Jean Castonguay – travelled to Havana in fall 1968 to receive revolutionary training.[52] Except for Castonguay, who took up arms in Central America, they stayed for eighteen months. The Cuban example remained influential for the actions of the FLQ until the kidnappings of James Cross and Pierre Laporte, which prompted the 1970 October Crisis, a moment when civil liberties were suspended in Quebec. When the release of the prisoners was negotiated, the members of the FLQ's *Libération* cell asked the Cuban government's lawyer in Montreal, Bernard Mergler, to help them. He negotiated their exile on the Caribbean island in return for the release of Cross, using for a moment the Cuban pavilion at Terres des Hommes (the continuing fair held on the site of Expo 67) as Cuban territory.[53] Cuba was then remembered as the ultimate refuge of this pro-independence guerrilla group.

Cuba's Achievements in Quebec Memory

Left-wing activists in Montreal did establish concrete ties with Cuba in the late 1960s, but these connections were rather short-lived as a result of the October Crisis and Cuba's good relations with the Trudeau government. We can safely say that Trudeau's successful visit to Havana in 1976 neutralized the idea of seeking support in the communist island for an independence revolution in the French-speaking province. Montreal left-wing groups remained fond of the Cuban example, but the hopes of the late 1960s largely vanished.

Interestingly, the ideals of social justice of the Revolution remained (indirectly) influential for a different type of French-Canadian activists in the 1970s: Catholic missionaries. Many missionaries working in Latin America during the Cold War experienced a process of radicalization as a result of the intense repression they witnessed or experienced in the countries governed by military regimes they worked in and their appropriation of Liberation Theology as a way to live and teach the Gospel in solidarity with the oppressed. Slowly but surely, they grew closer to popular movements – many directly influenced by the Cuban Revolution and the writings of Guevara – and joined their search for ways to secure more social justice for the masses. Even though most missionaries did not embrace fully the Cuban government's actions, they valued the alternative that Cuba represented on the world stage, and worked to preserve good relations with the regime. In 1970, for example, the oblates working in the impoverished regions of South America submitted a brief to the Canadian Department of External Affairs on these regions' horrendous socio-economic conditions. They explained why they understood and morally supported popular movements seeking a radical overhaul of their nations' oppressive socio-economic structures, and they recommended Canada abstain from any policy of reprisal against any Latin American state: "No state, however powerful, has the right to excommunicate a whole people from the human community and to deprive it of its natural relations with its own economic and political region. And we applaud the determination of Canada to persist in a policy of exchanges with Cuba, when the United States practically compelled other States of the Continent to break relations with Cuba."[54] Maurice Lefebvre, one of the missionaries who signed the brief, was killed by Bolivian dictator Hugo Banzer's forces during the 1971 coup d'état. His speech at La Paz University honouring Ernesto Guevara had made headlines in the capital a few months earlier; the military regime later explained that, like *el Che*, Lefebvre had been importing revolutionary ideas into Bolivia.[55]

Seen as a martyr – much like the Salvadorian Oscar Romero and the Canadian Raoul Léger, who were also killed for their support of an oppressed population defending itself against brutal regimes – Lefebvre, who did not shy away from collaborating with Cuban-inspired popular movements fighting for greater socio-economic justice in Latin America, became an inspiration for keeping the focus on condemning the continent's most repressive regimes. As a result, the Canadian Catholic hierarchy refrained from seriously denouncing Cuba – unlike its stance at the beginning of the 1960s – and expressed publicly its solidarity with left-wing resistance groups in Latin America, viewing them as victims of an unjust repression fuelled by a Washington-inspired national security doctrine. In this way, the Catholic hierarchy articulated a discourse on Cuba that was quite different from the dominant rhetoric of the Cold War.

They were not alone in maintaining this relatively positive image of the island in Quebec.[56] Various writers offered positive appreciations of the 1959 Revolution in the following decades. Many were influenced by Hubert Aquin, a member of the 1960s party, Rassemblement pour l'indépendance nationale (rally for national independence), who in 1965 published *Prochain épisode*, a novel that became a classic of *Québécois* literature. Aquin is actually at the juncture of the image created by left-wing activists and the memory of the Revolution entertained by novelists. Before publishing his novel, Aquin was director of the journal *Liberté*, and collaborated with *Parti pris*. He announced in a letter published in the newspaper *Le Devoir* in 1964 that he was going underground to join the FLQ. He was later arrested, and wrote his first novel in jail.

Prochain épisode – the novel was translated in English as *Next Episode* – is a story of espionage. It describes the actions of a *Québécois* terrorist who is on a mission in Switzerland to execute a Canadian federal double agent. The novel aims to show how Quebec's colonial story had been written in advance long ago, and how the only way to break out this predicament would involve the use of violence and concerted political action. Its opening line is one of the most famous in the literature of Quebec: "Cuba is sinking in flames in the middle of Lac Léman while I descend to the bottom of things."[57] Aquin evokes the Cuban victory, and later mentions a long series of revolutionary episodes inspired by the *foco* theory. According to the novel, these episodes are the inspiration for Quebec's own armed struggle.[58] For Aquin, Cuba is associated with two key elements: the ideas that alienation can be overcome through a revolutionary struggle, and that, if victory is to be achieved, people must be ready to pay the price. The numerous mentions of the 1953 Moncada attack and the 26th of July Movement's struggles attest to the difficulty of the task. In this way, the novel exemplifies a certain structure of feelings that emerged in the 1960s in Quebec's left-wing circles: a sentiment that Cuba was Quebec's "*grand-frère*" (older brother), to quote the lyrics of a Robert Charlebois song.[59] If Aquin's novel did not create direct bonds of solidarity with Cuba per se, it certainly contributed to crafting and preserving a certain association between Quebec's independence struggle and Cuban-inspired activism.

Although, as mentioned, the October Crisis and Trudeau's visit to Cuba largely neutralized the political impact of this association, literary references to this memory of activism remained alive in the decades to follow. *Prochain épisode*'s famous opening line has inspired subsequent writers, and was reproduced by Bernard Andrès as an epigraph to his 2007 novel, *Fidel, D'Iberville et les autres*, which makes many references to *Prochain épisode* in positioning the linkages between Cuba and Quebec at the centre of the story. Also a spy-thriller, but this time involving FLQ activists, *Fidel, D'Iberville et les autres* is not so much about revolutionary fervor in Quebec as about the various national liberation struggles throughout the Americas. The novel is an "uchronic political-fiction" based upon a profound knowledge of the historical links between Cuba and Quebec. In the story, while Cuba prepares itself to celebrate the three-hundredth anniversary of the death in Havana in 1706 of Pierre d'Iberville, a Canadian adventurer and pirate who travelled throughout North America on behalf of colonial New France, Fidel Castro disappears. The *Líder máximo* goes into hiding in Quebec's Côte-Nord region in the José-Martí and Hatuey mountains – named in honour of the two heroes of continental resistance. Andrès constantly juxtaposes *Québécois* and Cuban revolutionary heroes, showing how both governments (should) have political affinities, and describing how the histories of the two nations are interconnected – as a way of creating a fictitious America in which Quebec plays an inspirational role similar to that played by 1960s Cuba. The novel recycles the memory of the Cuban Revolution – as articulated by left-wing militants in Quebec – so that it overlaps a period in which the actions of the French in the Americas go far beyond the actual frontiers of Quebec. In a crucial scene of the novel, d'Iberville, the hero from New France, liberates Castro and brings him back to Cuba to defend the Revolution:

> In a funny *chasse-galerie* [a "flying canoe," a tale involving French-Canadian *voyageurs*], d'Iberville flew away with his *compañeros*. Along with Che, Cienfuegos and the cream of the crop of dead *barbudos*, Martí, Anadabijou and Hatuey were as enthralled as d'Iberville to discover the mountains that bear their names. Especially since at the foot of these hillocks resided another EMINENCE: the one whose delayed absence put the *Revolución* in peril. Everything was done to convince HIM to return to the country. As in the good old days, a new expedition brought back the hero from exile. Fifty years after Marea del Portillo, a new triumphant return happened aboard a *Granma* travelling, this time, not on waters but in the sky.[60]

A new, if fictitious, geopolitics emerges from Andrès's novel, one in which the Cuban-inspired Bolivarian projects of Hugo Chávez and Evo Morales include Quebec.[61] The literary reference goes on to show that the revolutionary utopia still inspires some *québécois* authors who wish the French-speaking province would renew the kinds of collective projects of the sixties and seventies.

In *Le fils du Che*, a novel published a year after that of Andrès, Louise Desjardins also invokes the militant memory of Cuba's Revolution as articulated in Quebec in the 1960s to frame her story about a Montreal family in crisis. Alex, a fourteen–year-old teenager has been educated by his grandparents – communist activists – and by his rebellious mom. His fondest dream is to get in touch with his absent father. Alex comes to believe – from political stories circulating in the family, his grandparents' revolutionary heroes, and the Guevara posters displayed in the house – that he is the son of a revolutionary leader in hiding. The education he has received and the social ideals he defends lead Alex to claim that Guevara is the person he imagines "when I think of my father."[62] We eventually learn that Alex's father is a Chilean exile who teaches Spanish in a college in Montreal. But the image of revolutionary Cuba, the activist stories of resistance he has heard through the years, and the values transmitted by his grandparents push the teenager to invent an idealized father-figure that gives sense to his life – maintaining along the way a militant memory of revolutionary Cuba that is meaningful in Quebec. That the story makes his father actually a Chilean refugee suggests that it could be read symbolically to mean that Cuba was the gateway to lasting bonds of solidarity with Latin American left-wing groups more broadly. Indeed, as well as establishing concrete links with Cuba, progressive groups in Quebec lobbied in the 1970s to force Canada to accept more political refugees from South and Central America, and created humanitarian non-governmental organizations that staunchly denounced the human rights abuses of Latin American dictatorships.

Conclusion

The three literary works examined above refer to Cuba to transmit a revolutionary heritage intended to give legitimacy to the idea that a national liberation struggle in Quebec is both desirable and possible. The urgency is not the same since the days of *Parti pris* and the publication of Aquin's novel, but the representation of Cuba by Quebec's left-wing writers has not changed much – although the reference is more nostalgic than anything else.

Yet, as we mentioned at the outset, this is an incomplete view of the representation of Cuba in Quebec: left-wing activists have not been alone in discussing the "Cuban model." From the 1960s onward, the journal *L'Action nationale* articulated a disapproving stance, with articles such "the truth about Cuba" and "Castro faced by fiasco."[63] The mass media have also been much more critical of the Cuban regime than have the left-wing writers. Daniel Gay aptly demonstrates that the "natural solidarity" some claimed Quebec had for Cuba and Latin America is not reflected in the editorials of the province's main newspapers.[64] Criticism of the regime increased in the 1980s and 1990s, especially after the fall of the Soviet Union appeared to represent a momentous challenge to the very survival of the Revolution.

The deep economic crisis that followed the end of Soviet support forced the Cuban regime to seek alternative sources of revenue. One was the tourist industry, which has created new bonds between Cuba and the *Québécois*, and Canadians more widely, that could not have been imagined in the 1960s.[65] A body of literature has even emerged in Quebec around the rise of people travelling to the Caribbean island.[66] Illustrating the different attitude about the island these literary texts convey, Cathy Bazinet's "Cuba libre," published in 2010, tells of the encounter between a tourist and a hotel employee who invites her to his house. She discovers that the hotel employee's father is staunchly opposed to the young man's desire to study medicine, as he wants never to have to say that his son "is not a doorman at the National, he is only a neurosurgeon."[67] In this literature, the focus is not so much on the historic achievements, such as health care, and their inspiration for social movements in Quebec, as on the concrete economic and political problems faced by the Cuban population. Needless to say, the image of the island here is much bleaker.

But the idealism of the sixties has not disappeared completely. Hundreds of students from Quebec high schools, colleges, and universities still organize solidarity campaigns and visit the island with concerns that do not include going to an all-inclusive resort. Echoes of the 1960s activism are also still present in left-wing circles in Montreal. Claude Kanute's public talk, organized by socialist students at the Université du Québec à Montréal in June 2014, attests to this persistence. Entitled "La révolution cubaine, ou comment sortir le Canada du Québec," the talk aimed to answer the question: What teachings can we take from the

Cuban Revolution? Kanute explained that, "without being a model to copy, the revolutionary experience – which still seriously antagonizes American imperialism – might be an example to follow."[68] If many reports about Cuba now focus on the predicament of living under the conditions imposed by the socialist regime, for some left-wing circles in Quebec the Revolution still symbolizes a model of emancipation and national self-determination. The image of the Revolution crafted in the sixties lives on, but with much less influence than before.

NOTES

The research for this article was funded by the Social Sciences and Humanities Research Council Insight Development Grants Program for the project directed by Michel Nareau and co-directed by Maurice Demers, entitled "Mise en récit de l'Amérique latine au Québec: transferts de sens d'une autochtonie continentale (1940–2010)." This funding enabled us to hire Marcel Nault Jr as a research assistant. His assistance in identifying texts published in Quebec on Cuba helped us tremendously, and we want to acknowledge it.

1 "Fidel Castro à Montréal," *Affrontement*, radio broadcast, 26 April 1959, Archives de Radio-Canada, available online at http://archives.radio-canada.ca/c_est_arrive_le/04/26/, accessed 10 October 2013.
2 Jean Lesage's Liberal government justified this new role with the Gérin-Lajoie doctrine (1965), which explained that Quebec, as a province of a federal entity, has the right to engage in foreign relations and to sign international treaties in its field of constitutional competence (such as education and culture).
3 Michel Werner and Michel Espagne, eds., *Transferts: les relations interculturelles dans l'espace franco-allemand* (Paris: Éditions Recherche sur les civilisations, 1985); Robert Dion, *L'Allemagne de Liberté: sur la germanophilie des intellectuels québécois* (Ottawa: Presses de l'Université d'Ottawa, 2007).
4 Jean Ménard, "Hors du presbytère et des sentiers battus," interview by M.H.C., available online at http://smelaval.org/pt-br/node/123/le-pays. This and the following translations from French to English in this chapter are those of the authors except where noted.
5 Ibid.
6 Jacques Lacaille, *En mission dans la tourmente des dictatures, 1965–1986* (Montreal: Novalis, 2014), 17.

7 Chantal Gauthier and France Lord, *Engagées et solidaires: les Sœurs du Bon-Conseil à Cuba, 1948–1998* (Montreal: Carte Blanche, 2013), 85.

8 Ibid., 89.

9 Albert Sanschagrin et al., *Lutte pour l'Amérique latine: journée d'étude organi-sée par les Ligues du Sacré-Cœur, avec le concours de vingt associations, sous la présidence de S.E. Mgr Albert Sanschagrin et de S.E. Mgr Agustín Adolfo Her-rera* (Montreal: Le Gésu, 1961), 25–6.

10 Ibid., 36.

11 *Relations* published 117 articles, columns, and book reviews on Latin America from 1945 to 1960.

12 "L'agonie de l'Église de Cuba," editorial, *Relations* 240, December 1960, 311; Luigi d'Apollonia, "Au fil du mois: le témoignage de Juana Castro," *Rela-tions* 285, September 1964, 271; idem, "Guerre Froide," *Relations* 246, June 1961, 155.

13 The enthusiasm of these intellectuals differs from the editorial positions of Quebec's main newspapers, which were quite critical of the Revolution; see Daniel Gay, *Les élites québécoises et l'Amérique latine* (Montreal: Nouvelle Optique, 1983).

14 Adèle Lauzon, *Pas si tranquille* (Montreal: Boréal, 2008), 206.

15 Ibid., 198.

16 "Nouvelles de Cuba," *L'Action nationale* 61 (1971): 58.

17 Adèle Lauzon, "Essayer de comprendre," *Cité libre* 31 (November 1960): 28–30.

18 During the 1950s *Cité libre* published only one article that seriously dis-cussed the Latin American context. The Cuban Revolution changed this lack of interest, but before the arrival of Adèle Lauzon, who was the first to dedicate full articles to Cuba, mentions of the Cuban example were rather negative. After Lauzon's articles, *Cité libre* started to publish more about Cuba, including a few important ones. See, for example, André Cham-pagne, "À l'horizon, la guerre sainte?" *Cité libre* 38 (June 1961): 27–8; Alice Poznanska, "La contre-révolution cubaine végète en Floride," *Cité libre* 41 (November 1961): 11–13; and François Piazza, "Punta del Este: la farce est jouée," *Cité libre* 45 (March 1962): 18–19.

19 "Cité libre (1950–2000)," Bibliothèque et Archives nationales du Québec, available online at http://collections.banq.qc.ca/ark:/52327/2225350.

20 Pierre Elliott Trudeau is one of the intellectuals who founded the journal in 1950 and later wrote many articles for the publication in opposition to the Duplessis government.

21 Adèle Lauzon, "Cuba," *Les Écrits du Canada français* 14 (1962): 259–309.

22 Pierre Rajotte, "Introduction," in *Le voyage et ses récits au XXe siècle*, ed. Pierre Rajotte (Quebec City: Nota bene, 2005), 16.

23 Claude Faux, cited in Lauzon, "Cuba," 261.

24 René Despestre, cited in ibid., 263.

25 Ibid., 277.

26 Ibid., 281.

27 Ibid., 294.

28 Sean Mills, *The Empire Within: Postcolonial Thought and Political Activism in Sixties Montreal* (Montreal; Kingston, ON: McGill-Queen's University Press, 2010), 34.

29 Robert Major, *Partis pris: idéologies et littérature* (Montreal: Hurtubise HMH, 1979), 26.

30 Lise Gauvin, *Parti pris littéraire* (Montreal: Les Presses de l'Université de Montréal, 1975), 55–74.

31 André J. Bélanger, "La recherche d'un collectif," in *Ruptures et constantes, quatre idéologies du Québec en éclatement: La Relève, la JEC*, Cité libre, Parti pris (Montreal: Hurtubise HMH, 1977), 137–93. Sean Mills also has a section on *Parti pris* in his book about activism in Montreal in the sixties; see Mills, *Empire Within*, 51–61.

32 This overview was realized thanks to an index compiled by Joseph Bonenfant, ed., *Index de "Parti pris"* (Sherbrooke, QC: Université de Sherbrooke, Centre d'étude des littératures d'expression française, 1975), 116.

33 Robert Major notes: "the discovery of Althusser at the beginning of the fourth year coincided with a disillusion with direct action [the failure of the Mouvement de libération populaire even after its adhesion to the Parti socialiste du Québec] and is the occasion to elaborate a new conception of revolutionary practices in the journal. This new theoretical practice, defined by Chamberland, will push *Parti pris* to become more interested in current events … [T]he number of references to Latin America, the USA and Che Guevara [is] sharply increasing" (ibid., 44).

34 Jacques Brault, "Un pays à mettre au monde," *Parti pris* 2, no. 10–11 (1964): 9–25.

35 Jacques Poisson, "La difficile naissance de Presse-Québec," *Parti pris* 2, no. 2 (1964): 247.

36 Robert Major, "*Parti pris*: idéologies et literature" (PhD diss., University of Ottawa, 1979), 40.

37 The special edition is *Parti pris* 5, no. 4 (1968).

38 Gilles Dostaler, "Situation révolutionnaire dans les républiques andines," *Parti pris* 5, no. 4 (1968): 17–28.

39 Lise Rochon, "Exposé: la réforme agraire à Cuba," *Parti pris* 4, nos 5–6 (1967): 63–70.

40 Gabriel Gagnon, "Les leçons de l'Amérique latine," *Parti pris* 4, nos 3–4 (1966): 103–7.

41 Ibid., 103.

42 Ibid., 106. Conditions in Latin American shantytowns were not described (nor probably understood) in depth.

43 Ibid.

44 Ernesto [Che] Guevara, "Créer deux, trois … de nombreux Vietnam, voilà le mot d'ordre!" *Parti pris* 5, nos 2–3 (1968): 38–46.

45 Ernesto [Che] Guevara, *Journal de Bolivie, 7 novembre 1966–7 octobre 1967* (Montreal: Parti pris, 1969). The book includes an introduction by Fidel Castro.

46 Pierre Vallières, "Cuba révolutionnaire," *Parti pris* 5, no. 1 (1967): 21. This point of view is similar to that defended at the same time by Pierre Vadeboncœur in the review *Socialisme*; see "Les salauds contre Cuba," *Socialisme*, nos 3–4 (1964): 79–88.

47 Vallières, "Cuba révolutionnaire," 21.

48 Ibid., 21–2.

49 Roger Soublière, "Hasta la victoria siempre!" *Parti pris* 5, no. 7 (1968): 37.

50 Ibid.

51 Louis Fournier, *FLQ: Histoire d'un mouvement clandestin* (Montreal: Québec Amérique, 1982), 124.

52 Ibid., 192–3.

53 On the Cuban experience of this FLQ cell, see Jacques Lanctôt, *Les plages de l'exil* (Montreal: Stanké, 2010).

54 Missionnaires Oblats de Marie Immaculée, "Canada's External Relations with Latin America," brief submitted to the Canadian Government (Montreal, 1970), 19.

55 Guy L. Côté, dir., *Les deux côtés de la médaille: risquer sa peau*, documentary (Montreal: Office national du film du Canada, 1974).

56 To be fair, it has to be said that Cuba's image remained controversial in Catholic circles, as Castro's own rapprochement with the Vatican waited for years. Catholic publications in Quebec more easily celebrated the Sandinista regime.

57 Hubert Aquin, *Prochain épisode* (Montreal: Le Cercle du livre de France, 1965), 7. The quote was translated by Sheila Fischman. The English translation was published by the New Canadian Library under the title *Next Episode*, which won the annual CBC book competition Canada Reads in 2003.

58 Ibid.

59 Robert Charlebois, "Mon ami Fidel" [My friend Fidel], from album *Longue Distance* (Solution, 1976).

60 Bernard Andrès, *Fidel, D'Iberville et les autres* (Montreal: Québec Amérique, 2007), 175.

61 Ibid., 205.

62 Louise Desjardins, *Le fils du Che* (Montreal: Boréal, 2008), 85.

63 "Documents: la vérité sur Cuba," *L'Action nationale* 59, no. 10 (1970): 963; "Actualités: Castro devant le fiasco," *L'Action nationale* 60, no. 2 (1970): 155–6.

64 Daniel Gay, *Les élites québécoises et l'Amérique latine* (Montreal: Nouvelle Optique, 1983).

65 Close to a million Canadian and *Québécois* tourists go to Cuba each year; see "Les Cubains, 2e touristes dans leur pays derrière les Canadiens," *La Presse* (Montreal), 8 July 2011, available online at http://www.lapresse.ca/voyage/destinations/amerique-latine/cuba/201107/08/01-4416192-les-cubains-2e-touristes-dans-leur-pays-derriere-les-canadiens.php.

66 Sophie Létourneau, "Des pesos," in *Polaroïds* (Montreal: Québec Amérique, 2006); Pierre Karch, *Noëlle à Cuba* (Sudbury, ON: BCF, 2007); Cathy Bazinet, "Cuba libre," *Biscuit chinois* 13 (2010): 30–6.

67 Bazinet, "Cuba libre," 35.

68 Quote included on the poster of the event held at the Université du Québec à Montréal on 29 June 2014.

PART TWO

Canada and Cuba in the Shadow of the US:
Structures and Economies

6 Trust and Affectivity in Contemporary Canada-Cuba-US Relations: Transcending the Past in Shaping the Future

CALUM McNEIL

The bilateral relationship with the United States is of overwhelming importance to Canada politically and economically. Canada has always struggled with the costs and benefits of engaging with its southern neighbour. Yet geographic proximity and economic interdependence have resulted in the largest bilateral trading relationship in the world and a relatively demilitarized border. Generally this relationship has produced measurable benefits for both states. Canada has gained relatively secure access to what is still the world's largest market, and has established bilateral defence agreements that have guaranteed Canadian security at a relative discount.[1] The United States has gained relatively unhindered access to Canadian commodities, manufactured goods, and services, while also achieving its ends regarding continental security. The relationship, however, is fundamentally asymmetric, which tends to leave Canadian policy-makers vulnerable when their interests and those of Washington[2] are in conflict. Such has been the case with both states' Cuba policies, as Canada has chosen to maintain normalized relations with Havana since the Revolution, while the United States has chosen a more punitive policy of embargo. Given the vulnerability of Canada to US political and economic pressure, it is worth considering how this pressure has affected state-to-state and substate interactions between Cuba and Canada.

In this chapter, I first argue that US Cuba policy has affected the trajectory and tenor of Cuba-Canada relations in ways often unacknowledged. Specifically, US policy has contributed to the symbolic importance and discursive construction of the Cuban "other" in Canadian foreign policy discourse. Although this terrain has been covered in various ways, I believe it is important to consider both *how* and *why* the triangulated nature of US-Canada-Cuba relations has functioned to incline and entrench certain routinized policy preferences. Second, I argue that, although the triangular relationship is often framed as a frustrating problematic inhibiting more fruitful Cuba-Canada relations, it can also be framed as a way to better understand how interstate trust-building – in this case between Canada and Cuba – can occur under difficult circumstances.

Theoretical Considerations: What Is Trust?

Perhaps the best example of trust in international relations is the bilateral relationship between Canada and the United States. Long characterized as sharing the world's longest undefended border, the two have little to fear from each other – even with the heightened security arrangements introduced after 9/11. Yet to make this seemingly obvious claim begs the question of what we are talking about when we characterize state-to-state relations as "trustful." After all, global politics is the realm of self-interested power politics: how can one speak of trust in a truly meaningful fashion?

Trust is generally accepted to refer to "an attitude involving a willingness to place the fate of one's interests under the control of others … based on a belief, for which there is some uncertainty, that potential trustees will avoid using their discretion to harm the interests of [the trustor]."[3] In addition it is understood that the attitude of trust is not sufficient in and of itself to cause trusting relationships. Trusting relationships vary in scope and intensity.[4] There is never a situation in which two or more actors trust one another unconditionally – consequently, in a trusting relationship, the trustor always makes assumptions about the likely behaviour of the trustee; this discretion entails that there is always some uncertainty – and risk – inherent in the decision-making process.[5] This has direct relevance to our ability to distinguish empirically between relationships involving trust and distrust. In both relationships we see evidence of risk, but in distrustful relationships we also find evidence of binding commitments that eliminate the possibility of betrayal. This does not mean that monitoring does not take place in trustful relationships; rather, it means certain types of monitoring are appropriate if actual trust-building is to take place. For example, before-the-fact oversight is more likely to place limits on the agency of trustees (those who are being trusted) than after-the-fact oversight; before-the-fact oversight, in rigidly mapping out exactly what is expected of the trustee in implementing an agreement, indicates an unwillingness to leave the mode of implementation in the trustee's hands. As Aaron Hoffman explains, "where there is more discretion there is more trust, [therefore] after-the-fact oversight is more consistent with trusting relationships than before-the-fact oversight."[6] This means that in policies designed to forge trust between two or more agents, the trustor must rely on subjective estimates of the *likelihood that the trustee will honour the trust*. This involves a necessary amount of risk for the trustor, given the absence of binding agreements to compel the "trustee" to fulfil its obligations.[7]

In addition it is rare that two actors are equal in terms of their material power relative to each other. Thus, as Deborah Welch-Larson argues, when two adversarial actors cooperate, trust acts as a necessary, but not sufficient, condition facilitating that cooperation. In many cases where the asymmetries in the relationship are particularly pronounced, trust-building can be facilitated only by the stronger actor's taking action to instil trust in the weaker side.[8] Trust therefore entails the stronger actor's accepting only the presupposition that the trustee believes itself obliged to fulfil that trust to the extent it is able and willing.[9] This implies that trust involves dialogue between both actors and a normative assumption on the part of the trustor that the trustee is "upright, honourable, truthful, loyal and scrupulous."[10]

In what follows, I offer a brief overview of the history of US and Canadian relations with Cuba to illustrate how trust and distrust have become deeply embedded in these inter-state interactions. I then focus on the post–Cold War period, and compare the Track I and Track II provisions of the US Cuban Democracy Act and the extraterritorial components of the Helms–Burton Act to the Canadian policy of engagement exemplified by the 1997 14 Point Declaration. I do this to highlight both how trust can be understood to exist in Cuba-Canada relations and how it has been manifestly in Canada's self-interest to take the necessary risks involved in trust-building. My analysis of Tracks I and II of the Cuban Democracy Act and Helms–Burton functions to illustrate the fundamental and deeply embedded distrust that continues to exist in US-Cuba relations even as the two countries begin the process of normalization. I also consider the positive and negative roles of US policy in the development of trust, respect, and understanding between Canada and Cuba. I conclude by highlighting how Cuba-Canada relations continue to benefit from the commitment to engagement and the multilayered social interactions it entails. I argue that these interactions potentially offer a validation rooted in an understanding of US self-interest of how and why the normalization of US-Cuba relations might be unfolding.

A Brief History of Canada-US-Cuba Relations to 1989

Trust requires risk. How we interpret the degree of risk has much to do with the mutual conceptions the actors have of one another. These representations are fluid, and evolve through time. This temporal dimension of risk and perceptions of trustworthiness have implications for the kinds of decision-making calculations likely to be embraced when actors formulate foreign policy. In the case of US-Cuba relations, the evolution of these contingent representations is important, as they have loomed so large in Cuba's post-Revolutionary history.

US trade with Cuba had its genesis in 1762, when British forces captured Havana and encouraged trade with their thirteen colonies. Throughout the nineteenth century, US interest – both economic and political – in Cuba grew dramatically. Washington, indeed, believed Cuba's annexation by the United States to be inevitable, but it was content to allow Spanish sovereignty over the island to continue so long as stronger powers did not gain influence or control over the wider region. Offers were made to purchase the island from Spain in 1848 and 1854.[11] Southern Democrats became interested in Cuba's annexation in the early 1850s as a means to maintain the balance between abolitionist and slave-holding states in the Senate. This desire for Cuba was epitomized by the so-called Ostend Manifesto of 1854, in which US diplomats advocated seizing Cuba militarily from Spain if the latter failed to agree to sell its colony to the United States.[12] By the late nineteenth century, more than 90 per cent of Cuba's sugar production was being exported to the United States, and the colony was on the verge of its second war of independence against Spain in three decades. When the war erupted in 1895, the United States waited three years to intervene, by which point the Spanish forces had been worn down and the countryside laid to waste. The US military intervention was fuelled by jingoistic nationalism, yellow journalism, a presumption of US superiority and hegemony in the Caribbean, and a pragmatic desire to secure US economic and strategic interests in Cuba by stabilizing the political situation. It is also important to note that many Americans were motivated by a genuine desire to liberate Cubans that had its roots in the United States' self-identification as a beacon of freedom and democracy. The Teller Amendment to the war resolution, however, declared that the United States would not claim sovereignty over Cuba at the end of hostilities. At the same time, little substantive consideration was given to Cubans' desires regarding their post-intervention future.

The presumption of US superiority in US-Cuba relations was evident from the outset,[13] and quickly codified in the 1902 Platt Amendment, which declared, among other things, that the United States had "the right to intervene for the preservation of Cuban independence, the maintenance of a government adequate for the protection of life, property, and individual liberty."[14] Acceptance of the conditions deemed necessary by Washington to end US military occupation of Cuba represented a humiliating compromise for those who had fought for and dreamed of a truly sovereign Cuban republic.[15] Yet the view persisted in Washington that the amendment's measures were necessary to protect Cuba from foreign intervention – and the Cuban people from themselves. As Louis Pérez elegantly words it, "Washington interpreted its actions by its presumed motives; Cubans interpreted Washington's motives by their actions."[16] The Platt Amendment reflected not only presumed notions of US superiority, but also representations of Cubans as childlike; hence Washington's determination to reserve the right to intervene in Cuban affairs – for the Cuban people's own good. This lack of trust in Cuban agency – in the capacity of the Cuban people and their state to chart their own destiny – had profound repercussions that continue to plague US-Cuban relations today.

The triumph of the 26th of July Movement was aided by the social and economic inequities prevalent in 1950s Cuba and a reflection of nationalistic appeals to a thwarted dream of national self-determination. Within the prevailing representational framework in the United States, where Cubans were understood to owe the United States a debt of gratitude and to exist comfortably within Washington's sphere of influence, Cuba's Revolution and eventual turn to the far left was interpreted as an intentional affront. It shattered complacent preconceptions of Cuba in the US public imaginary: where proximity between the United States and Cuba had been reflected metaphorically as familial in character,[17] it was now reconfigured as imminent peril.[18]

The policy of embargo functioned not simply as a tool of reactionary containment within a Cold War frame, but also as a way to discipline the revolutionary government by attempting to deny it the respect it demanded as a sovereign state. The bifurcation of the Cuban state from the Cuban people followed logically as well: the state apparatus and the Castro brothers, in particular, are framed as malevolent dictators, their political system as beyond the pale and self-evidently inferior to the US system. The Cuban people, however, are viewed with pity, and in this way assumed to be victims of an oppressive governmental apparatus. By entrenching a discursive construction of the Cuban people as "pitiable," Washington avoided acknowledging its problematic conception of the Cuban "other" and the symbolic humiliation this acknowledgment might entail. The entrenched parochialism of US policy left Washington ill-equipped to understand the emergence, much less the legitimacy, of the Revolution. It shattered Washington's capacity to "trust" the Cuban government, and led to the routinization of perceiving US-Cuban differences as a threat. The embargo has not simply been an economic tool that makes life difficult for Havana; it has also been a way to sustain a particular understanding of the American collective self vis-à-vis the Cuban "other."

Canada's engagement with Cuba has always functioned in the shadow of Washington's relationship. When the United States ended its reciprocity treaty with British North America in 1866, a delegation representing the various colonies was sent out to seek trading opportunities in Latin America – including the Spanish colony of Cuba.[19] Canadian investment in Cuba accelerated in the late nineteenth century, especially after the Spanish-American War. The Canadian presence was largely felt in the banking sector, with the Royal Bank playing a leading role.[20] Trade with Cuba represented only a fraction of total Canadian trade – as it still does – though it spiked briefly during the Second World War.[21] It was this brief, but substantial growth in trade that resulted in Canada's opening its first diplomatic mission in Cuba.[22]

As Cuba began to experience the economic impact of US policy after the Revolution, it searched for alternate sources. Canada's proximity, resources, and history of investment in Cuba made it an ideal partner.[23] Ottawa, moreover, unlike Washington, saw the Revolution as rooted in Cuba's social, political, and economic inequalities.[24] It was at this point that Canadian engagement with Cuba came into conflict with US strategic objectives. Canadian policy-makers, while they attempted to maintain a visible and robust commitment to their Cold War ally, also wished to continue a policy that increasingly became perceived as a sovereignty issue.[25] Personal animosity between Prime Minister Diefenbaker and President Kennedy – born out of the latter's perceived ignorance of Canada and insistence upon Canadian acquiescence to Washington's Cuba policy – also encouraged a continuation of engagement.[26] Diefenbaker's handling of the Cuban missile crisis – and of Canada-US relations more generally – led to his ouster as prime minister in 1963. Yet the Pearson Liberals did not end the policy of engagement, and when Pierre Trudeau became prime minister, a renewed push to expand Canadian trade in Latin America took place.

This so-called Third Way strategy reached its high point in Trudeau's visit to Cuba in 1976 – the first visit by a NATO head of government – and although subject to some domestic and international criticism, it led to a lasting friendship between the two leaders and considerable goodwill towards Canada on the part of the Cuban public. This period also marked the beginning of Canadian tourism to the island.[27] Yet little outside of discussion was accomplished regarding Cuba's foreign policy of intervention in Angola, as Trudeau failed to persuade Castro that the policy was not in Cuba's national interest. By 1980 all forms of Canadian development assistance to Cuba were suspended, and although Canadian engagement was sustained, not until the end of the Cold War would Cuba regain any prominence in Canadian policy.

Three dynamics should be stressed in understanding Canada-Cuba relations. First, Canada's Cuba policy has always been influenced by the United States' Cuba policy. Second, since 1959, Canada's Cuba policy has reflected a desire to assert both Canada's autonomy and a particular geopolitical identity,[28] as well as the pursuit of economic advantage in the Cuban market. Third, the reality of the potent influence of the United States on both Canada and Cuba means that the pursuit of these aspects of Canadian policy requires a delicate and often confusing balancing act domestically and internationally. Yet if one is to talk about "trust" as a key and important element of Cuba-Canada relations, and risk taking as an inherent aspect of trust, then one needs to ask not only how engagement has involved trust-building, but why it has been worth it for Canadian policy-makers to take the risk.

Distrust in Post–Cold War US-Cuba Relations

The United States has categorically refused to allow Cuba the discretional agency necessary for its policy initiatives towards Cuba to be considered in any way emblematic of trust. This is unsurprising, as a key tenet of post-revolutionary US-Cuba policy is the destruction of the Cuban political system. Canadian policy, by contrast, with few exceptions has allowed Cuba to adopt the role of trustee – that is, to determine the success of trust-based initiatives in the inter-state relationship.

Two key pieces of US legislation that became law in the early and mid-1990s exemplify the profound lack of trust between Washington and Havana. The Cuban Democracy Act (CDA) of 1992 was built upon a sense of opportunism and a supposition that the economic implosion Cuba faced in the early 1990s would quickly result in the end of the Castro-led government. It was believed that, given Cuba's troubles, the United States should seize the opportunity to promote a peaceful transition to democracy.[29] The Act sought to achieve this end by strengthening economic pressures brought to bear on the Cuban state (known as Track I), combined with attempts to increase bilateral relationships at the non-governmental level (known as Track II).

The CDA is a textbook case in before-the-fact oversight. It insists that the president may waive economic sanctions and take steps towards ending the embargo if he determines that the Cuban state has met the standards for democratic transition set forth in the Act.[30] Among these conditions are the holding of "free and fair elections under internationally recognized observers," and movement "toward establishing a free market economic system."[31] Thus Track I is characterized by a monologue in which the terms of normalization are dictated by Washington; the Cuban system has no legitimacy for Washington, and hence no legitimate voice in its own defence. As we have seen, this has been a consistent theme in US-Cuban relations since 1959. In addition, Track 1 places the onus of risk on Cuba – with Washington offering nothing unless it judges its preconditions to have been met. The Track I legislation, moreover, affects Canada and other states by preventing subsidiaries of US corporations from trading with Cuba and foreign ships docking in Cuban ports from unloading or loading cargo in US ports for six months.[32] Track I is meant to hasten the demise of the Cuban political system by providing an "incentive" for engaging states to reconsider their policies and to starve Cuba of desperately needed capital. Making matters worse is that this approach was adopted at a time of extreme desperation and deprivation for the island state, and has only added to the suffering of the Cuban people.

Track II diplomacy, by way of contrast, involves "unofficial interactions between people from countries or groups in conflict for the purpose of promoting peaceful solutions to international disagreements."[33] Although the CDA's provisions for increased interpersonal interaction between Americans and Cubans are framed in humanitarian terms, these Track II provisions also embody a belief in the potential for people-to-people contacts to develop a Cuban civil society capable of challenging and ultimately overturning the Cuban government.[34] Again this component of the legislation reflects misguided assumptions regarding the legitimacy of the Cuban system – or, from Washington's perspective,

the lack thereof – and reflects one of the pitfalls of distrustful social interactions: a lack of quality information in sufficient quantity. This can be
understood as a function of the embargo, which is not simply economic
but about restricting the movement of people. Limiting social interaction
limits the possibility of learning and transcending enmity. It is also an
effective means of fixing a particular understanding of the Cuban "other"
that does not confound the normative foundations of American identity.

The Cuban Liberty and Democratic Solidarity (Libertad) Act of 1996
(the Helms–Burton Act) represented the tacit acknowledgment of the
failure of the embargo. Indeed, once Cuba was "embargoed," the United
States had few options for further punitive action against Havana save
military invasion. Hence the passing of this particular piece of contentious legislation into law four years after the CDA and its emphasis on
strengthening the extraterritorial implications of the former Act. Title III
of Helms–Burton provides a means through which US citizens can sue
investors in property found to be expropriated by the Cuban government after the Revolution, and Title IV of the Act allows Washington to
ban business people and their families from entering the United States
if they are found to be "trafficking" in expropriated property.[35] In addition, Helms–Burton specifically excludes either of the Castro brothers
from any role in the transition process or a future non-revolutionary
government, and gives the president the right to determine whether or
not a transition is actually taking place.[36]

Again we see a reiteration of distrust in Washington's punitive
approach to Cuba. This time Washington compounded its error by
extending this "distrust" to its trading partners, in this way implying
either that US trading partners cannot be trusted of their own accord
to do "the right thing" and refrain from engaging Havana or that they
fail to recognize the error of their ways and need to be "encouraged"
to adopt the right policy approach. This again is reflective of the historical triangulation of US-Canada-Cuba relations in which Washington has either prevented Canadian overtures at engagement or actively
demanded an end to them. Moreover, we can again see the problematic
functioning of distrust in US-Cuba relations. In this instance a piece of
legislation, Helms–Burton, that faced significant opposition was passed
into law as a result of fundamental miscalculations on the part of the
Clinton administration.[37] This, I argue, is a quintessential case of the
irrational nature of Washington's Cuba policy and how the entrenched
distrust it has brought about has damaged Washington's relations with
its allies and throughout Latin America. The embargo itself has also

facilitated the entrenchment of this distorted and parochial "vision of Cuba" for Americans by limiting their contact with the island and magnifying their reliance for this view upon highly politicized groups such as the Cuban American National Foundation and right-wing neoconservative politicians such as the late Jesse Helms.

Trust-Building, Self-Interest, and the Merits of Engaging Cuba

As we have seen, Canada has maintained a consistent if varying policy of engagement with Cuba since formal diplomatic relations were established in 1945, and has had a presence in the Cuban economy since the mid-nineteenth century. At the end of the Cold War, Ottawa perceived Cuba's difficulties to be rooted in Havana's struggles adjusting to the new economic order – one in which particular forms of democracy and free market economics would be the universal norm. It was believed that this was a function of debate within the Cuban leadership regarding the necessity and scope of reform and the lack of Cuban government ability to achieve a successful transition.[38] In this context Canada was understood to be well positioned to pressure Havana to make the necessary political and economic changes, while also providing needed capital and training.[39] The impetus to Canada's policy was therefore not radically dissimilar from that which informed Washington's approach to Cuba: the assumption of the inevitability of "regime" change.[40] It also reflected a desire to use the economic distress of the early 1990s as an opportunity to engender reform. The difference was in how this change was to be facilitated in policy. Canada assumed that the Cuban government was well supported domestically and should be treated as such; Washington refused to acknowledge Havana's legitimacy, and actively sought to end the post-revolutionary political and economic system.

After the Chrétien Liberals won a majority government in 1993, the pace and scope of Canada's engagement with Cuba began to increase.[41] Canadian development assistance was reinstituted in 1994, and by 1995 Canada had become Cuba's largest trading partner. Then-foreign minister André Ouellet argued that it was in Canada's self-interest to reduce hemispheric tension by engaging diplomatically with Havana to achieve what appeared to be a nascent peaceful transition.[42] There was logic in Ottawa's fear of destabilizing the Cuban government, insofar as it might also destabilize the region. Dialogue and an incremental approach were believed to be the best means of achieving Cuba's sociopolitical transformation – yet Cuban policy-makers repeatedly have proved unreceptive to foreign interventions in their domestic politics – regardless of the form they take.[43]

Moreover, this more robust engagement with Cuba occurred as Canada's biggest trading partner was ratcheting up its attempt to isolate Havana and punish those who chose to engage with it. The pressure on Canadian policy that emerged as a result of Helms–Burton had the ironic effect of strengthening Canada's commitment to engagement with Cuba. As Julie Sagebien argues, "[o]pposition to Helms–Burton is based on its extraterritoriality, not on Cuba-Canada solidarity. Helms–Burton has, unfortunately, had a perverse effect – it has pushed Canadian policy over to the Cubans' anti-American camp and it has narrowed the leeway of policy options for the Canadian government."[44] Although Sagabien rightly notes the self-interest in Canada's policy, she also inadvertently highlights an ironic aspect of US policy – namely, its capacity to focus Canadian policy on Cuba and its role in providing a key motive for trust-building between the two states. There was therefore pressure on Ottawa to demonstrate that the "constructive" aspect of engagement actually was capable of producing results.

The high point of Cuba-Canada relations in the1990s was the 1997 Canada-Cuba Joint Declaration (CCJD) on Cooperation on Political, Social and Economic Issues. The CCJD, which emerged out of a visit to Cuba by Ouellet's successor, Lloyd Axworthy, in January 1997, contained fourteen initiatives broadening and deepening the two countries' bilateral relations. As Michael Bell et al. note, "the first five [initiatives, in particular] constituted a significant expansion and diversification of the bilateral relationship."[45] These areas were sensitive for Cuba, and represented a breakthrough in cooperation between the two states.[46] The CCJD offered Canada an opportunity to share its expertise and experience with Cuba while providing a more intimate glimpse into areas of Cuban political life previously hidden from view.[47] The CCJD also reflected a desire on the part of Cuban policy-makers to enhance political and economic ties between the two nations. These ties were valuable in providing investment, technical expertise, and political support in the face of increasingly punitive US policy initiatives.[48] The CCJD also avoided – to a certain extent – the impression of Canadian paternalism regarding Cuba and its policies, although Cuban officials made it clear that Canada "is not for us a teacher that gives us orders or certifies or decertifies us."[49]

The CCJD is a case study in trust-building, as Canada took a risk in publicly committing to an agreement that did not bind Cuba to particular behavioural outcomes, but, rather, showed a willingness to trust that Cuba would also take Canada's interests into account. It was understood that implementing the declaration would be difficult for Cuba – particularly in areas pertaining to human rights. Consequently Cuba's progress in implementing the agreement was expected to be incremental and sporadic – indeed, this gradual implementation was possible only because of the oversight incorporated into the CCJD. Cuba viewed the agreement in pragmatic terms; Foreign Minister Axworthy seemed to concur when he characterized it as "a start ... a work in progress."[50]

The US attitude towards the initiative was hostile, believing it conferred legitimacy on the "Castro regime" and gave it breathing space to endure in the face of US sanctions.[51] The Clinton administration and key elements in Congress wanted a more aggressive emphasis on human rights and a commitment to democratic reforms.[52] This was consistent with Washington's preferred policy approach of before-the-fact oversight – itself emblematic of the distrust of Cuba held by US policy-makers. In contrast, Canada's after-the-fact oversight was undertaken by the Department of Foreign Affairs and International Trade (DFAIT), which essentially sought to monitor progress on the various points itemized in the declaration. DFAIT clustered the fourteen points into three separate groups according to their political sensitivity in Havana, which reflected the empathy and trust Ottawa was willing to give its Cuban counterparts. DFAIT found progress on all but one point in the least sensitive grouping, that pertaining to joint research and cooperation in health and environmental projects. On issues in the second grouping, Cuba signed a bilateral sports agreement and four basic conventions on international terrorism, and renewed the anti-hijacking agreement.[53] On the most sensitive elements of the CCJD, Bell et al. explain:

> Items 1 to 5 of the CCJD were the most difficult, but these had always been things that Canada believed would take more time. Cuba, however, was being very cautious, but the Canadian side was encouraged nonetheless. A draft of the Umbrella Dialogue Fund Memorandum of Understanding was close to completion. A copy of the Hathaway Report on legal and judicial cooperation had been given to the Cubans. Parliamentary technical team visits were under way. The Citizens' Complaints Commission proceeded slowly. Canada was pushing for a follow up visit by [Max]

Yalden's successor at the Canadian Human Rights Commission, but Cuba was delaying its response. However, the visit of former British Columbia Ombudsman Stephen Owen was approved for February.[54]

Although the achievement of the CCJD does not seem as significant in retrospect, given how quickly Cuba-Canada relations cooled after 1997, it can be seen as validating Canadian trust-building via engagement for three reasons.[55] First, it did achieve real progress in bilateral relations, which other states noticed. Among other things it encouraged others, including the European Union, to engage more robustly with Cuba.[56] This, in turn, served Canada's national self-interest insofar as it reduced Canada's exposure to Helms–Burton's extraterritorial measures by effectively spreading the geopolitical scope of their potential impact. Second, in Latin America, the CCJD promoted a distinct Canadian identity positively juxtaposed with that of the United States. This promotion of a particular conception of Canada's "collective self" has been an ongoing aspect of Canadian foreign policy since 1945; it also functions to support broader, transformative, systemic goals consistent with Canada's interest as a relatively small trade-dependent nation. Finally, the robust commitment to engage – although premised upon commitments similar to those of US policy – allowed Cuba-Canada interactions to grow at the substate level, which have continued to develop even as other actors, such as China and Venezuela, have become larger players than Canada in Cuba's trade portfolio (see Table 6.1).

This is the final irony of the effect of US policy on Cuba-Canada relations in this period: by increasing economic and political pressure on Cuba during a time of profound weakness, it created a context in which both Cuba and Canada had a greater incentive to take risks in their engagement with each other. The relative success of Canada's engagement served to further undermine US policy by encouraging others to treat Cuba in a similar fashion. Finally, the extremely punitive nature of US policy in this period encouraged a remarkable resourcefulness on the part of the Cuban people and the Cuban government. It contributed to Havana's desire to diversify its trading relationships strategically, and in this way encouraged diplomatic innovations such as medical diplomacy with Venezuela, whereby Cuba's medical expertise was used in exchange for much-needed petroleum.

Table 6.1. Total Merchandise Trade with Selected Countries, Cuba, 2012

Trading partner	Value (millions of Cuban pesos)
Venezuela	8,562,849
China	1,695,899
Spain	1,156,085
Canada	938,294
Netherlands	791,811
Brazil	756,230
United States	509,047
Mexico	510,611

Source: Cuba, Oficina Nacional de Estadistícas e Información, "Trade in Goods in Selected Countries and Geographical Areas" (Havana, 2013), available online at http://www.one.cu/aec2012/esp/20080618_tabla_cuadro.htm, accessed 3 June 2014.

Why Value Cuba-Canada Trust-Building?

State-to-state interactions are key in discussing trust-building, but it is also important to consider the trusting relationships facilitated at the substate level. The complexity of Cuba-Canada social interactions is such that their outcome is not easily discernible. What one can say is that there has been real value for both states in pursuing more amicable and trusting relations because of the possibilities created by person-to-person engagements. In the period since the CCJD, much has happened to transform Canada's footprint in Cuba. As we have seen, Canada's share of merchandise trade has declined relative to others, and now ranks behind that of Venezuela, China, and Spain.[57] Canadians continue to travel to Cuba in increasing numbers, both in absolute terms and as a percentage of total tourist arrivals,[58] despite growing public and media criticism of Cuba. Heather Nicol notes that Canadian media accounts of Cuba since the late 1990s have adopted an increasingly anti-Castro tone (see the chapter by Olga Rosa González Martín in this volume). These accounts are partly the result of increased attention to and familiarity with Cuba, but they also reflect public US criticism of Canada's Cuba policy. As Nicol argues, "[s]ensitive, perhaps, to American criticisms of the Chrétien visit, the Canadian press began to adopt a more aggressively anti-Castro rhetoric. Some newspaper editorials claimed that Canada was oblivious to human rights violations in Cuba and that the government policy of constructive engagement had failed."[59]

These broad-based encounters are also having an impact on Cuba-Canada business relations. As former Canadian ambassador Mark

Entwistle argues, Ottawa has often been guilty of frustrating Canadian exporters to Cuba. In effect, more often than not, Canadian businesses have had to support themselves as they try to secure access to and thrive in the Cuban market.[60]

Cuba miraculously has managed to maintain extraordinarily high ratings in the United Nations Human Development Index, despite the economic readjustments of the past twenty years and the most recent global financial meltdown. In the 2013 *United Nations Human Development Report*, Cuba ranked fifty-ninth in the world, just missing out on "very high human development" ranking.[61] Only Argentina, Chile, and Uruguay ranked higher in Latin America. Cuba's highly educated and literate workforce is also reflected in its health and biotechnology sector. Currently Canada's International Development Research Centre and Queen's University are cosponsoring with the Swiss Agency for Development and Cooperation a program involving Cuba worth more than $1 million. In Cuba, researchers are studying the country's health system, which distinguishes itself from that of Canada in its high levels of community participation. They hope to use Cuba's approach to health care as a template to help more people in the Global South receive essential services.[62]

The Cuba-Canada relationship has also facilitated academic exchanges, of which this author has been a part. Cuban academics can travel to Canada much more easily – though there are still difficulties – than they can to the United States. As Sheryl Lutjens points out, only since the Obama administration took office has there been a tentative move to open the United States to increased academic interaction with Cuba.[63] She notes that Marazul Charters sent three thousand people to Cuba for non-family travel in 2009 – up from two thousand the year previously.[64] The US embargo and lack of trust at the inter-state level has also harmed US and Cuban academic projects, with US academics often bewildered when seemingly straightforward initiatives collapse. As Milagros Martínez Reinosa explains, this is often due to the inability of US academics to comprehend that it is not they whom the Cuban government distrusts, but the ends to which the US government might use their projects' results.[65] Conversely, the Clinton administration's policy of allowing student exchanges with Cuba was stunningly popular – by 2004, Cuba was one of the top fifteen destinations for US students studying abroad.[66] Not only did these students receive an exceptional education; the experience of being in Cuba also had a profound impact on how they viewed the country and its people.

As Martínez notes: "The young people who have participated in these programs ... have connected with the Cuban people in an experience truly classifiable as people-to-people diplomacy... They see how Cuba, unjustly included by the State Department in all its lists of fearsome countries, receives them in friendly fashion. They are surprised ... to find that young Cubans have much more in common with them than they have imagined."[67]

As a result of the "Commission for Assistance to a Free Cuba," however, these initiatives were severely curtailed by 2005.[68] Lutjens notes that, in 2012, permits continued to be denied to Cuban academics seeking to enter the United States, while US doctors were prevented from attending an international conference on orthopedics in Havana.[69] What we see here is evidence of routinized competitive behaviour born out of deep-seated and misguided distrust. The benefits that accrued to Americans and Cubans when greater interactions have been allowed have been offset by the continuing US enmity to the existence of Cuban difference. The good faith negotiations and confidence-building measures that preceded the decision announced on 17 December 2014 by the US and Cuban heads of state were a necessary first step for any kind of trust to emerge, and with that the possibility of fruitful and mutually beneficial engagement.

Conclusions: Cuba-Canada Trust-Building as a Template for US-Cuba Normalization?

The irony of US policy towards Cuba is that, in attempting to compel its allies to adopt its own hardline stance, the United States has provided the impetus and continuing rationale for a real-world demonstration of inter-state trust-building. Triangulation should not be viewed simply as undermining Cuba-Canada relations, but also as productive of them. The kind of triangulation brought about by hostile US policy continues to encourage Canadian engagement with Cuba by making it a sovereignty issue for Canada. The punitive nature of US policy and its lack of international legitimacy – particularly since the end of the Cold War – gives Canada an opportunity to present itself in a positive light relative to its southern neighbour, especially in Latin America. Trust-building in Cuba has also given Canadians and Cubans growing opportunities for mutually beneficial learning.

More broadly, by focusing on the concept of trust – its historicity and its policy relevance – one can gain a much more nuanced insight into seemingly intractable problems in international relations. US-Cuban relations are often reduced to a fatalistic and simplistic problem resulting from congressional politics, lobbying by Cuban-Americans, or economic self-interest. These explanations are not wrong per se, but they tend to sidestep the human and emotional aspects of politics that are so transparently evident in the way Washington and Havana relate to each other. I argue that, in grounding an analysis of the triangulation of US-Canada-Cuba relations on the concept of trust, one can take a first step towards considering how perception, representation, and emotion shape the rationality of foreign policy-making in subtle and often profound ways.

NOTES

1 Canada, Department of National Defence and Canadian Armed Forces, "The Canada-U.S. Defence Relationship," Backgrounder (Ottawa, 4 December 2014), available online at http://webcache.googleusercontent. com/search?q=cache:xHKTlYDI-xAJ:www.forces.gc.ca/en/news/article. page%3Fdoc%3Dthe-canada-u-s-defence-relationship/hob7hd8s+&cd =1&hl=en&ct=clnk&gl=ca, accessed 29 July 2015. The North American Aerospace Defense Command (NORAD) signed in 1958 is the obvious example; other agreements include the Permanent Joint Board of Defence, the Military Cooperation Committee, and the recently signed Canada-US Civil Assistance Plan.
2 I use the term "Washington" to refer to the US government broadly. Its usage normally refers to policy or approaches that have been consistent over a long period and span many administrations.
3 Aaron M. Hoffman, "A Conceptualization of Trust in International Relations," *European Journal of International Relations* 8, no. 3 (2002): 377.
4 Ibid., 378. Hoffman argues that intensity refers to the strength of an actor's perception of trustworthiness in others, while intensity refers to the discretion trustors grant trustees over their interests.
5 Ibid.
6 Ibid., 390.
7 Ibid., 378.
8 Deborah Welch Larson, "Trust and Missed Opportunities in International Relations," *Political Psychology* 18, no. 3 (1997): 727.
9 Hoffman, "Conceptualization of Trust in International Relations," 381.
10 Ibid.

11 Louis A. Pérez, *The War of 1898: The United States and Cuba in History and Historiography* (Chapel Hill: University of North Carolina Press, 1998), 5. President James Polk offered $100 million in 1848; six years later, President Franklin Pierce upped the amount to $130 million.

12 Lars Schoultz, *Beneath the United States: A History of US Policy toward Latin America* (Cambridge. MA: Harvard University Press, 1998), 35.

13 Louis A. Pérez, *Cuba in the American Imagination: Metaphor and the Imperial Ethos* (Chapel Hill: University of North Carolina Press, 2008).

14 United States, Library of Congress, Hispanic Division, "Teller and Platt Amendments" (Washington, DC, n.d.), available online at http://www.loc. gov/rr/hispanic/1898/teller.html, accessed 29 July 2015.

15 Lester D. Langley, *The Cuban Policy of the United States: A Brief History* (New York: John Wiley & Sons, 1968), 125. Langley notes that Washington turned a deaf ear to Cuban protests against the Platt Amendment's provisions regarding Cuban sovereignty; the Cuban delegation felt compelled to accept the cession of naval bases and the right of US military intervention as preferable to the likely continuation of military occupation.

16 Pérez, *Cuba in the American Imagination*, 182.

17 Familial in the sense of paternalism, with the United States as the dominant patriarchal figure in the relationship.

18 Pérez, *Cuba in the American Imagination*, 253.

19 Raúl Rodríguez Rodríguez, "Canada, the United States and Cuba between 1959 and 1962: The Triangular Relation as Seen in Cuban Diplomatic History," Working Paper (Cambridge, MA: Harvard University, Cuban Studies Program, 2010), 11.

20 Ibid., 13.

21 Michael Bell et al., "Back to the Future? Canada's Experience with Constructive Engagement in Cuba," ICCS Occasional Papers 21 (Miami: University of Miami, Institute for Cuban & Cuban-American Studies, 2002): 7. Trade amounted to $1.4 million in the 1930s and only began to increase substantially when the Trudeau Liberals adopted a policy of pragmatic trade diversification in the 1970s. Between 1969 and 1981 trade increased from $48 million to $648 million. For further information on the Cuba-Canada trade relationship, see the chapter by Luis René Fernández Tabío, in this volume.

22 Hal Klepak, "Canada, Cuba and Latin America: A Paradoxical Relationship," in *Our Place in the Sun: Canada and Cuba in the Castro Era*, ed. Robert Wright and Lana Wylie (Toronto: University of Toronto Press, 2009), 26.

23 Rodríguez, "Canada, the United States and Cuba," 3.

24 Ibid., 40.

25 Dennis Molinaro, "Calculated Diplomacy: John Diefenbaker and the Origins of Canada's Cuba Policy," in Wright and Wylie, *Our Place in the Sun*, 90. Molinaro argues that the hostile relationship between Kennedy and Diefenbaker played a decisive role in making engagement an issue pertinent to Canadian nationalism and sovereignty – the implication for Molinaro being that, had Nixon beat Kennedy, Canada might well have joined the embargo.

26 Ibid., 89.

27 Klepak, "Canada, Cuba and Latin America," 29.

28 Lana Wylie, *Perceptions of Cuba: Canadian and American Policies in Comparative Perspective* (Toronto: University of Toronto Press, 2010). That engagement with Cuba has become a foundational commitment in Canadian foreign policy is evident by the fact that successive Conservative and Liberal majority and minority governments have sustained it. Engagement with Cuba has been informed by, and has come to epitomize many aspects of, Canadian identity.

29 Cuba Democracy Act, sec. 6001 (6), available online at http://www.treasury.gov/resource-center/sanctions/Documents/cda.pdf, accessed 29 July 2015.

30 Ibid., sec. 6006.

31 Ibid.

32 Ibid., sec. 6005.

33 James G. Blight and Philip Brenner, *Sad and Luminous Days: Cuba's Struggle with the Superpowers after the Missile Crisis* (Lanham, MD: Rowman & Littlefield, 2007), 170.

34 Cuba Democracy Act, sec. 6004, g.

35 Cuban Liberty and Democratic Solidarity (Libertad) Act of 1996, title III, sec. 302; title IV, sec. 401, available online at http://www.treasury.gov/resource-center/sanctions/Documents/libertad.pdf, accessed 29 July 2015.

36 Ibid., title II, sec. 205–7.

37 Richard Gott, *Cuba: A New History* (New Haven, CT: Yale University Press, 2005), 303–7. The key factor in these dual miscalculations was the shooting down of two small aircraft operated by the Jose Basulto–led "Brothers to the Rescue." Despite Cuban protests, Washington failed to appreciate the seriousness with which Havana took the overflights. For its part, the extreme and violent Cuban response grossly underestimated not only Washington's reaction, but also that of the US public writ large. Gott notes that the exporters and many policy-makers – including the president – felt the legislation self-defeating.

38 Bell et al., "Back to the Future?" 14.

39 Ibid., 15.
40 Calum McNeil, "To Engage or Not to Engage: An (a)ffective Argument in Favour of a Policy of Engagement with Cuba," *Canadian Foreign Policy Journal* 16, no. 1 (2010): 155–7.
41 Cristina Warren, "Canada's Policy of Constructive Engagement with Cuba: Past, Present and Future," Background Briefing (Ottawa: Canadian Foundation for the Americas, 2003), 2. Then-foreign minister André Ouellet sought more robust Canadian involvement in Cuba; this was to be achieved by more high-level visits, a renewal of aid, and a more vocal opposition to the US approach to Cuba in international forums.
42 Bell et al., "Back to the Future?" 16.
43 Klepak, "Canada, Cuba and Latin America," 33–4; Mark Entwistle, "Canada-Cuba Relations: A Multiple-Personality Foreign Policy," in Wright and Wylie, *Our Place in the Sun*, 292.
44 Julia Sagebien, *Canadians in Cuba: Getting to Know Each Other Better* (Halifax: Dalhousie University, Centre for International Business Studies, 1998), 71.
45 Bell et al., "Back to the Future?" 17.
46 Ibid., 18.
47 Ibid.
48 Peter McKenna and John M. Kirk, "Canadian-Cuban Relations: Muddling Through the 'Special Period,'" in Wright and Wylie, *Our Place in the Sun*, 184–5.
49 Robert Wright, "'Northern Ice': Jean Chrétien and the Failure of Constructive Engagement in Cuba," in Wright and Wylie, *Our Place in the Sun*, 204.
50 Ibid., 202.
51 Wylie, *Perceptions of Cuba*, 57.
52 Bell et al., "Back to the Future?" 19.
53 Ibid., 18.
54 Ibid., 20.
55 Warren, "Canada's Policy of Constructive Engagement," 7–8. Ministerial visits were suspended in 1999 and the relationship did not begin to "warm" again until 2002 – by which point Ottawa was focusing more on securing Canada's commercial interests.
56 Bell et al., "Back to the Future?" 17.
57 Entwistle, "Canada-Cuba Relations," 286.
58 Cuba, Oficina Nacional de Estadístícas e Información, "Trade in Goods in Selected Countries and Geographical Areas" (Havana, 2013), available online at http://www.one.cu/aec2012/esp/20080618_tabla_cuadro.htm, accessed 3 June 2014. Between January and August 2013, Canadians

accounted for 41 per cent of all tourists visiting Cuba. A total of 660,384 Canadians travelled to Cuba in 2007; by 2012 that number had increased to 1,071,696.

59 Heather N. Nicol, "Canadian-Cuba Relations: An Ambivalent Media and Policy," *Canadian Foreign Policy Journal* 16, no. 1 (2010): 104.

60 Entwistle, "Canada-Cuba Relations," 287.

61 United Nations Development Programme, "Summary Human Development Report 2013" (New York: UNDP, 2013), 15, available online at http://hdr.undp.org/sites/default/files/hdr2013_en_summary.pdf, accessed 29 July 2015.

62 Canada, International Development Research Centre, "IDRC in Cuba" (Ottawa, n.d.), available online at http://www.idrc.ca/EN/Documents/Cuba-eng.pdf, accessed 29 July 2015.

63 Sheryl Lutjens, "The Subject(s) of Academic and Cultural Exchange," in *Debating U.S.-Cuban Relations: Shall We Play Ball?* ed. Jorge I. Domínguez, Rafael Hernández, and Lorena G. Barberia (New York: Routledge, 2012), 226.

64 Ibid., 227.

65 Milagros Martínez Reinosa, "Academic Diplomacy: Cultural Exchange between Cuba and the United States," in Domínguez, Hernández, and Barberia, *Debating U.S.-Cuban Relations*, 243.

66 Ibid., 245.

67 Ibid.

68 Ibid.

69 Lutjens, "Subject(s) of Academic and Cultural Exchange," 227.

7 Cuba-Canada Economic Relations: The Recognition and Respect of Difference

LUIS RENÉ FERNÁNDEZ TABÍO

The economic relationship between Canada and Cuba, for the most part, has been characterized as a prosperous and positive exchange for the two countries and their people. Even so, there have been periods of tension, particularly after 1959, due to the geopolitical location of the two countries relative to the United States. This has resulted in their relations frequently being influenced by the hegemonic power of the United States and its intentions for Cuba. US foreign policy on Cuba, defined in the context of domination, control, and subordination, remains in direct conflict with the fundamental interests of Cuban sovereignty and independence. In the growing economic integration of Canada with the United States, the persistence of US policy to facilitate the so-called transition of Cuba within US terms contributes to underlying tension in the area even as the current movement towards normalization progresses. The location of Canada in relation to the two implies that the process of Canadian foreign policy formation will also be affected.

In this chapter I argue that Cuba-Canada relations could function within a different framework as a kind of new paradigm for North-South relations in the western hemisphere in the face of US hegemony. Despite geopolitical and ideological obstacles, Canada and Cuba have benefited over time from good business, providing a stable and prosperous foundation on which to base their future relations. Of note is that the force behind the increasing trade and investment between Canada and Cuba is not necessarily driven by monetary gain in the traditional sense of economic development. Rather, Canadians and Cubans appear to be comfortable with each other at a basic human level that allows them to bypass obstacles persistently set in place by the United States.

Perhaps the significance of this relationship could be explained better as a kind of mutual understanding about the making of a new history – as the outcome of the sharing of a common geographic position in relation to the United States.

Historical Background

In one form or another, Cuba's being in the neighbourhood of the United States has always meant that the island nation has had a certain and particular kind of socio-economic and political reality. It is hardly possible to examine Cuba's current history – neither its economic activities nor its cultural development and national identity – without drawing attention to the historical context of Cuba's interaction with the United States. During the initial stages of the Cuban Revolution, it was not an option for the new government to be treated as an equal of the United States. Upon meeting Fidel Castro for the first time, during the Cuban leader's unofficial visit to the United States in 1959, Vice President Richard Nixon took on the role of patriarch of the Cuban nation to set the tone that Cuban sovereignty and independence would not be taken seriously. As Louis A. Pérez Jr notes, "[t]he affirmation of national sovereignty and self-determination and the demand for control – control over their resources, control over their lives, control over their future, much of which had been derived from U.S. sources – were simply not accepted at a face value in the United States."[1]

This subordination of Cuba to the United States dates back to colonial times, with a succession of US governments expressing an interest to purchase, annex, or subordinate the island as a possession or protectorate under neocolonial status, justified for the most part within the framework of US security.[2] Although the majority of Spanish colonies in Latin America gained their independence around 1825, Cuba did not, and endured a second and very costly war against Spain (1895–98) under the leadership of Antonio Maceo and José Martí, who, among a new generation of Cuban patriots, were explicit that Cuba, as a nation, had at all costs to maintain its independence from the United States. Martí had lived for many years in exile in the powerful northern country, carefully observing the long-standing and deeply imbedded US interest in Cuba. It was clear to Martí and the other leaders of the struggle for Cuban independence that Cuba had not only to confront Spain, a declining power, but also to remain steadfast against the rise of US expansionism, including its desire to control and subordinate Cuban independence and sovereignty to serve its own interests.

As a young nation in the 1870s, Canada faced similar challenges with respect to post-colonial designs on its economic development through both London and Washington. At that time, Canada had limited relations with Cuba, and until 1945 relations between the two countries were handled for the most part through Canada's High Commission in London. Despite attempts on the part of Prime Minister Alexander Mackenzie in 1876 to initiate trade relations with Cuba and the Dominican Republic in the Caribbean region, the British government was more concerned on how this might impact the British Antilles. As well, it was easier for Spain to sell its excess Cuban sugar to the United States, a major market only 145 kilometres to the north, than to focus on markets elsewhere in the hemisphere. As John Kirk and Peter McKenna point out, Canada's purchase of 28,372 tons of sugar in 1895 compared to the 769,000 tons that went to US refineries shows that the United States was already a geopolitical and economic obstacle to the development of Cuba-Canada economic relations.[3]

Following the Cuban War of Independence, the United States declared war on Spain, transforming the conflict into the Spanish-American War, as articulated through a US lens. The United States then began its legacy of nation-building by establishing a military government in Cuba from 1899 until 20 May 1902, when the US occupation ended and Cuba formally became independent. The United States, however, maintained its perceived prerogative to control Cuba politically and economically by imposing the Platt Amendment as an appendix to the Cuban Constitution of 1901. As Louis Pérez Jr has written, "Cuba's war of liberation had produced foreign intervention, not independence, and when the US military occupation ended, the condition imposed on the exercise of national sovereignty had rendered meaningless all but a cynical definition of independence."[4] This included the right to have naval bases on Cuban territory, and the base at Guantánamo was duly established.[5] At this point Cuba became a kind of US protectorate with semi-colonial status. Throughout Cuban history, the issue of independence has been a central imperative and primary motivation for the Cuban government's political and economic approaches to the island's internal and external affairs. The issue of Cuban sovereignty, on its own terms, remains a complex and challenging process to this day, as it is neither accepted by the US government nor can it be resolved by Cuba's succumbing to US interests.[6]

In the early years of their respective stages as independent nations, Cuba-Canada relations moved through different periods of development. Canadian engagement with Cuba was limited, following Cuba's formal separation from Spain in 1898. This was in part due to the development of Canadian external diplomatic representation out of the High Commission in London, not on Canada's own terms as a nation-state; only in 1944 did Prime Minister Mackenzie King call for Canadian representation in Cuba (and Peru and India).[7] Thus, formal diplomatic relations between Canada and Cuba were not long in place before the triumph of the Revolution in January 1959. Since then, Cuba-Canada economic and diplomatic relations have been influenced by the interactions with various Canadian prime ministers, beginning with the level of oppositional influence in the Canadian Parliament and/or the international environment. Later, the United States instilled a set of economic definitions of Cuba that has had both direct and indirect influences on the way Canada views the island. The US factor became an important, if not decisive, element in the nature, characteristics, and development of bilateral Cuba-Canada relations.[8] With few exceptions, the Canadian government has refrained from public criticism of US policy, either by effective action in contradiction to US policy toward Cuba or by challenging the projection of the US in the region, particularly when the issue has been seen as sensitive with respect to national security.

On the other hand, Canadian governments since 1959 have attempted to articulate a different approach towards Cuba. Worthy of note is that Canada was one of two countries in the western hemisphere that did not break formal relations with Cuba at the time of the Revolution, although Canada's underlying position remained that Cuba should aim to make its economic and political systems correspond with capitalist liberal values. The general difference between the United States and Canada has been explained as their having very different founding myths, which have contributed to how the two nations approach and negotiate international issues.[9] Mark Entwistle, Canada's ambassador to Cuba from 1993 to 1997, suggests the two countries have "different political cultures, values and self-identities,"[10] which influence their respective approaches in articulating the problem of Cuba.

In a different way than Cuba, Canada has also had to negotiate its position of asymmetry in relation to its imperialist neighbour to the south in terms of size, market dependency, and political and economic power, which has always limited Canada's ability to influence or oppose US policy. This lack of balanced interdependency between the two nations means that Canada continuously has to redefine itself with respect to, and in relation with, the US position as world leader. This, in turn, has allowed the United States to impede Cuba-Canada relations. Over the years, electoral pressure might have influenced broader attempts to differentiate Canada from the United States, so that Canadians can believe they are not subordinate to the so-called American way.

At the same time, Canada's not speaking out against US policy could also be read as ambivalence about relations with Cuba. Robert Wright describes Canada's Cuba policy after the Revolution as ranging from constructive engagement to benign neglect, with the former associated with the Liberal governments of Pierre Trudeau and Jean Chrétien and the latter with the approach of Conservative leaders John Diefenbaker and Stephen Harper. Of note is the adjective "benign," a reference to "the most anti-Castro of Tories," who nonetheless made a point of not following their US neighbours to "subject Cuba to punitive trade and diplomatic sanctions."[11] As Canada chose not to join the United States in breaking formal relations with Cuba after the imposition of the 1961 blockade, the key difference between the two countries has been in their different tactics in relation to Cuba. Canada might not have wanted to provide aid and comfort to the so-called enemy, but it also believed that the steps taken by the United States were not necessarily the best way of resolving the issue.[12] Beginning in the 1990s, the United States used the strategic exercise of third-party intervention to draw Canada into the conflict. Both the 1992 Torricelli Law and the 1996 Helms–Burton Law affected Canada's practice of commercial trade and investment with Cuba, even though Canada was not their direct target.

Revisiting Past Instruments in Cuba-Canada Relations

Some features of the relationship between Canada and Cuba imply mutual respect despite ideological, political, and economic policy differences. By focusing on these features, it is possible to rethink Cuba-Canada relations as a way of exploring a new paradigm in North-South cooperation. Traditional responses to the Cuban question have shifted back and forth between economic sanctions and isolation on the one hand,[13] and constructive engagement on the other. In suggesting a new approaches, however, my intent here is neither to denounce neoclassical approaches to economic and political relations nor to reject ideological referencing. Rather, it is to suggest ways of situating economic and political relations that merge within existing frameworks away from the otherwise binary approaches and responses that reflect dominant power structures, without considering other world views. Highlighting the positive human exchanges that have occurred between Canada and Cuba over time could contribute to redefining and adjusting government policy practices, institutional frameworks, and regulations so as to improve relations between the two countries. This, in turn, could be useful as a lens through which to examine the theoretical basis of the United States-Cuba conflict and the normalization process, which in turn could affect Cuba-Canada relations.

Trade and commerce should not be understood as independent factors that define or promote bilateral relations without considering that economic relations are also social relations. The key is in recognizing that the success of trade and business is in the nature of human relations, for even without official or measurable credit exchanges there remain intense interactions in a social context that can promote basic human understanding. Tourism, in particular, is the primary example in the Cuba-Canada case, but investment, trade, and business relations of all kinds are grounded in the same fundamental human principles.

The US system of sanctions against Cuba – referred to in the United States as an embargo and in Cuba as an economic and financial blockade – has established the context in which Cuba-Canada economic relations have evolved over the past fifty years. As a theoretical approach, the effectiveness of this political instrument, whose aim has been to cause the collapse of the Cuban government, is dependent on "the adherence of all members states to their application."[14] The fact that the Revolution has not collapsed in fifty years is evidence of the failure of the economic blockade, but this is not to imply that the blockade has not damaged Cuba or its relations with other countries. The blockade itself has been highly destructive in that it has both reduced Cuba's economic dynamism and import capacity as a nation-state and eroded its capacity to develop trading partners elsewhere. Nevertheless the result of persistent intimidation of the United States' claim of extraterritorial control of Cuba and its oppressive intention with respect to the island since 1959 have given Canada an opportunity to develop and strengthen bilateral relations with Cuba on its own terms. This relationship might not have occurred had Canada remained in the competitive shadow of the United States, and it has contributed to the relative importance of Canada in the eyes of the Cuban government.

The broader shift in international economic and political conditions has also been a contributing factor to the evolution of Cuba-Canada relations.

The rise of conservatism in the United States with the election of Ronald Reagan in 1980 unfolded as a new philosophy of neoclassical political-economic reforms, which spread across Latin American countries and resulted in a period of debt crisis that has come to be known as the lost decade for development. The so-called Washington Consensus emerged with a new flow of economic integration, influenced by the promise of new free trade agreements that presumed to aid development in Latin America by opening the door to liberalization and the reduction of state intervention in the market economy. This process introduced a hostile economic and political environment against the socialist principles of the Cuban society, as well as other social movements in Latin America dedicated to development and social change.

By the end of the 1980s, the Cuban economy was beginning to feel the impact of the debt crisis. This was not fully realized until the fall of the Berlin Wall and the collapse of socialism in Europe. This had a pronounced impact on the Cuban economy, which entered a significant crisis in the early 1990s that has come to be known as the "Special Period in Time of Peace." The collapse was a profound shock to Cuba's economic structure, significantly reducing economic growth and trade – including trade with Canada. With the abrupt end of Cuba's economic relations with the former Soviet Union, however, a shift in Cuba-Canada economic relations began. Between 1989 and 1994 Canadian exports to Cuba fell as a result of capital shortages faced by Cuba. A reorientation of Cuban exports, once part of a special trading arrangement with the Soviet Union, resulted in a shift of Canadian imports and indications of recovery between 1995 and 1998.

Throughout the 1990s, with the swirl of globalization, the debt crisis, neoliberal structural adjustment, the Washington Consensus, and the new impulse to free trade agreements as ways to increase economic growth and development, Cuba took steps to adjust to these conditions – within the terms and context of the Revolution – which, in turn, resulted in a growing role for Canada in the Cuban economy. In 1989, for example, only a little over 1 per cent of Cuban exports headed to the Canadian market; by 1992, that share had risen to almost 11 per cent. Interestingly, although Cuban exports in general rapidly decreased between 1989 and 1992 due to the impact of the Special Period, exports to Canada increased during that time. By 1998 16 per cent of Cuban exports, worth $232.5 million, were going to Canada; approximately 76 per cent of this amount consisted of raw materials for the manufacture of nickel. Key exports from Canada to Cuba during that time were food products such as grain, which accounted for about 20 per cent of total imports to the island.[15]

Canada was the most important foreign investor in Cuba during the initial stage of economic readjustment. Canada not only provided much-needed financial resources; it also participated in worthwhile projects to support the Cuban economy both technologically and in terms of access to Canada's important market. Because of the extraterritorial nature of US sanctions against Cuba, access to information on foreign investment in Cuba is maintained with great discretion by Cuban authorities, but a leisurely drive from Havana to Matanzas reveals Canadian and Cuban flags dotting the industrial landscape to mark joint ventures for the production of natural gas. By 1999 Canadian investment in Cuba was estimated at around US$600 million, or 35.2 per cent of the total foreign investment in Cuba – a clear indication of the stability and economic results of bilateral cooperation.[16] Sherritt International continues to be the most relevant and well-known face of foreign investment in Cuba, initially involved in nickel mining but gradually expanding to oil extraction, energy production, telecommunications, and tourism, all of which have evolved out of interpersonal human contacts. Ian Delaney, Sherritt's former chief executive officer,[17] links the significance of personal relations with economic growth and stability in how foreign investors need to "believe that they are investing in long-term relations with an entire nation."[18]

By the end of the 1990s, Canada already ranked first among sources of tourists in Cuba, with 276,350 Canadians visiting in 1999, accounting for 17.2 per cent of all tourists arriving that year.[19] By 2007 Cuba had become the fifth most preferred tourist destination for Canadians, after the United States, Mexico, the United Kingdom, and France. In 2015 1.3 million Canadians visited the island, representing almost 40 per cent of all tourists arriving in Cuba, despite a decline in the Canadian currency and a mild winter.[20] According to Cuban tourism minister Manuel Marrero, "Canada has been Cuba's number one outbound market since 1998. Forty-four per cent of Cuba's arrivals are repeat customers. Canada is a crucial market to us and remains our top priority."

Towards a New Paradigm for Economic Relations

The end of the Cold War did not bring a reduction of US economic sanctions against Cuba, but rather the strengthening of the blockade via the Torricelli and Helms–Burton acts, both of which carry extraterritorial

implications. There was a general assumption among the US political class that Cuba's socio-economic system would collapse with the
pressure of these impositions and with economic adjustment reforms
in place to initiate Cuba's transition to a liberal democracy and market
economy. As an official response, Prime Minister Jean Chrétien initiated
a constructive engagement policy as an alternative to the two US laws
that, in some ways, was intended to counteract the otherwise destructive elements of the US position. Examples of the dualism Canada has
taken on in the face of US policy range from interest in the direction of
a peaceful transition, to additional assistance in the form of seed money
for specific development projects, to facilitating non-governmental
assistance for humanitarian aid, and to supporting interested outsiders
in setting up business relations in Cuba. Cristina Warren outlines how
the policy also called "for Cuba's readmission into the Organization of
American States and participation in the Summit of the Americas process," while maintaining concerns about human rights.[21] This could be
translated as the Canadian government's overall preference for Cuba
to take on a capitalist-style political and economic structure, while preserving economic and social rights under the cloak of socialism.

The election of George W. Bush to the presidency of the United States
in 2001 brought another change in US policy towards Cuba – in particular, his rejection of the two-track approach and people-to-people diplomacy of the Clinton administration. The attacks of 11 September 2001
shifted US foreign policy towards unilateralism, militarism, and a neoconservative approach. With the end of people-to-people exchanges,
the practical elimination of academic exchanges, and the reduction of
travel and remittances, the Bush administration added another layer to
the blockade. In general terms, security became a high-level concern,
and the new political approach severely affected Cuba's economic relations and the development of an already fragile infrastructure, but did
not collapse its socio-economic or political system.

At the same time, with changes in the international and economic
political environment, there emerged new possibilities for the Cuban
economy and its international economic relations, including the export
of health services of high aggregated value and electoral results in Latin
America that were more favourable to the left. Cuba's gross domestic product began growing more rapidly, from 8.4 per cent in 2004 to
11.8 per cent in 2005 and to 12.5 per cent in 2006.[22] This growth could be
explained by increased cooperation with Venezuela, by various agreements Cuba signed with respect to the Bolivarian Alternative for the

Americas – an integration process of trade and commerce – and by a marked development in relations with China, including investment, trade, and cooperative exchanges.

Improvements in the Cuban economy and Cuba's gradual structural integration into the regional and world economies have affected Cuba-Canada economic relations for the better, despite the relatively small size of the Cuban market, increased US restrictions due to the strengthening of the economic blockade, and post-9/11 influences of the US media on the Canadian psyche. In 2008, Cuba was Canada's fourth-largest export destination in Latin America and its sixth-largest source of imports from the region.[23] That year, bilateral merchandise trade between the two countries reached a peak of $1.56 billion. Canadian merchandise exports to Cuba, including machinery, inorganic chemicals, and cereals and vegetables, rose by 37.5 per cent in 2008 to a record $722 million. Due to the decline of commodity prices and the world economic crisis, however, imports from Cuba declined by 48.9 per cent in 2009 to $440 million, and included the purchase of mineral ores, copper, tobacco, beverages, and fish and other seafood. Imports from Cuba have increased slightly since then, rising to $483 million in 2013, while Canadian exports to the island totalled $454 million.[24] In 2014 and 2015 Cuban imports from Canada declined to $408 million and $365 million, respectively.[25]

The Promise of Change

The election of Barack Obama as US president in 2008 fuelled great expectations of change in response to two wars without easy solutions in Iraq and Afghanistan, the spiralling impact of an economic crisis, and discontent about US domestic and foreign policy. A new approach to US policy towards Cuba also appeared to be in the cards, partly as a result of pressure from the US business sector – which was then exporting food and agricultural products to Cuba in cash. US agricultural exports to Cuba reached a maximum of US$685 million in 2008, but by 2014 had declined to US$286 million, principally due to US economic sanctions, US demands that Cuba pay in cash (while other countries provided credit), and the Cuban government's desire to diversify its sources of supply.[26] Another sign of change was in the posture of the Cuban exile community in Miami, which was now advocating closer relations with Havana. The United States, it seemed, had been defeated in its attempt to isolate the island.[27] Despite initial expectations, however, the Obama administration did very little to change the United States-Cuba relationship between 2008 and 2014. In practical terms, Obama maintained the main features of the George W. Bush administration's two-track approach – namely, reinforcing the blockade while easing some restrictions on communications, including the sending of remittances and the ability of Cuban-Americans to travel to Cuba. These changes, however, were minimal, and incorporated the issue of conditionality for negotiations with the Cuban government – a position unacceptable to Cuba as it represented a hegemonic precondition inconsistent with Cuban sovereignty and independence.

Nevertheless, on 17 December 2014 Obama and Raúl Castro, in separate but simultaneous televised broadcasts, informed their nations of the results of their secret eighteen months of negotiations to liberate prisoners for humanitarian reasons and to initiate a step-by-step process to re-establish diplomatic links, improve communications and travel, and make progress on issues that were not part of the bilateral conflict. Nevertheless most of the obstacles to fully normalized relations remained: the US economic and financial blockade, the illegal military base in Guantánamo that had also been transformed into a prison, and the program to influence Cuba's internal economic and political system.[28] These changes were undoubtedly positive and opened new opportunities, but Donald Trump's June 2017 revisions to US policy towards Cuba will have an impact on progress toward normalization, particularly with respect to tourism, which once again is prevented for individual US citizens, who will now have to travel in groups through a licensed provider. President Trump's restrictions on US currency going to Cuba's military will also affect the tourist sector, since the Cuban military is deeply involved in many businesses on the island, including tourism ventures. Some optimists see the possibility that the new US multi-millionaire president eventually might adopt a more pragmatic approach to Cuba and eliminate the economic blockade. Such a decision would create thousands of new jobs – one of Mr Trump's more repeated goals – and benefit US enterprises at a time when Cuban migration to the US is already subject to agreement and understanding between the two governments, including on deportation. Nevertheless, no one excludes stagnation of the bilateral relationship or even a complete rollback of the progress made under Obama. Increased competition for Canadian business in Cuba also should not be excluded, although Canada has an advantage because of the trade relations and investments that have been established and maintained over the fifty-year US economic and financial blockade.

Indeed, as the US moves incrementally to new forms of engagement with Cuba, Canada could further normalize its relations with the island. Canada has already conducted its trade relations with Cuba in a way that has gained the trust of Cubans, and the tone of future trade negotiations is likely to be set by Cuba's view of Canada's engagement as different – as downplaying pretensions of transforming the Cuban reality, as constructive engagement would imply.

In practical terms, this is not a discussion about the growing importance of Canada for Cuba's reinsertion into the world economy, nor does it imply that Cuba should compromise its own economic and political orientation in exchange for Canadian trade and investment – in particular because trade, investment, and increased participation in the tourist industry have not happened as the result of a specific government policy. Indeed, this relationship for the most part has evolved by Canadians coming to Cuba on their own initiative and taking advantage of opportunities at the margins of the US economic blockade. In doing so, Canadians have accepted such risk factors as the practical challenge of doing business in a infrastructure that has been compromised by a fifty-year economic blockade, and the possibility of being penalized, in whatever form, by the US government.

Some political advisers might assume that the economic importance of Canada for Cuba's reinsertion means Canada has real leverage to change the Cuban economy through constructive engagement.[29] For its part, the Obama administration – in wanting to reinstall the two-track approach to facilitating the transition of Cuba to capitalism and a liberal representative democracy using more communication, diplomacy, and soft power – itself recognized the failure of the extreme US policy of isolating Cuba. Entwistle reminds us that, "to the degree that political change is the core objective of the policy of either, or perceived to be, it makes no difference at all whether one follows a policy of isolation or one of engagement. Both will fail."[30] Both policies have indeed failed because Cubans see them as affecting the sovereignty and independence of Cuba, which remain key in Cuban political discourse.

In recent years, Canadian engagement with Cuba, particularly in trade and economic exchange, has developed and stabilized despite enormous difficulties. It has been promoted by private business and non-governmental organizations and marked by people-to-people relations at a genuine personal level. These relationships are an expression of the potential for the formation of a new pattern based on respectful relations in a human dimension.

Concluding Remarks: Towards a New Exchange Paradigm

The key terms for a new paradigm for North-South and inter-American relations, using the Cuba-Canada experience, could be formulated based on respect for differences between policies and political and economic systems, legitimated by national identity and history and by the will of their peoples. As nation-states, Canada and Cuba have many distinct features, including different political and economic systems, levels of development, and specific sets of international relations. Other factors have worked in favour of a normal recognition of differences to establish new patterns of relations in a progressive, cooperative, and respectful manner – politically, economically, socially, and otherwise.

Economic, political, social, and cultural relations among countries, governments, and other organizations, however, should not be based on the intention to change the other. Cuba does not define its economic relations with Canada on the basis of Canada's willingness to make changes in its socio-economic and political sectors that are part of its structure as a nation. The Cuban people, and the Cuban government on an official level, might have their own views on Canadians' limited access to free health services, on education as a universal right, or on the treatment of First Nations. Such topics might be part of discussions among governments, peoples, and organizations, but they need not be an instrumental part of the terms and conditions for the relationship between the two nations.

However far the current normalization process progresses, the United States and Cuba will not have a truly "normal" relationship until the United States gives up its goal of transforming the political and socio-economic nature of Cuba. Political instruments to influence the other country's systems, whether through soft or hard power, should not be part of the relationship. Clearly, from personal exchanges to the broader elements of international relations, attempting to influence the other as part of an established relationship is a normal and healthy pattern of human social behaviour – as long as it is not used as a pretext to judge, evaluate, or sanction the other based on values that have developed out of different histories, economic structures, experiences, and/or roles in international relations. Unique priorities borne out of historical experiences and traditions in one society could well be part of the daily lives of its citizens, but deemed intolerable or unacceptable in another society. In the broader history of humankind, war has been used as an instrument of power to conquer, dominate, and exploit others, but it is not the only way to subordinate and change others. Economic sanctions, isolation, and even constructive engagement can imply as much violence as an act of war, and should not be accepted as normal behaviour or discourse within the context of international relations.

Future exchanges between Canada and Cuba should be based on respect for each other's ideological, political, and economic differences as sovereign independent states – on recognition of the failure of economic sanctions, attempts at regime change, transition policies, and even Canada's constructive engagement to transform Cuba. The only engagement that would be truly constructive is one defined and based on mutually respectful recognition of the other, rather than on one that operates within the asymmetric triangular United States-Canada-Cuba interaction.

At a time when the hegemonic capacity of the United States is declining and new forms of relations in Latin America and the world are emerging, it is important for Canada to continue to develop an understanding of, and relations with, Cuba that signify respect for the island's sovereignty and independence and its right to form its own national identity. This approach, though not completely new, could be based on the right of the Cuban people to their own national socio-economic and political system as a model of a relationship based on recognition of, and respect for, differences. This approach would also involve a respectful distancing of Canada from US policy on Canada's own terms as a nation, paving the way not only for the development of broader, meaningful exchanges between Cuba and Canada, but also as a paradigm for strengthening North-South relations more generally.

NOTES

This is an Accepted Manuscript of an article published in *Canadian Foreign Policy Journal* on 30 August 2010, available online at http://www.tandfonline.com/doi/abs/10.1080/11926422.2010.9687299#.VX6OePlVhHw. It has been updated and revised for inclusion in this volume.

1 Louis A. Pérez Jr, *On Becoming Cuban: Identity, Nationality, and Culture* (Chapel Hill: University of North Carolina Press, 1999), 491.
2 Jane Franklin, *Cuba and the United States: A Chronological History* (Melbourne, NY: Ocean Press, 2006), 3–8.

3 John M. Kirk and Peter McKenna, *Canadá-Cuba: sesenta años de relaciones bilaterales* [Canada-Cuba: sixty years of bilateral relations] (Havana: Editorial de Ciencias Sociales, 2007), 15–16.
4 Louis A. Pérez Jr, *Cuba and the United States: Ties of Singular Intimacy* (Athens: University of Georgia Press, 2003), 113.
5 The Cuban government has called for the return of the territory of the Guantánamo Naval Base on the grounds that it is an illegitimate occupation that violates Cuban sovereignty. This demand has become particularly sensitive in light of its recent use as a prison where abuses and violations of human rights have been well documented.
6 William M. LeoGrande and Julie M. Thomas, "Cuba's Quest for Economic Independence," *Journal of Latin American Studies* 34, no. 2 (2002): 325–63.
7 Ivison S. Macadam, "Canada and the Commonwealth," *International Affairs* 20, no. 4 (1994): 519.
8 Peter McKenna and John M. Kirk, "Canadian-Cuban Relations: Muddling Through the 'Special Period,'" in *Our Place in the Sun: Canada and Cuba in the Castro Era*, ed. Robert Wright and Lana Wylie (Toronto: University of Toronto Press, 2009).
9 John W. Holmes, "Canada and the United States in World Politics," *Foreign Affairs* 40, no. 1 (1961): 105–17. Ironically, US policy on Cuba has always been presented as inspiring Cuba's socio-economic transformation, branded with concepts that have value for the Cuban way – liberty, freedom, human rights, and democracy – but laden with the intent to reinsert the island into a so-called market economy and Western style of representative democracy.
10 Mark Entwistle, "Canada-Cuba Relations: A Multiple-Personality Foreign Policy," in Wright and Wylie, *Our Place in the Sun*, 291.
11 Robert Wright, "'Northern Ice': Jean Chrétien and the Failure of Constructive Engagement in Cuba," in Wright and Wylie, *Our Place in the Sun*, 195.
12 Holmes, "Canada and the United States in World Politics," 107.
13 Canada, Global Affairs Canada, "Canadian Economic Sanctions" (Ottawa, 2016), available online at http://www.international.gc.ca/sanctions/index.aspx?lang=eng&menu_id=1&menu=R/, accessed 7 April 2017. Canadian governments, in principle, have disagreed with the US imposition of economic sanctions and isolation against Cuba, but officially Canada does not exclude its use in other cases.
14 M.S. Daoudi and M.S. Dajani, *Economic Sanctions, Ideals and Experience* (London: Routledge & Kegan Paul, 1983), 167.
15 Comisión Económica para América Latina y el Caribe (CEPAL), *La economía cubana: reformas estructurales y desempeño en los noventa* (Mexico City: Fondo de Cultura Económica, 2000), 33.

16 US-Cuba Trade and Economic Council, "Foreign Investment and Cuba" (New York, 2001).

17 Since January 2012 David Pathe has been president and CEO of Sherritt Corporation. According to the company, "[h]e has played an important role in enhancing Sherritt's strategy to focus on strengthening its core businesses of being a low-cost global nickel producer, balanced with its unique Cuban energy business and Cuban oil"; see http://www.sherritt.com/English/Company-Profile/Management/default.aspx, accessed 13 May 2017.

18 Rachel Pulfer, "Castro's Favourite Capitalist," *Walrus*, 12 December 2009, available online at https://thewalrus.ca/castros-favourite-capitalist/, accessed 7 April 2017.

19 CEPAL, *Cuba: evolución económica durante 1999* [Cuba: economic evolution in 1999] (Santiago de Chile: CEPAL, 2000).

20 Francesca Spizzirri, "Cuba's Tourism Minister Says Canada Remains Cuba's 'Top Priority,'" *Travel Week*, 10 May 2016, available online at http://www.travelweek.ca/news/cubas-tourism-minister-says-canada-remains-cubas-top-priority/, accessed 13 May 2017.

21 Cristina Warren, "Canada's Policy of Constructive Engagement with Cuba: Past, Present and Future," Background Briefing (Ottawa: Canadian Foundation for the Americas, 2003), 2.

22 CEPAL, *Economía cubana*, 120.

23 Simon Lapointe, "Canadian Trade and Investment Activity: Canada–Cuba," Publication 2010-87-E (Ottawa: Library of Parliament, 4 November 2010), available online at http://www.lop.parl.gc.ca/Content/LOP/ResearchPublications/2010-87-e.pdf, accessed 13 May 2017.

24 World Integrated Trade Solution, "Product Exports by Canada to Cuba 2013" (Washington, DC: World Bank, 2014), available online at http://wits.worldbank.org/CountryProfile/Country/CAN/Year/2013/TradeFlow/Export/Partner/CUB/Product/all-groups, accessed 31 July 2015.

25 Cuba, Oficina Nacional de Estadísticas e Información, *Anuario estadístico de Cuba 2015* (Havana, 2016), table 8.6, available online at https://thecuban-economy.com/wp-content/uploads/2016/11/ONEI-AEC-2015-SECTOR-EXTERNO.pdf, accessed 13 May 2017.

26 Mark A. McMinimy, "US Agricultural Trade with Cuba: Current Limitations and Future Prospects" (Washington, DC: Congressional Research Service, 1 October 2015), available online at https://fas.org/sgp/crs/row/R44119.pdf, accessed 13 May 2017.

27 McKenna and Kirk, "Canadian-Cuban Relations," 178.

28 William M. LeoGrande and Peter Kornbluh, *Back Channel to Cuba: The Hidden History of Negotiations between Washington and Havana* (Chapel Hill: University of North Carolina Press, 2014), 419.

29 Julia Sagebien, *Canadians in Cuba: Getting to Know Each Other Better* (Halifax: Dalhousie University, Centre for International Business Studies, 1998).

30 Mark Entwistle, "The Measure of a Revolution: Cuba, 1959–2009" (remarks at a conference, Queen's University, Kingston, ON, 9 May 2009).

8 Cuba-Canada Relations under Stephen Harper: Missed Opportunities (Again)

JOHN M. KIRK AND PETER McKENNA

We can't turn a blind eye to the fact that Cuba is a communist nation, and we want to see progress on freedom, democracy and human rights, as well as on economic matters.[1]

Stephen Harper, 19 April 2009, Port of Spain, Trinidad and Tobago

The early years of the Conservative government headed by Stephen Harper indicated clearly the direction of his foreign policy towards Latin America and the Caribbean. For some time now we have followed with interest relations between Canada and Cuba; this chapter provides an analysis of more recent developments in the bilateral relationship. In an earlier publication in 2000 we analysed the advantages of closer bilateral ties and, rather naively, asked: "Canadian-Cuban Relations: A Model for the New Millennium?"[2] We examined the evolution of the relationship, which at the time offered a stark alternative to that being pursued by Washington, talked about the sweeping changes taking place on the island, and discussed the policy of "constructive engagement" then being implemented by Ottawa. At the time, we believed that Ottawa would push ahead, taking advantage of its privileged relationship with Cuba while US enmity mistakenly continued, and while Cuban influence in Latin America and the Caribbean grew rapidly. This seemed to be an intelligent, pragmatic, and practical approach – with clear benefits for Canada. Under the Harper government, however, this obviously did not happen.

Much of what we chronicled at that time remains pertinent many years later. Cuba is again in the midst of sweeping economic change under the pragmatic leadership of Raúl Castro, who has noted his intention to step down in 2018, while opening the door to a dramatically different Cuba. Havana is keen to have increased foreign investment – new legislation encouraging foreign investment was announced in July 2013 – and in this regard China and Brazil have made their intentions clear with large investments and trade credits in a number of industries and sectors. Major political changes have also occurred within the Communist Party of Cuba, where technocrat Miguel Díaz-Canel has been singled out as the heir apparent after Raúl Castro steps down. In Cuban society, too, there have been significant changes: Cubans can buy and sell cars and houses and leave the country for up to two years, and some 470,000 are now self-employed. These changes would have been unthinkable just a few years ago.

In addition, remarkable events in Latin America as a whole have marked the beginning of a radically new approach to development in the region, resulting in a new consciousness about both the region's potential role and the need for a distinctly updated relationship with the United States. The massive shadow cast by Hugo Chávez following his first election in 1998 until his untimely death in 2013, the formation of the Community of Latin American and Caribbean States in late 2011, and the strengthening of the dozen or so left-of-centre governments known as the "Pink Tide," all illustrate this phenomenon well. (For further information, see Rosa López-Oceguera, in this volume). This process also occurred at a time when the US presidency of Barack Obama, in the midst of wrenching economic change at home and major foreign policy challenges in the Middle East and beyond, clearly lost a tremendous amount of influence, and interest, in Latin America during his first term,[3] although his gambit in December 2014 to revitalize US-Cuban relations undoubtedly helped to repair the earlier damage from Washington's tepid response to the Americas.[4] Likewise, President Donald Trump's reversal of some of the normalization policies enacted by Obama has reversed this repair process. In sum, there have been major changes in both Cuba and Latin America as a whole.

Meanwhile, despite the Harper government's rhetoric about its strong commitment to the region, its actions indicated a major disconnect with these dramatically new developments.[5] Put simply, the Harper government misread the underlying dynamics in Latin America's political evolution, the nature and scope of change taking place in Cuba, and a golden opportunity to strengthen bilateral relations with Havana significantly – and, by extension, with the region as a whole.

We start our analysis on the basis that Cuba plays a major role in the Americas – one far bigger than its small population (some 11.2 million) and geographical size (less than twice the size of Nova Scotia) would indicate. This is due to several factors – the extremely successful medical cooperation programs throughout the region, as well as those in education, sports, and culture; Cuba's far-sighted foreign policy supporting the region's right to self-determination and rejection of all foreign interference; the material support for a number of nations in the region (regardless of their government's ideology) in the wake of natural disasters; and the very symbolism of the Cuban Revolution's survival, just 145 kilometres away from its self-declared enemy and the only remaining superpower.

We also believe that the right-leaning government headed by Mr Harper did not realize the significance of this blend of factors, and as a result did not appreciate the advantages afforded by closer ties with Havana. (Another school of thought argues just the opposite – namely, that the prime minister read the dynamics well, but was ideologically opposed to them. Although Mr Harper's right-wing ideological bent indeed had a significant influence upon his policy decisions, we believe that commercial interests were the more significant factor in his analysis.) Moreover, the Harper government seemed unaware of the larger issue: the powerful regional currents that had developed over the past decade – which led to the increased isolation of Canada in the Americas. This can be seen in pronouncements by leading countries in the hemisphere at recent Summits of the Americas in Port of Spain and Cartagena and in the formation of the Community of Latin American and Caribbean States, a regional organization that deliberately excludes both Canada and the United States.

By contrast, Mr Harper's pronouncements on political developments clearly indicated a rather short-term interpretation, influenced more by ideology and trade expansion than by pragmatism – or, we would argue, by long-term, Canadian interests in Latin America. Minister of International Trade Ed Fast summarized this bluntly in the fall of 2013, noting that economic interests would be the centre of Canadian foreign policy, resulting in a national "economic diplomacy."[6] The prime minister showed interest in increased Canadian investment in the region, vigorously supporting mining companies despite their poor record, which has resulted in weakening human rights, the destruction of indigenous communities, and disregard of environmental concerns. Apart from supporting economic linkages, however, the Harper government's interest in developing a long-term strategy for the region was extremely limited.

A further element in our analysis is that Canada has a series of natural advantages in terms of bilateral ties that so far have not been properly exploited. That Canada and Mexico were the only two countries not to break diplomatic ties with revolutionary Cuba in 1962, despite great pressure from Washington to do so, is still greatly appreciated in Havana. Likewise, the strong personal ties between Fidel Castro and Pierre Trudeau – who in 1976 became the first leader of a NATO country to visit Cuba – are worth noting. This profound friendship was illustrated by Castro's participation as an honorary pallbearer at Trudeau's funeral in October 2000. In addition, the sizeable number of Canadian tourists who head to the island every winter – approximately 1.3 million annually, representing approximately 40 per cent of the total number of tourists to Cuba – highlights the economic importance of the Canadian market for Cuba. Indeed, the airport terminal from which international visitors to Havana usually leave was inaugurated by Prime Minister Jean Chrétien (with Fidel Castro) during an official visit in April 1998. Many other people-to-people facets of the relationship bear scrutiny, yet perhaps the most striking of all in symbolic terms of this potential bilateral rapprochement is the fact that every year some two million Cubans across the country participate in the Terry Fox Run – a household name on the island – to raise money for cancer research. In sum, there is clearly a solid basis for a strong bilateral relationship, should the Canadian government wish to take advantage of it.

We suggest, however, that this potential has been needlessly ignored, and we provide some illustrations of the major faux pas and errors of judgment by the Harper government. With a new government headed by Justin Trudeau now in place, we would encourage Ottawa to consider both the broader picture of developments in the region and the significant changes in Cuba today and in US-Cuba relations, and grasp fully the advantages for Canada of a closer relationship with the island.

The Early Years of the Harper Government's Approach to Cuba

Stephen Harper was sworn in as Canada's twenty-second prime minister in February 2006. He was subsequently re-elected in 2008 with another minority government, and in May 2011 emerged with a solid majority mandate. From confidential communications with several government ministers and diplomats in recent years, it is clear that Harper's own role in setting foreign policy was of paramount importance: members of the Department of Foreign Affairs and International

Trade and Development (usually abbreviated as DFAIT, now Global Affairs Canada) often learned of diplomatic initiatives from the Prime Minister's Office, or "the centre." It is also clear that the prime minister had certain priorities in his foreign policy outlook – and they most assuredly were not based on multilateralism and peace-building missions. In particular he favoured strong support for Washington and Israel – indeed, his unabashedly pro-Israeli bias at the expense of Arab sensibilities was controversial and was probably responsible, in part, for Canada's losing (to Portugal) its bid for a seat on the UN Security Council in 2010. (In passing, it is worth noting that Cuba was one of the few countries that supported Canada's bid.)

The early years of the Harper government's approach to Latin America revealed the prime minister's rather limited view of the Cuban revolutionary government – and some rather embarrassing gaffes. On 21 May 2008, for instance, DFAIT issued a statement expressing the government's solidarity with the people of Cuba in their struggle for freedom. What then-foreign minister Maxime Bernier failed to appreciate was that the date on which the document was released happened to be the anniversary of the election in Cuba in 1902 of a pro-US president following three years of US military occupation – fervently celebrated by Cuban-Americans in Miami, but rejected vigorously in Havana. The Canadian statement was released shortly after a similarly worded document was issued in Washington strongly supporting the position of the Cuban exile community. In other words, the Harper government had thrown its diplomatic weight behind the George W. Bush administration and its bitter opposition to the Cuban government. Such support for Cuban exiles and the small domestic opposition to the Cuban government was a first for Ottawa, and understandably caused much consternation in Cuban diplomatic circles.

Was this a simple error of judgment, or did it reflect a deliberate ideological position? Although the Harper government – and it is important to emphasize the influence of the prime minister himself in initiating and developing policy – had narrow ideological views on many aspects of foreign policy, we believe this action was not done deliberately to mark a new, somewhat negative, stage in Cuba-Canada relations. Rather, we view it as an example of ignorance and lack of experience – and as an attempt to curry favour with official Washington.

Elsewhere we have analysed some of these errors and clear ideological stances of the Harper government in its early days.[7] For instance, the sale of Regina-based CU Electronic Transaction Services (CUETS) to a subsidiary of the Bank of America in October 2007 meant that Canadian Mastercard credit card holders belonging to credit unions could no longer use their cards in Cuba (since this was prohibited by US law). Canada does have legislation to counter such processes – the Foreign Extraterritorial Measures Act – yet the Harper government raised not one claim or objection. Ottawa's dismal hurricane relief support following the massive devastation in Cuba of hurricanes Gustav and Ike in 2008 – even less than that provided by Namibia, Algeria, and Trinidad and Tobago – also spoke volumes about the lack of importance accorded Cuba by the Harper government.

No issue, however, caused more tension between Ottawa and Havana than that of human rights. For the Harper government, the concept revolved around questions of civil and political rights – in particular, the revolutionary government's failure to respect these. But Ottawa never attempted to place this emphasis against the ongoing tensions between Washington and Havana and decades of US hostility against Cuba, much less to analyse the prominence of social, cultural, and economic human rights inside the country. Instead, a simplistic, and consistently critical and unbalanced, interpretation was given. In January 2009, Peter Kent, then minister of state for foreign affairs, put his government's position well: Many Canadians "are too willing to accept a candy-coated vision of what life in Cuba really is … Canadians should be realistic … There certainly have been improvements in many ways, but it still is a dictatorship, any way you package it."[8] The undiplomatic tone of the spokesperson for the Canadian government on Latin American affairs did not go unnoticed in Havana. Understandably the Castro government became concerned about the combination of unusually hawkish statements and the apparent lack of respect shown by Ottawa towards things Cuban.

This commitment to western-style liberal democracy and the need to respect civil and political human rights became a mantra for the Harper government's foreign policy. (There were, of course, inconsistencies in the approach, since allies of the government – for example, Israel, Bahrain, Saudi Arabia, Mexico, Honduras, and Colombia – were rarely attacked. Moreover, the abuses of the social, cultural, and economic human rights of First Nations people in Canada – who live six years less than the Canadian average – were also largely ignored.) Suffice it to say, however, that Ottawa consistently criticized Cuba's approach to the human rights question – even though the Cubans were willing to engage in a balanced, fact-based, and wide-ranging discussion of human rights concerns. Significantly both Cuba and Canada were elected to the UN Human Rights Council in 2006 – Cuba received the support of 135 nations, Canada 130. (In November 2013 Cuba was elected for a second three-year period with the support of 148 nations, beating out Mexico with 135 and Uruguay with 93.) In June 2007, however, bilateral tensions arose when 46 (of the 47) member states of the Council voted in favour of a consensus document that, among other things, criticized Israel's treatment of Palestinians in the Occupied Territories, and called for the removal of special *rapporteurs* investigating the human rights situations in Cuba and Belarus. True to form, Stephen Harper's Canada was the lone voice opposing the document.

Ottawa's criticism of human rights in Cuba, ironically, ignored one area where there is ample evidence of human rights abuses: the US military base at Guantánamo. One looks in vain for criticism of the abuses of the "enemy combatants" well documented by Amnesty International and others. Highlighting the disconnect between the systemic abuses and the deafening silence of the Harper government – even when Canada's own Omar Khadr, arrested at age fifteen, was subject to these very abuses – was an extraordinary document published on 1 February 2007 in the *Globe and Mail* newspaper in which six former Canadian foreign ministers, both Liberal and Progressive Conservative, took the Harper government to task for its silence on the abuse of human rights in the Guantánamo prison camp. The six – Joe Clark, Lloyd Axworthy, Flora MacDonald, Bill Graham, John Manley, and Pierre Pettigrew – condemned the human rights abuses there, and called on Mr Harper to lobby President Obama to close the naval facility. They added: "We urge Prime Minister Harper to speak up. He must press the U.S. government to deal with the Guantánamo detainees, and all other detainees held in the 'war on terror,' in a manner consistent with international human-rights standards. He should appeal to the United States to respect the rule of law and close Guantánamo."[9] The Harper government, however, issued no public criticism of the degrading treatment of prisoners or "detainees" being held there.

Bilateral Economic Relations

It is instructive to compare the evolution of Stephen Harper's views on Cuba and those on China, both countries having a single-party communist government and widely criticized for their civil and political rights records. When he first came to power, Mr Harper was a steadfast critic of the Asian giant, criticizing its human rights abuses, disregard for the environment, record of industrial espionage, and regional territorial disputes. Yet following his first visit in 2009 and again in 2012, with follow-up visits by then-foreign minister John Baird and a number of parliamentarians, Mr Harper's approach changed dramatically, with terms such as "friend," "ally," and "strategic partner" frequently employed. Shortly before his own visit to China, Baird explained clearly the rationale for this change in strategy: "China is incredibly important to our future prosperity ... My government gets it and as Canada's new minister of foreign affairs I get it." The minister brushed aside the thorny question of differences in ideology and human rights: "Even the best of friends can have legitimate differences of opinion."[10] After Xi Jinping took over from Hu Jintao as China's president, then-defence minister Peter MacKay and trade minister Ed Fast visited China to strengthen bilateral ties with the new leadership, while in July 2013 Baird returned to China.

This political U-turn undoubtedly was prompted by the growth in bilateral commercial relations. Mr Harper put it succinctly: "China's economic engine needs fuel; resources to power and supply its factories; food to feed its workers. Canada has an abundance of natural and agricultural resources to share with China."[11] Bilateral trade by late 2015, the end of Mr Harper's term as prime minister, was valued at $21 billion in exports and $64 billion in imports. Foreign investment had grown exponentially from $10.9 billion in 2010 to $20.58 billion in 2015.[12] Chinese investment in Canada has "specifically focused on the oil and gas industry, including conventional oil and gas, as well as non-conventional assets such as oil sands, shale oil and tight oil."[13] In particular, the controversial $15 billion purchase of Nexen Inc. in 2013 by the giant Chinese state-controlled oil company CNOOC, despite widespread opposition in Canada, clearly revealed Beijing's interest in expanding its investments in the country. It is estimated that in 2012 Chinese business interests injected $22.9 billion into various mergers, joint investments and acquisitions in Canada.[14]

Undoubtedly this massive investment and commercial influence by Chinese government-operated enterprises moderated Ottawa's earlier criticisms of policies adopted by Beijing. By way of comparison, Cuba has little to offer in expanded trade, and none in terms of state investment in Canada. Indeed, while trade with China has been skyrocketing in recent years, trade with Cuba has been decreasing – in part because of fluctuations in the price of nickel – which is shipped to the Sherritt

Table 8.1. Cuba-Canada Trade, 2009–13

Year	Canadian exports to Cuba	Canadian imports from Cuba
	($ millions)	
2011	462.4	702.6
2012	421.9	539.7
2013	467.6	497.9
2014	448.1	562.4
2015	495.0	520.1

Source: Canada, Embassy of Canada to Cuba, "Factsheet: Cuba" (Havana, 2015), available online at http://www.canadainternational.gc.ca/cuba/bilateral_relations_bilaterales/fs-cuba-fd.aspx?lang=eng, accessed 28 June 2017.

International refinery in Fort Saskatchewan, Alberta, and makes up the overwhelming bulk of all Canadian imports from Cuba – and the 2008–09 global economic downturn. (See Luis René Fernández Tabío, in this volume, for a detailed analysis of bilateral economic relations.) Data from a Canadian government website illustrate the stagnant nature of bilateral trade during this period – see Table 8.1.

Regardless of the drop in price of nickel on the world market, trends are immediately clear: imports from Cuba have been dropping dramatically, from $702 million in 2011 to $520 million in 2015, aside from an increase in 2014 valued at $562 million. There was an increase in exports to the island during Harper's second term, from $462 million in 2011 to $495 million in 2015, but bilateral merchandise trade fell some 17 per cent between 2011 and 2012 alone. Given the importance of trade in shaping the Harper government's foreign policy – to the detriment of other key factors – the deteriorating nature of bilateral trade with Cuba did not bode well for any change in the direction of Ottawa's frosty approach to Cuba. To further demonstrate the drop in bilateral trade, it is worth putting this in historical perspective: during the Trudeau government's period in office in the early 1980s, Canada exported some $649 million in goods (in 1981 dollars) to Cuba, several times more than it exports today.

It is also instructive to note that Cuba's imports from the United States steadily decreased from $464.5 million in 2012 to $180.2 million in 2015.[15] Indeed, despite their strained relationship, the United States exports more merchandise to Cuba than Canada does – allegedly a country with stronger linkages to the revolutionary government. Although much of this can be explained by long-term trade planning by both Havana and Washington – for the time when their diplomatic relations are normalized and the embargo is dropped – it clearly illustrates how Canada has lost ground in its commercial relationship with Cuba, even though Toronto-based Sherritt International is still the most important single foreign investor in Cuba,[16] and Canadians make up 40 per cent of all tourists to Cuba.

Ambivalent Political Signals from Ottawa

Despite the apparent lack of interest in encouraging bilateral trade ties, it is significant that in its latter years the Harper government dispatched – albeit for lightning-quick visits – high-ranking members of DFAIT to Cuba, among them, in early 2012, Diane Ablonczy, the junior foreign minister for the Americas and consular services. It is interesting to compare her visit and the postponed visit of her predecessor, Peter Kent, almost three years earlier.

Kent had displayed an extremely confrontational attitude towards Cuba before his trip, with a clear penchant for megaphone diplomacy. Ablonczy, in contrast, praised the reform process and Cuba's general economic liberalization under Raúl Castro. In Cuba she met with the ministers of foreign affairs, tourism, and foreign trade and with the vice-president of the Council of Ministers to discuss ways of improving bilateral relations. In a two-hour meeting in Ottawa with one of the authors of this chapter shortly after her return from Cuba, Ablonczy expressed her pleasure with the successful visit and the wide-ranging discussions that had been undertaken. In particular, she referred to the "extraordinary enthusiasm of the Canadian business community for Cuba."[17] She was clearly aware of the significant changes being implemented in Cuba as the modernization process continued apace, and she counselled greater Canadian involvement.

Deputy Foreign Minister Morris A. Rosenberg also travelled to Cuba within a year of Ablonczy's visit, and reported similar observations to the Prime Minister's Office. Then, in February 2013, Foreign Minister Baird visited. His emphasis, like that of the previous two officials, was on creating employment in Canada – again highlighting how, for the Harper government, commercial advantages for Canada trumped everything else. Baird's visit, although extremely brief – part of a five-country tour of the Americas in just seven days – nevertheless had significant symbolic importance. It was the first by a Canadian foreign affairs minister since Lloyd Axworthy's in 1999. Economic liberalization and respect for human rights were key items on Baird's agenda, and increasing trade and investment opportunities for Canadian businesses, and assessing the future of a post-Raúl Cuba were his principal talking points. In our subsequent discussions with Canadian and Cuban officials and representatives of the business sector who had met with Baird, we noted how all stressed his commitment to expanding bilateral trade and his genuine interest in the process of economic liberalization in Cuba. Speaking later in the Dominican Republic, Baird noted: "There is no doubt there is ... a generational change of leadership and we will do everything we can to support a generational change and outlook."[18]

Although the three visits suggested a certain degree of openness on the part of the Harper government to engage Cuba, it is apparent that the government had no clear policy on how best to strengthen bilateral diplomatic relations – and had no particular interest in doing so unless there were large commercial benefits involved. Two examples, in particular, underscore the Harper government's somewhat petty approach to dealings with Havana.

The first relates to the diplomatic response to Cuba's recommendation that Peter Kent's visit be postponed after his rather undiplomatic remarks. (The visit, originally scheduled for May 2009, eventually took place in November, and by most accounts was extremely successful.) Shortly after the postponement, Cuba's minister of foreign investment, Rodrigo Malmierca, who was supposed to attend the annual shareholders' meeting of Sherritt International in Toronto, could not do so because Canadian immigration officials – perhaps in response to the Kent postponement – issued his travel visa only on the very day of the meeting, too late for him to arrive in time.

The second example of petty politics can be seen in the delay in approving the appointment of a new Cuban ambassador to Canada, Julio Garmendía Peña. In summer 2012, following the end of her term, his predecessor, Teresita Vicente, had gone through the normal farewell ceremonies for diplomats, and at the end of June the Cubans had requested Canada's permission to receive the new ambassador. Ottawa decided, however, to delay the approval, possibly out of concern for the fate of two Armenian-Canadian businessmen accused of corruption in Cuba – as we discuss later. This led to a major inconvenience for the Cuban diplomats, who had to wait until February 2013 before Ambassador Garmendía was given permission to present his credentials.

These picayune squabbles were, of course, totally unnecessary, and did little to develop any meaningful understanding between the two countries. But they do reveal a certain mean-spiritedness and ideological pettiness at times by the Harper government towards Havana. (It is worth noting that the Cuban government took the moral high ground and rapidly granted approval of Canada's nomination for its new ambassador, Yves Gagnon, at the end of Ambassador Matthew Levin's tenure in 2013.)

Far more significant than diplomatic pettiness towards Cuba, however, was the Harper government's apparent misreading of events in Latin America and the Caribbean. In the past fifteen years, the political tectonic plates have shifted radically throughout the region – yet Ottawa appeared to be out of touch with the enormity of these changes. Likewise, it failed to appreciate a fundamental rejection of US policies to isolate Cuba from the inter-American fold, a sentiment expressed throughout most of the hemisphere. This lack of awareness can be seen in comments made and positions taken by Mr Harper during Summits of the Americas held in Trinidad and Tobago (2009) and Colombia (2012).

Prior to the 2009 summit, there was a palpable sense of coming confrontation between the left-of-centre ALBA countries and those of a more conservative bent, mainly over the absence of Cuba at the meetings. The previous summit, held in Argentina in 2005, had proved a disaster, and as the 34 leaders gathered in Port of Spain, chatter about Cuba – the one country deliberately not invited – was expected to dominate the discussions. In the end, the leaders retained a certain degree of cordiality, largely because of the disarming charm offensive and intelligent strategy adopted by US president Barack Obama. At the same time, there were clear divisions among those present: the final document of the summit had just one signer – Prime Minister Patrick Manning of Trinidad and Tobago. Much discussion had taken place about the need for Cuba to take part in the meetings, and many attendees were disgruntled by the exclusion of the Caribbean's largest country. Stephen Harper, though, made his feelings on the subject clearly known through his ideological filter: "Obviously Canada has historically had good relations with Cuba and we'd like to see a certain normalization of Cuba's relationship with the rest of the hemisphere ... At the same time, I'm told this is the first summit where every leader around the table has been elected in a competitive electoral process ... but that is not the case in Cuba today and I'd like to see that change."[19]

If the member countries managed to avoid Cuba's dominating the agenda of the 2009 summit, the same could not be said for the 2012 gathering in Cartagena, Colombia. Three headlines from leading Canadian media reporting on the conclusion of the summit and Canada's role at the meetings spoke loudly: "Harper, Obama split with Latin American leaders on Cuba" (CTV, 15 April 2012); "Stephen Harper out of step with Latin America over Cuba" (*Toronto Star*, 19 April 2012); and "Canada, U.S. scuttle Summit of the Americas statement" (Canadian Press, 15 April 2012). In the end, it came down to the stand taken by two leaders – Obama and Harper – whose position on Cuba went against that of all other countries present. Even conservative Colombian president Juan Manuel Santos, the host of the summit, declared it unacceptable to isolate Cuba, siding with the majority who demanded that Cuba participate in any future summits. Mr Harper, however, strongly supported Obama's vetoing any Cuban presence at future summits, again justifying his position on the basis of the lack of Western-style liberal democracy in Cuba. In the end, there was no final communiqué, because there was no consensus. The Canadian prime minister defended his position as being a matter of "principles," and noted: "And when we take principled positions, we are prepared to argue that and discuss them. But obviously we don't have our positions dictated by any one country, or frankly, by any group of countries."[20] Mr Harper did go out of his way to stress that Canada's Cuba policy was not the mirror image of Washington's approach: "We don't have an embargo against Cuba and we don't support the complete isolation of the people. We believe that engaging Cuba is one of the tools by which we can hope to move it towards democracy and towards greater human rights."[21] He then went on to suggest that such a strategy had also encouraged other countries – without naming any – to work towards greater democratization and respect for human rights. As far as he was concerned, "We do believe that the Summit of the Americas should be restricted to democratic countries and that Cuba should be encouraged to come as a democratic country in the future. It's our contention that the Canadian policy is the way to get that kind of result."

The Harper government's insistence that only truly "democratic" countries could participate in the summits was not a new stance for Canadian foreign policy. The so-called Democracy Clause, which restricts participation to liberal, democratically elected governments, had been adopted unanimously by all leaders, including Canada's Jean Chrétien, at the 2001 summit in Quebec City. The rationale was that advances in democracy within the region had been hard won, and had to be protected – although human rights abuses in Guatemala, Colombia, Mexico, Paraguay, and Honduras, did not prevent these countries from attending. To put it mildly, the Canadian government has pursued a policy of selective indignation in its acceptance of "democracy."

The intransigence of the US and Canadian position on Cuba further deepened the differences between the thirty-three members of the Community of Latin American and Caribbean states (representing some six hundred million people) on the one hand, and the United States and Canada on the other. As one former Canadian diplomat put it: "Once again Prime Minister Stephen Harper is odd man out with other political leaders, angering fellow hemispheric politicians by his veto blocking Cuba as a participant in Summit of the Americas gatherings."[22] To a large degree, this can be explained by the prime minister's extremely conservative ideological concerns. Unfortunately, however, he seemed unaware that Cuba has normal diplomatic and commercial relations with every country in the hemisphere, and is moving to do so with the United States, and all of them wanted Cuba to participate in the summit in Panama. Although Canada's position on Cuba's participation was not entirely clear at that time, Cuba did attend the April 2015 Summit in Panama City with (finally) the support of Canada.

The Harper government did explore, albeit superficially, the possibility of enhancing bilateral trade: Ablonczy, Rosenberg, and Baird, during their visits to Cuba, all focused on developing business opportunities for Canadians. But was the government's view of Cuba based purely on Mr Harper's ideological dislike of left-wing governments or on what was perceived as Cuba's lack of importance in the region. It is abundantly clear that the prime minister viewed foreign policy through a somewhat simplistic filter, but we argue that the lack of economic value that Cuba-Canada trade offered was the main determinant in Stephen Harper's relationship with Cuba. (The major about-face in trade with China once Mr Harper became aware of its value to Canadian trade would appear to support this argument.)

The comparative lack of trade potential afforded by the Cuban market – compared with that in countries with right-wing governments, such as Colombia and Mexico – meant that, under Mr Harper, Ottawa did little to develop Canada's relationship with Cuba, a stance that could well prove harmful to Canada's long-term interests in the wider region.

The Corruption Scandal: The Cases of Yacoubian and Tokmakjian

The trials and tribulations of the bilateral relationship were complicated enough without the emergence of the case of two Armenian-Canadian businessmen – Sarkis Yacoubian, head of Tri-Star Caribbean, and Cy Tokmakjian, owner of the Tokmakjian Group – arrested in Cuba in 2011 for alleged corruption. The coverage of the case, the length of time the two men were held in custody, statements by Raúl Castro, and the severity of the sentences, all made this an extremely significant issue in Cuba. That the two men at the centre of the corruption scandal were Canadian citizens undoubtedly aggravated bilateral tensions.[23]

Some background is useful to understand the Cuban reaction to this episode. Since taking over from his brother in 2008, Raúl Castro has made badly needed economic reform the central goal of his government. Significant changes have taken place in this regard, and clearly the Cuban government is attempting to lead the economic system in a radically new direction. Within this massive and ambitious reform program, the problem of corruption is a major challenge, threatening to derail any progress. Although small-scale corruption has been a constant in Cuba for decades, Castro made it clear from the outset that corruption at the higher levels would not be tolerated – and would be dealt with harshly.

To support his initiative, he established the comptroller-general's office, granting the new position a seat on the powerful Council of State, and providing critical support for its activities and investigations. A crackdown on corrupt practices rapidly became a priority of Castro's far-reaching economic reform program: before the two Canadian businessmen were taken into custody, dozens of high-ranking Cuban bureaucrats (including several deputy ministers) had been arrested and given lengthy prison sentences. An Associated Press report of 24 May 2013, for example, noted: "Dozens of Cuban government officials and state company executives have been imprisoned for graft, while more than 150 foreign businesspeople and scores of small foreign companies have been kicked out of the country."[24] The eradication of corruption writ large is a major objective of the government of Raúl Castro, and all who are found guilty of participating in it – foreigner and Cuban alike – can expect no mercy.

Yacoubian and Tokmakjian were arrested in July and September 2011, respectively, and their multi-million-dollar businesses – importing automobiles and heavy machinery for a number of key industries – were closed down. Yacoubian's trial took place in May 2013; he was found guilty of all charges and sentenced to nine years in prison – the prosecution had requested twelve. In September 2014 Tokmakjian was sentenced to fifteen years for bribery and tax evasion.[25]

The case against each man was straightforward, and depended to a large degree on evidence provided by Yacoubian, a former partner of Tokmakjian who later became a fierce rival. Given the lack of an open bidding system in Cuba for the purchase of many goods from abroad, both men often paid bribes, including at the deputy minister level, for information leading to the awarding of contracts – particularly in the ministries of construction, transportation, and tourism. Yacoubian implicated several other foreign companies as well as his former employer, resulting in a major nationwide investigation of the process for importing foreign goods. Usually foreigners guilty of such crimes are deported, so the attention paid to the case was unprecedented, revealing the importance paid to it by the Cuban leadership, and perhaps intended as a warning against temptation for Cuban officials in this field.

The case understandably took its toll on the Cuba-Canada diplomatic relationship. Cultural differences in the practice and application of law led to misunderstandings, with Canadian diplomats expressing concern about the longevity of the process and the opaque nature of the evidence-gathering and of the trial itself, both very different from their Canadian equivalents. Requests to receive updated information from the Cuban government were widely ignored. In early 2012 Canadian officials were disturbed when Cuban bureaucrats and members of the Communist Party of Cuba were invited to see a video on the corruption in which the Canadian businessmen and several high-ranking Cuban officials were involved. The video, entitled *Metástasis*, showed how bribes by Canadian businessmen had spread rapidly like a cancer among Cuban officials who worked with them. The primary cancer cell, as revealed in the documentary, was Cy Tokmakjian himself. The documentary was introduced by Raúl Castro, admonishing Cuban government officials to guard against corruption; it ended with a warning that this example of corruption – starting with a Canadian businessman and spreading like wildfire throughout the governmental structure – constituted a serious threat to national security.

The government of Raúl Castro has invested enormous political capital in its economic reform program, and given its emphasis on the need, as part of that program, to eradicate corruption, an example had to be made. Unfortunately, the Cuban government's lack of subtlety and the lamentable presence of two Canadians at the centre of the scandal were not helpful in strengthening bilateral relations. As one diplomat confided to us, "You can't show a video to all the senior officials in government accusing Canadians of being at the centre of corruption in the country without having a bad effect on the relationship." It was also thought that, in light of the damning documentary, it could prove difficult for Tokmakjian to get a fair trial. Since the men have now been released and a message sent to the Cuban bureaucracy about the government's absolute rejection of corruption, normal diplomatic engagement can be resumed.

A useful barometer of the direct impact of these corruption cases on Canadian investment interest in Cuba was the International Fair of Havana, the thirty-first edition of which was held in November 2013. At the commercial exposition some fourteen hundred businesses from sixty-five countries, including Canada, exhibited their wares. Media coverage emphasized the greatest growth in participation from Spain, Brazil, Germany, Panama, and South Korea, while particular attention was paid to companies from Venezuela, Russia, Brazil, Spain, Italy, and Mexico. Canada was largely overlooked, although fifty-seven Canadian companies and organizations – including twenty-eight participating for the first time – were among the exhibitors.[26] Canada remains one of the largest investors in Cuba, but this is largely due to the major investments of one company, Sherritt International.

Cuba-US Rapprochement and Cuba-Canada Relations

It is not surprising that Canadians were at the centre of trying to foster some sort of rapprochement between Washington and Havana in 2014. In fact Canada has been playing the role of intermediary between the US and Cuban governments for over fifty years. According to some US officials, Canada's involvement in the most recent secret talks was nothing short of "indispensable." Canada undoubtedly was the bridge that was needed to bring the two sides together.

Prime Minister Harper tried to downplay Ottawa's role, however, by pointing out that his government did not mediate or direct the discussions between the two parties. In an interview with the CBC, Mr Harper noted: "I don't want to exaggerate Canada's role. We facilitated places where the two countries could have a dialogue and explore ways of normalizing the relationship."[27] From most media accounts, Canadian officials offered to host the secret meetings – seven or so over an eighteen-month period – in Canada as a friendly and constructive site. It was the Canadians' job to make sure that the face-to-face negotiations between the Cubans and the Americans did not go off the rails. Working behind the scenes, Canada's role was to keep both sides talking to each other – and not shouting over their respective heads.

Canada was viewed as a useful interlocutor because of its amicable relations with both Cuba and the United States. In short, Canada had the crucial ingredient of trust in the eyes of the two governments. (It is also clear that Washington appreciated Canada's honest-broker role, and it has been suggested that Ottawa undertook it at the request of the Obama administration.) For their part the Cubans appreciated Canada's policy, since 1959, of dialogue, commercial exchange, and principled engagement. Although relations between Canada and Cuba have not always been smooth or cordial – witness Ottawa's refusals to invite Cuba to Summits of the Americas and the Harper government's tough line – neither side has deemed it necessary to shut down the channels of diplomatic communication. And the Cubans understood full well that Canada – which has been a long-standing critic of the US embargo against Cuba since the early 1960s – was not going to stab them in the back.

For its American friends, Canada had "street cred" because Canadian officials in Cuba have been sharing intelligence with them on the country for over fifty years. They also knew that Canada's goals for Cuba since 1959 have been the same as theirs – namely, political liberalization, respect for basic human rights, and an open economy – while the two countries have differed sharply on the means of securing those policy objectives.

It is worth mentioning, though, that the normalization of Cuba-US relations could have both positive and negative implications for Canada. Canada might well benefit from seeing greater demand in Cuba for infrastructure projects (trading on its good name as a long-time friend), investment opportunities in certain specialized sectors (such as oil and mineral development, along with financial and banking services), and from sharing its expertise on tourism management. But recent developments could also have a negative effect on Canada's commercial relationship with Cuba, which, as we have seen, amounts to roughly $1 billion annually in two-way trade. Although Canadian companies are highly regarded on the island, they could easily get squeezed out by their US competitors, leading to a sharp decline in trade and investment dollars between Canada and Cuba. Lastly, a good part of Canada's influence in Cuba is tied to Havana's completely dysfunctional relationship with Washington. But as Cuba-US relations take on greater importance over the long term, Canada's leverage in the country is likely to wane.

Concluding Remarks

Foreign relations with any country should be based on the bedrock of national interests, preferably long-term ones. These interests can be strengthened through financial support for cultural activities, people-to-people exchanges, and development assistance. For instance, disbursements in Cuba by the Canadian International Development Agency in fiscal year 2010/11 were some $6.47 million, mainly in the areas of food security and support for economic growth – a modest contribution but an important symbolic step that generates goodwill in Havana. Ottawa also provided $500,000 in emergency assistance after Hurricane Sandy devastated eastern Cuba, causing $8 billion in damages. Such help, however, whether in real or in symbolic terms, has been far too little and infrequent. The Harper government's approach to Cuba – indeed, to Latin America as a whole – subordinated long-term national interests to a narrow ideological position and the pursuit of mostly trade possibilities.

By times, ideology is trumped by commercial and financial concerns – as is the current case with China. Yet unlike the situation of Canadian ties with China – where rapidly growing trade and investment interests play an enormous role in the government's decision to downplay both human rights concerns and the single-party rule by the Communist Party – Cuba has comparatively little to justify similar treatment. (It is worth remembering that total annual trade between Cuba and Canada is less than one day's bilateral trade between Canada and the United States.) The Harper government was uninterested in cultivating relations with revolutionary Cuba largely because of ideological incompatibility. The prime minister had a hard time getting past what he perceived as Cuba, the land of godless communists. And there were those around the cabinet table – such as Jason Kenney, Peter Van Loan, Julian Fantino, and Maxime Bernier – who were equally uncomfortable with reaching out to the Cubans. In short, the ideological proclivities of the Harper Conservatives supplanted any reasonable discussion of how cordial relations with Cuba could enhance Canada's position in the Americas, help secure the country's overall foreign policy objectives, and better position itself for the eventual normalization of Cuba-US relations, including the lifting of the US embargo.

This narrow ideological bent was also seen in several key elements of the Harper government's foreign policy. In 2007, it is worth recalling, Mr Harper offered the Canadian model for the consideration of Latin America, seeing it as compromise between what he saw as the only two alternatives found in the region: "unfettered capitalism and Cold War socialism."[28] Shortly after being elected with a majority government in 2011, moreover, Mr Harper made clear his foreign policy agenda when he noted in his victory speech that his government had a purpose: "It is no longer to please every dictator with a vote at the United Nations ... We know where our interests lie and who our friends are."[29]

Another example was Canada's official statement on the death of Venezuelan president Hugo Chávez in 2013, which offered condolences to the people of Venezuela and expressed Mr Harper's interest in working with Chávez's successor: "At this key juncture, I hope the people of Venezuela *can now build for themselves a better, brighter future based on the principles of freedom, democracy, the rule of law and respect for human rights*" (emphasis added).[30] Adding the word "now" seemed to imply that Venezuela had been lacking in these fundamental principles, even though Chávez had been elected on several occasions in democratic processes since 1998 that had been highly regarded by international electoral observers, and with a far greater degree of popular support than Mr Harper had obtained.[31]

These examples illustrate Stephen Harper's rather Manichean approach to foreign relations. Although there was some pragmatic evolution of his approach to diplomacy over his term in office – as in his policy towards China – his ideas remained anchored to a bedrock of conservative ideological thought. In this world view, support for Israel remained absolute, while a rather one-dimensional view prevailed towards Latin America: leftist governments in Venezuela, Ecuador, Bolivia, and Nicaragua were regarded with suspicion, while conservative-minded governments in Costa Rica, Colombia, Honduras, and Mexico were seen favourably. Needless to say, despite the many logical advantages offered by closer ties between Canada and Cuba, a strengthening of bilateral relations could not have happened under the Harper government.

In light of these opportunities and benefits, what should the govern-ment of Justin Trudeau do to bolster Canada's increasingly weak rela-tionship with Cuba? From the outset, it is important that the Cubans know that Ottawa policy-makers are not doing Washington's bid-ding or acting as its stalking horse in multilateral forums such as the Organization of American States and the Summit of the Americas.[32] It is also necessary to convey the message that Canada's Cuba policy is not one-dimensional or held hostage within a strictly human rights box. Cubans would welcome additional ministerial visits – especially by Canada's international trade minister – although a visit by a rank-ing Cuban government minister is also long overdue. (Other people-to-people contacts across a wide swathe of sectors would also serve to place the relationship on a more solid bilateral footing.) Ottawa could send out a signal by having a Canadian warship make a cour-tesy visit to Havana harbour, something Britain, Spain, and several other NATO countries have already done, or by arranging a baseball game between teams from each country – the Toronto Blue Jays and the Cuban national team.[33] The International Book Fair in Cuba is another excellent opportunity for Ottawa to pursue a "soft power" approach. And finally, given the large Haitian population in Quebec and Cuba's enormous contribution to public health care in Haiti, Canada and Cuba have an excellent opportunity to collaborate on the delivery of health care there. Such simple initiatives need only the political will and inter-est to be undertaken.

Ottawa now must overcome the ideological blinkers of the Harper era, and recognize that the much-maligned Washington Consensus failed fully a decade ago – that Latin America is no longer under the sway of US hegemony, but has evolved dramatically in recent years. As Jorge Heine has noted, "[o]ver the past decade – the region's most suc-cessful – there has been a sea-change in its politics, its economies and its foreign relations. Yet many observers continue to look at Latin Amer-ica through a Cold War lens."[34] Given these trends, and recent efforts to revitalize the Washington-Havana relationship, it is important for Ottawa to realize Cuba's importance, a fact that eluded Mr Harper.[35] A simplistic, ideologically driven analysis of political currents is of lit-tle value in understanding the current complex reality of the region in general, and Cuba in particular. Canada must not let the relationship with Havana wither on the vine. It now has a tremendous opportunity to enhance bilateral relations with Cuba, and to develop an effective foreign policy for the entire hemisphere.

NOTES

1 Quoted in Ria Taitt, "Canada: Embargo up to U.S., Cuba," *Miami Herald Online*, 19 April 2009.
2 Peter McKenna and John M. Kirk, "Canadian-Cuban Relations: A Model for the New Millennium?" in *Cuban Transitions at the Millennium*, ed. Eloise Linger and John Cotman (Largo, MD: International Development Options, 2000), 351–71.
3 In early July 2013 political leaders from South America criticized Washington for rerouting the airplane of Bolivian president Evo Morales (on his return from a summit meeting in Russia) and forcing it to land in Austria on the suspicion that US National Security Agency whistle-blower Edward Snowden was on board. See Juan Karita, "South American leaders demand apology in plane row," *Miami Herald Online*, 5 July 2013.
4 Tavia Grant, "'Isolation has not worked': Obama and Castro signal U.S. trade embargo against Cuba must end," *Globe and Mail*, 18 December 2014; see also Ryan Dube, "Donald Trump's line on Cuba unsettles Latin America," *Wall Street Journal*, 28 November 2016, available online at https://www.wsj.com/articles/donald-trumps-line-on-cuba-unsettles-latin-america-1480372939.
5 See John M. Kirk and Peter McKenna, "Canada and Latin America: Assessing the Harper Government's Americas Strategy," in *Communautés atlantiques: asymétries et convergences*, ed. Dorval Brunelle (Montreal: Éditions IEIM, 2012), 133–58. See also Peter McKenna, ed., *Canada Looks South: In Search of an Americas Policy* (Toronto: University of Toronto Press, 2012).
6 Mike Blanchfield, "Countries with dubious human-rights records buoy Canadian arms exporters," *Globe and Mail*, 9 December 2013.
7 John M. Kirk and Peter McKenna, "Stephen Harper's Cuba Policy: From Autonomy to Americanization?" *Canadian Foreign Policy* 15, no. 1 (2009): 21–39.
8 Cited in Mike Blanchfield, "Canada can play a role in emerging Cuba: MP," *National Post*, 6 January 2009.
9 Joe Clark, Lloyd Axworthy, Flora MacDonald, Bill Graham, John Manley, and Pierre Pettigrew, "Speak up, Mr. Harper – Guantánamo is a disgrace," *Globe and Mail*, 1 February 2007.
10 Cited in Paul Wells, "What about the whole communist thing?" *Maclean's Online*, 22 July 2011.
11 Quoted in Wenran Jiang, "The Dragon Returns: Canada in China's Quest for Energy Security," in *Issues in Canada-China Relations*, ed. Pitman B.

Potter and Thomas Adams (Toronto: Canadian International Council, 2011), 179.

12 Michaël Lambert-Racine, "Trade and Investment: Canada-China," Publication 2016-68-E (Ottawa: Library of Parliament, 19 September 2016), available online at https://lop.parl.ca/Content/LOP/ResearchPublications/2016-68-e.html#show/hide.

13 Yuen Pau Woo, "Chinese Lessons: State-owned Enterprises and the Regulation of Foreign Investment in Canada," *China Economic Journal* 7, no. 1 (2014): 21–38.

14 Olesia Plokhii and James Munson, "Canada top target for Chinese foreign investment last year," *iPolitics.ca*, 13 February 2013.

15 See United States, Department of Commerce, "Foreign Trade: Trade in Goods with Cuba" (Washington, DC, 2017), available online at https://www.census.gov/foreign-trade/balance/c2390.html#2011, accessed 15 June 2017.

16 Sherritt is particularly important in the mining of nickel and oil/gas exploration. In 2012 the Moa Joint Venture project produced 38,054 tonnes of nickel and cobalt. Sherritt Oil also operates three commercial oil fields in Cuba, which in 2012 produced 20,164 barrels of oil per day, approximately half of Cuba's national oil production. See Sherritt International Corporation, *2012 Annual Report* (Toronto, 2013), 6, 14.

17 Minister Ablonczy exaggerated somewhat. As has been noted, Canadian trade with Cuba has decreased in recent years, and if it were not for the huge value of Sherritt's importation of nickel ore, it would appear very small indeed. A lack of coverage by the Export Development Corporation for Canadian businesses exporting goods to Cuba and diplomatic ambivalence from Ottawa largely explain this.

18 Tim Harper, "Baird treads softly in Latin America," *Hamilton Spectator*, 23 February 2013.

19 "Obama foresees positive relations with Cuba," *CTVNews.ca*, 19 April 2009.

20 Quoted in Mark Kennedy, "Division on Cuba ends Summit of Americas on frosty note," *Ottawa Citizen*, 16 April 2012.

21 Ibid. All quotes in this paragraph are drawn from this same source.

22 Harry Sterling, "Stephen Harper out of step with Latin America over Cuba!" *Toronto Star*, 20 April 2012. In the same report, Sterling quotes summit host President Santos, noting that the denial of Cuban participation was "unacceptable," and referring to the exasperating "ideological stubbornness" that had excluded Cuba's participation. In part, the consensus position within Latin America and the Caribbean to invite Cuba to the

April 2015 summit in Panama bolstered Obama's interest in normalizing relations with Havana.

23 For further information, see Marc Frank, "Canadian, British executives face corruption charges in Cuba," *El Nuevo Herald Online*, 29 April 2013; idem, "Canadian businessman goes on trial in Cuban corruption crackdown," *Reuters*, 23 May 2013; idem, "Britons freed, Canadian jailed for 9 years in Cuban graft case," *Reuters*, 20 June 2013; idem, "Corruption trial of Canadian trader ends in Cuba, with verdict soon," *Reuters*, 25 May 2013; Julian Sher, "Canadian entrepreneur who blew whistle on Cuban corruption faces 12-year term," *Toronto Star*, 16 May 2013; Julian Sher and Juan O. Tamayo, "Canada's ambassador to Cuba to attend Toronto man's corruption trial in Havana," *Toronto Star*, 23 May 2013; and Julian Sher, "Toronto man sentenced to 9 years in Cuba on corruption charge," *Toronto Star*, 20 June 2013.

24 See "Cuba silent on Canadian's corruption trial," *Associated Press*, 24 May 2013. In an insightful article, Domingo Amuchastegui notes the commitment of the government of Raúl Castro to the anti-corruption campaign: "Potential investors must realize that the old Cuba is being left behind, and that as part of the many changes taking place, there is now a general comptroller as well as audits, laws, regulations and controls ... Local Cubans have already gotten the message and are now paying their share of the consequences"; see "Raúl warns foreign investors: Play by the rules – or else," *CubaNews* 21, no. 7 (2013): 7.

25 Daniel Trotta, "CEO's gifts to Cubans led to 15-year sentence," *Globe and Mail*, 4 October 2014.

26 "Canadá entre los tres principales inversores en Cuba," *Prensa Latina*, 5 November 2013.

27 Quoted in Campbell Clark, "Canada plays host: Seven secret meetings were held over 18 months in Ottawa and Toronto," *Globe and Mail*, 18 December 2014. It is worth mentioning that the Harper government – no doubt with an eye towards its conservative-minded electoral base – went out of its way to downplay Canada's involvement in the Cuba-US discussions. It should also be said that no one within "Fort Pearson" was willing to talk about Canada's role as mediator between the two sides.

28 Yasmine Shamsie and Ricardo Grinspun, "Missed Opportunity: Canada's Re-engagement with Latin America and the Caribbean," *Canadian Journal of Latin American and Caribbean Studies* 35, no. 69 (2010): 186.

29 Tonda MacCharles, "Harper vows to make Tories 'Canada's party,'" *Toronto Star*, 11 June 2011.

30 Stephen Harper, "Statement by the Prime Minister of Canada on the Death of Venezuelan President Hugo Chávez Frías" (Ottawa: Office of the Prime Minister, 5 March 2013).

31 His sending of a lowly parliamentary secretary to the Chávez funeral service was also seen as a slight by the Venezuelan political leadership.

32 For more on what Canada should do to cultivate stronger relations with Cuba, see Peter McKenna and John M. Kirk, "Through the Sun and Ice: Canada, Cuba, and Fifty Years of 'Normal' Relations," in *Canada Looks South: In Search of an Americas Policy*, ed. Peter McKenna (Toronto: University of Toronto Press, 2012), 170–2.

33 Since this chapter was written, there have been some important developments in the bilateral relationship. In November 2016 the HMCS *Fredericton* made an official visit to Havana, the first by a Canadian navy vessel in fifty years. That same month Prime Minister Justin Trudeau also visited Cuba, and was received by President Raúl Castro, while in March 2016 Cuban Foreign Minister Bruno Rodríguez made an official visit to Canada. Clearly a different tone had been struck in the bilateral relationship.

34 Jorge Heine, "Canada re-engages with Latin America," *Toronto Star*, 22 February 2013.

35 The role of Raúl Castro at the December 2013 funeral ceremonies for Nelson Mandela further illustrated the importance of Cuba in the developing world. The Cuban president was one of just six foreign leaders to address the massive crowd, the others being the presidents of India, Namibia, Brazil, and the United States, and the vice-president of China. Castro was introduced by Maleka Mbete, former speaker of the National Assembly of South Africa and former deputy-president, as being the president of "a tiny island, a people who liberated us."

9 Canadian Foreign Policy and the Inter-American System: Implications for Relations with Cuba

ROSA LÓPEZ-OCEGUERA

Translated by Peter Gellert

In the second decade of the twenty-first century, Canada faces a number of major foreign policy challenges, among them those linked to its deep integration with the United States. These include the structural and systemic crisis of global capitalism and its economic, social, and environmental effects; the growing militarization of international relations, with a pronounced interventionism sanctioned by the UN Security Council and led by the United States under the cover of NATO; and growing mass protests and mobilizations in several regions around the world, reflecting disagreement, questioning, and opposition to such policies by international civil society.

In the context of Cuba and the inter-American system more specifically, foreign policy and strategic challenges are posed by ongoing projects for South-South integration, including the creation of intra-regional institutions that exclude the United States and Canada. Moreover, as Luis René Fernández Tabío, Cynthia Wright, and Lana Wylie (in this volume) note, one important reason the United States was forced to make a diplomatic opening to Cuba was that Latin American and Caribbean states made it clear they were not prepared to tolerate the exclusion of Cuba from hemispheric summits. The long history of the United States' successfully isolating Cuba from the Caribbean and Latin America (with the exception of Mexico) was decisively ended. This, in turn, was the outcome of political shifts in Latin America, including the so-called pink tide, and also of Cuba's decades-long commitment to building links and institutions within Latin America, the location of its most important allies.

Canada, of course, has always enjoyed relatively stable diplomatic relations with revolutionary Cuba while also remaining a major US ally – indeed, Canada at times has used precisely those diplomatic channels to spy on Cuba for the United States (Don Munton, in this volume). At the same time, for all its tensions, it was precisely the fact that Canada was – and is – a key ally of the United States that has made it at times invaluable for Cuba including, for example, in facilitating various moments of back-channel diplomacy. In recent years, however, the deepening of the profound integration between Canada and the United States, including with respect to security issues, has raised new issues and questions for analysis. In this chapter, I consider the costs for Canada of its growing identification with the international and regional policy of the United States, which has affected its image and presence in Latin America and the Caribbean and, consequently, its national interests (see also John M. Kirk and Peter McKenna, in this volume). In particular, I focus on the possible implications for Canada's relations with Cuba in the context of a complex, changing, and contradictory inter-American system. I suggest that the challenges facing Canadian foreign policy in relation to that system – if prevailing trends continue and consolidate in the post–Stephen Harper context – might prove insurmountable and, therefore, existing Canadian relations with Latin America and the Caribbean will be dramatically affected.

This chapter is divided into four sections. I begin with a historical examination of Canada's relationship to the inter-American system. Prior to 1990 Canadian foreign policy in the western hemisphere was centred mainly on the United States and the Caribbean, with the rest of the region virtually relegated to second place. Following the end of the Cold War, and based on the new global context of regional integration that led to globalization, Canadian foreign policy included a shift towards Latin America. Canada's entry into the Organization of American States (OAS), the signing of the North American Free Trade Agreement (NAFTA), and its support for the Central American peace process were among the developments that signalled a gradual outreach to the region.

Yet the inter-American system was already displaying unequivocal signs of obsolescence and irrelevance when Canada became a full member of the OAS in 1990. Thus, in the second section, I consider the political transformations that have taken place in several important Latin American countries since the end of the past century. Without being totally anti-systemic, these movements pursue paths different from the dictates of the hegemonic policies institutionalized by the United States in the inter-American system, thus contributing to the crisis in the system.

The third and fourth sections consider the deepening Canada-US alignment and its implications for Cuba-Canada relations. Security has been given a priority following the 11 September 2001 attacks, and Washington's redefining of global terrorism has imposed profound changes on the other two North American countries – namely, Mexico and Canada. One consequence was a slowing of the level of trade among the NAFTA member states and the disruption of integrated production chains. In response, Canada began to forge further bilateral agreements with countries outside North America, precisely starting with those in Latin America. Such adjustments have not resulted in significant changes with respect Canada's relationship with Cuba; instead, previous bilateral relations have prevailed, with an emphasis on economic issues, including trade, tourism, cooperation, and investment, despite ongoing differences concerning political issues, such as human rights.

Still, two questions remain: to what extent will Canada risk antagonizing Latin American and Caribbean states by aligning itself with a US policy towards Cuba that – despite normalization – remains imperial at its core? And to what extent will Canada align itself with the hemispheric bloc in favour of Cuba – and thereby risk US disapproval?

Canada and the Inter-American System: A Historical Overview

It is a commonplace in specialized studies on relations between Canada and Latin America to state that, until 1989, such ties were intermittent, distant, and ambivalent. For example, according to Jack Ogelsby, despite occasional contacts, Latin America as a region was regarded as far away and problematic.[1] Peter McKenna, describing Canada's relationship with the inter-American system, concludes that, "throughout the history of pan-Americanism, Canada was a more passive than active spectator."[2] Similarly James Rochlin notes that, until recently, Canada has played a minor role in matters concerning the western hemisphere.[3]

The reasons for this are historical, and are linked to US designs on the Americas. US hegemonic claims on the hemisphere, reinforced by the First International Conference of American States, held in Washington, DC, in 1889, were based on the newly emerging conception of Pan-Americanism, in which the United States reclaimed the spirit of the Monroe Doctrine of 1823. Over the next fifty years the United States opposed Canadian participation in what were shaping up as the supporting elements of the inter-American system, mainly because

Washington regarded Ottawa as an agent of British interests. Even after Canada obtained the authority to design its own international relations in 1926 with the Balfour Declaration, and then in 1931 with the Statute of Westminster, the United States resolutely and repeatedly objected to its integration in hemispheric institutions.

The reaction of some Latin American countries was different. Since the founding of the Pan American Union in 1910, most of its Latin American members were in favour of Canada's participation in the new body. As a symbolic gesture, a chair with the name of Canada was prepared for the hall where the plenary session was to take place, but it would remain empty in the basement of the Pan American Union, and later the OAS, until recent times. This almost unanimous Latin American position was based on the perception that Canada, through its connection with the British Empire, could act as a counterweight to the growing hegemony of the United States in the region. This support for Canada's formal incorporation in the inter-American institutional framework, however, only reinforced the opposition of the United States, which led Canada to be even more cautious in its political involvement in hemispheric affairs.

Cuba, of course, was isolated from the inter-American system soon after the triumph of the Revolution in 1959 because of the hostile policy of the United States. The US-Cuba conflict during the Cold War was not simply bilateral; it had multilateral dimensions from the start because of the island's symbolic value within US policy towards the hemisphere and towards the Third World more generally. US hostility had its roots in Cuba's disengagement from the US domination of Latin America – domination already institutionalized in the inter-American system. What made Cuba particularly unacceptable, however, was its adoption of a nationalist political project of economic and social development radically opposed to capitalism. Most US attacks and campaigns directed against Cuba focused on the island's international political projection. For example, Cuban foreign policy was the target of Joint Resolution 230 – signed into law on 3 October 1962 by President John Kennedy – that stated the need to impede by whatever means the "expansion" of the Cuban Marxist-Leninist regime beyond its borders and its "subversive activity" in the hemisphere.

Changes in the international correlation of forces that led to the end of the Cold War and the advent of the worldwide strategic-military unipolarity of the United States put an end to the long period of

Canada's political ambiguity in relation to its full participation in the inter-American system. Indeed, the 1980s were especially marked by Canada's reluctance to join an inter-American system weakened by the clear unilateralism displayed by the United States in successive critical cases, such as the Malvinas conflict, the invasion of Grenada, and the prolonged war in Central America – as well as the continued isolation of Cuba. But with the end of the Cold War, the Progressive Conservative government of Brian Mulroney, differentiating itself from previous Liberal governments, wanted to make Canada a full member of the inter-American system. In the contradictory transition in international relations from the late 1980s to the early 1990s, and in the context of the formation of economic blocs, "hemispheric regionalism" and deepening relations with Latin America became a priority for Canada. As a first step in integrating into the hemisphere, Canada signed NAFTA, along with the United States and Mexico, which became the major axis of Canadian economic and trade policy.

The growing incorporation of Canada into the inter-American system in the 1990s was characterized by its active promotion of initiatives in inter-American relations. For example, Canada hosted the First Parliamentary Conference of the Americas in Quebec City in 1997, and Prime Minister Jean Chrétien headed up two Team Canada–type missions to the region. Canada hosted the Pan American Games in Winnipeg in 1999, the OAS General Assembly in 2000, and the Third Summit of the Americas in Quebec City in 2001. A few days prior to that summit, in a clear expression of the Canadian government's political will in terms of integration into the western hemisphere, Secretary of State for Latin America and Africa David Kilgour declared that "the first challenge that Canada had to face on the road to the Quebec summit was to accept that our destiny, our future prosperity and stability, is intimately linked to the region. This has not been obvious to Canadians. We have directed our sights toward other regions. We have placed greater attention on other regions and made greater efforts to develop our relations with other partners."[4]

The Quebec City summit was one of three that formed the preamble to the launching of the Free Trade Area of the Americas (FTAA) in 2005.[5] This ambitious project first stalled, and finally was allowed to die at the Fourth Summit of the Americas in Mar del Plata, Argentina, in November 2005. The defeat of the FTAA was the result of major shifts in the region, a theme to which I now turn.

Recent Political Changes in Latin America and the Caribbean: Towards South-South Integration

In two hundred years of independence, and even though it is the Third World region with the longest history of integration in the international market, Latin America has not received much attention in international relations. Recent changes, however, in the internal and external political cal policies of a number of Latin American countries – mainly in South America, but also in Central America and the Caribbean – finally could make the region an international player. This would pose an enormous challenge to the hegemonic pretensions of the United States, and also for Canada, which increasingly has chosen to accompany its neighbour in such efforts, as we shall see.

This Latin American awakening – which some in the North have sought to stigmatize and demonize as "a wave of populism" – has seen the arrival of progressive governments in a number of countries. It has had as its main driver the failure of neoliberal policies imposed by international financial institutions such as the International Monetary Fund (IMF) and the World Bank – representatives and instruments of finance capital and its main interests, the transnational corporations. Neoliberal structural adjustment programs began to be developed in Latin America in the early 1980s, although even in the 1970s Chile under Pinochet and Argentina under the military governments became pioneers and advanced students of the "Chicago boys." Under the name "Washington Consensus," an international agenda of structural reforms began to be implemented to convert neoliberal ideas into state projects. This included advocating a reduction in the role of the state in the economy – specifically in terms of income redistribution, through privatization, the elimination of subsidies and social welfare programs, and more openness to foreign investment, among other measures.

The result of these changes in the short and medium term was an exponential increase in poverty as the popular classes saw their social gains come under attack on the job and in government benefits within the context of already weakened mechanisms of social protection. The subsequent increase in criticism and protests was met by public institutions unable to resolve the demands imposed upon them. At the same time, the transversal success of neoliberal ideology significantly decreased the differences between the main political parties, while the corruption fuelled by the privatization of public assets – a true lubricant facilitating agreements among the elites – further discredited politics

and politicians. The gap between the represented and their representatives widened, with the latter increasingly perceived as a selfish caste
regardless of the acronym of their party.

Social movements born in the heat of the negative effects of neoliberalism had radical expressions that, by the second half of the
1990s and the early 2000s, led to the fall of governments in several
Latin American countries. As an unambiguous sign of the strength of
democracy with participation from the popular masses, as opposed
to the traditional political give-and-take among the elites, a number of progressive governments were elected. Although of different
ideological origins, the leaders of these governments included Hugo
Chávez in Venezuela in 1998; Luiz Inacio (Lula) da Silva in Brazil
in 2002; Néstor Kirchner in Argentina in 2003; Tabaré Vázquez in
Uruguay in 2004; Evo Morales, an indigenous leader of the country's coca growers, in Bolivia in 2006; Rafael Correa in Ecuador in
2007; and, in that same year and after a sixteen-year absence, Sandinista leader Daniel Ortega was voted back into office as president
of Nicaragua.[6]

Even though in no case has the performance in office of these progressive governments been without pitfalls, conflicts, and disputes,
all of them can claim clear achievements on the social front – mainly
poverty reduction, raising educational levels, attention to health care,
and defence of natural resources. This has guaranteed them the support
of broad sectors of the population. And despite significant differences,
a minimum common agenda of these governments can be identified.
This includes:

- the incorporation in national life of large layers of the population
  formerly relegated to the margins and outside the social coverage
  networks and official recognition – particularly indigenous peoples
  and *Afrodescendientes* – with policies promoting inclusion and the
  decolonization of state apparatuses;
- the recovery of previously privatized natural resources of crucial
  importance to the domestic economy and the return of the state to
  its role as being in charge of order and protecting property and as
  a promoter and coordinator of development and diversification, of
  the redistribution of wealth, and of ensuring the population's main
  social needs;
- the affirmation of national sovereignty as a key principle in foreign
  affairs, thus breaking with US tutelage – including the promotion of

"post-liberal" regional integration characterized by an emphasis on political and social relations before trade and commercial ties; and
• a national-popular interpellation that identifies the impoverished majorities with "the nation," and links the defence of both in a permanent political mobilization that, along with the large number of elections, is the lever through which the government tries to dismantle the state it inherited from the national oligarchies; in some cases, such as in Venezuela and Bolivia, this process has taken on characteristics of a refounding of the national state through the adoption of new constitutions and other participatory tools such as referendums and consultations.

The most significant impact, however, of the policies followed by these progressive governments at the regional level has been the commitment to integration, not only in discourse, but also in the creation of institutions that reflect new conceptions of the region as a whole. This, I argue, represents an unprecedented challenge for the inter-American system and the ideological, political, and economic fundamentals that have underpinned it – and thus also a challenge for Canadian policy towards the hemisphere, including, potentially, Cuba – in several ways. First, the integration projects are entirely South-South, a radical departure from the trend that prevailed in the 1990s, when North-South integration schemas were prioritized with the goal of creating an FTAA and Canada signed many free trade agreements with countries in the region. Second, the integrationist effort is built on new conceptual bases that go beyond purely trade and commercial interests and extend to other areas of cooperation with a view to social development based on solidarity, and focused on issues that have a high impact on the poorest strata of the population, who unfortunately make up the majority in the countries of the region. Thus, projects such as the Bolivarian Alliance for the Peoples of Our America (ALBA)[7] are outside the total domination of the market. The aim is to raise the standard and quality of life of the broad masses, and includes goals such as the elimination of illiteracy, strengthening family farming and food security, and restoring sight to millions of people. In short, the emphasis is on satisfying the needs of the population as a priority beyond market mechanisms and capital accumulation.

Third, integration is conceived broadly to include energy, a new regional financial architecture, and bodies for conflict resolution and reaching consensus-based political agreements. The question of energy, for example, has already been concretized in a series of actions, one of the most important of which is the oil agreement among Caribbean countries (Petrocaribe).[8] Apart from ALBA, there are other regional energy integration agreements such as Petrosur, whose most spectacular project is the construction of a 7,000-kilometre pipeline from Venezuela to Argentina, with branches to northeast Brazil and Peru. This integrationist momentum also poses the need to create the region's own financial architecture, the centre of which would be the Banco del Sur,[9] to contribute to South American financial autonomy and to promote regional equilibrium, giving a potential tool to the poorer countries with less access to credit in international financial organizations. Also needed is a South American stabilization fund that would serve as a lender to countries experiencing payments crises, thus assuming the IMF's function without its conditions and policy recommendations. In terms of consensus-based political agreements, UNASUR (Union of South American Nations),[10] since its birth in 2008, has proved its importance by participating in resolving conflicts among and within its member countries. These have included the conflict due to Colombia's military incursion into Ecuador against the Revolutionary Armed Forces of Colombia (FARC) guerrillas, the secessionist conflict in several Bolivian departments, and the violent actions of opposition groups in Venezuela.

In short, a tremendous transformation is under way in the political geography of Latin America and the Caribbean. These integrationist projects with a high social content represent a decisive step towards higher goals in terms of the role and place of the region in international relations, which could lead to the formation of a power bloc for the first time in 250 years of history. However, given that, under his rule, Venezuela was one of its main proponents and ideologues, the unfortunate death of Hugo Chávez in early 2013 could have negative repercussions on this integration effort if forces opposing such a policy manage to overthrow the government of Nicolás Maduro as representative of Chávez's project.

Finally, at the geostrategic level, 2011 ended with one of the most momentous developments of the past fifty years: the birth in Caracas of the Comunidad de Estados Latinoamericanos y Caribeños (the Community of Latin American and Caribbean States, or CELAC). This institution represents an alternative to the OAS, since the thirty-three independent countries of Latin America and the Caribbean are also members of CELAC, but – unlike the OAS – the United States and

Canada are explicitly excluded. CELAC is the culmination of a decade of efforts to build an organization to reach consensus-based political agreements grounded in the integrationist process. Its birth in Caracas was not accidental, linked as it is to Simón Bolívar's project for Latin American unity in the struggle for independence in the nineteenth century; it also reflects the central role Chávez played in this process. CELAC aims to represent the interests of a subcontinent of developing countries, which would speak with one voice despite differences and even conflicts among some of its members. But, crucially, it should also be a counterweight to the political and economic hegemony of the United States. The presence of Cuba in CELAC and as part of the first "troika" of the *pro tempore* presidency (Chile, Cuba, and Costa Rica) points in this direction. The successful holding of CELAC's second summit in Havana was a welcome development, showing that, despite its recent creation and the great diversity of its members, CELAC has the commitment of the countries in the region to carry out an integrationist project that transcends purely economic issues. At a time when the global trend towards multipolarity and the end of the old hegemonic pretensions of the Great Powers is becoming clear, CELAC could represent a firm basis for the positioning of the southern part of the hemisphere as a power bloc in the international arena.[11]

Before turning to the implications of these developments in Latin America for Cuba-Canada relations, one first needs to survey the recent operations of Canadian capital in Latin America, shifts in the Canadian state's policies towards the region, and the consequences of Canada's deep alliance with the United States.

The Increasing Alignment of Canadian and US Foreign Policy: An Approximation

As the economic integration between Canada and the United States intensifies and deepens, so too does the political alignment. Under the Stephen Harper government, first elected in 2006, Canada made a distinctly rightward turn that was not well received by most Latin American and Caribbean countries; moreover, Canada's socio-economic problems, such as those plaguing indigenous communities, worsened under the Harper government. In contrast to the United States, Canada is perceived by Latin America as a relatively egalitarian society, with a progressive social security and health care system and a gentle and non-interventionist foreign policy interested in maintaining peace.

Canada was appreciated in the hemisphere as a country with respected institutions, including a vibrant parliament due to its valuing of the separation of powers, the legislative process, and the opposition, and with a foreign policy that had an occasional air of independence.

Along with economic integration, conservatives in both Canada and the United States have pushed for deeper continental integration on a number of security issues, thereby allying Canada more closely with the global military power. Any observer of Canadian politics can see the radical changes in Ottawa's overall foreign policy that came with aligning the country with the most aggressive policies of the United States. Canada's repeated unconditional support for Israel, for example, is well known. As analyst Campbell Clark wrote in his balance sheet of Canada's international policies in 2011, "in a year when the world shook from financial crises and Arab uprisings, Canada's place in it was shifting, too. Even before Canada pulled out of a ground war in Afghanistan in July, it joined an air war in Libya. When it was over, Mr. Harper touted victory, and promised a military ready for more. He blocked part of a G8 leaders' statement urging peace talks on Israel, and bucked the UN majority in vocally opposing a Palestinian bid for statehood."[12]

In terms of Canada's policy towards Latin America, the fundamental orientation continues to be its traditional emphasis on economic relations, including the defence of the interests of Canadian investors and large banks such as the Bank of Nova Scotia and mineral and mining companies. There has also been sustained momentum in the negotiation of bilateral and multilateral free trade accords. At the political level, the Harper government was identified with the policy approach of the United States and right-wing Latin American governments, to the degree that its main allies were precisely the most reactionary governments or those closest to the United States, such as that of Colombia. The country's convergence with policy orientations set by the United States – whether in relation to Latin America or to the rest of the world – became apparent in the positions Ottawa's representatives adopted in international institutions and agencies. For example, together with its two North American neighbours – Mexico and the United States – Canada prevented the OAS from considering a resolution condemning Israel for its attack on a humanitarian aid flotilla bound for Gaza. Four other examples, involving Honduras, Venezuela, Colombia, and Mexico, further illustrate Canada's rightward orientation to Latin America.

Within the OAS, Canada was among those that early on advocated the reinstatement of Honduras, whose government was established after a military coup. Indeed, Canada's image in the hemisphere was very negatively affected by its support for the 2009 Honduran coup that overthrew the constitutional government of Manuel Zelaya, which was expressed during a 2010 visit to Honduras by Peter Kent, Canada's secretary of state for the Americas. Ignoring human rights abuses committed under the government of Porfirio Lobo, Kent fulfilled his promise to promote the normalization of Honduras's relations with the rest of Latin America and the Caribbean. In November 2009, under the military dictatorship and in the context of repression and intimidation, Lobo had won fraudulent elections that were boycotted by the domestic anti-coup movement; both the OAS and the European Union had refused to send official observers. Nonetheless, once Lobo was installed as president, Kent said that Canada would "support President Lobo's efforts as he moves to fully reintegrate Honduras into the international and hemispheric community, including in the Organization of American States."[13] Canada, the largest mining investor in Honduras, aspired to see its interests significantly bolstered if Lobo and the right-wing were to adopt a new mining law that would increase the rights of foreign capital.[14]

During his tour of the region before visiting Honduras, Kent stopped in Venezuela, where he failed to meet any representatives of the democratically elected government of Hugo Chávez, but did get together with a number of groups associated with the ultra-right opposition. On 28 January 2010, after his return to Canada, Kent said in a press release that "there was shrinking democratic space in Venezuela" under Chávez. "During my recent visit to Venezuela," he said, "I heard many individuals and organizations express concerns related to violations of the right to freedom of expression and other basic liberties."[15] These comments provoked a response by Chávez on his weekly television program, *Aló Presidente*. Referring to Harper, Chávez said he would not accept advice from an "ultra-right" government that had just "closed" Parliament – alluding to Harper's notorious suspension of Parliament from 30 December 2009 to 3 March 2010 to avoid a debate on abuses committed by Canadian troops in occupied Afghanistan.

In March 2010, while presenting legislation to implement the Canada-Colombia Free Trade Agreement, international trade minister Peter Van Loan failed to utter a single word about the shameful human rights violations committed by the regime of Colombia's Álvaro Uribe or Uribe's close ties to the paramilitary networks that operated with impunity throughout the country. Instead, in a press release, the Department of Foreign Affairs and International Trade claimed that, "[t]he Canada-Colombia Free Trade Agreement will provide greater market access for Canadian exporters of goods such as wheat, pulses, barley, paper products and heavy equipment," adding that "an increasing number of Canadian investors and exporters are entering the Colombian market, and it is also a strategic destination for Canadian direct investment, especially in mining, oil exploration, printing and education."[16]

Finally there is Mexico. Since 1994, when the free trade agreement with the United States and Canada entered into effect, mining in Mexico has increased exponentially. More than two hundred Canadian companies operate throughout the country, which is rich in minerals and has a perfect terrain for mining activity. Canadian mining companies have the support and permission of the Mexican federal government and state authorities to exploit Mexican land, which makes their stay and activities in the country very easy – and they pay low taxes to set up operations. The only resistance these Canadian companies have encountered is that of the local inhabitants, who complain that mining leaves no resources or benefits on the land. Everything is sent abroad, back to the North. In dealing with such resistance, the companies resort to violent repression. They usually have armed security services that, with the approval of local authorities, confront, shoot, and kill demonstrators who protest the presence of the mining companies. Raúl Delgado Wise, researcher at the Center for Development Studies at the Autonomous University of Zacatecas, reports on the situation in the desert municipality of Mazapil with respect to the Peñasquito mine, owned by the Canadian company, Gold Corp. Inc.: "it has meant a drain on resources for the State, because tax revenue does not stay there; production only leaves a trail of tremendous ecological destruction."[17] Nor is Mexico the only Latin American country where Canadian mining practices are a source of conflict. Gold Corp. has projects in Argentina (Cerro Negro) and Chile (El Morro). In Peru the case of the Conga mine in the Cajamarca region sparked considerable uproar and protests due to the danger posed by emptying four lagoons.[18] Additional projects are under way in Brazil and Panama – indeed, Latin America is full of them.

Implications for Cuba-Canada Relations

Relations between Canada and Cuba since the Cuban Revolution – already a period spanning more than half a century – have not always been particularly warm, except during the government of Pierre Trudeau. The most complex and tense point in their bilateral relations has been the issue of human rights. Although Canada has voted against the US blockade against Cuba in the UN General Assembly since the 1980s, Ottawa has also actively acted in favour of, and voted for, resolutions that condemned or tried to re-condemn Cuba in the UN Human Rights Commission in Geneva. At the same time, many analysts consider Cuba-Canada relations a model of a relationship between a large, developed, capitalist country and a small, undeveloped island that is trying to defend its sovereignty and independence through its own national project of a socialist nature. In other words, despite some instances of disagreement, respect for differences and the quest for mutual benefit has prevailed through trade and investment.

Canada never broke off relations with Cuba, which means that Ottawa did not adhere to the policy of hemispheric isolation and hostility directed against Cuba by Washington since the victory of the Revolution in 1959. Initiated by President Dwight Eisenhower, this policy essentially remains unchanged to this day. It was adopted by the OAS in 1962 at the behest of the United States, and was accepted by all Latin American countries except Mexico. Of course, the resolution calling for the breaking of diplomatic and trade relations with Cuba was not binding on Canada, which was not at that time a member of the conclave, but it was clear that maintaining an independent policy towards Cuba, in the context of the Cold War, was a display of autonomy, capacity for political self-determination, and reaffirmation of national sovereignty by Canada. Although weakened under the Harper government, there has been a recognition for over fifty years that the relationship with Cuba resonates with broad sectors of the Canadian public. Undoubtedly, that Canada's position on Cuba is at variance with that sustained by Washington is an integral part of its political culture and national identity.

Today, however, there is more on the agenda than maintaining normal diplomatic and trade relations with Cuba amid a policy of isolation imposed by the United States against the island. As we have seen, important changes in Latin America and the Caribbean have deepened Cuba's insertion into the hemisphere. Havana now has relations with all the countries of the region; what is more, these countries increasingly and more insistently are demanding the inclusion of Cuba in all hemispheric forums under conditions of full equality. This was clearly expressed through the unanimous Latin American position in favour of

Cuba's participation in hemispheric institutions and events, such as its joining the Rio Group in December 2008, a month before the inauguration of Barack Obama. It was also seen in San Pedro Sula, Honduras, during the 39th General Assembly of the OAS in 2010, at which the hemisphere's foreign ministers voted unanimously (including the US representative) to lift Cuba's 1962 suspension from the organization.

In contrast, the first two Summits of the Americas that took place during the Obama administration, in 2009 in Port of Spain and in 2012 in Cartagena, proved to be a total failure, even ending without the adoption of a final declaration, mainly because of the absence of Cuba from the conclave, which most countries in the region considered unacceptable. Indeed, Havana's participation became a litmus test of the announced change in US policy towards Latin America and Caribbean, which had been perceived as a symbol of old Cold War thinking and of Washington's hegemonic ambitions in the hemisphere. Several heads of state in Latin America, such as Rafael Correa of Ecuador and Evo Morales of Bolivia, indicated they would not participate in the 2015 summit in Panama unless Cuba was invited without any preconditions. As the Introduction and other chapters in this volume make clear, this pressure from the Latin American states was an important factor behind the Obama administration's 17 December 2014 decision to normalize relations.

Maintaining normal relations with Cuba has, historically, legitimized Canada's position in the eyes of most Latin American governments, and has contributed to the perception that Ottawa is a hemispheric player with independent positions somewhat different from those of the United States. Today, however, there is another underlying challenge for the country's foreign policy towards Latin America and the Caribbean: the increasing displays of independence on the part of many countries in the region (embodied primarily in the creation of CELAC) indicating that perceptions of the positive role Canada might play in inter-American relations have changed. The big question at this juncture is whether Canada will continue to align itself with US policy towards Cuba that, despite normalization, remains imperial at its core, thereby antagonizing the vast majority of countries in the region. Alternatively, will Ottawa join the regional chorus in favour of Cuba, and partially recover its former prestige and admiration among Latin American and Caribbean countries, even though it might face US disapproval?

Final Thoughts

Two decades after its full incorporation into the inter-American system, Canada once again faces major challenges in its relations with Latin America and the Caribbean, especially in regard to its role and presence in this system. Many factors have contributed to this conjuncture, including the social movements that have arisen in response to more than twenty-five years of neoliberal policies and that unleashed a dynamic that put an end to the formation of a FTAA; the election of governments in various Latin American and Caribbean countries that, to varying degrees, reject the hegemonic pretensions of the United States; the relative loss of US influence in the international system and the clearly militaristic orientation Washington has taken to recover its previous position; the return to the past in terms of US policy towards Latin America with the re-emergence of de facto military coups, such as in Venezuela in 2002 and in Honduras in 2009, the secessionist revolt of the Bolivian oligarchy (2006–09), and a coup attempt in Ecuador in 2010; and, finally, the creation of regional organizations such as ALBA and UNASUR outside the framework of the inter-American system. The regional integration process is exemplified by the 2011 establishment of CELAC, a body for consensus-based political agreement that is Latin American and Caribbean, without the presence of the United States or Canada, and with the full participation of Cuba.

All these developments require alignments and decisions that Canada cannot postpone. The Latin American regional environment, which Canada decided to join so late in the game, is, together with the entire international system, in transition. The impact of this transition on the current and future evolution of relations between Cuba and Canada remains to be seen. What is clear is that Canada's relationship with Cuba cannot be understood outside the Latin American and inter-American context in which it is embedded. Moreover, if Ottawa's foreign policy continues in the direction it has taken in recent years – and if prevailing trends in Latin America continue and are consolidated – Canada will be unable to confront the challenges facing the inter-American system, with radical implications for Canada's traditional relations with Latin America and the Caribbean.

NOTES

1 J.C.M. Ogelsby, *Gringos from the Far North: Essays in the History of Canadian-Latin American Relations, 1866–1968* (Toronto: Macmillan of Canada, 1976).
2 Peter McKenna, *Canada and the OAS: From Dilettante to Full Partner* (Montreal; Kingston, ON: McGill-Queen's University Press, 1995).
3 James Rochlin, *Discovering the Americas: The Evolution of Canadian Foreign Policy towards Latin America* (Vancouver: UBC Press, 1994), 12.
4 David Kilgour, Remarks to the international conference on "Hemispheric Integration beyond Free Trade," Université Laval, Quebec City, 17 April 2001.
5 "Un système de coopération interaméricaine," *Radio-Canada*, 14 May 1999, available online at http://ici.radio-canada.ca/regions/quebec/dossiers/2010/sommetdesameriques/enProfondeur_sommet.asp.
6 As can be seen, many of these countries underwent severe crises of the political system that produced a new political cycle of reform and refoundation of the state, as in Venezuela, Bolivia, and Ecuador. In other cases, changes at the ballot box have brought progressive governments to power, as in Brazil, Uruguay, Argentina, Paraguay, and Peru.
7 ALBA arose in December 2004 in Havana, when Venezuela's Hugo Chávez and Cuba's Fidel Castro initialled its creation as a form of integration and unity for Latin America and the Caribbean based on a model of independent development with a priority placed on regional economic complementarity. This would allow for a commitment to promote the development of all the participating countries and strengthen cooperation through mutual respect and solidarity. The current members of ALBA are Antigua and Barbuda, Bolivia, Cuba, Dominica, Ecuador, Nicaragua, Saint Vincent and the Grenadines, and Venezuela.
8 Petrocaribe was born as a result of a Venezuelan initiative on 29 June 2005 at the first summit, held in Puerto La Cruz, 220 kilometres east of Caracas. Its underlying concept is based on fair and equitable sharing among Caribbean countries and the solution of asymmetries in access to energy resources. It also has led to the creation of joint ventures in several member states to concretize cooperation projects, coupled with work designed to expand infrastructure for the storage and distribution of crude oil and derivatives. Petrocaribe's member countries are Antigua and Barbuda, the Bahamas, Belize, Cuba, Dominica, the Dominican Republic, Grenada, Guatemala, Guyana, Haiti, Jamaica, Nicaragua, Saint Kitts and Nevis, Saint Vincent and the Grenadines, Suriname, and Venezuela. In addition,

St Lucia, El Salvador, Costa Rica, and Puerto Rico have expressed interest in participating.

9   The Banco del Sur was founded on 9 December 2007 in Buenos Aires. Its creation was agreed to at a meeting of South American economy ministers held in Rio de Janeiro in October that year, in which those from Argentina, Bolivia, Brazil, Ecuador, Paraguay, Uruguay, and Venezuela participated. The ministers said they hoped the bank could help improve the availability of liquidity and revitalize investment in the region, as well as aid in the development of its infrastructure.

10 UNASUR was born in Brazil in May 2008, at which time its Founding Charter was signed by twelve members: Argentina, Bolivia, Brazil, Colombia, Chile, Ecuador, Guyana, Paraguay, Peru, Suriname, Uruguay, and Venezuela.

11 CELAC was founded on 2–3 December 2011 in Caracas in the framework of the Third Summit of Latin America and the Caribbean on Integration and Development and the 22nd Summit of the Rio Group. The presidency *pro tem* went to Chile. CELAC's first summit was held in Santiago, Chile, on 28 February 2013, and the presidency *pro tem* was occupied by Cuba. The second summit was held in Havana on 28–29 January 2014, and Costa Rica held the presidency *pro tem* until the 2015 summit.

12 Campbell Clark, "John Baird crafts Canadian foreign policy with a hard edge," *Globe and Mail*, 28 December 2011.

13 Todd Gordon and Jeffery R. Webber, "Canada's Long Embrace of the Honduran Dictatorship," *CounterPunch*, 19–21 March 2010.

14 Ibid.

15 Ibid.

16 Ibid.

17 Víctor Martín Gómez, "El impacto de las mineras canadienses en México," *Rebelión*, 22 March 2012.

18 See "Promesas vacías de las mineras canadienses en México: la verdad expuesta / Mujeres indígenas protestan contra proyecto minero en norte peruano," *Zapateando*, 11 December 2011, available online at http://zapateando.wordpress.com/2011/12/20/promesas-vacias-de-las-mineras-canadienses-en-mexico-la-verdad-expuesta-mujeres-indigenas-protestan-contra-proyecto-minero-en-norte-peruano/, accessed 2 December 2013.

PART THREE

Constructing Canada and Cuba

10 Cuba in the Canadian Media:
To Be or Not to Be?

OLGA ROSA GONZÁLEZ MARTÍN

After the triumph of the Cuban Revolution in 1959, foreign policy became a major tool used by the Cuban state to guarantee its sovereignty, independence, and national integrity. Thus, new political and economic relations were established with new states, and existing ties with other countries were strengthened. This goal was achieved despite US efforts to isolate Cuba, especially in the western hemisphere where, following US pressure, only two countries, Mexico and Canada, maintained their relations with the island.

The then-prime minister of Canada, John Diefenbaker, maintained Canada's relationship with Cuba based on the principle that every state had the right to adopt the political system it considered the best. As Walter C. Soderlund, Ronald H. Wagenberg, and Stuart H. Surlin point out:

> Canada was a full partner of the United States in the Cold War as evidenced by military alliances such as NATO and NORAD. Nonetheless, a desire to conduct an independent foreign policy as a middle power frequently led Canada to adopt postures different from their ally. None has turned out to be as significant as Canada's independent policy on Cuba. An historical detachment from Latin America had meant that few Canadian vital interests had developed in the area that were threatened by the Cuban Revolution. Thus, Canadian policymakers did not accord Cuba the same prominence as did their American counterparts. Indeed, as time passed, the maintenance of some degree of normalcy in relations with Cuba was viewed as a testament to a "made in Canada" foreign policy.[1]

Since then, Cuba and Canada have maintained and increased their friendship and cooperation, mainly in the economic, cultural, scientific, and academic sectors. The Canadian government's assistance to the island in important sectors such as education, finance, and banking should be added to this list.[2] Nowadays, Canada is Cuba's fourth-largest economic partner, preceded only by Venezuela, China, and Spain.[3] In addition, Canada was Cuba's major source of tourists in 2013, when more than 1.1 million Canadians visited.[4] Therefore, paying attention to what is said about Cuba in the Canadian media is of vital importance for Cuba even though Cubans are aware that their country is not of much relevance to Canadian media gatekeepers.

Between 1988 and the end of the Cold War, Canadian media coverage of Cuba focused on the following topics: Cuba's military withdrawal from Angola; Mikhail Gorbachev's visit to Cuba and Cuban-Soviet relations; the trial and execution of General Arnaldo Ochoa; Cuba's economic crisis; Cuban human rights abuses; the Pan American Games; Fidel Castro as ruler and personality; and new insights into the Cuban Missile Crisis as gleaned from a series of meetings between Cuban, Soviet, and US participants.[5] Summaries by the Canadian Foundation for the Americas (FOCAL) of news reports between January 2003 and December 2005 focused on business and the success of Sherritt International in mining and energy in Cuba, Canadian tourists visiting Cuba, violations of human rights, and, especially in 2003, political repression in Cuba.

In her study of the Canadian media portrayal of Cuba between 2000 and 2009, Heather Nicol analyses 644,450 articles and identifies six lenses through which perceptions about Cuba were shaped: travel (the most substantive of all in her view); international news and information with stories about everyday life and events in Cuba (less than 25 per cent of all articles); complex foreign relations (Cuba-Canada, Cuba-US relations); culture, sports, and entertainment; weather; and "other" (Cuba as a metaphor for repression, although not exclusively).[6] She also states that

> the press is more critically positioned than a decade ago ... The result is ambivalence in the way in which Cuba is portrayed and understood, and more generally positioned in terms of attitude and popularized geopolitical perceptions. It is increasingly linked to what might be considered an Americanized media perspective at the same time that it is embedded within a tradition of foreign policy, which has consistently treated Cuba quite differently than has the United States ... While originally supportive of the Cuban Revolution ... the Canadian press has waxed and waned

in its enthusiasm towards Fidel Castro's Cuban experiment ever since ... This trend continues in the early twenty-first century. With the exception of the years surrounding the Helms–Burton crisis, the Canadian press has not been overwhelming in its support of Cuba.[7]

Based on these studies I would argue that, during the last decade of the twentieth century and the first decade of the twenty-first, the Canadian media changed the way they covered Cuba. Cuba was no longer the Robin Hood that Canadian newspapers touted at the beginning of the Revolution. Major news stories now were based on the famous triad – free elections, a free market, and a multiparty system – which has become the lens through which the media see, try to understand, and portray Cuba's reality.

According to FOCAL, the Canadian newspapers that have covered Cuba the most are the *Globe and Mail* and the *Toronto Star*,[8] but for the purposes of analysing media coverage in this chapter, I considered articles only in the former from January 2006 to summer 2012. I identified all topics regarding Cuba's domestic and foreign policy and the sections of the newspaper in which they were included, giving special attention to editorials and to the newspaper's sources. Although focusing on just one newspaper necessarily limits the analysis, it is important to point out that the *Globe and Mail* is not only a national newspaper; arguably, it is Canada's most important newspaper for people in the business, investor, and entrepreneurial class. It is also widely read by parliamentarians, policy-makers, and the political elite in Canada. In consequence, its readers represent a powerful segment of Canadian society even if the newspaper might not reflect Canadian general opinion.

From January 2006 to August 2012 – during which time Cuba elected a new president and Canada had a new prime minister, both of whom brought relevant changes to their respective governments – the *Globe and Mail* published a total of 2,194 articles that mentioned Cuba. Of these I chose a final sample of 221 items, none of which made it to the front page of the newspaper, that were about Cuba in particular.

As shown in Figure 10.1, coverage of Cuba in the *Globe and Mail* was the highest in 2006 and 2008. In fact 2006 was a turning point in Cuba's history. During that summer Fidel Castro fell ill, and as his health worsened, predictions of his death were made. Accordingly, reporting about Cuba reached a peak in August, when Castro stepped aside due to his poor health, and his brother Raúl – then second secretary of the Communist Party of Cuba and minister of the Cuban Revolutionary Armed

Figure 10.1. Articles about Cuba in the *Globe and Mail*, January 2006–August 2012

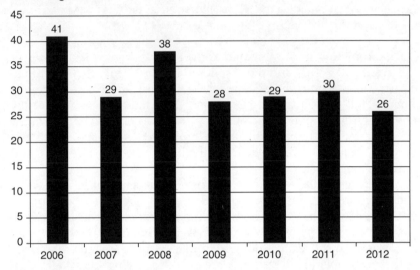

Source: Author's compilation.

Forces – became acting president of the republic. It was the first time in the history of revolutionary Cuba that Cubans were going to live under the leadership of a different president. The international community – the United States, in particular – expected Fidel Castro's absence, not to mention his death, would bring about a political crisis on the island, but nothing of the kind happened. In February 2008 Canadian media coverage of Cuba picked up again as presidential elections were held on the island and Raúl Castro was officially elected president. These events characterized the most dramatic changes in Cuba's institutional arena in fifty years.

Of the sample of 221 articles about Cuba in the *Globe and Mail*, 70.13 per cent were written by the newspaper's staff. Virtually all of the rest were produced by wire services, especially Reuters, AP, AFP, Canadian Press, and Bloomberg News, and authored by a group of fifteen Canadian, US, and European personalities, among them Álvaro Vargas Llosa, senior fellow at the Independent Institute in Oakland, California; Alex Neve, secretary-general of Amnesty International Canada; Peter Kornbluh, director of the Cuba Documentation Project at the National Security Archive at George Washington University;

Peter McKenna, professor at the University of Prince Edward Island; John Kirk, professor at Dalhousie University; and Ken Frankel, director of FOCAL. That such a large share of the articles was written by *Globe and Mail* staff is of particular interest considering that, during the 1990s, Canadian newspapers depended heavily on wire services. It suggests that, by then, the *Globe and Mail* was displaying a degree of journalistic independence. Through this journalistic discourse, the newspaper constructed a certain Cuban *reality* for its readers. Events were decontextualized and then recontextualized, a process that depends on the different ideological, political, economic, and social mediations that affect news-making.

As Figure 10.2 shows, news about Cuba appeared most often in the following sections of the newspaper: International News, Travel, Letters

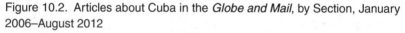

Figure 10.2. Articles about Cuba in the *Globe and Mail*, by Section, January 2006–August 2012

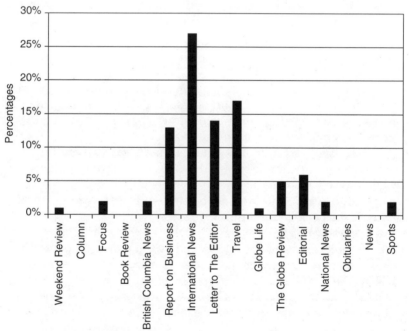

Source: Author's compilation.

to the Editor, Report on Business, Comment, and Editorial. The International News section alone devoted fifty-nine features to Cuba because of the dramatic political and economic changes the island was experiencing. In addition the Latin American political landscape was changing, and Cuba's position in the hemisphere was being strengthened thanks to the support of the "pink tide" of leftist Latin American governments. Numerous articles about Cuba also appeared in the Travel section – not surprisingly given low-cost Cuba's attraction for Canadian tourists and their need to know if it was safe to visit – and travel-related articles also appeared in other sections. Articles about how the changes in the island might affect the economic relationship between Cuba and Canada were also common. Lastly, Prime Minister Stephen Harper's policy on Latin America – and on Cuba, in particular – was subject to discussion in the Letters to the Editor, Comment, and Editorial sections.

The topics the *Globe and Mail* used most often to transmit the Cuban reality to its readers were the following (see Figure 10.3):

- *Fidel Castro's illness, his legacy, and the transition in Cuba* (fifty-five articles): under this topic the newspaper evaluated the achievements of the Revolution, its mistakes, and the future of the Cuban nation.
- *Economy and business* (forty-two articles): articles here focused on the economic reforms implemented by the government of Raúl Castro after his election as president.
- *Cuba as a tourist destination for Canadians* (twenty-six articles): these focused on Cuba as a cheap sun-and-sand paradise where Canadians could escape from their cold winter; some articles also mentioned potential safety concerns of tourists.
- *Bilateral relations between Cuba and the United States* (twenty-three articles): these articles discussed the Cuba policies of Presidents George W. Bush and Barack Obama; many also focused on the economic situation in Cuba and on the effect of Fidel Castro's personal absence on the bilateral conflict.
- *Bilateral relations between Cuba and Canada* (eighteen articles): articles on this topic discussed the role played by Canadian companies in Cuba and their future there under Raúl Castro's new leadership, as well as Prime Minister Harper's policy towards Cuba.
- *Human rights in Cuba* (ten articles): these articles discussed so-called violations of human rights on the island, often quoting individuals considered to be counterrevolutionaries and/or considered by the international community as dissidents.

Figure 10.3. Articles about Cuba in the *Globe and Mail*, by Topic, January 2006–August 2012

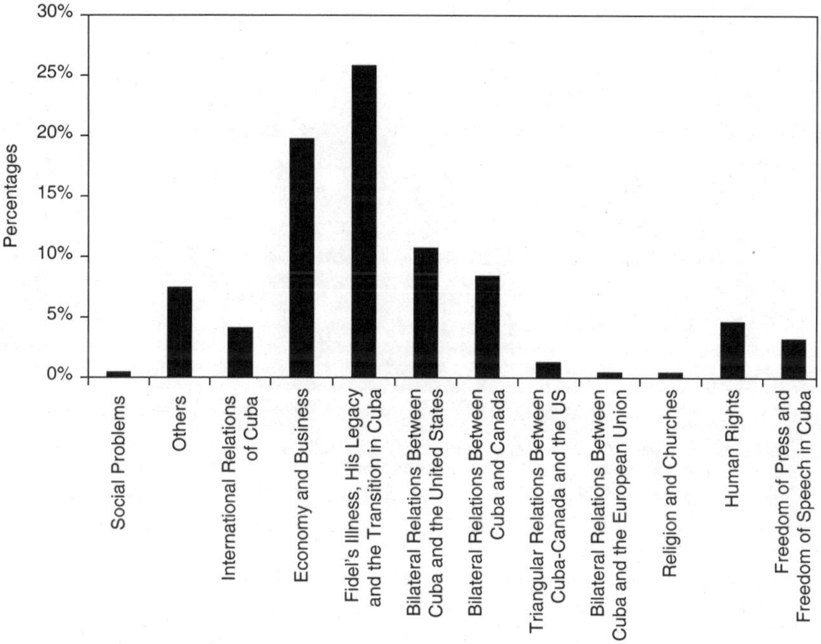

Source: Author's compilation.

As well as identifying the topics these articles covered, it is important to determine their sources because they are key to the construction of the newspaper's agenda in terms of its reporting about Cuba and they have a validating power that cannot be underestimated. The sources a journalist uses provide credibility and legitimize viewpoints that help to create a certain reality. Accordingly, the documents cited in the *Globe and Mail* articles came from the following sources:

- a hotel price index study;
- the Heritage Foundation's Index of Economic Freedom;
- Transparency International's Corruption Perceptions Index;
- the Reuters publication *Breakingviews*;

- "Reflections," a newspaper column by Fidel Castro in the Cuban media;
- Statistics Canada;
- the World Bank;
- a US State Department cable;
- a Human Rights Watch report;
- polls by the Institute for Cuban & Cuban-American Studies, in association with the University of Miami;
- a study by the Economist Intelligence Unit;
- a US Geological Survey estimate;
- Cuban Labour and Social Security Resolution 9;
- the communist youth newspaper *Juventud Rebelde*;
- the Saint John (NB) *Telegraph-Journal*;
- the magazine *Cigar Aficionado*;
- the Communist Party daily *Granma*.

The *Globe and Mail* articles also cited the following human sources (see Figure 10.4):

- *State sources*: includes all references to people involved in the functioning of a given government or the government-controlled institutions responsible for its administration. A total of thirty-nine people were quoted or referred to in the sample, the majority of them Cuban, followed by American, Canadian, Venezuelan, Caribbean, Chinese, and Spanish. State sources quoted most often were: Fidel Castro; Raúl Castro; Barack Obama, both as a presidential candidate and, after his election, as US president; Prime Minister Stephen Harper; late president of Venezuela Hugo Chávez; former US president George W. Bush; Ricardo Alarcón, former head of Cuba's National Assembly; and Secretary of State Hillary Clinton.
- *Political party sources*: includes all references to members of a political party. There were a total of eight such sources; of these, only US and Cuban sources were mentioned. The sources quoted most often were Fidel Castro as former first secretary of the Communist Party of Cuba; and Senator Lindsey Graham, a Republican from South Carolina.
- *Business company sources*: includes all references to representative members of the commercial, trade, and corporate sectors mentioned or consulted as sources of information. Of the total of thirty-one, relevant here is the number of Canadian sources mentioned (eighteen),

Figure 10.4. Articles about Cuba in the *Globe and Mail*, by Source, January 2006–August 2012

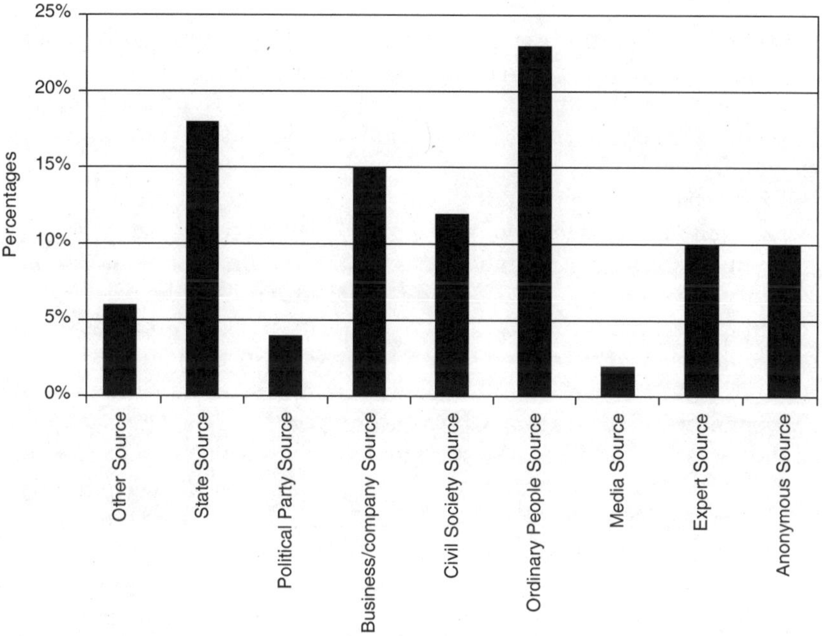

Source: Author's compilation.

followed by Cuban, US, and Spanish sources. Ian Delany, former chief executive officer of Sherritt International, was the Canadian business source quoted the most, followed by representatives of Pebercan Inc., Sunwing Vacations, Nolitours, Transat Holidays, and Hola Sun Holidays.

- *Civil society sources*: includes references to all members of an organized civil society such as non-governmental organizations, unions, churches, or organizations that do not represent a state or the business world. Twenty-five such representatives were quoted in the sample articles. Most frequently quoted were Human Rights Watch, Amnesty International, and John Graham, chairman of FOCAL.

- *Ordinary people as sources*: includes references to people as individual sources of information who spoke for themselves, not as a representative of a state, political party, business company, or civil society organization. These sources were the most often cited in the sample studied; a total of forty-nine ordinary people, most of them Cuban, were quoted, followed by Europeans and Canadians visiting the island.

- *Media sources*: includes references to a member, representative, or spokesperson of a media company; only five were quoted, most of them Cuban – in particular, the editor-in-chief of *Granma* newspaper and the editors of *Bohemia*, Cuba's oldest and most prestigious magazine.
- *Expert sources*: includes references to persons, such as professors, researchers, social and political scientists, and economists, who follow Cuba's internal dynamics and international relations or who study the political, economic, and social situation of the western hemisphere more broadly. A total of twenty-two such sources were quoted, most of them Americans, followed by Canadians and only one Cuban, perhaps suggesting either that US and Canadian experts were more available than Cuban sources or that the *Globe and Mail* did not know or did not wish to quote Cuban sources. Nevertheless, the fact is that the most important changes in Cuban society in fifty years were being analysed without taking into account what Cuba specialists living on the island had to say about them.
- *Anonymous sources*: includes all specifically unidentified sources or those the author of article chose to refer to as anonymous. Out of twenty-one anonymous sources in the 221 sample articles, most were identified broadly as Cubans, followed by two Americans and one European tour operator.
- *Other sources*: refers to all sources mentioned that do not fit any of the previous categories; there were twelve such miscellaneous sources, nine of them Cuban musicians, athletes, baseball players, and novelists.

How did the *Globe and Mail* combine all these elements to transmit the Cuban reality to its readers? Let us look at how the newspaper covered the most frequent topics.

FIDEL CASTRO'S ILLNESS, HIS LEGACY, AND THE TRANSITION IN CUBA

Fidel Castro's departure from the scene and the passing of the reins of government to brother Raúl was analysed in fifty-five articles. In twenty-three of these, the *Globe and Mail* presented Fidel in the kinds of traditional clichés his opponents had always used: "Cuba's long-time dictator who had been in power for 49 nine years,"[9] "the last of the Cold Warriors,"[10] who had "designated" his "brother," his "long-term lieutenant ... Fidel-Lite"[11] to rule the "only Communist-run nation" in the hemisphere.[12] Through such statements, the *Globe and Mail* implied there was a lack of democratic participation in Cuba. Instead of helping the reader to understand why Raúl had been "designated," it led them to believe he had been "appointed" merely for being Fidel's "younger brother," implying that Cuba was being ruled by a dynasty.[13] In fact, Raúl Castro has led Cuba in a different manner from that of Fidel, and although the newspaper reported Raúl's decision to encourage a national debate, it did so in a way that suggested this was *rare* in Cuba. One article, for instance, stated: "Cuban university students, in a rare public challenge to authorities, openly criticized government restrictions on access to the Internet, hotels and travel abroad,"[14] the last phrase strengthening the alleged lack of public participation in the decision-making process in Cuba.

The articles also implied that Raúl Castro not only had been "designated" just for being the younger brother, but that he did not have the necessary leadership qualities or capacity to do the job. An article published on 2 August 2006 questioned Cubans' support for Raúl even though the Cuban media had been preparing the Cuban people for the "succession" by presenting him as the right man to succeed Fidel. A Canadian academic, Archibald Ritter, was quoted in the article as saying, "[t]here's some question as to how long Raúl could maintain support ... Some people think he would have to rely increasingly on violence,"[15] at a time when stability was so necessary not only for Cuba, but also for the United States, "whose private nightmare of a post-Castro Cuba includes its emergence as a major narcotics shipment centre in the Caribbean, and a centre for organized crime."[16]

The idea of possible instability in Cuba was reinforced by quoting anonymous Cuban sources who were reported to have said: "This is a very critical moment ... it's true we want [Fidel Castro] to recover, because nobody wants a radical change."[17] In an article on 7 August 2006, *Globe and Mail* correspondent Alan Freeman quoted an ordinary Cuban woman named Luisa who, he said, "despises Cuba's Communist government, yet admits that she became anxious when she heard that Fidel Castro temporarily ceded his presidential powers last week after surgery for gastrointestinal bleeding." Freeman further reported Luisa as saying, "He's like a grandfather to me ... It's very strange. I hate the government, but when this happened I was scared. It's very complicated." Freeman described another ordinary person as being "convinced that political change is inevitable," that he thinks "Fidel sustains the revolution in Cuba. It's a revolution he created. I think there is no other leader that would be able to sustain what he has been able to do for so many years."[18] Such statements might have given readers of the *Globe and Mail* the impression that the Revolution is all about Fidel Castro himself, but although Fidel was the historical leader, he needed the support of ordinary Cubans – what many Cubans describe as the social basis of the Revolution.

The *Globe and Mail* also stated that Fidel Castro was "leaving uncertain the future of his Caribbean Communist experiment ... the dictatorship ... [where] dissidents languish in Cuban jails." Foreign Minister Maxime Bernier accordingly said it was necessary to continue "to monitor developments in Cuba," with the hope that the end of Castro's rule "will open the way for the Cuban people to pursue a process of political and economic reform."[19] Among all such reporting about Cuba's future, however, not a single expert Cuban source was quoted – only a "dissident" demanding more democratic liberties. A more balanced view of what the "Caribbean Communist Experiment" has meant in social terms would have helped readers to gain a broader idea of the Cuban *reality* over the past fifty years.

The *Globe and Mail* also reported, in a somewhat contradictory way, that Fidel Castro had betrayed the ideals of the Revolution. In a column published in February 2008, it stated that "the political philosopher who most inspired Mr. Castro was Franklin Delano Roosevelt, and up to the moment his movement seized power in Cuba, Fidel cited the New Deal as the model for Cuba's transformation." The author quoted the old editors of *Bohemia*, Cuba's most prestigious magazine, as saying that Fidel Castro told them "the new government will decline any relations with dictatorial states ... first of all the Soviet Union," but, "at the last moment, in the summer of 1959, something changed."[20] This, of course, left *Globe and Mail* readers without any context regarding what had happened in Cuba and its conflict with the United States. The question of why Fidel Castro's ideas had changed was left unaddressed in historical terms.

Another article comparing Fidel Castro's original vision to the Revolution concluded that his legacy was mixed: there was "high literacy and free health care on the one hand, political repression and economic hardship on the other."[21] Yet the article did not address how a highly educated population accepted political repression. Repression takes place in dictatorships and, as James W. Winter points out, "[i]lliteracy and ignorance are the hallmarks of dictatorship."[22] This is not the case in Cuba. What about the national consensus in Cuba?

The "moribund revolution" – as the *Globe and Mail* characterized the Cuban Revolution in an article on 21 April 2011 – was supposed to be resuscitated by discussing a document that contained "311 modifications to a law designed to chart a course away from the economic stagnation in which the communist country is mired ... [T]he paper, however, has not been made public. The lack of transparency is just one sign, analysts say, that despite Cuba appointing new leaders to the Communist Party and taking half-measures toward privatization, reality will essentially remain unchanged for average Cubans."[23] The document in question is known in Cuba as *Lineamientos de la Política Económica y Social del Partido y la Revolución*, and it was not secret, but discussed by the Cuban population over three different periods – December 2010–February 2011, 8–10 April 2011, and 17–18 April 2011. The first draft was discussed throughout Cuba in more than 160,000 meetings. Originally, the document had 291 *Lineamientos* (guidelines). A revised document was released after the public consultations that reflected the results of the national debate. The revised version, entitled *Información sobre el resultado del Debate de los Lineamientos de la Política Económica y Social del Partido y la Revolución*, was published in May 2011. The *Globe and Mail* article, therefore, was hardly accurate even though it quoted Cuban state sources such as Marino Murillo, the vice-president in charge of implementing the *Lineamientos*, and Teresita Vicente, Cuba's ambassador to Canada.

THE CUBAN ECONOMY AND BUSINESS

Economic matters were discussed in forty-two *Globe and Mail* articles over the study period. The first, published on 16 January 2006, focused on China as the island's second-largest trading partner after Venezuela. The author noted, however, that Chinese companies "worry about collecting payment for their increasing sales of durable goods,"[24] suggesting that Cuba was not a trusted partner, even though the volume of business between China and Cuba would indicate that a certain degree of trust must be present.

The paper also reported that "Cuba has declared an end to the daily blackouts that have wreaked havoc on peoples' lives and the economy since the 1991 collapse of the Soviet Union. The change was reported by official media yesterday."[25] The source of this positive development, however, was quoted as the "official" media, which tended to diminish its relevance since Cuba has been criticized for its "state-controlled" media and, by implication, non-existent freedom of the press.

Despite the Cuban economy's recovery from the early post-Soviet era, the *Globe and Mail* devoted an entire article to the dual currencies in use – the regular Cuban peso and the Cuban convertible peso (CUC) – and how that system affects people. Two Canadian experts with different opinions were quoted. "They've displaced the U.S. dollar, but they've done so with this convertible currency. The result is that they've still got this bifurcated, dual economy which is dysfunctional," said Archibald Ritter, an economist at Carleton University in Ottawa.[26] On the other hand, John Kirk, an expert on Latin American studies at Dalhousie University (and a contributor to this volume), considered that "[t]he average Cuban lives a lot better than the average Latin American"[27] in terms of life expectancy, impressive infant mortality statistics, and free education. Ritter was also quoted as saying that, although "Cuban living standards have improved since the worst of the economic crisis after the Soviet fall, they have not recovered to pre-1989 levels,"[28] and Kirk stated that "an estimated 70 per cent of Cubans have access to CUCs," but "low-paid workers ... don't have enough pesos at the end of the month to buy any CUCs."[29] This idea was reinforced by quoting ordinary people. A fifty-seven-year-old Cuban night watchman, for example, complained about his low wage and his inability to feed his wife and three children, and compared his situation to that of a younger technician who, because he worked in a hotel, could afford to buy expensive toys for his daughter. Thus, even articles that seem balanced because they quoted ordinary Cubans and their experiences reinforced the idea that Cuba's economy was dysfunctional.

The *Globe and Mail* also covered the economic reforms introduced and implemented by the government of Raúl Castro in this period. An editorial published in October 2009 said that Cuba "may at last be moving toward a market economy." The editorial continued, however: "[i]n all this, there is little or no sign of political reform. Perhaps Cuba is headed for the time being toward a Chinese-style market economy without democracy. But in the Western hemisphere, in the neighbourhood of the United States, it seems unlikely that, with a comparatively open economy, a one-party, indeed almost one-family, state can long continue."[30] So, even when a market economy was at last being implemented, Cuba was still doomed to fail not only because a market economy and "lack of democracy" were incompatible, but because no state with such characteristics could survive having the United States as a neighbour. Yet the Cuban Revolution had survived for fifty years. Cuba continues to have a strong social consensus, and the economy has experienced other periods of economic reform. For example, in the 1990s the Cuban government introduced measures aimed at boosting the Cuban economy that permitted not only foreign investment in the island, but the ownership of private property, too.

In another editorial, the *Globe and Mail* stated that, even when announcements such as the "laying off" of "500,000 state employees ... show[ed] the desperate state of the economy," they were a "welcome first step." It also said that, "to expect state employees, especially the least enterprising, to succeed in the private sector is politically risky" – as Carleton's Archibald Ritter was quoted as saying, "[o]nce people aren't reliant on the goodwill of the state, they are much less manageable. So there is a political risk,"[31] implying that these changes might provoke a political crisis.

CUBA AS A DESTINATION FOR CANADIAN TOURISTS

Canadian tourism in Cuba was the third most popular topic covered by the *Globe and Mail*. The general theme of the articles was Cuba as an inexpensive sun and beach vacation destination, but seven articles were less enthusiastic. One stated that, although "Cuba is rarely thought of as a hotbed of crime ... the Department of Foreign Affairs is warning tourists that increasing numbers of Canadians have been victims of pickpocketing, theft and assault – especially in Havana's Old Havana, Centro Havana, the Malecon, and Vedado and on the beaches of Playas del Este and Varadero. Those who are mugged and stripped of identification and money should contact the Canadian embassy before the local cops, who may just toss them in jail until their identity is confirmed and their solvency restored."[32] To that warning one could add the *Globe and Mail*'s reporting of one issued by the Canadian Association of Tour Operators that, in 2006, Cuba "was losing out to other Caribbean destinations because of the lack of adequate service for tourists, theft of luggage at airports and hotels, and a failure to attend to complaints."[33] Perhaps such reports induced some tourists to vacation elsewhere.

Cuba-US relations were next on the list of topics covered, with a total of twenty-three articles. Migration to the United States was one of the themes the *Globe and Mail* addressed. Consistent with its earlier tone, the paper reported that Cubans had "fled" their country,[34] but failed to provide history or context. For instance, the articles did not address the peculiarities of the special treatment the United States provides Cuban migrants under the Cuban Refugee Adjustment Act of 1966, which allows Cubans to apply for permanent resident status within one year of their arrival in the United States – an opportunity not given any other group or nationality. No additional information was given to readers about the history of migration between Cuba and the United States, which did not begin in 1959 but in the nineteenth century. Instead the paper implied that this migration was a simple response to the "Castro regime" and its "lack of democracy."

The paper also used the US term "embargo," rather than the Cuban term "blockade," to describe US policy towards Cuba.[35] An editorial described the "embargo" as "an anachronistic leftover of the Cold War that should have been lifted years ago," and went on to say that "Washington should show more respect for its neighbours' laws and get rid of a ridiculous embargo that still plays well with Cuban expatriate voters in Florida but whose dubious limited value in pressuring the Castro regime was gone long ago."[36] Although this would seem on the surface to support Cuba, the editorial implicitly accepted the underlying US rationale for the policy, as it stressed that the blockade should be lifted because it had been ineffective in "pressuring the Castro regime." The editorial did not, for instance, critique US policy as a violation of international law, or comment on its negative impact on the Cuban people who are suffering because of it.

A comment published by the paper equated the "Castro regime" and the "embargo," and quoted the US government as saying it was "not going to lift the U.S. embargo on Cuba just because Fidel Castro has formally stepped aside as the island's leader. Washington's view is that nothing has really changed in Havana and that as long as Cuba suffers under Communist tyranny, the ban on trade and travel must stay." The author of the comment went even further by stating: "The caution is well justified. With Mr. Castro's brother, Raul, in charge, there is no sign yet of a change or even a softening of what can still rightly be called the Castro regime." The author then quoted US senator John McCain: "I think we should make it very clear that once free elections are held, that the political prisoners are released and human-rights organizations are functioning in Cuba, that we would be willing to provide whatever aid and assistance that's necessary ... [A]nything short of that ... might serve to prop up a new regime." The author also quoted Barack Obama: "Fidel Castro's stepping down is an essential first step, but it is sadly insufficient in bringing freedom to Cuba."[37] Again the lifting of the blockade was linked to political issues in Cuba, not to its inhumane nature or violation of international law.

BILATERAL RELATIONS BETWEEN CUBA AND CANADA

Cuba-Canada relations were discussed in eighteen articles that focused mainly on economic issues. The bottom line was that Canadian companies were going to "be monitoring any developments after an ailing Fidel Castro transferred his duties to his younger brother Raul."[38] Nonetheless, Cuba was still presented as a stable trading partner interested in continuing business with companies such as Sherritt International, the largest foreign investor on the island.[39] Three months later the *Globe and Mail* reported that, although business in other areas was being conducted as usual, there were some problems with the payments on the part of Cuba's oil company to Pebercan Inc.: "Cuba's state-run oil company is behind in $69-million (U.S.) of payments to its Canadian partners in a heavy oil-producing block on the north side of the island."[40]

The newspaper also reported that Canada could help "nudge [Cuba] toward democracy after an ailing Fidel Castro is gone," quoting US Assistant Secretary of State for the Western Hemisphere, Thomas Shannon. The US official also said that "Canada, Mexico, and other countries in the region share with the United States the desire to see Cubans transform their country into a democracy. The fact that Canada and others trade with Cuba while the United States maintains an economic embargo is simply a matter of different tactics ... The tactical differences can actually work to the advantage of our larger objective."[41] Since Canadian officials normally emphasized the distinctiveness of Canada's policy towards Cuba, this remark might have been unwelcome in Canada.

HUMAN RIGHTS IN CUBA

Ten articles focused on the issue of human rights in Cuba. For example, attention was given to an exhibition organized by a so-called independent Cuban curator in a famous Cuban private restaurant because, in Cuba, artists can show their work, but censorship is employed by, for instance, limiting access to galleries.[42] The *Globe and Mail* also focused on "the lack of freedom of press in Cuba," commenting that the US-based Committee to Protect Journalists had noted that "Cuba has jailed 25 journalists, more than any other country except China."[43] An editorial on 23 November 2009 regarding the human rights situation argued that, despite "market reforms at home, a loosening of travel restrictions from its old enemy to the north, and Fidel Castro out of the picture[, a] new Human Rights Watch report ... shows that, under the rule of Raul Castro, Fidel's brother, Cuba continues to oppress even the loneliest dissenter. Canada must work with other nations to demand political reform." The paper then called on the international community and Canada to implement what it defined as "[a] multilateral approach, in which Canada should be at the forefront ... For example, countries in the Americas and Europe could demand the release of all political prisoners within a certain time or institute travel bans and asset freezes against Cuban leaders."[44] The paper then called for the same blockade that, in another editorial, was considered to be "an anachronistic leftover of the Cold War that should have been lifted years ago."[45] Such lack of consistency could only lead one to wonder if the paper was being hypocritical and if it considered that the internal affairs of Cuba should be solved by others, not by Cubans themselves.

The *Globe and Mail* also discussed the death of Orlando Zapata Tamayo, a Cuban dissident considered a counterrevolutionary by the Cuba authorities, and who died after a hunger strike, an incident widely reported by the international media. In covering it the *Globe and Mail* quoted Amnesty International, US secretary of state Hillary Clinton, Spanish prime minister José Luis Rodríguez Zapatero, Reyna Luisa Tamayo (Orlando Zapata's mother), and Marta Beatriz Roque, another dissident, all of whom accused the Cuban government of the violation of human rights and murder.[46] The newspaper stated: "Raul Castro, the Cuban president, took the unusual step of expressing public regret for Mr. Zapata's death ... [and] used the occasion not to announce a political opening, but to deny that the deceased was mistreated and to attack the U.S."[47] In another editorial the paper questioned if "ordinary Cubans actually believe that all political opponents are U.S. mercenaries, and that another country is responsible for what happens inside Cuban prisons." The conclusion agreed with a quote from a researcher with Human Rights Watch, Nik Steinberg, who said Cuba "is an incredibly effective, repressive state machine."[48] The fact that after Mr Zapata's death the Cuban government released fifty-two "prisoners of conscience" was not considered in another editorial as "evidence of "political tolerance by the Communist dictatorship" because "there is still much need for reform in this one-party state. There are justifiable fears that as long as 'Cuba's draconian laws' remain in place, in the words of Human Rights Watch, new generations of innocent Cubans exercising their right to freedom of expression will take the place of those just released."[49]

Conclusion

The *Globe and Mail*'s coverage of Cuba over the period from January 2006 to August 2012 presented a biased and unfavourable picture of the country that stressed that, even as Fidel Castro passed power to his brother, the "designated" successor, Cuba's human rights violations would continue and thus so should the blockade. The newspaper argued that political reforms were necessary even though it recognized that economic reforms had been implemented. However, the paper presented the economic reforms as necessary to save the "moribund revolution" inherited by Raúl Castro. The paper might have overcome this bias by consulting a wider base of sources, including Cuban experts and other sources living on the island, which might have given the analysis of events in Cuba a wider perspective.

As well, Cuba-Canada relations and foreign policy were not as well represented in the newspaper as bilateral relations between Cuba and the United States. Canada's unbroken diplomatic relationship with Cuba was regarded as an example of an independent foreign policy, yet Canada's policy towards Cuba was seen as determined by the triangular relationship among Cuba, Canada, and the United States. This view is not likely to change in the near future despite the diplomatic opening between Cuba and the United States begun by presidents Obama and Castro. Moreover, now that President Donald Trump, following his announcement of 16 June 2017, has reversed this progress, what Heather Nicol calls the "Americanization" of Canadian media perspectives on Cuba might well remain a distinctive feature of Canadian media portrayals of Cuba. We shall have to wait and see.

NOTES

I would like to thank the David Rockefeller Center for Latin American Studies at Harvard University and Dr Linda Rodríguez, a post-doctoral fellow at New York University for assisting me in locating and sending to Cuba all the documents used to select the sample for this chapter.

1 Walter C. Soderlund, Ronald H. Wagenberg, and Stuart H. Surlin, "The Impact of the End of the Cold War on Canadian and American TV News Coverage of Cuba: Image Consistency or Image Change?" *Canadian Journal of Communication* 23, no. 2 (1998): 217–31.
2 For a characterization of Cuba-Canada relations in this period, see Pavel Consuegra Montes, "Las relaciones cubano-canadienses en los noventa y la influencia de los Estados Unidos," in *Los retos frente a la internacionalización, lo público, lo privado y la identidad en América Latina y Canadá*, ed. Delia Montero Contreras and Raúl Rodríguez Rodríguez, 51–76 (Havana: Empresa Editorial Poligráfica Félix Varela, 2005).
3 Cuba, Oficina Nacional de Estadísticas e Información, *Anuario estadístico de Cuba 2013* (Havana, 2013), 183–5.
4 Cuba, Oficina Nacional de Estadísticas e Información, *República de Cuba: panorama económico y social* (Havana, April 2014), 38.
5 Soderlund, Wagenberg, and Surlin, "Impact of the End of the Cold War."
6 Heather N. Nicol, "Canada-Cuba Relations: An Ambivalent Media and Policy," *Canadian Foreign Policy Journal* 16, no. 1 (2010): 103–18.
7 Ibid., 109, 112.
8 Olga Rosa González Martín, "La opinión pública de Estados Unidos y Canadá hacia Cuba: un estudio comparativo," in *Políticas públicas, relaciones bilaterales e identidad en Canadá*, ed. Delia Montero Contreras and Raúl Rodríguez Rodríguez (Havana: Editorial Félix Galván, 2007), 111–32.
9 "Fidel's retirement and its impact for Sherritt and the Caribbean," *Globe and Mail*, 29 February 2008, Report on Business: International, B13.
10 Paul Koring, "Castro lets go of power; brother likely to succeed him; After half a century, the fiery and loquacious revolutionary – who outlasted nine U.S. presidents – quietly steps aside," *Globe and Mail*, 20 February 2008, International News, A12.
11 Ibid. In the entire sample, Fidel Castro was mentioned 142 times; he was called "dictator" 19 times and Cuba was identified as a "dictatorship" 25 times. The term "communist" was used 116 times; "repressive" was used 10 times.
12 "Raul Castro good for Cuba, government observers say," *Globe and Mail*, 18 January 2007, International News; World in Brief, A14.
13 Anthony Boadle, "Cubans touting smooth transition," *Globe and Mail*, 9 August 2006, International News, A10.

14 "Cuban students speak out against restrictions," *Globe and Mail*, 8 February 2008, International News, A15.

15 Estanislao Oziewicz, "Brother expected to 'be there for some time,'" *Globe and Mail*, 2 August 2006, International News, A10.

16 Stephen Handelman, "How Chavez complicates post-Castro transition," *Globe and Mail*, 2 August 2006, International News, A10.

17 Alan Freeman, "Vendors weigh Cuba's future in street markets of Havana," *Globe and Mail*, 3 August 2006, International News, A1.

18 Alan Freeman, "Sipping rum and cola, waiting for a Cuba libre," *Globe and Mail*, 7 August 2006, International News, A1.

19 Koring, "Castro lets go of power."

20 Doug Saunders, "How Fidel missed his Mandela moment," *Globe and Mail*, 23 February 2008, Focus, F3.

21 Marina Jimenez, "Dec. 2, 1961/Castro declares he's a Marxist-Leninist," *Globe and Mail*, 2 December 2010, International News, A2.

22 James W. Winter, "Fidel Castro, Jimmy Carter and George W. Bush in the Canadian News Media: A Critical Analysis" (Windsor, ON: University of Windsor, 2006), 18.

23 Sonia Verma, "Cuba's challenge: Open up economy, but stay communist; Historic gathering of top-ranking officials debate a secret document aimed at lifting country out of stagnation," *Globe and Mail*, 21 April 2011, International News, A19.

24 Anthony Boadle, "China becomes Cuba's no. 2 trading partner; Only Venezuela supplies more goods to island nation; Canada drops to fourth," *Globe and Mail*, 16 January 2006, Report on Business: International, B6.

25 "Havana says good night to 15 years of blackouts," *Globe and Mail*, 13 June 2006, International News, A18.

26 Quoted in Alan Freeman, "A tale of two pesos; Subsidized goods are so shoddy, ordinary Cubans will do almost anything to get convertible pesos," *Globe and Mail*, 12 August 2006, Focus, F2.

27 Quoted in ibid.

28 Quoted in ibid.

29 Quoted in ibid.

30 "Edging toward markets," *Globe and Mail*, 22 October 2009, Editorial, A20.

31 Quoted in "Going private," *Globe and Mail*, 20 September 2010, Editorial, A14.

32 Laszlo Buhasz, "Crime in Cuba," *Globe and Mail*, 14 January 2006, Travel, T2.

33 Rosa Tania Valdes, "Prices, not politics slow Cuba tourism; Tourists finding better value elsewhere," *Globe and Mail*, 7 March 2007, Travel, T6.

34 "U.S. sends home Cubans who land on bridge piling," *Globe and Mail*, 10 January 2006, International News, A14; see also Sean McNeely, "Close but no cigar for these Cubans," *Globe and Mail*, 29 April 2006, Travel, T4.

35 An embargo takes place when one country imposes economic sanctions upon another country and the economic relations between those two countries is regulated by the imposed sanctions. A blockade takes place when the economic sanctions imposed by one government upon another affect the economic and financial relations of that country with third countries.

36 "A reach too far," *Globe and Mail*, 10 February 2006, Editorial, A14.

37 Marcus Gee, "Enough with the embargo," *Globe and Mail*, 29 February 2008, Comment, A19.

38 Tavia Grant, "In Cuba, it's business as usual; Despite Castro's transfer of power and uncertain prospects, Canadian companies don't expect big changes in the near future," *Globe and Mail*, 2 August 2006, Report on Business, B1.

39 Ibid.

40 "Cuba owes Canadian oil firms $69-million (U.S.)," *Globe and Mail*, 28 December 2006, Report on Business, B5.

41 Jeff Sallot, "U.S. sees strategic advantage in Ottawa's Cuban ties," *Globe and Mail*, 19 December 2006, International News, A10.

42 Sarah Milroy, "Art in Cuba: freedom?" *Globe and Mail*, 8 April 2006, Weekend Review, R8.

43 "Power struggles," *Globe and Mail*, 14 June 2006, Editorial, A20.

44 "Unreformed tyranny," *Globe and Mail*, 23 November 2006, Editorial, A14.

45 "A reach too far," *Globe and Mail*, 10 February 2006, Editorial, A14.

46 "Cuba's other face," *Globe and Mail*, 2 March 2010, Editorial, A16.

47 Ibid.

48 "No end to repression," *Globe and Mail*, 8 March 2010, Editorial, A12.

49 "A dictator blinks," *Globe and Mail*, 12 July 2010, Editorial, A12.

11 "Not Miami": The Cuban Diasporas in Toronto and Montreal

CATHERINE KRULL AND JEAN STUBBS

Tourism and migration rarely receive serious consideration in foreign policy international relations analyses. Yet these international travellers often assume important roles in mediating relations between different societies. This chapter explores why Cubans have chosen to migrate to Canada, their experiences and perceptions once there, and how they relate to Canada and their country of birth.

To conceptualize the diasporic relationship between the Hispanic Caribbean and the United States, Jorge Duany draws on the insightful threefold classification of contemporary migrant-sending states set out by Peggy Levitt and Nina Glick Schiller.[1] The first and most common type, the "strategically selective state," encourages expatriate engagement with the home country, but does not grant citizenship and other rights (examples in the Americas include Haiti and Barbados). The "transnational nation-state," the second type, incorporates its overseas nationals, granting them dual citizenship (the Dominican Republic, El Salvador, and Mexico fit this model). The third is the "disinterested and denouncing state," which treats émigrés as no longer citizens and even as traitors (with Cuba the prime instance). Duany himself adds a fourth type, the "transcolonial state," with large migrant populations abroad that, despite common citizenship with their new countrymen, tend to be seen as foreigners in the "mother country" (for example, Puerto Ricans in the United States).

Categorizing Cuba as a "disinterested and denouncing state" might well have been accurate in describing Cuba-US migration a decade ago, when Levitt and Glick Schiller developed this typology, but it fails to capture Cuba in terms of its migration flows to other countries where Cuban émigrés do not lose their citizenship rights and are not seen as traitors.[2] Moreover, this categorization fails to apply to the United States today, especially in the wake of the January 2013 immigration reforms permitting Cubans freedom to travel overseas, the result of a twenty-year process of piecemeal openings[3] and the process of normalization of US-Cuban relations initiated in December 2014. Depending on the citizenship laws of a country, Cubans who opt to stay abroad can often apply for new citizenship. Thus Spain has a "grandchildren's law" that could allow 180,000 Cubans to "gain citizenship once all the applications have been processed." Canada, on the other hand, has a multifarious process whereby immigrants can settle and seek Canadian citizenship in a number of ways: family sponsorship, refugees, special selection for Quebec, and more.[4] And, in this context, many Cubans abroad send remittances to their families in Cuba, an important source of support on the island.[5] Indeed, remittances are relatively more important for Cuba, which received US$3.5 billion from that source in 2013, than for Mexico, which, with ten times Cuba's population, received US$22 billion.[6] These incongruities lead us to posit a fifth classification for Cuba as a post-1989 migrant-sending state, the "interested transnational state" – one that is especially applicable to Canada as an alternative destination for the Cuban diaspora.

Canada can also be characterized as an "interested transnational state" when it comes to receiving immigrants from Cuba. As the Soviet Union imploded and the United States tightened and extra-territorialized its trade embargo with the 1991 Torricelli and 1996 Helms–Burton Acts, Cuban government strategies in the face of crisis included promoting international tourism and alternative sources of trade and investment. These were accompanied by a changing mindset regarding overseas migration whereby increasing numbers of Cubans also sought alternative migratory destinations. The attraction of Canada was grounded on a track record of friendly international relations, direct investment, people-to-people contact generated by the large number of Canadians who visit Cuba annually, and policies that facilitate immigration and multiculturalism.

Coinciding with the period following Cuba's 1959 Revolution, Canada's immigration and multiculturalism reforms revolved around respecting the French-speaking and the dominant English-speaking cultures as what were termed the "two Founding Nations."[7] Following major reforms in the 1970s and 1980s, this extended to embrace the aboriginal "First Nations" and, subsequently, fast-growing other European and non-European immigrant groups.[8] This process accelerated in the

1990s, such that Canada at the start of the twenty-first century boasted a multiplicity of peoples, cultures, and languages, including significant numbers from the Caribbean and Latin America. In fact, until recently, Spanish was the language most spoken in Canada after its official languages, English and French.[9] And over the past few years there has been a 32 per cent increase in the number of persons who report speaking Spanish most often at home.[10]

Numbering more than twenty-one thousand on current estimates,[11] the Cuban diaspora remains small in comparison with other diasporas in Canada and Cuban diasporas elsewhere, such as in the United States (overwhelmingly the prime destination since 1959, with approximately two million Cuban migrants),[12] trailed by Spain (with 125, 263).[13] From an insignificant number in 1989, however, Canada's Cuban diaspora grew at a rate of over a thousand a year on average over the ten-year period from 2001 to 2011.[14] And although Cubans are dispersed across Canada, approximately 82 per cent reside in Toronto and Montreal. Indeed, Spanish is fast becoming, after French and English, the third language in Montreal, which also boasts the largest number of Spanish-speakers in the country (Statistics Canada 2011).[15] Both Toronto and Montreal have been major recipients of immigrants, including Latin Americans in waves mainly triggered by political events: Chileans in the 1970s, Central Americans in the 1980s, Peruvians in the 1990s, and, since then, more economic and professional migrants and Caribbean migrants. From the 1950s onwards, Toronto has seen an influx from the English-speaking Caribbean territories, while Haitians have flocked to Montreal. This development, in turn, allows for important comparative ethnic analysis in the two major urban cityscapes that Cubans find themselves having to negotiate.

When characterizing this post-1989 Cuban migration to Canada, the receptiveness of both Cuba and Canada challenges us to explore the category of "interested transnational state," as well as the broader concepts of "diaspora" and "transnationalism." Exploring why Cubans have chosen to emigrate to Canada, their experiences and perceptions once there, and how they relate to their host and home countries raises a range of issues, some of which we outline here. First, we provide a brief overview of Canadian immigration history as it has affected the contemporary Cuba-Canada relationship, paying particular attention to multiculturalism and immigration. We then focus on Toronto and Montreal, comparing and contrasting their separate histories and development, factors that frame the experiences and perceptions of

Cubans who have settled there. We highlight issues surrounding the commodification of Cuba, the development of political and cultural imaginaries, and the importance of race and ethnicity. Our concluding remarks suggest further avenues of enquiry regarding Cuban-ness and "moving on." Given the size of the Cuban community in the United States (particularly in Florida), the probability of family members living in the United States, and the similarity of this US-Cuban community to the home country in terms of language, culture, geography, and climate, why have so many Cuban émigrés chosen Toronto and Montreal, not Miami?

Immigration and Multiculturalism in Canada

Cuban immigrants to Canada, especially since 1989, have encountered an increasingly restrictive immigration system, especially after the advent of the Conservative government led by Stephen Harper in 2006. Nonetheless, like the whole of the Americas, Canada's demographic and economic development has been shaped largely through immigration, such that its immigration levels have been among the highest in the Western world. It is important, therefore, to understand some of the complexities of Canada's history of immigration and multiculturalism before turning to the more recent post-1989 Cuban migratory experience in Canada.

Immigration policy has long been a high priority for Canada. It has also been for the most part highly discriminatory in practice. As Jacklyn Neborak has argued, "this has resulted in constantly changing parameters for the 'ideal immigrant,' with definitions built upon a range of rationales, from racial premises to economic motives."[16] It is not surprising, then, that for the most part Canadian migration has favoured primarily western Europeans and white Americans. Beginning in the 1960s, however, Canada's immigration policies have undergone several significant reforms. Most important, in 1962, the federal government tabled regulations that eliminated colour, race, and nationality as criteria for denying immigrants entry to Canada. And in 1966, the government tabled a White Paper that recognized immigration as a major contributor to the national goals of population and economic growth, while recommending a preference for skilled labourers. In 1967 the points system was introduced, which reinforced, among other things, the preference for skilled labour, an existing family network, employability, education, and ability to speak one of the Canada's two official languages. Another significant change occurred with the 1976 Immigration Act, which not only formally recognized refugees as a legitimate class of immigrants, but also restricted the points system to the independent class and, to a lesser degree, the assisted relatives class. Immigrants applying under the humanitarian and family class were now exempt from meeting the points criteria. A fifth immigration category, the business class, was added to the Immigration Act in the 1980s; immigrants applying under this designation were required to bring enough financial capital to Canada to launch a business or invest in the domestic economy.

Although less explicitly discriminatory than in earlier days, these policies were nonetheless controversial. By the early 1990s immigration had become a highly charged issue on the political agenda, leading the newly elected Liberal government to pledge to overhaul Canada's immigration and citizenship policies. In the House of Commons, Minister of Immigration Sergio Marchi tabled "A Broader Vision: Immigration and Citizenship Plan for 1995–2000," a document casting immigration not as a domestic issue but as one that needed to take into account the global context. In 1994 and 1995, considerable consultation between various levels of government and private groups ensued. Much of the debate was dominated by the right-wing Reform Party (later the Canadian Alliance Party, and then the Conservative Party), which argued that immigration levels should be reduced and guided by economic needs, not by social or humanitarian imperatives. This meant that immigrants should be selected based on neoliberal constructions of what they could contribute to Canadian society, rather than place demands on state-financed services. The notion that the ideal immigrant should be self-sufficient won out, and a new points system was introduced with the aim of shifting immigration percentages over a five-year period (1995–2000) from 43 per cent economic and 51 per cent family to 53 per cent and 44 per cent, respectively (and reducing the numbers of refugees from 23.2 per cent in 1991 to 13.2 per cent in 2000).[17]

Following the September 2001 terrorist attacks, the Liberals under Prime Minister Jean Chrétien replaced the 1976 Immigration Act with the Immigrant and Refugee Protection Act (IRPA), which aimed, in effect, to open the door to the kinds of immigrants Canada desired and close it to the rest. It did so by 1) tightening the eligibility requirements for refugees, skilled immigrants, and business immigrants; 2) extending family entitlements to same-sex and common-law relationships;

and 3) increasing the government's power to arrest, detain, and deport any landed immigrant suspected of being a security threat. This direction was consolidated under the Harper Conservatives. As Neborak explains,

> The IRPA enables anyone holding the position of the Citizenship and Immigration Minister to capitalize upon security as a justification to exercise unilateral power and discretion. This has been illustrated in the form of a series of amendments and proposed changes that have emerged under Citizenship and Immigration Minister Jason Kenney, such as the new selection system for the Federal Skilled Worker Program, the *Faster Removal of Foreign Criminals Act*, and the series of recent changes to the Family Class, which involve freezing parent and grandparent applications in 2011, introducing the Super Visa for temporary entry, and the most recent May 2013 proposed package of reforms to the Family Class.[18]

Another reform came in the way of Bill C-11, the Balanced Refugee Reform Act, which slightly increased the number of new refugees accepted each year – the number increased from 232,811 in 1991 to 280,636 in 2010[19] – accelerated the speed of approval (primarily for refugees coming from "safe" countries), and increased funding to facilitate their integration into Canadian society.[20] In March 2005 it was reported that "[p]rocessing of new asylum claims is down to three months from more than 20 months under the old system, with the backlog reduced by two-thirds to 9,877 claims – one-fifth of them in the system for more than three years – from the peak of 30,750 in 2012."[21] Also new was the exponential growth of temporary foreign workers – rising from 73,050 in 2015 to 78,720 in 2016, suggesting a total of between 700,000 and 750,000 over the preceding decade – although very few of them have attained permanent resident status, which "has had some critics likening this disposable workforce to modern-day slavery."[22]

These post-9/11 changes mark the growing internationalization of Canada's immigration policy, including the sharing of information with other governments.[23] More than half of immigrants are selected according to education, knowledge of one of Canada's two official languages, and age, with the goal of a large proportion holding a university degree and a high-status professional position. Selection based on country of origin is wide ranging, with variations according to potential immigrants' destination within Canada. Meanwhile, illegal Cuban immigration has not posed much of a problem, because

Canada's porous border with the United States means that, if they choose, undocumented Cubans largely can head south.[24] Although it is impossible to assess accurate numbers, it is interesting that several Cubans in our study mentioned they knew Cubans living in Canada who were heading for the United States because, given the recent and ongoing attempts to normalize US-Cuban relations, they feared the Cuban Adjustment Act would soon be abolished and they would no longer have the opportunity.

It is important to note that Quebec has had its own immigration policy. Since 1867 immigration has remained largely the preserve of the federal government, but with the Quiet Revolution of the 1960s and growing demands by both federalist and separatist Quebecers for greater control over policies to preserve the province's francophone culture, the Quebec government slowly acquired more control over its immigration policy. The province established a separate immigration department in 1968, and provincially controlled immigration emerged as a means to both strengthen Quebec's francophone society and, with declining birth rates, sustain population levels.[25] In 1991 Ottawa and Quebec City agreed to the "Canada–Quebec Accord" giving Quebec the primary responsibility for immigration to the province. By this means, with subsequent federal-provincial clarifications, including partial federal funding, Quebec set its own annual immigration objectives and established provincial offices abroad to screen and select immigrants.

These various and significant changes in immigration policy have had an impact. Over the course of just over two and a half decades, Canada has experienced rapid changes in its population; today, Cubans are but one of a plethora of visible minorities in the country. The 2011 census and Statistics Canada's 2011 National Household Survey both testified to the country's remarkable ethnic diversity, with the presence of more than two hundred ethnic groups, thirteen of which have surpassed the one million mark in number. Other numbers are equally staggering: the proportion of foreign born (20.6 per cent of the total population) is the highest among the G8 countries; more than two million people migrated to Canada from 2001 to 2011; and more than six million (almost 20 per cent of the total population) identify as belonging to a visible minority group, with South Asians, Chinese, and blacks accounting for about 61 per cent of the visible minority population, followed by Filipinos, Latin Americans, Arabs, Southeast Asians, West Asians, Koreans, and Japanese. As is the case with the immigrant population in general, most people who identify as a visible minority live in

Ontario, Quebec, Alberta, and British Columbia; 70 per cent reside in Toronto, Montreal, and Vancouver. The largest visible minority groups in Toronto are South Asians, Chinese, and blacks; in Montreal it is blacks, Arabs, and Latin Americans.[26]

Until recently, migration from Latin American countries was negligible. Between 1966 and 1975 there were only 39,155 Latin American migrant landings in Canada. But starting in the 1990s, the demographic profile of Latin Americans in Canada shifted considerably. From 1996 to 2001 the number of Canadians claiming to be of Latin American origin increased by 32 per cent. As Alan Simmons has argued, the "migration stream from Latin America to Canada arose on the foundation of a combination of special circumstances: violence in sending countries; variable barriers to migrant entry to the United States; an independent Canadian immigration and refugee policy; and relatively high income and employment opportunities in Canada."[27]

By 2001 there were almost a quarter of a million Canadians of Latin American origin, making them one of the largest non-European-based ethnic groups as well as one of the fastest-growing ethnic groups in the country. They were mainly young (under age twenty-five), conversant in one of the two official languages, and, although more likely to have a university degree, more likely to have a lower income than the overall population. The number of Latin American migrants in Canada continues to increase, rising by 121 per cent over the five-year periods of 1996–2000 to 2001–06; they are currently the fourth-largest source of immigration to Canada.[28]

A number of studies have highlighted the specific histories of Latin American and Caribbean migrants in Toronto and Montreal, as well as their ethnic and cultural presence in these cities – ranging from restaurants, bars, clubs, and other small businesses to events such as concerts and art exhibitions – and the ethnic and racial discrimination issues they face.[29] We draw on these works as we consider exploratory comparative aspects of the commodification of Cuba, the development of political and cultural imaginaries, and the factors of race and ethnicity in Montreal and Toronto.

Canada and Cuba: The Unique Relationship

Canada's post-1989 approach to immigration has been conducive for Cuban migration, as "Canada's generous accommodation of thousands of Cuban and Chilean refugees during the 1960s and 1970s made it an attractive option for would-be immigrants and refugees from throughout the Americas over the next few decades."[30] Canadian immigration policy thus has encouraged Cubans to come to Canada on work, travel, student, and family visas, as well as to claim refugee status.[31] Moreover, well before the Revolution that brought Fidel Castro's regime to power, there had been a long history of economic and political ties between Canada and Cuba.[32] Canadian trade with the island dates back to the late eighteenth century. After 1898, when Spain's colonial power collapsed and the United States replaced it as the dominant power in Cuba, Canadian companies began investing substantially in the island. Ottawa and Havana established formal diplomatic relations in 1945, and there were private initiatives in Cuba such as that of the Matanzas-based branch of the missionary Les Sœurs de Notre-Dame du Bon-Conseil.[33] When the Cuban Revolution succeeded, Canada was one of only two countries in the Americas (the other was Mexico) that did not break relations with the new government. Although some Canadian leaders and elements of the Canadian public initially showed concern about a communist regime emerging in the Caribbean, the decision to have normal relations devolved from two issues: first, preserving and extending the economic dimension of the relationship; and, second, defending Canada's foreign policy sovereignty, such that Canada would not allow its interests to be dictated by the strongly anti-Cuban United States.[34]

The advent of Pierre Trudeau as prime minister in April 1968 proved a watershed in Cuba-Canada relations. Trudeau had entered Quebec politics in the 1960s during the Quiet Revolution,[35] winning a federal seat in his Montreal riding in 1965, rising in the Liberal Party, and, after becoming prime minister, dominating Canadian politics until his retirement in 1984. He supported Canadian national unity, and he was both uneasy about Washington's Cold War crusades and supportive of Cuba's efforts to maintain its sovereignty vis-à-vis the United States. Trudeau formed a strong personal friendship with Fidel Castro, and his government expanded Canada's ties with Cuba.[36] Although sometimes buffeted by ideological differences – including, during the later years of the 1993–2006 Liberal government and especially during the subsequent Conservative government – the relationship has endured, often in the face of stiff US opposition.[37]

Thus, in the crisis years of the early 1990s with the onset of the "Special Period" in Cuba – triggered by the fall of the Berlin Wall, the disintegration of the Soviet Union, the collapse of Cuba's trade relations with the Soviet bloc, and the tightening of the US blockade – Canadian multinational corporations such as Sherritt International invested heavily on the island. Moreover, Canadian companies helped build Cuban infrastructure, such as the international terminal at Havana's José Martí Airport. Canada's contemporary Cuba policy has been well documented elsewhere.[38] A 1999 assessment by the Canadian Foundation for the Americas (FOCAL) explains best why Chrétien's Liberal government embarked in 1994 on policy of "constructive engagement" as part of a strategy to encourage peaceful transition in Cuba:

> As the last bastion of communism in the Western Hemisphere, Cuba remains a dilemma and a priority within the Americas, a region increasingly committed to closer political and economic ties. Although the island's political and economic crisis has diminished the island's security risk in the region, the real possibility of significant economic and political chaos in Cuba continues to pose uncertainty for the region's democratic, political and economic stability.
>
> Closer to home, Cuba has become a priority for Canada's foreign policy towards the Americas. Since 1994, Canada has staked itself on a high-profile policy of constructive engagement towards the island. As a result, Canada's deepened political and economic ties with the communist island have heightened the interest for Canadians in developments taking place within Cuba.[39]

Canada saw Cuba as an opportunity to invest profitably in cooperative ventures and develop tourism, especially for "snowbirds" hoping to escape the harsh Canadian winter.[40] By 2003 Canada was the number one source of tourists travelling to Cuba; less than a decade later, more than one million Canadians were doing so each year.[41]

Cuba similarly viewed Canada in a favourable light, courting Canadian trade, investment, and tourism, and seeking to market its exportable items ranging from rum and cigars to culture (especially music and art). Perhaps most important in a transnational sense, through significant Canadian tourism people-to-people contacts have blossomed, and many Canadians and Cubans now have some understanding not only of the problems their countries face relative to the United States, but also of each other's politics, culture, and society. Hence Canada is not unknown to Cubans who emigrated there in increasing numbers. Indeed, for Cubans, the process of immigration to Canada differs significantly from that to the United States in that the former is a legal, government-to-government process reflecting the context of Canada's well-established connection to the island. Initially Havana allowed small openings for immigrants to move to Canada; today there is an almost open door to emigration. Curiously, however, tourism and migration are rarely given centre stage in analyses of foreign policy and international relations; our analysis addresses this major lacuna.

Cubans in Canada

Cuba's post-1989 out-migration has been driven less by political considerations and more by the economic challenges of the past quarter-century. Other factors also come into play, especially the efforts of Cubans to seek personal and professional advancement, including through studying or seeking work opportunities abroad, or marrying out, all while not cutting ties back home. This pattern of emigration brings to the fore the question of why Cubans choose to emigrate to Canada, especially to Toronto and Montreal, and how these cities are experienced and perceived by Cubans once they arrive.

Cubans have proven themselves savvy when it comes to locating opportunities, and Canada scores high in that respect. As Joe Friesen has argued, "[b]etween now and 2021, a million jobs are expected to go unfilled across Canada ... We need to radically boost immigration numbers. With the right people, Canada can be an innovative world power. Without them, we'll drain away our potential."[42] Cubans we interviewed expressed the view that Canada was attractive as a cosmopolitan country of opportunity, preferable by far to the United States, where politics is of paramount importance. A thirty-six-year-old male remarked: "The Cubans here [in Toronto], and I know them, have some kind of different opinions than Miami ... The Cubans in Miami have different positions and they go there for different purposes." And, as one thirty-three-year-old female said, she and her husband came to Canada "for my son so that he would have more options and a healthier relationship with Cuba. He could not have that in Miami. We did this for him." Along the same lines, a fifty-year-old female who has lived in Toronto since 2009 stated that her adopted country was a safer place to raise her children:

> All Cubans want to go to United States, but I didn't like it to live. My grandfather fought very hard against [Fulgencio] Batista's regime. He was tortured because of his political ideas. To my family and me, Batista is synonymous with the United States. Moreover, criminal rates are very high in United States; anyone can carry a gun ... I don't like that either. I don't believe in the American Dream either. Everything over there is

competition and about having success. On the other hand, Canada gave me the opportunity to emigrate with the kids to a quieter and safer society. However, I could have got a better job in United States easily, whether in Miami or in New York. But that would have meant to sacrifice the security of my kids on behalf of my own personal realization. My decision to leave Cuba was actually taken thinking of my kids and their future. I knew that Cuba's future was going from bad to worse.

When asked why she and her husband did not go to Miami, a sixty-year-old female explained: "I don't like it. I went to Miami with my husband in 1994. At the end, we came back to Cuba. We didn't like the lifestyle of Miami. Miami is still not appealing to me."

There is also a perception among many Cubans that there is less racism in Canada, although that perception may be challenged in reality:

Canadians seem to be less racist ... Canadians are most polite. They are careful not to show anything explicit. For example, I work at a school wherein the owner is a female Chinese ... The other day the teacher classified Russians as tax cheaters. He forgets that I am half-Russian! But these are very soft comments because it is not very easy to be openly racist in Canada. (Fifty-year-old female)

On television you see that everything in Canada is fine, that everything is quiet, with no violence and everyone was happy. Canada appealed to us ... The shock was a little hard because the truth is that [Canadians] do not discriminate openly but when you start interacting with them you realize that people here are quite racist and discriminate against you. (Thirty-one-year-old male)

Canada has always been seen, at least in Cuba, as a first world country that is highly developed, quiet and safe. Although, when you get here you realize that this is not as you imagined. (Forty-two-year-old male)

Equally, Cubans are clear as to which city they wanted to live in and why: "In Toronto, Cubans tend to have opportunities. Black Cubans like me prefer it here. The wealthy Cubans also have a preference for Toronto but in a different part of Toronto, they also like exclusive areas in Ottawa like Gatineau. Cubans who were connected to the Party prefer to go to Quebec or to Gatineau" (thirty-four-year-old male).

In a general sense, a crucial aspect of the decision to emigrate seems to be an understanding that Canadian society in both its English- and French-speaking dimensions offers Cubans an immediate home.

Although being new Canadians and building new lives, there is no question of having to surrender their language while learning a new one, to change their politics, or to weaken their own culture. In Canada, Cubans have a network of other Cubans on whom they can draw; moreover, when time and circumstance permit, they can more easily travel back to Cuba to see family and friends – something difficult for Cuban-Americans to do, given the ongoing US embargo and anti-Cuban legislation. In the words of four Cubans interviewed:

> I have many Cuban friends here. There are Cuban things between us … they helped me, like where I can stay. (Thirty-nine-year-old male, Toronto)

> In Cuba, maybe she would not be my friend, but here it is different, she is my friend here, she is Cuban. (Twenty-four-year-old female, Toronto)

> But yes I think that the North in particular, is different from the US, it is better and remember Canada is very far from the Cuban mentality, Canada is very far from the Cuban idea of living. (Twenty-one-year-old male, Toronto)

> I did not look for having Cuban friends here. It just happened. But it is easier to become friends with people who have more similarities with you, and the language is important for that. I wasn't looking for Cuban friends, but it is natural to feel closer to Cubans because of the same culture and idiosyncrasy. (Sixty-year-old female, Toronto)

Cosmopolitan Toronto

The answer to "Why Canada?" is, of course, complicated by the existence of English- and French-speaking Canada, because immigrants to both parts of the country confront two dissimilar societies and cultures. Notable in this light is that the two main sites where Cubans have settled should present diverging realities and visions of Cuba. Toronto, on the one hand, has a visually significant Cuban presence – restaurants, small businesses, clubs, a music scene, and a solidarity movement – and respects Cuba as a place holding up against the tremendous pressures put upon it by the United States. Montreal, on the other hand, lacks a Cuban-based infrastructure in the way of restaurants and small businesses. It does, however, have its music scene and solidarity movement, and there are Quebecers (both federalist and separatist) who see Cuba as a place of revolutionary success that can guide them in protecting and further developing their own progressive society and language rights, if not independence.

Cubans interviewed in Toronto singled out the differences they saw between Cubans who choose to live in Toronto or Montreal:

To the east of the Yonge Street area [a main Toronto thoroughfare], we are talking about many Cubans who are not wealthy. So you have Cubans living here who are black Cubans, mulatto Cubans, they didn't have a job in Cuba or they are only musicians, and they would live in this area ... The Cubans who came here, white Cubans who came in the 1980s, they'll go to Montreal. In Toronto you have interesting Cubans living here. (Thirty-two-year-old male)

I stay in contact with everybody in the Cuban community here in Toronto because for me ... this is not a place for a political campaign, not like Quebec, not at all. Not from whatever side. This is a cultural space. (Twenty-seven-year-old male)

When you go to Montreal, even though French is close to Spanish, they have the perception that in Toronto you will do better ... but it is more about political issues in Montreal, about Cuban political issues. (Thirty-one-year-old female)

The Greater Toronto Area in many ways epitomizes the popular perception of modern multicultural Canada. With a population of more than six million, the majority of its citizens are of non-British origin: European, South Asian, East Asian, African, and Caribbean. Accordingly it has a rich and diverse cultural life.[43] In this milieu, Cubans in Toronto have constructed a strong ethnic and cultural presence that appeals to the Cuban diaspora as well as to Latin Americans and to Caribbean migrants and others in the city.

The Cubans we interviewed often were adamant that certain criteria, such as food and language, are essential to an ethnic/cultural presence. When asked what was important to feeling or being Cuban, one woman answered: "*Yucca con mojo*, white rice, black beans, and pork. I actually eat more 'Cuban food' here than in Cuba ... I like calling the grocery '*la bodega*.' My daughter criticizes me when I do that ... I also keep saying '*oigo*' when I answer the phone. I am very proud of using '*oigo*' because Cubans are the only people who use that expression to answer the phone ... it means that a person is Cuban, with a similar life story as you. Now, my daughter has adopted '*oigo*' as a mark of identity too. I like that! I am very proud of her!" Likewise, another woman noted: "I don't know how to define Cubans. Maybe in relation to what we eat (black beans and *yucca con mojo*); maybe our smile. Cubans smile every time that we meet someone."

Toronto boasts a number of Cuban-owned or Cuban-themed restaurants that serve traditional Cuban dishes – Julie's, La Cubana, Cuba's Latin Restaurant, Mambo, and La Cubanita are some examples. They vary from those in trendy areas such as Danforth Avenue to small cafes in neighbourhoods outside the city centre. It is also common to see other restaurants and bars feature Cuban-themed events. For example, the trendy Sky Bar hosted "A Cuban Affair: … A warm summer evening dedicated to saluting the Cuban lifestyle … we divulge into the Cuban culture and tradition. Come experience a taste of … HAVANA: A Salute to all things Cuban." Julie's Café, one of the more popular, centrally located, authentic Cuban eateries, advertises itself as a "Casually cool Cuban cantina on downtown's west side," and tells its customers that it "serves up authentic dishes, a cozy environment, and good vibrations – all of which will make you feel as though you have stumbled into a neighbourhood dinner party."

Among the Cuban diaspora, music has played a large role, and the music scene in Toronto has a number of popular Cuban bands and musicians who play in some of the Cuban, Latino, and pan-Latino restaurants and clubs, including Lula's Lounge, Skybar, Epic Lounge, Julie's Restaurant, Los Cabos, and Mambo Lounge. These bands and musicians also appear to play at some of the most popular Toronto venues with a regularity much greater than one might expect: "their impact on the musical life of the country far outweighs what the numbers would indicate."[44] Cuban musicians from the island who tour Canada tend to play to sold-out audiences when in Toronto – in the past few years alone, musicians and groups performing in Toronto have included Carlos Varela, Chucho Valdés, Roberto Linares Brown, Compay Segundo, Orishas, Los Van Van, X Alfonso, and Los Muñequitos de Matanzas. The city has gained such a reputation as a Cuban musical centre that Jane Bunnett, a Toronto-based Canadian soprano saxophonist, flutist, bandleader, and multiple Grammy nominee and Juno Award winner, was moved to comment: "In recent years, Cuban musicians mention Toronto as a place that they would like to get to. In the past, people told [me] that they wanted to relocate to Miami or New York, but more and more [I am] hearing that Cubans see our city as a desirable place to live and work."[45]

Cigar stores are another feature of life in Toronto. Selling one of the premier cultural exports of the island, they do so with an aura of Cuban culture. An advertisement for Frank Correnti Cigars – "Cuban in every way" – is a case in point: "Like his Father and Grandfather before him, every bale of tobacco is chosen personally, IN CUBA. The cigars are made completely by hand in the old Cuban tradition using CUBAN cigar rollers. Relationships with CUBA go back over a century because making Cigars is not about politics or business, but about Passion and Respect. Cigar Makers are a universal family. They do what they do out of a Love of The Leaf."[46] The prominent presence of the phrase "Cuban cigars" on the windows and signs of many stores throughout Toronto is testament to the popularity of what is seen as a quintessentially Cuban commodity.

It is also not uncommon to see Cuban émigré writers, filmmakers, and artists featured at events, book launches, and exhibits. In Accents Bookstore, which is Cuban owned and specializes in books on Cuba, discussion groups are held to converse about the latest Cuban novel, and people can either listen to visiting Cuban scholars, poets, and writers passing through the city or just meet to deliberate about political and economic events on the island. Art exhibits have included an exhibition by Carlos Garaicoa at the Royal Ontario Museum (2006); *Cardboard Beach*, an installation by Los Carpinteros at the David Pecaut Square in downtown Toronto (2014); *The Possibility of Everything*, an exhibition that included Cuban artists such as Glenda León (2014); and *Before Day Breaks*, with Cuban artists such as Yoan Capote, Los Carpinteros, and Wilfredo Prieto (2014). The recent CineCuba film festival "[strove] to open the window to Canadians to see the real Cuba through film," while the Diaspora Film Fest presented two good films about Cuba: *Una noche* and *Amor crónico*. Indeed, there are so many Cuban events in Toronto that a web site, "Cuba in Toronto," has been created to help Torontonians track them all.[47]

Such events have come to serve as key focal points for members of the Cuban diaspora in Toronto and its surrounding suburbs. They do so by enabling the members of the diasporic community to keep up to date with issues in Cuba, dialogue with Cuban residents and visitors, and establish and strengthen networks among themselves. At the same time, these spaces are frequented by Canadians with an interest in Cuban affairs, so that, at a certain level, the transnational bonds among the émigré community, Canadians more generally, and Cuban-based guests are strengthened. Accents Bookstore is typical: "It has become a community space for performances and presentations, discussions, debates, consultations, workshops and classes on Cuba."[48]

Canadian solidarity groups that support Cuba have been a fixture since the early 1960s. With more of a transnational emphasis on sharing culture, food, and friendship than politics – though politics is important – perhaps the most important group, due to its size and nationwide presence, is the Canadian-Cuban Friendship Association (CCFA). Toronto's branch is particularly active and has come to provide an enabling role for greater contact between Canadians sympathetic to the Revolution and society in Cuba and the Cuban diaspora in Canada. The CCFA and other solidarity groups play a major part both in fundraising for their activities in Cuba, including hurricane relief, the purchase of ambulances, providing grants for Canadian students to do volunteer work in agricultural and other endeavours in Cuba, and sponsoring national speaking and musical tours for prominent Cubans visiting Canada.[49] They also help new Cuban-Canadians adjust to life after they have emigrated. For some émigrés the solidarity groups are where they make their first contacts with other Cubans after arrival and begin to carve out their place. A Cuban émigré solidarity group in Toronto – La Asociación de Cubanos "Juan Gualberto Gómez," founded in 2007 and connected to the CCFA – has as its first goal "Promover y difundir la cultura e identidad cubana en Toronto" (to promote and spread Cuban culture and identity in Toronto).[50]

Not all Cubans in Toronto, however, find unbridled success or have a positive émigré experience. Despite the glittering goal of a multicultural society, the realities of class and race can often be at variance with the ideal. In the words of one twenty-six-year-old male:

> In Cuba, I am Cuban first. In Canada, I am Afro-Cuban … [W]hen you are in Cuba you're Cuban, but when you're here you're black, you're mulatto, you're this and that … [W]hen you arrive [in] Canada, you have the cost of the housing, the racism behind the process of how to get a job, or how to get a house, or how to deal with the landlord, [then] they will say "let me go back." I met Cubans like this, black Cubans. I am a black Cuban, I am very black; at the same time there is a very universal term that people use in Toronto: "Afrocentric." I do not match totally with that term because I am Cuban … it definitely has another connotation, but definitely I am part of the new black Cuban diaspora around the world.

The strong Caribbean presence – 6 per cent of the Toronto population,[51] a three-week annual August Caribbean Carnival, Caribana, an area of Toronto called Little Jamaica, and many Caribbean restaurants and venues – can also add to this disjunction, not least the representation that people from the Caribbean are anglophone, despite the presence of Afro-Latino/as.

The Cuban community in Toronto has developed a strong sense of its unique identity within one of the strongest centres of the multicultural mosaic of English-speaking Canada. It has seen increased members of the diaspora since the onset of the debilitating "Special Period" on the island primarily because the political milieu in Toronto – and anglophone Canada – is not ideologically polarized like that experienced by the Cuban-American community in Miami. This is not to suggest that problems of integrating with Canadian society do not exist; racism, for instance, is sometimes palpable. Our interviews indicate, however, that, in building new lives and having the chance for economic betterment, Cuban-Canadians have found a place where they can thrive and still maintain their Cuban identity.

Politicized Montreal?

In Montreal the situation is different. Solidarity groups have also played an important role in making new Cuban-Canadians there feel welcome, smoothing the paths for housing and employment, and maintaining ties with Cuba. However, events held in Montreal can also be highly politicized and off-putting for some Cubans who might have left Cuba for primarily economic reasons and want to distance themselves from politics. The legacy behind this politicization is the more charged political relationship that Quebecers in general, and Montrealers in particular, have had with Cuba. As noted above, many Quebecers have identified with the symbolism of the Cuban Revolution, which occurred just as the Quebec's Quiet Revolution began. Fidel Castro himself visited Montreal in April 1959 to seek business ventures and investment and to strengthen political ties with Canada. A leading scholar of 1960s Montreal has observed: "[T]he significance of the Cuban revolution resided in its destruction of a myth according to which the struggle against economic dictatorship was doomed to failure. From [Che] Guevara, activists were also beginning to believe that they could not sit back and wait for the right conditions for social transformation, but that these conditions needed to be actively fostered."[52]

Although by no means a 1960s radical, Pierre Trudeau's positive attitude towards Cuba was prototypical of many Quebecers' feelings about the island. As an associate professor of law at the Université de Montréal from 1961 to 1965, he was exposed to the city's vibrant pro-Cuban spirit. This spirit was on display at the 1967 World's Fair held in Montreal, where Cuba's presence, through its modernistic pavilion, its sale of cigars and rum, and its welcoming atmosphere, proved a turning point in creating a positive image of Cuba in both Quebec and the rest of Canada, even if many visitors were not so receptive to the subtle ideological promotion.[53]

Montreal then witnessed a radical turn in the late 1960s and early 1970s, one fractured by race and nation. A recent landmark study highlights how the French and the British had been seen not only as the two founding nations, but also as the two founding "races," something evidenced in the concept of "White Niggers" adumbrated by Pierre Vallières.[54] Drawing on the language of Black Power and French Caribbean figures such as Aimé Cesaire, Frantz Fanon, and Édouard Glissant, Vallières' work dramatically highlighted the plight of French Quebec, contributing to a shift in *Québécois* consciousness. At the same time, however, as David Austin argues, it obscured the presence of the not-insignificant number of real blacks in Montreal, which for a period became a veritable centre of Black Power and the British Caribbean left. Of two catalyst groupings, the Caribbean Conference Committee and the C.L.R. James Study Circle, the latter was small and based in Montreal, although it also had members in Toronto, Ottawa, and other parts of Canada, the United States, and the Caribbean. It formed the footing for a new Caribbean left in Canada and brought to Montreal the influential Trinidadian political thinker and historian C.L.R. James, Trinidadian economist Lloyd Best, Jamaican writer and sociologist Orlando Patterson, Grenadian-Trinidadian calypsonian Mighty Sparrow, and Barbadian writer George Lamming. This effort laid the groundwork for the 1968 Congress of Black Writers at McGill University, which was a seminal event attended by well-known black thinkers and activists from across Canada, the United States, Africa, and the Caribbean, including C.L.R. James, Stokely Carmichael, Miriam Makeba, and Walter Rodney. Many of these speakers, it might be added, were also visitors to Cuba around that time. Within months a black-led protest at Sir George Williams University (now Concordia University) raised fears that Montreal would become a hotbed of international black radical politics.[55]

Two years later, in October 1970, elements of the Front de libération du Québec (FLQ) attempted to destabilize the pro-federalist provincial government of Quebec through two terrorist acts: kidnapping the British trade commissioner, James Cross, and abducting and assassinating

Quebec cabinet minister Pierre Laporte.[56] Among FLQ radicals, building an independent and socialist Quebec *à la* Cuba was a goal. Although the terrorists in the Laporte case were apprehended and, after trial, imprisoned, the FLQ cell involved in the Cross kidnapping received safe passage to Cuba with Fidel's support after successful negotiations for Cross's release. After spending four years in Cuba and three in France, the exiles returned to Montreal in 1977 through the mediation of a separatist government in Quebec – they pleaded guilty, served short prison terms, and were released.

How much of an impact this political history has had on the present day is a moot question, but what is evident is that, whether through politics, or tourism, or culture, Cuba figures in the Quebec imaginary. In rallies and demonstrations in Quebec over the years, the Cuban image has had prominence with posters of Che and Cuban flags. A good case in point is one of the largest political protests in Quebec since the Second World War, which involved about ten thousand trade unionists, left-wing activists, the unemployed, and university students marching on McGill University in 1969.[57] Photographs published in the media show placards with Che's image alongside Quebec and Cuban flags; protestors argued that "Capital speaks English, labour speaks French … Turn McGill over to the Francophone working class."[58] John Hellman, a professor at the time in the Department of History and Classical Studies at McGill, recalls that "students would interrupt … There was a guy that would sit up in the front row, … a tough guy [dressed] like Che Guevara. I would be talking about nineteenth-century France … and he would get up and he would say, 'Professor, for heaven's sakes, I mean, this is a story about class struggle, about the poor against the rich, what are you going off on a tangent again for?'"[59]

Given Quebec's identification with the Cuban Revolution, what is surprising, then, is the extent to which the Cuban cultural presence is far less visibly tangible in Montreal than in Toronto. There is almost an absence of Cuban restaurants, bars, or clubs in this cosmopolitan city. As expressed in one blog posting in 2012: "I just want to confirm that there is no Cuban restaurant in Montreal. CUBA & SAVEUR TROPICALE is closed, right? And CAYO COCO is closed as well? I am part Cuban and I want to introduce my guy to Cuban food. Not a 'Cuban *sandwich*' but just regular typical Cuban restaurant food and/ or pastries. Let me know please. Thanks." In response a couple of people pointed out that there were two other small Cuban restaurants in Montreal, but, as one women explained: "I don't know if I'd actually call Café Cubano a restaurant. It is a tiny hole-in-the-wall café bar, perhaps there are a couple of dishes beyond the traditional Cuban sandwich. The new B del M is not far from there, just a bit north and east. That rather desolate strip on St. Hubert north of Jean-Talon is slowly and painfully becoming a spot for small independent restaurants, especially Latin American." There is also the Havana Resto Lounge, but the only thing Cuban is its name, as it serves "creative fusion cuisine from France and Italy."[60]

In terms of Cuban cultural events, a thirty-one-year-old Cuban man stated: "I don't like how Cuban culture is shown here [in Montreal]. In the summer there is a festival called 'Weekend du Monde' where every week is dedicated to different countries ... I went to Cuba's week and I did not like it. That was not Cuba ... There was only one stand selling Cuban food and the rest was all Dominicans selling Dominican food as Cuban food. Panamanians wearing their typical costumes danced pretending they were Cubans. It did not have anything to do with Cuba." Likewise, a thirty-three-year-old Cuban bank clerk said: "There is a celebration every year here, the Weekend du Monde, at Saint Helen's Island, and at Jean Drapeau's park. There is a Cuban day, but according to what I hear, there is nothing Cuban about it. It is a bunch of Peruvians playing salsa and I am not interested in that."

Also telling is the absence of Cuban-to-Cuban networks in Montreal. The Cubans we interviewed, especially those who have come to Canada in the past few years, made remarks such as: "I have found strange the behaviour of the Cubans I have met here. Cubans don't like to be in contact with other Cubans" (middle-aged female). "I know Cubans who do not like to connect with other Cubans. I don't understand that. How are you going to deny your people? Your country?" (forty-two-year-old male). "In Cuba, people have solidarity. Here in Montreal Cubans are more reserved ... they would never ask me to come in to chat here" (fifty-year-old female).

Although Cuban-centred venues in Montreal have proved few and ephemeral, some major Cuban cultural events have been held. An outstanding one was in 2008, when Montreal's much-celebrated Museum of Fine Arts hosted "¡Cuba! Art and History from 1868 to Today, the largest Cuban state-sponsored exhibit of Cuban art ever assembled, with many pieces being shown outside the country for the first time."[61] Emphasizing the strong state-to-state relationship between Quebec and Cuba, it is noteworthy that this Cuban state-sponsored exhibit took place only in Montreal and no other Canadian city.

As in Toronto, alongside art, music has played an important role for Montreal's Cuban diasporic community, especially in the context of the city's famed jazz festivals. Again, however, specific Cuban music venues are in short supply. Thus, Cubano's Club and Le Code Bar are no longer regular salsa venues, though in 2013 Diese Onze Jazz Club on Rue St Denis proved popular by running weekly "Les Lundis Cubains" events with local-based Cuban musicians; and on Sundays, Cuban musicians could be found among those open-air drumming at Les Tam-Tams du Mont Royal. There are no Cuban bookstores of the kind found in Toronto, so outside the occasional music venues, the only other events tend to be organized by the solidarity groups.

Cubans in Montreal express mixed feelings about this historical and cultural baggage: "They understand Cuba in Quebec. There are more opportunities in Toronto, but here is better" (twenty-two-year-old female). "The people of Quebec support our revolution ... there is solidarity here" (twenty-six-year-old female). "They are like Cuba ... A small population trying to fight a large enemy ... an enemy who wants to take away their identity, their culture" (twenty-six-year-old male). Speaking of when Fidel went to Montreal in October 2000 as a private citizen to mourn at Trudeau's state funeral, one Cuban commented: "They [Montrealers] have been friends with Cuba for a long time. Fidel was even at Trudeau's funeral ... there is respect" (thirty-four-year-old male).

Other Cubans simply want to get on with their lives, away from politics, and find the more politically charged reality in the city, especially linked to francophone separatists, hard to handle: "Montreal isn't an easy city, and the *Québécois* aren't easy either," said one Cuban. Others echoed his words, expressing the desire to distance themselves from any political or cultural stereotyping.[62] A forty-two-year-old man said he was disappointed at how aloof people were in Quebec: "You are just another number ... you see people on the subway or on the bus and everyone goes with the phone or I-pod and no one looks at anyone. This is very shocking to Latin people." Another man (age thirty-three) explained that Montreal is "a city in decay, it is falling apart." An established university professional resented his children having to go to French school: "I left Cuba so as not to have to be told what to do, and now I'm being told what to do with my children. If anything makes me leave, it will be that."[63] Several such professionals interviewed in 2013 had family and friends in Miami, visited them regularly, and were considering their options. Several who had made the move had done so not only for familial reasons, but also to be in a warmer climate. Moreover, a few held the belief that Florida politics was in transition, especially in 2012 when the majority voted for the Democratic presidential nominee, Barack Obama; one recently relocated Cuban art curator said she left Montreal for family reasons, but also in part because Miami itself was changing.

Another reason Cubans have chosen to come to Quebec is that they believed their chances of leaving Cuba were more likely if they went through the province's immigration process than through the process in another country. As one thirty-one-year-old male explained: "We submitted our application to the immigration program in Montreal because it was the easiest way to leave the country. If there was a chance to go to another place, I would have gone elsewhere." Similarly, a thirty-three-year-old male referred to Quebec's immigration program as "affordable" and "quick."

In short, unlike in Toronto, the Cuban diaspora in Montreal has long existed – even before the increased emigration after the "Special Period" – in a strongly political milieu constrained by the sovereignty movement in French-speaking Canada, one that seeks to promote a unicultural, rather than a multicultural, society. There are much fewer social and cultural manifestations of Cuban-ness in Montreal, including restaurants and other cultural venues, than in Toronto. Still, the Cuban community in Montreal exists; it still attracts new Cuban immigrants and, with its own problems, remains an expression of the island's culture in a place that is not Miami. In the words of one Cuban living in Montreal, "the United States could have been another way out ... but it would have only been a [stopover], especially if we had gone to Miami. I was not interested in living there and I am not interested now." Yet another explained: "I didn't consider moving to the USA as most Cubans do because I am a victim of all the anti-Yankee propaganda in Cuba that they have been shoving into our brains for over fifty years, and besides, the USA seemed to me to be a violent society, with major problems regarding the health care system." Like their compatriots in Toronto, Cuban-Canadians in francophone Montreal have found a place where they can thrive and still maintain their Cuban identity.

"Moving On" and Carrying Cuban-ness within

In the United States the metaphor for creating "Americans" from diverse ethnic and racial backgrounds is that of a "melting pot," and whether or not it reflects actual lived experiences, the allegory in Canada is that of a "cultural mosaic."[64] Canada is often internationally perceived as a place where one can live and express oneself as one pleases, a place that does not necessarily diminish one's heritage, culture, or identity. Cubans can identify with these sentiments. In the words of one twenty-four-year-old male: "If I lose my connection with being Cuban, I would change completely. I would be another person. I will never be Canadian like other people here because I am Cuban." He carries his "Cuban-ness" within, in contradistinction to the society and cultures around him in Canada, including Cuban culture. "You don't need to be in Cuba, because you have the Cuban inside you. Whatever place you go to, even if there are no Cubans around you, you have your own Cuba inside you ... That's why it's good to be living in Canada ... I'm still Cuban." Similarly, a fifty-year-old female observed: "I am not sure if I received this Cuban-ness from Mom or my Grandma, but my Mom could have been living in Brazil or elsewhere and she continued to say that her permanent address was in Havana. She used to say: 'I am not living in Cuba, but I am from Cuba and this is my home.' This is the same feeling I do have, too. We are very proud of being Cubans ... So the Cuban identity is something rooted in me ... my love for Cuba, no one can take that from me." And yet another female emphatically stated: "I am Cuban. Cuba is my nation. But I like living in Canada more than living in Cuba."

Alongside the ease of travel to and from Cuba, the Internet and social media have emerged as powerful tools for strengthening transnational Cuban diasporic ties and a transnational sense of self:

I write friends e-mails ... to my family and say hi to them. So yes, I still have contact with them. This is important. Some of them have gone to Miami and they send me Facebook mail; so, yes, my friends I keep in contact with on the computer. (Eighteen-year-old male)

I miss the Cuban people but I don't need to be in Cuba – I can have anything Cuban on the Internet. I can e-mail my Cuban friends. I have YouTube. (Twenty-one-year-old male)

It is something important to me. I keep in touch with all my friends and family who are living out of Cuba, wherever we are. (Fifty-year-old female)

I am far away from my friends and family in Cuba, but I still know that they are there and I can talk with them anytime I want using the computer. It will never be like seeing them but it is a good thing that you can talk with them ... We send e-mails ... We are still in communication. (Twenty-six-year-old female)

At the same time, the Internet was a source of struggle for older Cubans immigrating to Canada. As one woman said: "I was over forty-five years old when I came here. It is difficult immigrating at that age. I know how everything works in Cuba. I know how to behave; I know how to interact with people. Here I know nothing of that ... It was very hard for me when I had to ask for some help, and people didn't give me any orientation. People usually said: 'Look it up on the Internet' ... You lose your confidence ... This was one of the events that triggered my depression."

It is also interesting to examine the reactions of Cubans living in Canada to the attempts by US president Obama and Cuban president Raúl Castro in 2014–15 to restore diplomatic relations; almost all viewed these efforts as positive, especially the re-opening of the Cuban embassy in Washington in July:

> To me, it is the most important news in terms of politics that I have heard in a long time. I was very happy ... It was a total surprise. I really didn't expect something like this to happen. (Thirty-three-year-old male)

> I went to Cuba recently; I was there a few days after the announcement was made. I really noticed an honest happiness coming from most of the people. People are generally happy and have lots of hope. But I think that sense of hope doesn't have real foundations. (Thirty-eight-year-old male)

> I watched Obama's speech from beginning to end. And then Raúl's ... I felt really happy and I was like God, this is the beginning of something good, the beginning of whatever it is, the beginning of the end of the blockade, the beginning of the end of all these years of hate and division between a border and another one. (Twenty-five-year-old male)

Cubans in Canada remain sceptical, however, as to whether this will translate into better social, economic, and political outcomes for Cuba:

> I still don't believe that half the things that people were saying will happen will actually happen ... I am sceptical because I don't believe in this change of a political position from the US side towards Cuba. It feels to be, at least from the Cuban side, as if it's some kind of pretend happiness. (Thirty-two-year-old male)

> We cannot allow [Americans] to come to Cuba with an attitude of colonizing. We need to be alert because I know that there will be many American tourists that will have a big influence on Cubans. We need to be very careful because they will go to Cuba and they will tell Cubans about their

story of success and about how capitalism is the best thing in the world. The US should not be against what we have had as politics until now, right? (Twenty-nine-year-old female)

If Obama leaves the presidency without doing anything else related to this change, well, we really need to see what's going to happen with the next president of the US. Of course Raúl will remain where he is. (Thirty-two-year-old male)

The Cubans to whom we spoke were adamant that changes in US-Cuba relations would have little impact on their own lives; they also speculated that restored relations might have a negative impact on Canada's relationship with Cuba:

Nothing has really changed at all, really. There has been no change in regards to the relations with my family in Cuba or my friends there in the US. (Thirty-eight-year-old male)

This hasn't affected my everyday life in Canada; it really hasn't changed at all. (Twenty-five-year-old male)

If American companies get in the way as well as American tourism, then the whole relationship between Cuba and Canada will be altered. That is because American tourism in Cuba will change the prices there. Things won't be so readily available to Canadians. (Fifty-one-year-old female)

Cuba has kept up something that is really authentic for a long time, an autonomy, an authenticity that is very important, which is very rich, ... And if the Americans come here now and get involved, they are going to invade the Cuban market ... In a couple of years, we will have McDonalds in Cuba for sure! (Thirty-two-year-old male)

Americans are very possessive and very imperialistic. Very domineering. Cuba and America don't fit together. Their mindsets don't fit each other ... The thing is that Canadians are not very happy about Americans going to Cuba as tourists ... They feel like they won't be able to go because Americans are going to screw everything up ... I think Cuba is going to get very expensive, and Cuba is already expensive. If Americans start visiting Cuba, things will be much more expensive. The change will be very drastic. (Thirty-three-year-old male)

Importantly, even in the face of normalized Cuba-US relations, Cubans living in Canada continue to feel confident that their decision to move to Canada, rather than to the United States, remains the correct one:

> I have noticed that starting from December 17th [Obama's December 2014 announcement], a lot of [Cuban] people have commented to me that either themselves or [Cuban] people they know have decided to abruptly move to the US. What I mean is maybe it was something that they hadn't considered before or at least they hadn't considered doing it in such a rush. And now all of a sudden they decide to do it because once they heard that diplomatic relations will improve, they think that the Cuban Adjustment Law will be removed and all the immigration privileges that Cubans enjoy when they want to move to the US will be over. So Cubans want to take that step now before it is no longer possible. This is true for Cubans in Cuba and in Canada. But I am not considering it, neither is my family. Not at all ... It is not the right place for me ... I don't like the US in a general sense. And I want to live in Florida even less so; in Miami is where most Cubans move to ... I feel even less inclined to do so. (Thirty-eight-year-old male)

> There are people who resent Obama's and Raúl's changes. These people in Miami, these crazy old men who live in Miami, and I am sorry if I have to call them that but there is really no other way, these elderly who live in Miami, they are resentful about everything that Fidel has brought upon them ... I understand that pain and I understand the resentment, but being against a change that could translate into something positive for people who live in Cuba is not an option. (Twenty-six-year-old male)

> We went to Miami after Obama's speech. But after spending fifteen days in Miami, [my family] wanted to come back [to Canada] ... They feel free here ... So, you know, this [living in Canada] is of different value to them. (Fifty-year-old female)

> If a Cuban wants to move [from Canada] to the US, he will move whether there are relations with the US or none at all. Cubans who live in the US do so because they want to. Eliminating the Cuban Adjustment Act will not impact Cubans' decision to stay in Canada or come to Canada. Cubans come to Canada because of its government program dedicated to professionals, the Skilled Workers Program. The US does not have this. (Thirty-three-year-old male)

Optimism for normalized relations between Cuba and the United States has considerably dampened since the inauguration of President

Donald Trump in January 2017. Within six months of his presidency, Trump promised to cancel "the last administration's completely one-sided deal with Cuba," and attempted to stir up historical anti-Cuba emotions to past events such as the missile crisis: "We will never, ever be blind to it. We know what is going on and we remember what happened."[65] Still, although restrictions and sanctions against Cuba have since been tightened, formal diplomatic relations between the two countries have not yet been broken and the new embassies in Washington and Havana remain open.

Despite the differences between Montreal and Toronto, and between Quebec and elsewhere in Canada, the Cuban diaspora's realities and perceptions are far removed from those still dominant in Miami and, more generally, in the United States. Dissimilar historical, political, and social contexts, and the level of Cuba-Canada people-to-people contact and government ties, render Cuba as a fifth category to add to the Levitt, Glick-Schiller, and Duany typologies: that of the "interested transnational state." Cubans can come legally to Canada as a migrant-receiving state, and have chosen to do so in significant numbers to the major English- and French-speaking cities of Toronto and Montreal. Since the political implications of the 1959 Revolution are not anathema to the majority of Canadians or their governments, Cubans in Canada can, on balance, decide whether to participate in discussions and activities touching the Revolution and its ideals. In understanding itself as multicultural/intercultural – although more true in theory than in practice – the Canadian government encourages Cubans to see Canada as a place to pursue new opportunities without the need to sever connections with their homeland. They can stay or leave, and, if they can so engineer it, be part of the drift within Canada to Toronto as well as the drift across the border to warmer climes south, although not without reservations where Miami is concerned. Canada, and especially Toronto and Montreal, can become a second home where, as that one young Cuban remarked, they can "move on," carrying their "Cubanness" within.

NOTES

This chapter is part of a larger ongoing project on the new Cuban diasporas, which examines the complexities of transnational Cuban migration to Canada (particularly Toronto and Montreal) and western Europe (particularly London, Paris, Berlin, and Madrid).

Grounded on secondary research involving a growing international network of scholars, and primary research involving site visits, participant observation, and in-depth interviews, the project explores the ways in which commodities, generations, gender, class, race, and culture affect the experiences and perceptions of migration. Additionally the study considers the extent to which the new Cuban diasporas follow migratory patterns that are similar to or different from those of other migrant groups in new host countries, especially groups from the Caribbean and Latin America. The project would not have been possible without financial support from the Social Sciences and Humanities Research Council of Canada. For this and other sources of collaboration in terms of both funding and kind, we wish to express our thanks, in particular, to the University of London School of Advanced Study for funding and its member Institute for the Study of the Americas for hosting a workshop in London in December 2011 while also hosting Krull as a visiting fellow and Stubbs as associate fellow; the Institut des Amériques and our European colleague Christoph Singler for hosting a workshop in Paris in October 2012; and the Cuban Research Institute (CRI) at Florida International University – in particular CRI director Jorge Duany – for hosting the Symposium on The Cuban Diaspora in the World in Miami in March 2013 and the 9th Annual Conference on Cuban and Cuban American Studies on the theme "Dispersed Peoples: The Cuban and Other Diasporas" in May 2013. For facilitating our research in Canada, we wish to thank many colleagues for their generosity and time and for guiding our path along the way: notably, in Toronto, Cynthia Wright, who was generous with both her time and her knowledge of Cuban venues in the city; and in Montreal, David Austin, Steven High, Catherine LeGrand, Sean Mills, and Jarrett Rudy. Most of all, we thank the anonymous protagonists of our research, the many Cubans who are shaping the new diasporas and wanted their stories told.

1 Jorge Duany, *Blurred Borders: Transnational Migration between the Hispanic Caribbean and the United States* (Chapel Hill: University of North Carolina Press, 2011); Peggy Levitt and Nina Glick Schiller, "Conceptualizing Simultaneity: A Transnational Social Field Perspective on Society," *International Migration Review* 38, no. 3 (2004): 1002–39.
2 Levitt and Glick Schiller, "Conceptualizing Simultaneity."
3 Cubans no longer require an exit visa or a letter of invitation to travel abroad. Moreover, the length of time abroad has been extended from eleven to twenty-four months. A passport and visa from the destination country is all that is required. However, the government has the authority to deny travel for national security reasons or to prevent a "brain drain" from the island (of persons deemed vital).
4 Soledad Alvarez, "More than 180,000 Cubans could gain Spanish citizenship," *Latin American Herald Tribune*, 30 July 2015, available online at http://www.laht.com/article.asp?ArticleId=454784&CategoryId=14510; Canada, "Apply to Immigrate to Canada" (Ottawa, n.d.), available online at http://www.cic.gc.ca/english/immigrate/apply.asp.

5 Havana Consulting Group, "CUBA: The Fastest Growing Remittances Market in Latin America" (Miami, 23 June 2016), available online at http://www.thehavanaconsultinggroup.com/en-US/Articles/Article/20.

6 Ibid.; and D'Vera Cohn, Ana Gonzalez-Barrera, and Danielle Cuddington, "Remittances to Latin America Recover – but Not to Mexico" (Washington, DC: Pew Research Center, 15 November 2013), available online at http://www.pewhispanic.org/2013/11/15/remittances-to-latin-america-recover-but-not-to-mexico/.

7 Brigitte Glaser and Jutta Ernst, eds., *The Canadian Mosaic in the Age of Transnationalism* (Heidelberg: Universitätsverlag Winter, 2010); Augie Fleras, *The Media Gaze: Representations of Diversities in Canada* (Vancouver: UBC Press, 2011); Eve Haque, *Multiculturalism with a Bilingual Framework: Language, Race, and Belonging in Canada* (Toronto: University of Toronto Press, 2012).

8 Olivia Patricia Dickason and David Long, *Visions of the Heart: Canadian Aboriginal Issues*, 3rd ed. (Toronto: Oxford University Press, 2011); Natasha Netschay Davies, Lloyd Dolha, and Len O'Connor, *Smoke Signals from the Heart: Fourteen Years of the First Nations Drum* (Vancouver: Totem Pole Books, 2004).

9 Jack Jedwab and Victor Armony, "¡Hola Canadá! Spanish Is Third Most Spoken Language," *FOCALPoint* 8, no. 4 (2009): 14–16; Statistics Canada, "Figure 1: Number of Canadians whose mother tongue is one of the 22 immigrant languages reported by more than 100,000 persons, Canada, 2011" (Ottawa, 2015), available online at https://www12.statcan.gc.ca/census-recensement/2011/as-sa/98-314-x/2011003/fig/fig3_2-1-eng.cfm.

10 Statistics Canada, "Figure 1: Population growth (in percent) in number of persons who reported speaking one of the top 25 immigrant languages most often at home, Canada, 2006 to 2011" (Ottawa, 2015), available online at http://www12.statcan.ca/census-recensement/2011/as-sa/98-314-x/2011001/fig/fig1-eng.cfm.

11 Of the total number of Cubans living in Canada, 14,545 claimed multiple ethnic origin (that is, Cuban-Canadian) and 6,895 claimed single ethnic origin; see Statistics Canada, *2011 National Household Survey: Data Tables* (Ottawa, 2011), "Ethnic Origin (264), Single and Multiple Ethnic Origin Responses (3), Generation Status (4), Age Groups (10) and Sex (3) for the Population in Private Households of Canada, Provinces, Territories, Census Metropolitan Areas and Census Agglomerations," available online at http://www12.statcan.gc.ca/nhs-enm/2011/dp-pd/dt-td/Rp-eng.cfm?LANG=E&APATH=3&DETAIL=0&DIM=0&FL=A&FREE=0&GC=0&GID

=0&GK=0&GRP=0&PID=105396&PRID=0&PTYPE=105277&S=0&SHOW
ALL=0&SUB=0&Temporal=2013&THEME=95&VID=0&VNAMEE=&VNA
MEF=. The 2011 census figures, which are the most up-to-date at the time
of writing this chapter, recorded a total of 21,440 Cubans.

12 United States Census Bureau, "Census Bureau releases 2011 American
Community Survey estimates" (Washington, DC, 19 September 2012),
available online at https://www.census.gov/newsroom/releases/
archives/american_community_survey_acs/cb12-175.html. See also Statistics Canada, *2011 National Household Survey: Immigration and Ethnocultural
Diversity* (Ottawa, 2013).

13 For 2015, the International Organization for Migration figure for Cubans in
Spain was 125,263. http://www.iom.int/world-migration.

14 Organization of American States, *International Migration of the Americas:
Second Report of the Continuous Reporting System on International Migration in
the Americas (SICREMI) 2012* (Washington, DC: OAS, 2012), 259, available
online at http://www.oecd.org/els/mig/G48952_WB_SICREMI_2012_
ENGLISH_REPORT_LR.pdf.

15 According to the 2011 National Household Survey, 11,675 Cubans
resided in Ontario, with 7,720 in Toronto; of 5,860 Cubans living in
Quebec, 4,905 resided in Montreal. Alberta has the third-highest number of Cubans, approximately 1,800, the majority of whom are more or
less evenly distributed between Edmonton and Calgary. See Statistics
Canada, *2011 National Household Survey*.

16 Jacklyn Neborak, "Family Reunification? A Critical Analysis of Citizen-
ship and Immigration Canada's 2013 Reforms to the Family Class," RCIS
Working Paper 2013/8 (Toronto: Ryerson University, Ryerson Centre for
Immigration and Settlement, 2013), 3.

17 Gary P. Freeman, "The Quest for Skill: A Comparative Analysis," in *Migration and Refugee Policies: An Overview*, ed. Ann Bernstein and Myron Weiner
(London: Continuum, 1999), 98; Anne Milan, *Migration: International, 2009*
(Ottawa: Statistics Canada, July 2011), 4, available online at http://www.
statcan.gc.ca/pub/91-209-x/2011001/article/11526-eng.pdf.

18 Neborak "Family Reunification?" 6.

19 Milan, *Migration*, table 2.

20 "Spending for the program in 2010–2011 exceeds $1 billion – almost twice
the amount of the other six departmental programs combined"; see Jennifer Hyndman, *Research Summary on Resettled Refugee Integration in Canada*
(Toronto: York University, Centre for Refugee Studies, 2 May 2012), 6.

21 "Canada's refugee acceptance rate up despite asylum restrictions," *Toronto
Star*, 1 March 2015.

22 Canada, "Canada – Temporary Foreign Worker Program Work Permit
   Holders by Gender, Occupational Skill Level and Year in which Permit(s)
   Became Effective, Q1 2015–Q1 2017" (Ottawa, n.d.), available online
   at http://open.canada.ca/data/en/dataset/360024f2-17e9-4558-bfc1-
   3616485d65b9. For the critique, see Nicholas Keung, "Canada immigration:
   How a decade of policy change has transformed the immigration landscape," *Toronto Star*, 15 February 2013.
23 Yasmin Abu-Laban and Christina Gabriel, *Selling Diversity: Immigration,
   Multiculturalism, Employment Equity, and Globalization* (Toronto: University
   of Toronto Press, 2002).
24 This assumption is based on the absence of information on Cubans
   entering Canada illegally, unlike immigrants arriving from some other
   countries such as China. Reports do exist of some Cubans who are in
   Canada for a temporary visit – for a family visit, sporting event, conference, and so on – but then who cross into the United States with the
   aim of becoming a US citizen; see, for example, "Cubans leave men's
   team in Canada," *Yahoo News*, 13 October 2012, available online at
   https://sg.sports.yahoo.com/news/cubans-leave-mens-team-canada-
   170424313--sow.html. It is also interesting to note that, since Cuba
   loosened its travel restrictions for Cubans, there has been a significant increase in the number of Cubans crossing into the United States
   through Mexico; it has been estimated that approximately thirteen
   thousand crossed the border undetected between September 2012 and
   September 2013; see "Soaring number of Cubans are entering the United
   States through Mexican border," *Fox News World*, 29 October 2013, available online at http://latino.foxnews.com/latino/news/2013/10/29/
   soaring-number-cubans-are-entering-united-states-through-mexican-
   border/.
25 Catherine Krull, "Quebec's Alternative to Pronatalism," *Population Today*
   29, no. 8 (2001): 3–4; M. Vatz Laaroussi, "L'intergénérationnel dans les
   réseaux transnationaux des familles immigrantes: mobilité et continuité,"
   in *L'intergénérationnel: regards pluridisciplinaires*, ed. R. Hurtubise and A.
   Quéniart, 267–93 (Rennes, France: Presses de l'École des hautes études en
   santé publique, 2009).
26 Statistics Canada, *2011 National Household Survey*.
27 Alan B. Simmons, "Latin American Migration to Canada: New Linkages
   in the Hemispheric Migration and Refugee Flow System," *International
   Journal* 48, no. 2 (1993): 287.
28 Simon Houpt, "Targeting Canada's "invisible" Hispanic community,"
   Globe and Mail, 17 November 2011.

29 On Toronto, see Dwaine Plaza, "Migration caribéenne et intégration au Canada: à la poursuite du rêve d'ascension sociale (1900–1998)," in *Dynamiques migratoires de la Caraïbe* (Migratory dynamics of the Caribbean), Terres d'Amérique 6 (Paris: Karthala, 2007), 141–57; and Dwaine Plaza and Frances Henry, eds., *Returning to the Source: The Final Stages of the Caribbean Migration Circuit* (Kingston, Jamaica: University of the West Indies Press, 2006). On Montreal, see David Austin, *Fear of a Black Nation: Race, Sex, and Security in Sixties Montreal* (Toronto: Between the Lines, 2013); José del Pozo Artigas, ed., *Exiliados, emigrados y retornados: Chilenos en América y Europa, 1973–2004* (Santiago de Chile: RIL Editores, 2006), and idem, *Les Chiliens au Québec: immigrants et réfugiés, de 1955 à nos jours* (Montreal: Les Éditions du Boréal, 2009).

30 Maria Cristina Garcia, "Canada: A Northern Refuge for Central Americans," *Migration Information Source*, 1 April 2006, available online at http://www.migrationpolicy.org/article/canada-northern-refuge-central-americans.

31 "Canadian Embassy in Cuba" (Toronto: Migration Expert, n.d.), available online at https://www.migrationexpert.ca/visa/canadian-embassy/cuba.

32 Lana Wylie, *Perceptions of Cuba: Canadian and American Policies in Comparative Perspective* (Toronto: University of Toronto Press, 2010); and Peter McKenna and John M. Kirk, "Through Sun and Ice: Canada, Cuba, and Fifty Years of 'Normal' Relations," in *Canada Looks South: In Search of an Americas Policy*, ed. Peter McKenna, 149–79 (Toronto: University of Toronto Press, 2012), 149–79.

33 Chantal Gauthier and France Lord, *Engagées et solidaires: les Sœurs du Bon-Conseil à Cuba 1948–1998* (Montreal: Éditions Carte Blanche, 2013). The book was launched in May 2013 at the Sisters' Montreal headquarters at a well-attended event, including by some who had been among the first to go out to Matanzas, Cuba, when the Sisters opened in 1948. They continued their pastoral work in Matanzas until 1968.

34 Asa McKercher, "'Complicated and Far-Reaching': The Historical Foundations of Canadian Policy toward Cuba," in *Cuba in a Global Context: International Relations, Internationalism, and Transnationalism*, ed. Catherine Krull (Gainesville: University Press of Florida, 2014), 109–24; John M. Kirk and Peter McKenna, *Canada-Cuba Relations: The Other Good Neighbor Policy* (Gainesville: University Press of Florida, 1997).

35 Quebec and Ontario differ considerably in terms of their history, culture, language, politics, and legal system. Apart from Canadians acquiring their independence from Britain peacefully in 1867, colonial Quebec had been taken by the British from the French over a century earlier, in 1759, and,

given its relatively large population base at the time, had been allowed to keep French as its language, along with the Roman Catholic religion and French civil law. Accordingly, although English-speaking Protestant British North America adhered to English common law, what became the province of Quebec developed divergently from the rest of the nascent country. While much of Canada modernized over the century following independence and its population grew, by 1960 Quebec was just 25 per cent of the total population and, outside the major urban centres of Montreal and Quebec City, the province remained a largely traditional agrarian society. In 1960, a reformist Liberal government took power in the province and initiated the so-called Quiet Revolution designed to modernize Quebec by taking education away from the Church, enforcing women's rights, and beginning to build a modern economy based upon massive hydroelectric development. See Michael D. Behiels, *Prelude to Quebec's Quiet Revolution: Liberalism vs Neo-Nationalism, 1945–60* (Montreal; Kingston, ON: McGill-Queen's University Press, 1985); Catherine Krull, "From the King's Daughters to the Quiet Revolution: A Historical Overview of Family Structures and the Role of Women in Quebec," in *Voices: Essays on Canadian Families*, ed. Marion Lynn (Toronto: Nelson Canada, 1996), 369–96; and Yvan Lamonde, *La modernité au Québec*, 3 v. (Montreal: Fides, 2011).

Underpinning this movement lay the fear that Quebec's francophone society would be eroded by the greater wealth and growing anglophone population of the rest of Canada. Although the majority of Quebecers supported the federal government, a minority – including the Marxist, separatist, quasi-paramilitary Front de libération du Québec (FLQ) – mobilized for Quebec's separation and the creation of an independent state. In any event, the Quiet Revolution was a success: Quebec soon almost drew level economically with the rest of Canada and the provincial government introduced both new laws to protect the use of the French language and some of the most progressive social legislation, designed to bolster Quebec as a whole and its families in particular. The rest of Canada adhered to English as the common tongue, maintained its British-inspired political institutions and common law, and developed as a mixed economy blending free enterprise with national socialized health care and social services. See Gérard Bouchard, "Neoliberalism in Québec: The Response of a Small Nation under Pressure," in *Social Resilience in the Neoliberal Era*, ed. Peter Hall and Michele Lamont (Cambridge: Cambridge University Press, 2013), 267–92; and Catherine Krull, "Families First? An Assessment of Quebec's Family Policies," *Canadian Review of Social Policy* 59 (2008): 93–101.

36 Robert Wright, *Three Nights in Havana: Pierre Trudeau, Fidel Castro and the Cold War World* (Toronto: HarperCollins Canada, 2007).

37 Kirk and McKenna, *Canada-Cuba Relations*; Wylie, *Perceptions of Cuba.*

38 Robert Wright and Lana Wylie, *Our Place in the Sun: Canada and Cuba in the Castro Era* (Toronto: University of Toronto Press, 2009).

39 Canadian Foundation for the Americas, *Cuba Today: The Events Taking Place in Cuba and Issues for Canadian Policy* (Ottawa: FOCAL, 1999), 1.

40 Guidebooks proliferated. One, published in Quebec in 1997 by Jerzy Adamuszek, titled *Cuba Is Not Only Varadero*, took an evident knock at the sun, sand, and sea package-type holidays to Varadero Beach. Adamuszek, after completing his Master's at the University of Crakow in 1980, moved to Canada to realize his dream of travel, going first to the United States and then to Cuba on a reconnaissance trip in 1993 and around the island by bicycle in 1994, spending no foreign currency at the peak of shortages and hardships in the local peso economy. In his preface he writes: "The fall of the Berlin Wall and the disintegration of communist Eastern Europe have left us all wondering not if, but when the Castro regime in Cuba will also succumb to the influence of Western democracy. Before the inevitable happens, I wanted to see for myself what life was really like in one of the last bastions of Marxist ideology. Obviously, a true view could not be obtained by following the usual tourist paths; my idea was to penetrate the Cuban hinterland alone, by bicycle." See ibid., 13.

41 By 2003, Air Canada had increased its regular winter flights to twenty-five a week, flying from seven Canadian cities to Havana, Varadero, Holguin, Jardines del Rey, and Cayo Largo del Sur. After Canada followed Italy, France, Germany, Spain, and the United Kingdom, this last being the fastest-growing sender. "CANADIANS AND BRITONS give a new boost to Cuban tourism," *Cuban Review* (November 2003), was the front-page lead article in a special edition of the publication specializing in Cuban tourism, published in Toronto and London.

42 Joe Friesen, "Our time to lead: Why Canada needs a flood of immigrants," *Globe and Mail*, 4 May 2012.

43 Julie-Anne Boudreau, Roger Keil, and Douglas Young, *Changing Toronto: Governing Urban Neoliberalism* (Toronto: University of Toronto Press, 2009); Amy Lavender Harris, *Imagining Toronto* (Toronto: Mansfield Press, 2010); and David Miller and Douglas Arrowsmith, *Witness to a City: David Miller's Toronto* (Toronto: Cormorant, 2010).

44 Quoted in Angel Romero, "Interview with José Ortega of Lula Lounge Records in Toronto," *World Music Central*, 26 February 2013, available online at http://worldmusiccentral.org/2013/02/26/interview-with-jose-ortega-of-lula-lounge-records-in-toronto/.

45 Quoted in ibid.
46 Frank Correnti Cigars, "Cuban in Every Way" (Toronto, 2012); but see Jean Stubbs, "Transnationalism and the Havana Cigar: Commodity Chains, Networks, and Knowledge Circulation," in Krull, *Cuba in a Global Context*, 227–42.
47 See the web site http://cubaintoronto.com/.
48 Authors' interview with the owner of Accents, 2012.
49 As the head of the Toronto CCFA remarked about one of its events, it "featured Cuban music, dancing, and food, to the delight of hundreds of participants and passers-by"; authors' interview, with the head of the Canadian-Cuban Friendship Association, 2012.
50 For this and the group's six other objectives, see the web site of La Asociación de Cubanos "Juan Gualberto Gómez," at http://cubanosjgg. blogspot.ca/p/quienes-somos.html.
51 Colin Lindsay, "The Caribbean Community in Canada 2001," Cat. no. 89-621-XIE – No. 7 (Ottawa: Statistics Canada, 2007), available online at http://www.statcan.gc.ca/pub/89-621-x/89-621-x2007007-eng.pdf.
52 Sean Mills, *The Empire Within: Postcolonial Thought and Political Activism in Sixties Montreal* (Montreal; Kingston, ON: McGill-Queen's University Press, 2010), 69.
53 See Asa McKercher, in this volume.
54 Austin, *Fear of a Black Nation*; Pierre Vallières, *White Niggers of America: The Precocious Autobiography of a Quebec "Terrorist"* (Toronto: McClelland & Stewart, 1971).
55 Austin, *Fear of a Black Nation*.
56 Guy Bouthillier and Édouard Cloutier, eds., *Trudeau's Darkest Hour: War Measures in Time of Peace, October 1970* (Montreal: Baraka Books, 2010).
57 "On this day in history," *Globe and Mail*, 28 April 2013.
58 Ibid.; Bronwyn Chester, "McGill français and Quebec society," *McGill Reporter*, 8 April 1999, available online at http://reporter-archive.mcgill. ca/Rep/r3114/francais.html.
59 Sam Pinto, "Faded Red: The Rise and Fall of Radicalism at McGill," *McGill Tribune*, 4 November 2014, available online at http://mcgilltribune.com/ mcgill-marxism-faded-red/.
60 See "Havana Resto Lounge," *Yelp* (n.d.), available online at http://www. yelp.ca/biz/havana-resto-lounge-montrpercentC3percentA9al?osq=Cuban +Food.

61 "Cuban art shines at Montreal Museum," *CBC News*, 8 February 2008, available online at http://www.cbc.ca/news/canada/cuban-art-shines-at-montreal-museum-1.709920; Nathalie Bondil, *Cuba: Art and History from 1868 to Today* (Montreal: Montreal Museum of Fine Arts, 2009).
62 For further discussion about minorities maintaining their cultural identity, see Renée Desjardins, "2007: Translating Culture during the Bouchard-Taylor Commission," in *Translation Effects: The Shaping of Modern Canadian Culture*, ed. Kathy Mezei, Sherry Simon, and Luise von Flotow (Montreal; Kingston, ON: McGill-Queen's University Press, 2014), 142–61.
63 In Quebec, children must attend French school from grades 1 through 12, unless one of their parents previously attended an English-language school somewhere in Canada; children of immigrants living in Quebec must attend French school regardless of the type of school their parents attended. See "Canadian Schooling System," *Canada Visa.com: Immigration Forum*, 22 May 2011, available online at http://www.canadavisa.com/canada-immigration-discussion-board/school-admissions-read-all-about-it-here-t72241.0.html.
64 Cherif Rifaat, *Immigrants Adapt, Countries Adopt … Or Not: Fitting into the Cultural Mosaic* (Montreal: New Canadian Press, 2004); and Norman J. Threinen, *A Religious-Cultural Mosaic: A History of Lutherans in Canada* (Vulcan, AB: Today's Reformation Press, 2006).
65 Dan Merica, "Trump unveils new restrictions on travel, business with Cuba," CNN (17 June 2017), available online at www.cnn.com/2017/06/16/politics/trump-cuba-policy/index.html.

12 Taking Generation NGO to Cuba: Reflections of a Teacher

KAREN DUBINSKY

Since 2008 I have co-taught an annual course called "Cuban Culture and Society," offered by the Department of Global Development Studies at Queen's University, in conjunction with the University of Havana. The course takes place in Canada and in Cuba. In Canada the course is taught by a rotating group of Queen's instructors and graduate students who meet with students for twelve sessions (the equivalent of one Canadian university semester) prior to our departure.[1] In the two-week Cuban portion, students are taught by instructors from the University of Havana, as well as by Havana-based artists, musicians, and playwrights. The course is part of a formal agreement between the University of Havana and Queen's, which also sends students to Havana for longer periods of study (a semester abroad) and also brings one Havana-based professor to Queen's annually for up to a month, to study, give research talks, and meet colleagues and students.

In this chapter I want to reflect on our ongoing experiences of this institutional relationship. I focus specifically on the challenges and rewards of bringing Canadian undergraduate students to Cuba under the mantle of "development studies." The chapter contextualizes our experiences in the growing literature about international development studies education, particularly criticisms of its often superficial and colonial nature. Are such courses merely "voluntourism," or "edutainment"? What do Canadian students learn in a course like this? What are the particularities of Cuba in the world of international development studies? To what extent do educational excursions such as these heighten, diminish, or simply avoid complicated questions of global inequalities? Can these "exchanges" ever be considered reciprocal?

Educational ties between Cuba and Canada are a little-known feature of Cuba-Canada relations. Universities and colleges from across Canada have participated in partnerships with Cuban institutions since the 1960s, particularly in the areas of engineering, medical sciences, and agriculture. In the late 1960s Cuba asked the non-governmental organization (NGO) Canadian University Services Overseas for help in replenishing the technical expertise of Havana's engineering and animal health schools, whose faculties, like many professionals, had left the country in the aftermath of the Revolution. The request blossomed into a multiyear project funded by the Canadian International Development Agency (CIDA) that sent Canadian educators to Havana institutions and also brought a number of Cuban students to Canadian universities. Over time, Canadian university professors taught more than 120 postgraduate courses at the Ciudad Universitaria José Antonio Echeverría, Havana's main engineering school, and 70 Cuban students and professors visited Canadian institutions, where they were involved in 100 Master's research projects. Federally funded research projects continue in Cuba, while other ties between Canadian and Cuban universities take place in the context of exchange agreements funded by the universities themselves. In 2012 the Canadian embassy in Havana commissioned a report on Cuba-Canada educational ties, which listed forty-three Canadian universities and colleges with projects or exchange agreements with forty-eight Cuban partners: institutions of higher education, research, government, and civil society. Forty of these initiatives remain active.[2]

So the program I work within emerges from a long and surprisingly extensive history of Cuba-Canada educational exchanges. It also is part of another more recent trend: the huge growth in international experiential learning opportunities for Canadian students throughout the developing world. International educational programs, volunteer opportunities, and development tourism have all generated an enormous debate among educators and development studies scholars. In a recent anthology that brings together various views on the matter, Canadian educators Rebecca Tiessen and Robert Huish ask probing questions about the pursuit of "global competency" and cross-cultural understanding through international experiential learning. "Why," they ask, "does the quest for global citizenship matter? Does international experiential learning produce globetrotters or global citizens?"[3]

The varied categorizations, as well as the varied criticisms, of the global citizenship produced through international education are relevant to the work I do with students in Cuba. In reflecting on our experiences in Havana, in the context of a growing literature on international education in the developing world, my first challenge is to place ourselves among the myriad visitors. Canadians are hardly an unknown quantity in Cuba – over a million of us visit annually. Thus our experiences in Havana share similarities with recent trends in NGO-sponsored "development tourism" analysed by Australian anthropologist Rochelle Spencer. "Tourism" – particularly mass travel by people from the global North to warm places with beautiful beaches in the global South – is typically considered to be the opposite of what we are trying to achieve in Cuba – namely, "education." As Spencer and a host of commentators on modern tourism declare, tourism encourages encounters between locals and foreigners that are "artificial, asymmetrical, and unidirectional." The contrast between the travel-savvy, passport-wielding tourist and the supposedly place-bound Cuban becomes a mirror that magnifies global political inequalities. NGOs from around the "First World" have organized "study tours" – for which Cuba is a popular (though by no means the only) destination. Study tours, which emerge specifically from frustration with the superficialities of mass tourism, orchestrate what Spencer calls "specific forms of social interaction" in an attempt to transcend the limitation of mass tourism.[4] Through exchanging ideas and knowledge between specific groups of people, educational or "development tours" can, despite their brevity, "facilitate the establishment of new networks and international links." When foreigners and Cubans are linked together in specific projects or educational undertakings, so the argument goes, they are less likely to view each other through the one-dimensional lenses of "host/guest" or "us/them" typically offered by mass tourism and, of course, also fundamentally embedded in Western cultural thinking.[5]

Yet there are significant differences between the politicized, activist travellers who are attracted to NGO study tours, and the mainstream, young Canadian undergraduates who inhabit our classrooms. Our course is interdisciplinary, and attracts students from a range of departments such as Film, History, Political Science, as well as Global Development Studies, which hosts the course. Few of our undergraduates come from activist, much less leftist, backgrounds. At most they have an understanding of Cuba as part of the global South, about which they have learned from their university Development Studies classes and, increasingly, their own experience of travel and/or volunteering in the Third World previously, including trips they made during high school.

As Kathyrn Fizzell and Marc Epprecht have recently pointed out, the growth of international educational and volunteer opportunities in the developing world in Canadian high schools is another growing and little-studied addition to the curriculum.[6] Plenty of our students have previously visited Cuban resorts with their parents for March break vacation, but others have spent a two-week high school trip in Honduras building a school, or a semester in India, or a summer learning Spanish in Nicaragua, or taking secondary school courses in Brazil. A few are second-generation immigrants from the global South who have experience visiting grandparents in Venezuela, Lebanon, El Salvador, or India. We teach "Generation NGO," in the memorable phrasing of Alisha Nicole Apale and Valerie Stam's eponymous new anthology; referring to the increasing number of Canadian youth for whom "globalization" means an opportunity for travel, work, or study in the developing world.[7] Their curiosity about Cuba is motivated less by its revolutionary history than by its poverty. When we are there, they are inspired less by its political leadership than by its organic gardens and its cultural achievements.

Learning about or visiting Cuba from the perspective of Generation NGO leads to complicated but rich discussions about development, because Cuba is both the same as and different from its global South neighbours in so many respects. It has in many ways departed historically from the standard Third World economic development model that North American students learn about, but it also has a different relationship to, and role for, foreigners. Although it remains to be seen what role foreign NGOs will play in *la nueva Cuba* with growing private economic initiatives, historically the country has not relied on NGOs to provide social welfare, as have many other developing countries. International NGOs were few in number in Cuba until the 1990s, which were the boom years for NGO expansion around the world. There are approximately two thousand NGOs registered in Cuba, but only twenty international NGOs currently have a presence there.[8] Neighbouring Haiti, by way of contrast, was home to between three thousand and ten thousand NGOs (estimates vary), which delivered 70 per cent of health care and 85 per cent of education *before* the 2010 earthquake.[9] International NGOs do not operate with the same kind of autonomy in Cuba as they are accustomed to in other countries.[10] Because Cuba is not dependent on foreign NGOs for basic social services, it is not immersed in what some have termed the "White Savior Complex."[11] Cuba stands outside, at least to a certain extent, some of the many problems experienced by other developing countries with huge numbers of international NGOs: a depoliticized understanding of global poverty, the political and social dominance of the "aid industry," the ascendancy of the foreign expert.[12] Cubans do not appear in the repertoire of "oversimplified, decontextualized, and ahistorical" NGO-generated images of global poverty that saturate our media and our imaginations, analysed recently by Nandita Dogra.[13] Indeed, Cuba thinks of itself as a donor country, not a recipient country, which, at least in the field of humanitarian medical aid, it clearly is.[14] These realities themselves are tremendously instructive for young Canadian development studies students. After learning about the history of the Cuban literacy campaign, in which thousands of young Cubans fanned out throughout the country after the Revolution, teaching rural dwellers of all ages how to read, one of our students observed, clearly surprised: "As a Devs student, I hope to go do that kind of thing, teach literacy, to people in other countries, but in Cuba they did it themselves." The comment speaks volumes about what Cuban history has to say to Generation NGO.

Another issue Spencer identifies relevant to NGO study tours and educational experiences such as ours is politically sensitive: Who controls the agenda? In Cuba NGO study tours are administered by the Instituto Cubano de Amistad con los Pueblos (ICAP, or Cuban Institute for Friendship between Peoples). ICAP, a product of the Revolution, was founded in 1960 and works as a kind of clearing house for international tours, Cuban friendship associations, and donations. Spencer invokes the phrase "techniques of hospitality," which emerged from a study of international visitors to the Soviet Union in the 1930s, to describe the process of "selective presentations of reality ... which exposed tourists to those qualities of the country that would ensure a good impression." ICAP's techniques of hospitality emphasize Cuba's resilience. As Spencer puts it, the itineraries ICAP organizes for visitors send a clear message about "Cuba's capacity to reinvent itself in difficult times."[15] Politically uncomfortable topics simply do not appear on the tour agendas or in reading packages.

We have not faced issues of control and censorship so bluntly. Our relationship is not with ICAP but with the University of Havana. We have formed good working relationships with the professors who teach our students there, including those with whom we work to develop our roster of Havana scholars and artists. It is not that we have never disagreed about a speaker or a topic – we have. But because we have relationships, forged over time, that are trustful and respectful, we have been able to talk through our differences of opinion with our Havana colleagues. Our course approaches contemporary Cuba largely through cultural practice. During the twelve-session Queen's part of the course, we focus on Cuba's recent history, political economy, nation- and institution-building campaigns, social identities, and political tensions. We continue in this vein in Havana, but with a stronger emphasis on cultural politics and achievements. This is a tremendous asset because it opens a range of doors. As many have argued, the Third World that emerges from the First World "development gaze" is one-dimensional and desperate. It contains only, in the words of Nigerian writer Chimamanda Adichie, a single story: poverty. "Power," Adichie suggests, "is the ability not just to tell the story of another person, but to make it the definitive story of that person."[16] The stories – expressed in various media – our students hear in Havana can never reduce the place to a single narrative. Some of our instructors are professors at the University of Havana, others are professors whom we visit at the Instituto Superior de Arte or the Facultad de Arte de los Medios de Comunicación Audiovisual. Still others are a range of cultural producers from whom we have been privileged to hear: playwrights, filmmakers, musicians, and art curators, who express to us their (often extremely critical) works and perspectives openly. We visit cultural centres and institutions such as the Museo de Bellas Artes, Casa de Las Américas, Centro Cultural Pablo de la Torriente Brau, the Fábrica de Arte Cubano, and Casa de África. We have heard humorous commentaries from professors on the specifics of how censorship works on Cuban radio and TV and the various code words artists and commentators have learned to get around it. We have heard provocative songs about immigration conflicts, political leadership, and intergenerational political struggles. Filmmakers have told us about the problems they encounter with police when making documentaries about politically challenging subjects (such as homelessness in Havana), while others have described the profound sexism of the Cuban film industry. Other professors have spoken openly about racism in contemporary Cuba, and still others have made painfully irreverent jokes about the economic "failures" the country has experienced over the years. We tell our students that they can ask their instructors, Cuban and Canadian alike, anything, and I do not think any students have ever left the classroom feeling their question was evaded or sugar-coated.

Our students are not fed a steady diet of official discourse in the classroom, but in any case, as soon as they step outside the university they encounter other realities. One of Havana's many attractive features is its relative safety – although this should not be overstated – and our students' after-hours activities are largely of their own making. Even though most of them do not speak Spanish, they make friends with University of Havana students, go dancing with the staff in the hotels or residences we stay in, and find other Canadian or US students with whom to compare notes. They encounter the vibrant and varied youth culture in various corners of Havana recently described by US journalist Julia Cooke.[17] They also meet a range of Cubans, of all ages, who hang out on the Malecón or in clubs or parks. Sometimes their new Cuban friends invite them for dinner, to meet parents and other generations in the household. So from Cubans themselves, outside the classroom, they hear an enormous and diverging spectrum of political and social opinions. All of these conversations become part of the shared curriculum we discuss in ongoing seminars while we are there, and sometimes end up in their research essays as well. Often students hear something from someone they meet that contradicts what they have read in their textbook or heard from either their Canadian or their Cuban instructors. This can occasionally cause panic. Who is right? Should they believe authority, in the form of the professor or the textbook? What is the authority of someone who lives there? These are the conflicts that produce the best kind of discussions, because they open the door to honesty and complexity.

Another influential analysis of study-abroad courses was undertaken by South African historian Marc Epprecht, and our experiences with Canadian students in Havana resonate with some of his conclusions. Epprecht praises such experiences for pushing Canadian students beyond complacency, arguing that "the shock of immersion in a foreign culture disorients the student's faith in her/his own embedded assumptions about right and wrong. Such culture shock ideally forces her/him to reconstruct a truly global perspective."[18] But there are limits to the power of culture to shock. Students can be pushed only so far. Or maybe it is just that our two-week stints in Havana barely scratch the surface. I have watched intelligent, thoughtful, open-minded Canadian students forge seemingly fond and respectful friendships with Cubans of their generation, only to leave them open-mouthed as the Canadians discuss, in front of them, the amount of money they plan to spend to buy their fathers cigars, for example. (Once, mistrusting his English, a young Cuban friend asked me quietly, "did she just say she was going to buy $200 worth of cigars?")

Epprecht also sees the possibility that study-abroad programs might backfire, in pedagogical terms, by "hardening Northern students' pre-existing negative or exotic stereotypes about the South, by fostering a missionary zeal."[19] In my experience, Cubans have a way of quickly dispelling any zealous missionary-type feelings of pity or charity on their behalf. When learning that our course was housed in a Development Studies department, the response of a Cuban friend, herself a graduate student, was telling. "Oh, them," she said, rolling her eyes just slightly. The poverty our students encounter in Cuba is, of course, experienced differently than in other developing countries; it is a poverty that comes with declining but still adequate benefits such as health care and education. But that does not prevent our students from engaging in what some commentators call "lotto logic": a superficial understanding of global economic hierarchies in which "we" count our lucky stars for having had the "good fortune" to be born in Canada – as though what happens in the First World plays no role in shaping what happens in the Third.[20] Similarly, accompanying Generation NGO to Cuba has given me the opportunity to understand much about which "Canada" my students hail from. White students from small-town Ontario see racism for the first time – for example, when their new Afro-Cuban friend is harassed by Cuban police who assume he is preying on tourists. An upsetting yet educational moment – but when my students see this, they declare its impossibility in Canada. Similarly the overtly sexualized, sometimes aggressive nature of heterosexual relations on the streets of Havana initially comes as an unwelcome shock to the young females in our group. Sometimes this provides an opportunity for some complex reflections about different sexual cultures and the multiple ways in which patriarchal control and intimidation of women is exercised in different parts of the world, *including* Canada. Other students, shocked and frightened by a street culture they have never experienced, conclude that male sexual aggression is a wholly, uniquely Cuban phenomenon. I also regularly observe middle-class, suburban-dwelling Canadians wrenched by the sights of poverty in Havana, seemingly having managed to avoid it in Canadian cities and towns. "Why do you have to come all the way to Havana to notice poor people" is a question we grapple with constantly. One young woman was moved almost to tears when she reflected in class on what she believed was the horrible life of the elevator operators who worked in our university residence. She had never seen an elevator operator in her life, and believed it to be the worst job imaginable. Her classmates talked her through it: the elevators were old and actually quite complex pieces of equipment – perhaps this should be seen as skilled labour. The staff people at the residence were clearly fond of one another, and treated one another (not to mention us) really nicely; it seemed like a good working environment. All good points, but I continue to marvel that this young woman had never considered that there are worse jobs in the world than being an elevator operator.

Who benefits from international educational programs in the developing world? Most commentators come to the obvious conclusion. In a recent article on global citizenship education, Shelane Jorgensen and Lynette Schulz note that "the movement between the South and North is largely controlled by the North"; moreover, a particular slice of "the North": elites with disposable income. International education programs "require particular forms of economic, cultural, and social capital that preclude the majority of students from participating."[21] On the odd occasion that our group includes someone with no international travel experience, the student generally hides this fact, treating it as a slightly embarrassing illness.

If international education means that the world, or at least the "Third World" is little more than a "laboratory for testing an academic or career choice," in the words of Tiessen and Huish, it is no wonder that most academic commentators conclude that the benefits of international travel flow in only one direction.[22] Again, Cuba might be the exception here, but only for students from the United States. US commentators stress the important role that educational tours play in thawing US-Cuba relations – something political leaders clearly see as well, as George W. Bush curtailed many of these educational tours when he was in office. Lynne Bond, Sinan Koont, and Sky Stephenson believe the encounters between US students and their Havana hosts have been crucial in attempting to create "a culture of peace" between the two countries. Writing from their experiences bringing US students to Cuba for short-term courses such as ours, these authors observe that "nothing had a more profound impact on how students understood Cuba, its people, and, for that matter, themselves than the personal relationships the students established with Cubans and especially with those who were in positions that engendered relatively egalitarian, reciprocal friendships."[23] This Cold War–busting argument is less important in the Canadian context, as Canadians have not grown up believing Cuba was the Enemy. Arriving in Cuba from Canada is not an illegal, illicit, or even complicated move behind enemy lines.

I have no trouble understanding that the international educational experiences I facilitate teach a "cultural competence" that reproduces the social dominance of an elite slice of Canadian society. That is not particularly different from any aspect of teaching at a Canadian university such as Queen's, one of the educational destinations of choice for the Canadian Establishment.[24] But it does not end there. I prefer the question Leela Gandhi asked of an earlier generation of people who attempted to cross formidable boundaries in pursuit of friendship and education: "[W]hat ethical imperatives rendered some Europeans immune to the temptations of an empire which was a factory for making imperialist-minded citizens?"[25]

The great pleasure of teaching a course like this is to be part of a process of education like nothing else I have seen in a regular classroom. At their best our students understand the tremendous privilege it is to have an entire city – at least its central core – as one's classroom. At their best they learn from everyone. I can actually gauge how involved any particular group is, not by how they behave in the classroom – university students *always* know, at least by third year, what constitutes good behaviour in the classroom – but by how they interact with Cuban students, waiters in restaurants, instructors outside the classroom. Then I notice if boundaries have been crossed, even tentatively, or remain nervously defended.

The other side of the equation is more difficult to judge, and perhaps not for me to do so. Do Cubans benefit from our presence? Materially, yes. We pay tuition, and we bring much-needed supplies. I believe we have single-handedly kept the University of Havana Philosophy Department photocopier in toner for several years, and the professors at the Faculty of Arts and Letters show their students slides on several data projectors we have brought, in exchange for using their classrooms. Maybe that is all we can claim, but I think we can do better than that. The negotiation of the agreement between my university and the University of Havana is a real one. Both parties bring items to the negotiating table, and have to grapple with each other's positions. It is not, as my colleague and co-teacher Susan Lord put it, as though the University of Havana "is sitting around waiting for Northern universities to show up and start handing out photocopy toner." As I read the expanding literature that critically reviews the massive global expansion of international NGOs, in conjunction with the growth of international education programs, I appreciate even the modicum of reciprocity contained in our exchange with Cuba. Cuban instructors shape, and deliver, the content of the curriculum while we are in Havana. Cultural producers contribute to education alongside university professors. And we recognize also – in a tokenistic way – that at least one Cuban educator should have the same opportunities as thirty Canadian undergraduates: the chance to see new things and think new thoughts.[26] Relations with our Cuban instructors are enriched by the fact that by now at least five of them have spent at least two weeks with us at Queen's. But here too the benefits flow back to us as well: our course improves immeasurably as our Cuban instructors become more familiar with the knowledge levels and cultural contexts of our students and our community in Canada. I believe our course will achieve a level of what could really be called "reciprocity" or "exchange" only when we are able to invite Cuban students back to Canada with us, to take advantage of the same kind of horizon-opening experiences our students have in Havana.

There have been some smart, thoughtful studies about international education programs in the developing world. Yet discussions of reciprocity are notably absent. No one – not the commentators who analyse international education, nor the university administrators who help plan and fund such courses, nor professors like me who help to deliver them – seems to spend much time working towards reciprocity. It is instructive to recall the CIDA-funded project in the early 1970s I described at the beginning of the chapter, when over seventy Cuban professors AND students came to study in Canada. A 2014 Canadian embassy–sponsored study of Cuba-Canada educational ties counts thirty-four Cuban students who received Canadian government funding to study in Canada since 2000. That is only two students annually.[27]

We say goodbye to students in May when we land at Pearson Airport, and every year a few of them look at me earnestly, even tearfully sometimes, and say "thank you for the best experience in my life." I continue to hear from graduates of this course, and they continue to tell me that the experience was transformative. I conclude that the best part of this experience is the mixture of inspiration and confusion it provides Canadian students when they are back in Canada. I do not mean this in the sense that international NGO volunteers describe the mind-spinning movement between the Third and First Worlds of deprivation and excess. Visiting Havana under the mantle of "development education" helps them see how, as one former student put it, "our categories for dividing up the world into global South and global North betray common elements shared across borders. Inequality, creativity, poverty, dignity, and unwillingness to be missionized is as much a part of life in downtown Winnipeg as it is downtown Havana."[28]

NOTES

Thanks to my colleagues, fellow teachers, and friends for their comments on this chapter: Susan Belyea, Susan Lord, Freddy Monasterio, Scott Rutherford, and Zaira Zarza. Thanks also to my colleagues and friends in Havana who have helped to keep me, and this program, going.

1 Besides myself, the instructors who have been involved in this course at Queen's are Jennifer Hosek, Catherine Krull, Susan Lord, and Zaira Zarza.
2 All information about the history of Cuba-Canada educational relations is drawn from Rafael Betancourt, *Canadian Universities in Cuba* (Havana: Embassy of Canada and Canadian International Development Agency, 2012).
3 Rebecca Tiessen and Robert Huish, "International Experiential Learning and Global Citizenship," in *Globetrotting or Global Citizenship: Perils and Potential of International Experiential Learning*, ed. Rebecca Tiessen and Robert Huish (Toronto: University of Toronto Press, 2014), 3.
4 Rochelle Spencer, *Development Tourism: Lessons from Cuba* (Farnham, UK: Ashgate, 2010), 3.
5 Ibid., 66, 77.
6 Kathyrn Fizzell and Marc Epprecht, "Secondary School Experiential Learning Programs in the Global South: Critical Reflections from an Ontario Study," in Tiessen and Huish, *Globetrotting or Global Citizenship*, 112.
7 Alisha Nicole Apale and Valerie Stam, eds., *Generation NGO* (Toronto: Between the Lines, 2011).
8 Adrian H. Hearn, "Political Dimensions of International NGO Collaboration with Cuba," in *Cuba Today: Continuity and Change since the 'Período Especial,'* ed. Mauricio A. Font (New York: Bildner Center for Western Hemisphere Studies and City University of New York, Graduate Center, 2006), 209; and Christina Polzot, Program Coordinator, CARE International, Cuba, personal communication, 22 July 2014.
9 Vijaya Ramachadran, "Is Haiti Doomed to Be the Republic of NGOs?" (Washington, DC: Center for Global Development, 1 December 2012), available online at http://www.cgdev.org/blog/haiti-doomed-be-republic-ngos, accessed 22 July 2014.
10 Spenser, *Development Tourism*, 107.

11 The phrase is usually associated with Teju Cole, "The White-Savior Industrial Complex," *Atlantic*, 21 March 2012, available online at http://www.theatlantic.com/international/archive/2012/03/the-white-savior-industrial-complex/254843/, accessed 20 July 2014.

12 Good examples of such criticisms can be found in Firoze Manji, "The Missionary Position: NGOs and Development in Africa," *International Affairs* 78, no. 3 (2002): 567–83; Molly Kane, "International NGOs and the Aid Industry: Constraints on International Solidarity," *Third World Quarterly* 34, no. 8 (2013): 1505–15; and Nikolas Barry-Shaw and Dru Oja Jay, *Paved with Good Intentions: Canada's Development NGOs from Idealism to Imperialism* (Halifax: Fernwood, 2012).

13 Nandita Dogra, *Representations of Global Poverty: Aid, Development and International NGOs* (London: I.B. Tauris, 2014), 25.

14 See, for example, John M. Kirk and H. Michael Erisman, *Cuban Medical Internationalism: Origins, Evolution, and Goals* (New York: Palgrave Macmillan, 2009); and Robert Huish, *Where No Doctor Has Gone Before: Cuba's Place in the Global Health Landscape* (Waterloo, ON: Wilfrid Laurier University Press, 2013).

15 Spencer, *Development Tourism*, 130.

16 Chimamanda Adichie, "The Danger of a Single Story," *TED Talk*, July 2009, available online at http://www.ted.com/talks/chimamanda_adichie_the_danger_of_a_single_story, accessed 21 July 2014.

17 Julia Cooke, *The Other Side of Paradise: Life in the New Cuba* (Berkeley, CA: Seal Press, 2014).

18 Marc Epprecht, "Work-Study Abroad Courses in International Development Studies: Some Ethical and Pedagogical Issues," *Canadian Journal of Development Studies* 25, no. 4 (2004): 714.

19 Ibid., 711.

20 Fizzell and Epprecht, "Secondary School Experiential Learning Programs," 118.

21 Shelane Jorgensen and Lynette Schulz, "Global Citizenship Education (GCE) in Post-Secondary Institutions: What Is Protected and What Is Hidden under the Umbrella of GCE," *Journal of Global Citizenship and Equity Education* 2, no. 1 (2012): 11.

22 Tiessen and Huish, "International Experiential Learning," 3.

23 Lynne Bond, Sinan Koont, and Sky Stephenson, "The Power of Being There: Study Abroad in Cuba and the Promotion of a 'Culture of Peace,'" *Frontiers* 11 (August 2005): 114.

24 Our program fee, approximately $3,000, covers all travel, accommodation, meals, and excursion expenses for two weeks in Havana. This makes us

one of the lower-priced international post-secondary excursions, but it certainly remains a financial challenge for students.

25 Leela Gandhi, *Affective Communities: Anticolonial Thought, Fin-de-Siècle Radicalism, and the Politics of Friendship* (Durham, NC: Duke University Press, 2006), 2.

26 The Cuban professors and cultural producers we have hosted at Queen's since 2008 – some through our exchange agreement, others through other faculty initiatives – are as follows: María Caridad Cumaná (Fundación del Nuevo Cine Latinoamericano), Inés Rodríguez (University of Havana), Lourdes Pérez (University of Havana), Dannys Montes de Oca (Centro de Arte Contemporáneo Wifredo Lam), Gloria Rolando (Imágenes del Caribe, documentary filmmaker), René Francisco (Instituto Superior de Arte, artist), Julio César González Pagés (University of Havana), Carlos Varela (musician), Telmary Díaz (hip hop musician/poet), Soraya Castro (University of Havana), Francisco García Gonzáles (writer), Esteban Morales Domínguez (University of Havana), Enrique Beldarraín Chaple (Centro Nacional de Información de Ciencias Médicas), Carlos Alzugaray (University of Havana), Joaquín Borges-Triana (journalist, *El Caimán Barbudo*), and Xenia Reloba de la Cruz (journalist, *Casa de las Américas*). As well, in 2009, Queen's hosted a conference, The Measure of a Revolution, organized by Professor Catherine Krull to mark the fiftieth anniversary of the Cuban Revolution. The conference brought four hundred people to Queen's, including forty scholars and artists who attended from Cuba.

27 Betancourt, *Canadian Universities in Cuba*, 39.

28 Scott Rutherford, personal communication, 19 July 2014.

Bibliography

Abu-Laban, Yasmin, and Christina Gabriel. *Selling Diversity: Immigration, Multiculturalism, Employment Equity, and Globalization*. Toronto: University of Toronto Press, 2002.

Adamuszek, Jerzy. *Cuba Is Not Only Varadero*. St-Laurent, QC: Yunia Publications, 1997.

Adichie, Chimamanda. "The Danger of a Single Story." *TED Talk*, July 2009. Available online at http://www.ted.com/talks/chimamanda_adichie_the_danger_of_a_single_story, accessed 21 July 2014.

Aldrich, Richard J., and Michael F. Hopkins, eds. *Intelligence, Defence and Diplomacy: British Policy in the Post-War World*. Ilford, UK: Frank Cass, 1994.

Allard, Jean-Guy. "The Miami Mafia in Canada." *Granma*, 16 April 2004. Available online at http://www.latinamericanstudies.org/belligerence/canada.htm.

Allard, Jean-Guy. *Posada Carriles: cuatro décadas de terror*. Havana: Editora Política, 2006.

Allard, Jean-Guy. "Promotor de una 'lista de patrocinadores del terror,' EEUU da asilo a decenas de terroristas y prófugos." *Contrainjerencia*, 21 August 2011. Available online at http://www.contrainjerencia.com/?p=24321, accessed 12 February 2013.

Alvarez, Soledad. "More than 180,000 Cubans could gain Spanish citizenship." *Latin American Herald Tribune*, 30 July 2015. Available online at http://www.laht.com/article.asp?ArticleId=454784&CategoryId=14510.

Alzugaray Treto, Carlos. *Crónica de un fracaso imperial: la administración Eisenhower y el derrocamiento de la dictadura de Batista*. Havana: Editorial Ciencias Sociales, 2000.

Alzugaray Treto, Carlos. "Cuba: definiendo estrategias de política exterior en un mundo cambiante (2001–2011)." In *Cuba Futures: Cuba and the World*, edited by Mauricio Font, 1–46. New York: Bildner Center for Western Hemispheric Studies, 2011.

Alzugaray Treto, Carlos. "Cuba y el sistema internacional en la década de los '90." In *Problemas actuales de teoría sociopolitical*, edited by Emilio Duharte. Havana: Editorial Félix Varela, 2000.

Alzugaray Treto, Carlos. "Cuba's National Security vis-à-vis the United States: Conflict or Cooperation?" In *US-Cuban Relations: Shall We Play Ball?* edited by Jorge Domínguez, Rafael Hernández, and Lorena G. Barberia, 52–71. New York: Routledge, 2012.

Amario, Christine. "Coral Gables travel agency fire was arson." *Huffington Post*, 13 May 2012.

Amuchastegui, Domingo. "Raúl warns foreign investors: Play by the rules – or else." *CubaNews* 21, no. 7 (2013): 7.

Anderson, Norton. "Can we do business with Castro's Cuba?" *Financial Post*, 29 October 1960.

Anderson, Scott. "The Evolution of the Canadian Intelligence Establishment, 1945–1950." *Intelligence and National Security* 9, no. 3 (1993): 448–71.

Andrès, Bernard. *Fidel, D'Iberville et les autres*. Montreal: Québec Amérique, 2007.

Anglin, Douglas G. "United States Opposition to Canadian Membership in the Pan American Union: A Canadian View." *International Organization* 15, no. 1 (1961): 1–20.

Apale, Alisha Nicole, and Valerie Stam. *Generation NGO*. Toronto: Between the Lines, 2011.

Aquin, Hubert. *Prochain épisode*. Montreal: Le Cercle du livre de France, 1965.

August, Arnold. "Democracy Still in Motion: The 2013 Election Results in Cuba." *International Journal of Cuban Studies* 6, no. 1 (2014): 87–94.

Austin, David. *Fear of a Black Nation: Race, Sex, and Security in Sixties Montreal*. Toronto: Between the Lines, 2013.

Backhouse, Constance. *Colour-Coded: A Legal History of Racism in Canada, 1900–1950*. Toronto: University of Toronto Press, 1998.

Badella, Alessandro. "American Hybris: US Democracy Promotion in Cuba after the Cold War – Part 1." *International Journal of Cuban Studies* 6, no. 2 (2014): 157–88.

Badella, Alessandro. "Between Carter and Clinton: Obama's Policy Towards Cuba." *Caribbean Journal of International Relations & Diplomacy* 2, no. 2 (2014): 29–59.

Baker, Joseph. "The Ambitious Expo." *Canadian Architect* 52, no. 8 (August 2007): 43–4.

Bantey, Bill. *Bill Bantey's Expo 67*. Montreal: Gazette Publishing Company, 1967.

Bardach, Ann Louise, and Larry Rohter. "Key Cuban foe claims exile backing." *New York Times,* 12 July 1998.

Barry-Shaw, Nikolas, and Dru Oja Jay. *Paved with Good Intentions: Canada's Development NGOs from Idealism to Imperialism.* Halifax: Fernwood, 2012.

Bazinet, Cathy. "Cuba libre." *Biscuit chinois* 13 (2010): 30–6.

Behiels, Michael D. *Prelude to Quebec's Quiet Revolution: Liberalism vs Neo-Nationalism, 1945-60.* Montreal; Kingston, ON: McGill-Queen's University Press, 1985.

Beier, Marshall J., and Lana Wylie, *Canadian Foreign Policy in Critical Perspective.* Toronto: University of Toronto Press, 2010.

Bélanger, André J. "La recherche d'un collectif." In *Ruptures et constants, quatre idéologies du Québec en éclatement:* La Relève, *la JEC,* Cité libre, Parti pris, 137–93. Montreal: Hurtubise HMH, 1977.

Bell, José, Delia Luisa López, and Tania Caram, eds. *Documentos de la Revolución cubana 1959.* Havana: Editorial Ciencias Sociales, 2008.

Bell, José, Delia Luisa López, and Tania Caram, eds. *Documentos de la Revolución cubana 1960.* Havana: Editorial Ciencias Sociales, 2008.

Bell, Michael, Eugene Rothman, Marvin Schiff, and Christopher Walker. "Back to the Future? Canada's Experience with Constructive Engagement in Cuba." ICCS Occasional Papers 21. Miami: University of Miami, Institute for Cuban & Cuban-American Studies, 2002.

Berton, Pierre. "By God, we did it. And generally we did it well." *Maclean's,* June 1967.

Betancourt, Rafael. *Canadian Universities in Cuba.* Havana: Embassy of Canada and Canadian International Development Agency, 2012.

Biniowsky, Gregory. "The Cuba moment is finally ripe, and Ottawa isn't seizing it Havana." *Globe and Mail,* 22 March 2016. Available online at http://www.theglobeandmail.com/report-on-business/rob-commentary/the-cuba-moment-is-finally-ripe-and-ottawa-isnt-seizing-it/article29315672/, accessed 9 December 2016.

Blanchfield, Mike. "Canada can play a role in emerging Cuba: MP." *National Post,* 6 January 2009.

Blanchfield, Mike. "Countries with dubious human-rights records buoy Canadian arms exporters." *Globe and Mail,* 9 December 2013.

Blanchfield, Mike. "White House thanks Canada for hosting meetings between U.S., Cuba." *Huffington Post,* 17 December 2014. Available online at http://www.huffingtonpost.ca/2014/12/17/white-house-canada-cuba_n_6342342.html, accessed 13 August 2015.

Blight, James G., and Philip Brenner. *Sad and Luminous Days: Cuba's Struggle with the Superpowers after the Missile Crisis.* Lanham, MD: Rowman & Littlefield, 2007.

Boadle, Anthony. "China becomes Cuba's no. 2 trading partner; Only Venezuela supplies more goods to island nation; Canada drops to fourth." *Globe and Mail*, 16 January 2006.

Boadle, Anthony. "Cubans touting smooth transition." *Globe and Mail*, 9 August 2006.

Bolender, Keith. *Cuba Under Siege: American Policy, the Revolution and Its People.* Basingstoke, UK: Palgrave Macmillan, 2012.

Bolender, Keith. *Voices from the Other Side: An Oral History of Terrorism Against Cuba.* London: Pluto Press, 2010.

Bond, Lynne, Sinan Koont, and Sky Stephenson. "The Power of Being There: Study Abroad in Cuba and the Promotion of a 'Culture of Peace.'" *Frontiers* 11 (August 2005): 99–120.

Bondil, Nathalie. *Cuba: Art and History from 1868 to Today.* Montreal: Montreal Museum of Fine Arts, 2009.

Bonenfant, Joseph, ed. *Index de "Parti pris."* Sherbrooke, QC: Université de Sherbrooke, Centre d'étude des littératures d'expression française, 1975.

Bouchard, Gérard. "Neoliberalism in Québec: The Response of a Small Nation under Pressure." In *Social Resilience in the Neoliberal Era*, edited by Peter Hall and Michele Lamont, 267–92. Cambridge: Cambridge University Press, 2013.

Boudreau, Julie-Anne, Roger Keil, and Douglas Young. *Changing Toronto: Governing Urban Neoliberalism.* Toronto: University of Toronto Press, 2009.

Bouthillier, Guy, and Édouard Cloutier. *Trudeau's Darkest Hour: War Measures in Time of Peace, October 1970.* Montreal: Baraka Books, 2010.

Boyer, Harold. "Canada and the Cuban Revolution: A Study in International Relations." PhD diss., Simon Fraser University, 1972.

Brault, Jacques. "Un pays à mettre au monde." *Parti pris* 2, no. 10–11 (1964): 9–25.

Brenner, Philip. "Establishing, Not Restoring, Normal Relations between the United States and Cuba." *AU-SSRC Implications of Normalization: Scholarly Perspectives on U.S.-Cuban Relations.* Washington, DC: American University, Center for Latin American & Latino Studies, April 2015. Available online at http://www.american.edu/clals/Implications-of-Normalization-with-SSRC-Brenner.cfm, accessed 12 August 2015.

Brenner, Philip, Marguerite Rose Jiménez, John Kirk, and William LeoGrande, eds. *A Contemporary Cuba Reader: Reinventing the Revolution.* Lanham, MD: Rowman & Littlefield, 2007.

Buhasz, Laszlo. "Crime in Cuba." *Globe and Mail*, 14 January 2006.

Cabezas, Amalia L. *Economies of Desire: Sex and Tourism in Cuba and the Dominican Republic.* Philadelphia: Temple University Press, 2009.

Canada. "Apply to Immigrate to Canada." Ottawa, n.d. Available online at http://www.cic.gc.ca/english/immigrate/apply.asp.

Canada. "Canada – Temporary Foreign Worker Program Work Permit Holders by Gender, Occupational Skill Level and Year in which Permit(s) Became Effective, Q1 2015–Q1 2017." Ottawa, n.d. Available online at http://open.canada.ca/data/en/dataset/360024f2-17e9-4558-bfc1-3616485d65b9.

Canada. Auditor General of Canada. *Report*. Ottawa, 1996. Available online at https://fas.org/irp/world/canada/docs/oag96/ch9627e.html.

Canada. Commission of Inquiry into the Actions of Canadian Officials in Relation to Maher Arar. *Report of the Events Relating to Maher Arar: Factual Background*, vol. 2. Ottawa: Public Works and Government Services Canada, 2006. Available online at http://epe.lac-bac.gc.ca/100/206/301/pco-bcp/commissions/maher_arar/07-09-13/www.ararcommission.ca/eng/Vol_II_English.pdf.

Canada. Department of National Defence and Canadian Armed Forces. "The Canada-U.S. Defence Relationship." Backgrounder. Ottawa, 4 December 2014. Available online at http://webcache.googleusercontent.com/search?q=cache:xHKTlYDI-xAJ:www.forces.gc.ca/en/news/article.page%3Fdoc%3Dthe-canada-u-s-defence-relationship/hob7hd8s+&cd=1&hl=en&ct=clnk&gl=ca, accessed 29 July 2015.

Canada. Embassy of Canada to Cuba. "Canada-Cuba Relations." Havana, February 2013. Available online at http://www.canadainternational.gc.ca/cuba/bilateral_relations_bilaterales/canada_cuba.aspx?lang=eng, accessed 13 August 2015.

Canada. Embassy of Canada to Cuba. "Factsheet: Cuba." Havana, 2015. Available online at http://www.canadainternational.gc.ca/cuba/bilateral_relations_bilaterales/fs-cuba-fd.aspx?lang=eng, accessed 28 June 2017.

Canada. Parliament. House of Commons. *Debates*, 4th Session, 24th Parliament, vol. 107, 16 December 1960.

Canada. Parliament. House of Commons. *Debates*, 1st Session, 27th Parliament, vol. 14, 10 April 1967.

Canada. Parliament. House of Commons. *Debates*, 2nd Session, 27th Parliament, vol. 3, 17 October 1967.

Canada. International Development Research Centre. "IDRC in Cuba." Ottawa, n.d. Available online at http://www.idrc.ca/EN/Documents/Cuba-eng.pdf, accessed 29 July 2015.

Canadian Foundation for the Americas. *Cuba Today: The Events Taking Place in Cuba and Issues for Canadian Policy*. Ottawa: FOCAL, 1999.

Castro Mariño, Soraya, and Ronald W. Pruessen. *Fifty Years of Revolution: Perspectives on Cuba, the United States, and the World*. Gainesville: University Press of Florida, 2012.

Champagne, André. "À l'horizon, la guerre sainte?" *Cité libre* 38 (June 1961): 27–8.

Charette, Pierre. *Mes dix années d'exil à Cuba*. Montreal: Stanké, 1979.

Charlebois, Robert. "Mon ami Fidel." From album *Longue Distance*. Solution, 1976.

Chase, Michelle. "The Trials: Violence and Justice in the Aftermath of the Cuban Revolution." In *A Century of Revolution: Insurgent and Counterinsurgent Violence during Latin America's Long Cold War*, edited by Greg Grandin and Gilbert M. Joseph, 163–98. Durham, NC: Duke University Press, 2010.

Chester, Bronwyn. "McGill français and Quebec society." *McGill Reporter*, 8 April 1999. Available online at http://reporter-archive.mcgill.ca/Rep/r3114/francais.html.

Child, Marquis. "What Rusk told our NATO Allies." *Washington Post*, 10 May 1961.

Clark, Campbell. "Canada plays host: Seven secret meetings were held over 18 months in Ottawa and Toronto." *Globe and Mail*, 18 December 2014.

Clark, Campbell. "John Baird crafts Canadian foreign policy with a hard edge." *Globe and Mail*, 28 December 2011.

Clark, Joe, Lloyd Axworthy, Flora MacDonald, Bill Graham, John Manley, and Pierre Pettigrew. "Speak up, Mr. Harper – Guantánamo is a disgrace." *Globe and Mail*, 1 February 2007.

Cochrane, Robertson. "Controversy's rocking the Expo boat." *Toronto Star*, 18 April 1967.

Cochrane, Robertson. "Expo Cubans: Only one beard in a boatload." *Toronto Star*, 17 April 1967.

Cohn, D'Vera, Ana Gonzalez-Barrera, and Danielle Cuddington. "Remittances to Latin America Recover – but Not to Mexico." Washington, DC: Pew Research Center, 15 November 2013. Available online at http://www.pewhispanic.org/2013/11/15/remittances-to-latin-america-recover-but-not-to-mexico/.

Cole, Teju. "The White-Savior Industrial Complex." *Atlantic*, 21 March 2012. Available online at http://www.theatlantic.com/international/archive/2012/03/the-white-savior-industrial-complex/254843/, accessed 20 July 2014.

Collinson, Stephen. "2016 Republicans slam Cuba announcement." *CNN*, 19 December 2014. Available online at http://www.cnn.com/2014/12/17/politics/us-cuba-2016-reax/index.html, accessed 22 August 2015.

Collister, Eddie. "Cuba Expo pavilion guarded by police after shell found." *Gazette* (Montreal), 10 April 1967.

Collister, Eddie. "Cubans on arms, obstruction charges." *Gazette* (Montreal), 5 April 1972.

Comisión Económica para América Latina y el Caribe. *Cuba: evolución económica durante 1999*. Santiago de Chile: CEPAL, 2000.

Comisión Económica para América Latina y el Caribe. *La economía cubana: reformas estructurales y desempeño en los noventa*. Mexico City: Fondo de Cultura Económica, 2000.

Constantinou, Costas M. *On the Way to Diplomacy*, vol. 7. Minneapolis: University of Minnesota Press, 1996.

Consuegra Montes, Pavel. "Las relaciones cubano-canadienses en los noventa y la influencia de los Estados Unidos." In *Los retos frente a la internacionalización, lo público, lo privado y la identidad en América Latina y Canadá*, edited by Delia Montero Contreras and Raúl Rodríguez Rodríguez, 51–76. Havana: Empresa Editorial Poligráfica Félix Varela, 2005.

Cooke, Julia. *The Other Side of Paradise: Life in the New Cuba*. Berkeley, CA: Seal Press, 2014.

Cooper, Andrew F. *Canadian Foreign Policy: Old Habits and New Directions*. Scarborough, ON: Prentice-Hall, 1997.

Cooper, Andrew F., and Brian Hocking. "Governments, Non-governmental Organisations and the Re-calibration of Diplomacy." *Global Society* 14, no. 3 (2007): 361–76.

Cooper, Barry. *CFIS: A Foreign Intelligence Service for Canada*. Calgary: Canadian Defence & Foreign Affairs Institute, 2007.

Côté, Guy L., dir. *Les deux côtés de la médaille: risquer sa peau*. Documentary. Montreal: Office national du film du Canada, 1974.

Courneyeur, Felipe Stuart. "Cuban Palm Trees under Vancouver's Lions Gate: A Memoir of the 1960s Fair Play for Cuba Committees in Western Canada." n.p.: Felipe Stuart Courneyeur, 2014. Available online at https://johnriddell.files.wordpress.com/2014/09/cuban-palm-trees-under-vancouvers-lions-gate.pdf, accessed 7 August 2015.

Cuba. Oficina Nacional de Estadísticas e Información. *Anuario estadístico de Cuba 2013*. Havana, 2013.

Cuba. Oficina Nacional de Estadísticas e Información. *Anuario estadístico de Cuba 2015*. Havana, 2016.

Cuba. Oficina Nacional de Estadístícas e Información. "Trade in Goods in Selected Countries and Geographical Areas." Havana, 2013. Available online at http://www.one.cu/aec2012/esp/20080618_tabla_cuadro.htm, accessed 3 June 2014.

Cuba. Oficina Nacional de Estadísticas e Información. *República de Cuba: panorama económico y social*. Havana, April 2014.

Cuba Tourist Board in Canada. "Seven leading Cuban contemporary artists' works on display at new Toronto gallery." Press release, [December 2013]. Available online at http://gocuba.ca/client/news/show.php?news_id=49, accessed 13 August 2015.

Cull, Nicholas J. "'Public Diplomacy': The Evolution of a Phrase." In *Routledge Handbook of Public Diplomacy*, edited by Nancy Snow and Philip M. Taylor, 19–24. Abingdon, UK: Routledge, 2008.

Cull, Nicholas J. "Public Diplomacy: Taxonomies and Histories." *Annals of the American Academy of Political and Social Sciences* 616 (2008): 31–54.

Cumaná, Maria Caridad, Karen Dubinsky, and Xenia Reloba de la Cruz. *My Havana: The Musical City of Carlos Varela*. Toronto: University of Toronto Press, 2014.

Daoudi, M.S., and M.S. Dajani. *Economic Sanctions, Ideals and Experience*. London: Routledge & Kegan Paul, 1983.

d'Apollonia, Luigi. "Au fil du mois: le témoignage de Juana Castro." *Relations* 285, September 1964.

d'Apollonia, Luigi. "Guerre Froide." *Relations* 246, June 1961.

Davidson, Amy. "Barack Obama's Cuba Surprise." *New Yorker*, 17 December 2014. Available online at http://www.newyorker.com/news/amy-davidson/obama-administrations-cuba-surprise, accessed 13 August 2015.

Davies, Natasha Netschay, Lloyd Dolha, and Len O'Connor. *Smoke Signals from the Heart: Fourteen Years of the First Nations Drum*. Vancouver: Totem Pole Books, 2004.

del Pozo Artigas, José. *Les Chiliens au Québec: immigrants et réfugiés, de 1955 à nos jours*. Montreal: Boréal, 2009.

del Pozo Artigas, José, ed. *Exiliados, emigrados y retornados: Chilenos en América y Europa, 1973–2004*. Santiago de Chile: RIL Editores, 2006.

Desjardins, Louise. *Le fils du Che*. Montreal: Boréal, 2008.

Desjardins, Renée. "2007: Translating Culture during the Bouchard-Taylor Commission." In *Translation Effects: The Shaping of Modern Canadian Culture*, edited by Kathy Mezei, Sherry Simon, and Luise von Flotow, 142–61. Montreal; Kingston, ON: McGill-Queen's University Press, 2014.

D'Estéfano Pisani, Miguel A. *La política exterior de la Revolución cubana*. Havana: Editorial Ciencias Sociales, 2002.

Dickason, Olivia Patricia, and David Long. *Visions of the Heart: Canadian Aboriginal Issues*, 3rd ed. Toronto: Oxford University Press, 2011.

Diefenbaker, John G. *One Canada: Memoirs of the Right Honorable John G. Diefenbaker*. Toronto: Macmillan of Canada, 1976.

Diez Acosta, Tómas. *Octubre de 1962: a un paso del holocausto*. Havana: Editorial Política, 2008.

Dion, Robert. *L'Allemagne de* Liberté: *sur la germanophilie des intellectuels québécois*. Ottawa: Presses de l'Université d'Ottawa, 2007.

Dogra, Nandita. *Representations of Global Poverty: Aid, Development and International NGOs*. London: I.B. Tauris, 2014.

Domínguez, Jorge I., Rafael Hernández, and Lorena Barberia. *Debating U.S.-Cuban Relations: Shall We Play Ball?* New York: Routledge, 2012.

Donlan, Sandra. "Cuba's day marked by joyous celebration." *Gazette* (Montreal), 27 July 1967.

Dostaler, Gilles. "Situation révolutionnaire dans les républiques andines." *Parti pris* 5, no. 4 (1968): 17–28.

Duany, Jorge. *Blurred Borders: Transnational Migration between the Hispanic Caribbean and the United States*. Chapel Hill: University of North Carolina Press, 2011.

Dube, Ryan. "Donald Trump's line on Cuba unsettles Latin America." *Wall Street Journal*, 28 November 2016. Available online at https://www.wsj.com/articles/donald-trumps-line-on-cuba-unsettles-latin-america-1480372939.

Dubinsky, Karen. *Babies without Borders: Adoption and Migration across the Americas*. Toronto: University of Toronto Press, 2010.

Dupuy, Pierre. *Expo 67: The Official Souvenir Album*. Toronto: Thomas Nelson, 1968.

Eayrs, James. *The Art of the Possible: Government and Foreign Policy in Canada*. Toronto: University of Toronto Press, 1961.

Eayrs, James. *In Defence of Canada*, vol. 5, *Indochina: Roots of Complicity*. Toronto: University of Toronto Press, 1965.

Entwistle, Mark. "Canada-Cuba Relations: A Multiple-Personality Foreign Policy." In *Our Place in the Sun: Canada and Cuba in the Castro*, edited by Robert Wright and Lana Wylie, 282–301. Toronto: University of Toronto Press, 2009.

Entwistle, Mark. "The Measure of a Revolution: Cuba, 1959–2009." Remarks at a conference, Queen's University, Kingston, ON, 9 May 2009.

Epprecht, Marc. "Work-Study Abroad Courses in International Development Studies: Some Ethical and Pedagogical Issues." *Canadian Journal of Development Studies* 25, no. 4 (2004): 687–706.

Feinsilver, Julie M. "Fifty Years of Cuba's Medical Diplomacy: From Idealism to Pragmatism." *Cuban Studies* 41 (2010): 85–104.

Fizzell, Kathryn, and Marc Epprecht. "Secondary School Experiential Learning Programs in the Global South: Critical Reflections from an Ontario Study." In *Globetrotting or Global Citizenship: Perils and Potential of International Experiential Learning*, edited by Rebecca Tiessen and Robert Huish, 112–39. Toronto: University of Toronto Press, 2014.

Fleras, Augie. *The Media Gaze: Representations of Diversities in Canada.* Vancouver: UBC Press, 2011.

Forrest, V.A.C. "Catholic Church assesses Castro." *Ottawa Journal*, 18 January 1961.

Fournier, Louis. *FLQ: Histoire d'un mouvement clandestin.* Montreal: Québec Amérique, 1982.

Frank, Marc. "Britons freed, Canadian jailed for 9 years in Cuban graft case." *Reuters*, 20 June 2013.

Frank, Marc. "Canadian, British executives face corruption charges in Cuba." *El Nuevo Herald Online*, 15 May 2013.

Frank, Marc. "Canadian businessman goes on trial in Cuban corruption crackdown." *Reuters*, 23 May 2013.

Frank, Marc. "Corruption trial of Canadian trader ends in Cuba, with verdict soon." *Reuters*, 25 May 2013.

Frank Correnti Cigars. "Cuban in Every Way." Toronto, 2012.

Franklin, Jane. *Cuba and the United States: A Chronological History.* Melbourne, NY: Ocean Press, 2006.

Franklin, Jane. "Looking for Terrorists in Cuba's Health System." *Z Magazine*, June 2003. Available online at http://andromeda.rutgers.edu/~hbf/j/health.htm, accessed 25 September 2015.

Freedman, Lawrence. *Kennedy's Wars: Berlin, Cuba, Laos, and Vietnam.* New York: Oxford University Press, 2000.

Freeman, Alan. "Sipping rum and cola, waiting for a Cuba libre." *Globe and Mail*, 7 August 2006.

Freeman, Alan. "A tale of two pesos; Subsidized goods are so shoddy, ordinary Cubans will do almost anything to get convertible pesos." *Globe and Mail*, 12 August 2006.

Freeman, Alan. "Vendors weigh Cuba's future in street markets of Havana," *Globe and Mail*, 3 August 2006.

Freeman, Gary P. "The Quest for Skill: A Comparative Analysis." In *Migration and Refugee Policies: An Overview*, edited by Ann Bernstein and Myron Weiner, 84–118. London: Continuum, 1999.

Friesen, Joe. "Our time to lead: Why Canada needs a flood of immigrants." *Globe and Mail*, 4 May 2012.

Fulford, Robert. *This Was Expo.* Toronto: McClelland & Stewart, 1968.

Fursenko, Aleksandr, and Timothy Naftali. *"One Hell of a Gamble": Khrushchev, Castro, and Kennedy, 1958–1964.* New York: W.W. Norton, 1997.

Gagnon, Gabriel. "Les leçons de l'Amérique latine." *Parti pris* 4, nos 3–4 (1966): 103–7.

Gandhi, Leela. *Affective Communities: Anticolonial Thought, Fin-de-Siècle Radicalism, and the Politics of Friendship.* Durham, NC: Duke University Press, 2006.

Garcia, Maria Cristina. "Canada: A Northern Refuge for Central Americans." *Migration Information Source*, 1 April 2006. Available online at http://www. migrationpolicy.org/article/canada-northern-refuge-central-americans.

Gauthier, Chantal, and France Lord. *Engagées et solidaires: les Sœurs du Bon-Conseil à Cuba 1948–1998*. Montreal: Éditions Carte Blanche, 2013.

Gauvin, Lise. *Parti pris littéraire*. Montreal: Les Presses de l'Université de Montréal, 1975.

Gavshon, Arthur. "Canada set to mediate in the Cuba U.S Dispute." *Washington Post*, 11 May 1961.

Gay, Daniel. *Les élites québécoises et l'Amérique latine*. Montreal: Nouvelle Optique, 1983.

Gee, Marcus. "Enough with the embargo." *Globe and Mail*, 29 February 2008.

Gitlin, Todd. *The Sixties: Years of Hope, Days of Rage*. New York: Bantam, 1993.

Glaser, Brigitte, and Jutta Ernst, eds. *The Canadian Mosaic in the Age of Transnationalism*. Heidelberg: Universitätsverlag Winter, 2010.

Gleijeses, Piero. *Conflicting Missions: Havana, Washington, and Africa, 1959–1976*. Chapel Hill: University of North Carolina Press, 2002.

Glennon, John P., ed. *Foreign Relations of the United States, 1958–1960*, vol. 6, *Cuba*. Washington, DC: US Government Printing Office, 1991.

González Martín, Olga Rosa. "La opinión pública de Estados Unidos y Canadá hacia Cuba: un estudio comparative." In *Políticas públicas, relaciones bilaterales e identidad en Canadá*, edited by Delia Montero Contreras and Raúl Rodríguez Rodríguez, 111–32. Havana: Editorial Félix Galván, 2007.

Gordon, Todd, and Jeffery R. Webber. "Canada's Long Embrace of the Honduran Dictatorship." *CounterPunch*, 19–21 March 2010.

Gott, Richard. *Cuba: A New History*. New Haven, CT: Yale University Press, 2005.

Graham, John. "Bill Warden, 1934–2011: Diplomat, Bus Driver, Sailor, Spy." *Bout de Papier* 26, no. 1 (2011): 31–2.

Grant, George P. *Lament for a Nation*. Montreal; Kingston, ON: McGill-Queen's University Press, 2005.

Grant, Tavia. "In Cuba, it's business as usual; Despite Castro's transfer of power and uncertain prospects, Canadian companies don't expect big changes in the near future." *Globe and Mail*, 2 August 2006.

Grant, Tavia. "'Isolation has not worked': Obama and Castro signal U.S. trade embargo against Cuba must end." *Globe and Mail*, 18 December 2014.

Gronbeck-Tedesco, John A. "The Left in Transition: The Cuban Revolution in US Third World Politics." *Journal of Latin American Studies* 40, no. 4 (2008): 651–73.

Guevara, Ernesto [Che]. "Créer deux, trois … de nombreux Vietnam, voilà le mot d'ordre!" *Parti pris* 5, nos 2–3 (1968): 38–46.

Guevara, Ernesto [Che]. *Journal de Bolivie, 7 novembre 1966–7 octobre 1967*. Montreal: Parti pris, 1969.

Hammond, Georgina. "Everyone knows opening imminent as Expo pavilions shown to press." *Vancouver Sun*, 21 April 1967.

Handelman, Stephen. "How Chavez complicates post-Castro transition." *Globe and Mail*, 2 August 2006.

Harper, Stephen. "Statement by the Prime Minister of Canada on the Death of Venezuelan President Hugo Chávez Frías." Ottawa: Office of the Prime Minister, 2013.

Harper, Tim. "Baird treads softly in Latin America." *Hamilton Spectator*, 23 February 2013.

Harris, Amy Lavender. *Imagining Toronto*. Toronto: Mansfield Press, 2010.

Havana Consulting Group. "CUBA: The Fastest Growing Remittances Market in Latin America." Miami, 23 June 2016. Available online at http://www.thehavanaconsultinggroup.com/en-US/Articles/Article/20.

Havana Consulting Group. "Cuban émigrés sent more than $3.5 billion in in-kind remittances in 2013." Miami, 3 July 2014.

Hayden, Tom. *Listen Yankee! Why Cuba Still Matters*. New York: Seven Stories, 2015.

Haydon, Peter T. *The 1962 Cuban Missile Crisis: Canadian Involvement Reconsidered*. Toronto: Canadian Institute of Strategic Studies, 1993.

Hearn, Adrian H. "Political Dimensions of International NGO Collaboration with Cuba." In *Cuba Today: Continuity and Change since the 'Período Especial,'* edited by Mauricio A. Font, 209–27. New York: Bildner Center for Western Hemisphere Studies and City University of New York, Graduate Center, 2006.

Heine, Jorge. "Canada re-engages with Latin America." *Toronto Star*, 22 February 2013.

Hensler, Alistair. "Creating a Canadian Foreign Intelligence Service." *Canadian Foreign Policy* 3, no. 3 (1995): 15–35.

Herman, Michael. "Diplomacy and Intelligence." *Diplomacy & Statecraft* 9, no. 2 (1998): 1–22.

Hinch, Thomas D. "Cuban Tourism Industry – Its Re-emergence and Future." *Tourism Management* 11, no. 3 (1990): 214–26.

Hoffman, Aaron M. "A Conceptualization of Trust in International Relations." *European Journal of International Relations* 8, no. 3 (2002): 375–401.

Holmes, John W. "Canada and the United States in World Politics." *Foreign Affairs* 40, no. 1 (1961): 105–17.

Houpt, Simon. "Targeting Canada's "invisible" Hispanic community." *Globe and Mail*, 17 November 2011.

Hudson, Peter James. "Imperial Designs: The Royal Bank of Canada in the Caribbean." *Race & Class* 52, no. 1 (2015): 33–48.

Huish, Robert. *Where No Doctor Has Gone Before: Cuba's Place in the Global Health Landscape.* Waterloo, ON: Wilfrid Laurier University Press, 2013.

Hull, Chris. "Our Arms in Havana: British Military Sales to Batista and Castro 1958–59." *Diplomacy and Statecraft,* 18, no. 3 (2007): 593–616.

Hyndman, Jennifer. *Research Summary on Resettled Refugee Integration in Canada.* Toronto: York University, Centre for Refugee Studies, 2 May 2012.

James, Geoffrey. "Pavilion contrasts show Cuba's two faces." *Montreal Star,* 17 April 1967.

Jedwab, Jack, and Victor Armony. "¡Hola Canadá! Spanish Is Third Most Spoken Language." *FOCALPoint* 8, no. 4 (2009): 14–16.

Jensen, Kurt F. "Canada's Foreign Intelligence Interview Program, 1953–90." *Intelligence and National Security* 19, no. 1 (2004): 95–104.

Jensen, Kurt F. *Cautious Beginnings: Canadian Foreign Intelligence, 1939–51.* Vancouver: UBC Press, 2008.

Jensen, Kurt F. "Toward a Canadian Foreign Intelligence Service." *Bout de Papier* 22, no. 2 (2006): 21–3.

Jiang, Wenran. "The Dragon Returns: Canada in China's Quest for Energy Security." In *Issues in Canada-China Relations,* edited by Pitman B. Potter and Thomas Adams, 169–97. Toronto: Canadian International Council, 2011.

Jiménez Gómez, Rubén. *Octubre de 1962: la mayor crisis de la era nuclear.* Havana: Editorial Ciencias Sociales, 2003.

Jimenez, Marina. "Dec. 2, 1961/Castro declares he's a Marxist-Leninist." *Globe and Mail,* 2 December 2010.

Jorgensen, Shelane, and Lynette Schulz. "Global Citizenship Education (GCE) in Post-Secondary Institutions: What Is Protected and What Is Hidden under the Umbrella of GCE." *Journal of Global Citizenship and Equity Education* 2, no. 1 (2012): 1–17.

Kahn, E.J. "Our Far-Flung Correspondents: Expo." *New Yorker,* 10 June 1967.

Kane, Molly. "International NGOs and the Aid Industry: Constraints on International Solidarity." *Third World Quarterly* 34, no. 8 (2013): 1505–15.

Kapcia, Antoni. *Cuba in Revolution: A History since the Fifties.* London: Reaktion Books, 2008.

Kapcia, Antoni. *Cuba: Island of Dreams.* Oxford: Berg, 2000.

Karch, Pierre. *Noëlle à Cuba.* Sudbury, ON: BCF, 2007.

Karita, Juan. "South American leaders demand apology in plane row." *Miami Herald Online,* 5 July 2013.

Kenneally, Rhona Richman, and Johanne Sloan. *Expo 67: Not Just a Souvenir.* Toronto: University of Toronto Press, 2010.

Kennedy, Mark. "Division on Cuba ends Summit of Americas on frosty note." *Ottawa Citizen*, 16 April 2012.

Keung, Nicholas. "Canada immigration: How a decade of policy change has transformed the immigration landscape." *Toronto Star*, 15 February 2013.

Kimber, Stephen. *What Lies Across the Water: The Real Story of the Cuban Five.* Winnipeg: Fernwood, 2013.

Kirk, John. "Cuban-American groups threaten Canadian tourists." *Globe and Mail*, 11 October 1993.

Kirk, John M. "Foreword." In *Cuba Solidarity in Canada: Five Decades of People-to-People Foreign Relations*, edited by Nino Pagliccia, xiii–xix. Victoria, BC: Friesen Press, 2014.

Kirk, John M., and H. Michael Erisman. *Cuban Medical Internationalism: Origins, Evolution, and Goals.* New York: Palgrave Macmillan, 2009.

Kirk, John M., and Peter McKenna. "Canada and Latin America: Assessing the Harper Government's Americas Strategy." In *Communautés atlantiques: asymétries et convergences*, edited by Dorval Brunelle, 133–58. Montreal: Éditions IEIM, 2012.

Kirk, John M., and Peter McKenna. *Canada-Cuba Relations: The Other Good Neighbor Policy.* Gainesville: University Press of Florida, 1997.

Kirk, John M., and Peter McKenna. *Canadá-Cuba: sesenta años de relaciones bilaterales.* Havana: Editorial de Ciencias Sociales, 2007.

Kirk, John M., and Peter McKenna. "Stephen Harper's Cuba Policy: From Autonomy to Americanization?" *Canadian Foreign Policy* 15, no. 1 (2009): 21–39.

Kissinger, Henry. *White House Years.* Boston: Little, Brown, 1979.

Klassen, Jerome. *Joining Empire: The Political Economy of the New Canadian Foreign Policy.* Toronto: University of Toronto Press, 2014.

Klepak, Hal. "Canada, Cuba and Latin America: A Paradoxical Relationship." In *Our Place in the Sun: Canada and Cuba in the Castro Era*, edited by Robert Wright and Lana Wylie, 22–43. Toronto: University of Toronto Press, 2009.

Koring, Paul. "Castro lets go of power; brother likely to succeed him; After half a century, the fiery and loquacious revolutionary – who outlasted nine U.S. presidents – quietly steps aside." *Globe and Mail*, 20 February 2008.

Kornbluh, Peter. "A New Deal with Cuba: Caribbean Détente, After a Half-Century of Conflict." *Nation*, 23 December 2014. Available online at https://www.thenation.com/article/new-deal-cuba/, accessed 13 August 2015.

Kornbluh, Peter. "The Posada File: Part II." National Security Archive Electronic Briefing Book 157. Washington, DC: George Washington University, National Security Archive, 9 June 2005. Available online at http://nsarchive.gwu.edu/NSAEBB/NSAEBB157/.

Kröller, Eva-Marie. "Expo 67: Canada's Camelot." *Canadian Literature* 152/153 (1997): 36–51.

Krull, Catherine. *Cuba in Global Context: International Relations, Internationalism, and Transnationalism.* Gainesville: University Press of Florida, 2014.

Krull, Catherine. "Families First? An Assessment of Quebec's Family Policies." *Canadian Review of Social Policy* 59 (2008): 93–101.

Krull, Catherine. "From the King's Daughters to the Quiet Revolution: A Historical Overview of Family Structures and the Role of Women in Quebec." In *Voices: Essays on Canadian Families,* edited by Marion Lynn, 369–96. Toronto: Nelson Canada, 1996.

Krull, Catherine. "Quebec's Alternative to Pronatalism." *Population Today* 29, no. 8 (2001): 3–4.

Kushner, Marilyn S. "Exhibiting Art at the American National Exhibition in Moscow, 1959: Domestic Politics and Cultural Diplomacy." *Journal of Cold War Studies* 4, no. 1 (2002): 6–26.

Lacaille, Jacques. *En mission dans la tourmente des dictatures, 1965–1986.* Montreal: Novalis, 2014.

Lacosta, Walt. "Bomb a publicity stunt?" *Ottawa Citizen,* 23 September 1966.

Lambert-Racine, Michaël. "Trade and Investment: Canada-China." Publication 2016-68-E. Ottawa: Library of Parliament, 19 September 2016. Available online at https://lop.parl.ca/Content/LOP/ResearchPublications/2016-68-e.html#show/hide.

Lamonde, Yvan. *La modernité au Québec,* 3 v. Montreal: Fides, 2011.

Lanctôt, Jacques. *Les plages de l'exil.* Montreal: Stanké, 2010.

Langhorne, Richard. "The Diplomacy of Non-State Actors." *Diplomacy & Statecraft* 16, no. 2 (2005): 331–9.

Langley, Lester D. *The Cuban Policy of the United States: A Brief History.* New York: John Wiley and Sons, 1968.

Lapointe, Simon. "Canadian Trade and Investment Activity: Canada–Cuba." Publication 2010-87-E. Ottawa: Library of Parliament, 4 November 2010. Available online at http://www.lop.parl.gc.ca/Content/LOP/ResearchPublications/2010-87-e.pdf, accessed 13 May 2017.

Larsen, Sarah, and Susan Lord. "Cinema in Search of the Public in Cuba: A Translation of 'En Cuba el cine busca al publico' published in *Cine Cubano* 13 (1963)." *Public* 40 (2009). Available online at http://public.journals.yorku.ca/index.php/public/article/view/31977/29238, accessed 13 August 2015.

Larson, Deborah Welch. "Trust and Missed Opportunities in International Relations." *Political Psychology* 18, no. 3 (1997): 701–34.

Lauzon, Adèle. "Cuba." *Les Écrits du Canada français* 14 (1962): 259–309.

Lauzon, Adèle. "Essayer de comprendre." *Cité libre* 31 (November 1960): 28–30.

Lauzon, Adèle. *Pas si tranquille*. Montreal: Boréal, 2008.

Lawson, Bruce. "Cuba's day at Expo mixes air of fiesta with heavy security." *Globe and Mail*, 27 July 1967.

LeBlanc, Daniel. "Family hopes for release of Canadian businessman." *Globe and Mail*, 19 December 2014.

LeoGrande, William M. "What Trump misses about Cuba." *New York Times*, 1 December 2016. Available online at http://www.nytimes.com/2016/12/01/opinion/what-trump-misses-about-cuba.html, accessed 15 December 2016.

LeoGrande, William M., and Peter Kornbluh. *Back Channel to Cuba: The Hidden History of Negotiations between Washington and Havana*. Chapel Hill: University of North Carolina Press, 2014.

LeoGrande, William M., and Julie M. Thomas. "Cuba's Quest for Economic Independence." *Journal of Latin American Studies* 34, no. 2 (2002): 325–63.

Létourneau, Sophie. "Des pesos." In *Polaroïds*. Montreal: Québec Amérique, 2006.

Levitt, Peggy, and Nina Glick Schiller. "Conceptualizing Simultaneity: A Transnational Social Field Perspective on Society." *International Migration Review* 38, no. 3 (2004): 1002–39.

Lindsay, Colin. "The Caribbean Community in Canada 2001." Cat. no. 89-621-XIE – No. 7. Ottawa: Statistics Canada, 2007. Available online at http://www.statcan.gc.ca/pub/89-621-x/89-621-x2007007-eng.pdf.

Livermore, Daniel. "Does Canada Need a Foreign Intelligence Agency?" CIPS Policy Brief 3. Ottawa: Centre for International Policy Studies, 2009.

Lord, Barry. "A Visit to Expo '67." *Canadian Dimension* 4 (September–October 1967): 30–2.

Lowenthal, Mark. *Intelligence: From Secrets to Policy*. Washington, DC: CQ Press, 2006.

Lutjens, Sheryl. "The Subject(s) of Academic and Cultural Exchange." In *Debating U.S.-Cuban Relations: Shall We Play Ball?* edited by Jorge I. Domínguez, Rafael Hernández, and Lorena G. Barberia, 218–36. New York: Routledge, 2012.

Macadam, Ivison S. "Canada and the Commonwealth." *International Affairs* 20, no. 4 (1994): 519–26.

MacCharles, Tonda. "Harper vows to make Tories 'Canada's party.'" *Toronto Star*, 11 June 2011.

Major, Robert. *Partis pris: idéologies et littérature*. Montreal: Hurtubise HMH, 1979).

Major, Robert. "*Parti pris*: idéologies et literature." PhD diss., University of Ottawa, 1979.

Manji, Firoze. "The Missionary Position: NGOs and Development in Africa." *International Affairs* 78, no. 3 (2002): 567–83.

Martín Gómez, Victor. "El impacto de las mineras canadienses en México." *Rebelión*, 22 March 2012.

Martínez Reinosa, Milagros. "Academic Diplomacy: Cultural Exchange Between Cuba and the United States." In *Debating U.S.-Cuban Relations: Shall We Play Ball?* edited by Jorge I. Domínguez, Rafael Hernández, and Lorena G. Barberia, 237–55. New York: Routledge, 2012.

Martínez Reinosa, Milagros. "Cuba and the United States: New Opportunities for Academic Diplomacy." *LASAFORUM* 42, no. 2 (2011): 4–6.

Masey, Jack, and Conway Lloyd Morgan. *Cold War Confrontations: US Exhibitions and Their Role in the Cultural Cold War*. Baden, Germany: Lars Müller Publishers, 2008.

McDowall, Duncan. *Quick to the Frontier: Canada's Royal Bank*. Toronto: McClelland & Stewart, 1993.

McKenna, Peter. *Canada and the OAS; From Dilettante to Full Partner*. Montreal; Kingston, ON: McGill-Queen's University Press, 1995.

McKenna, Peter, ed. *Canada Looks South: In Search of an Americas Policy*. Toronto: University of Toronto Press, 2012.

McKenna, Peter, and John M. Kirk. "Canadian-Cuban Relations: A Model for the New Millennium?" In *Cuban Transitions at the Millennium*, edited by Eloise Linger and John Cotman, 351–71. Largo, MD: International Development Options, 2000.

McKenna, Peter, and John M. Kirk. "Canadian-Cuban Relations: Muddling Through the 'Special Period.'" In *Our Place in the Sun: Canada and Cuba in the Castro Era*, edited by Robert Wright and Lana Wylie, 163–94. Toronto: University of Toronto Press, 2009.

McKenna, Peter, and John M. Kirk. "Through Sun and Ice: Canada, Cuba, and Fifty Years of 'Normal' Relations." In *Canada Looks South: In Search of an Americas Policy*, edited by Peter McKenna, 149–79. Toronto: University of Toronto Press, 2012.

McKenzie, Robert. "Visitors cool to Cuba's Expo pitch." *Toronto Star*, 2 May 1967.

McKercher, Asa. "'Complicated and Far-Reaching': The Historical Foundations of Canadian Policy toward Cuba." In *Cuba in a Global Context: International Relations, Internationalism, and Transnationalism*, edited by Catherine Krull, 109–24. Gainesville: University Press of Florida, 2014.

McKercher, Asa. "A Half-hearted Response? Canada and the Cuban Missile Crisis, 1962." *International History Review* 33, no. 2 (2011): 335–52.

McKercher, Asa. "The Most Serious Problem? Canada-US Relations and Cuba, 1962." *Cold War History* 12, no. 1 (2012): 69–88.

McKercher, Asa. "Southern Exposure: Diefenbaker, Latin America and the Organization of American States." *Canadian Historical Review* 93, no. 1 (2012): 57–80.

McMinimy, Mark A. "US Agricultural Trade with Cuba: Current Limitations and Future Prospects." Washington, DC: Congressional Research Service, 1 October 2015. Available online at https://fas.org/sgp/crs/row/R44119.pdf, accessed 13 May 2017.

McNeely, Sean. "Close but no cigar for these Cubans." *Globe and Mail*, 29 April 2006.

McNeil, Calum. "To Engage or Not to Engage: An (a)ffective Argument in Favour of a Policy of Engagement with Cuba." *Canadian Foreign Policy Journal* 16, no. 1 (2010): 155–73.

McPherson, Alan. "The Limits of Populist Diplomacy: Fidel Castro's April 1959 Trip to North America." *Diplomacy & Statecraft* 18, no. 1 (2007): 237–68.

McQuigge, Michelle. "End of golden era for Canadian tourists in Cuba? Affordable vacations will be hard come by, experts say." *MoneySense*, 18 December 2014. Available online at http://www.moneysense.ca/spend/travel/end-of-golden-era-for-canadian-tourists-in-cuba/, accessed 13 August 2015.

Mickiewicz, Ellen. "Efficacy and Evidence: Evaluating U.S. Goals at the American National Exhibition in Moscow, 1959." *Journal of Cold War Studies* 13, no. 4 (2011): 138–71.

Milan, Anne. *Migration: International, 2009*. Ottawa: Statistics Canada, July 2011. Available online at http://www.statcan.gc.ca/pub/91-209-x/2011001/article/11526-eng.pdf.

Millar, Ruch Wayne. "Terrorist Provocations against Cuba: A Selection of Items Retrieved from News Sources, 1992–96." Saskatoon, SK, 18 April 1996. Available online at http://www.hartford-hwp.com/archives/43b/142.html.

Miller, David, and Douglas Arrowsmith. *Witness to a City: David Miller's Toronto*. Toronto: Cormorant, 2010.

Millin, Leslie. "Cuba lifts sugar-cane curtain to tell of the continuing revolution." *Globe and Mail*, 11 April 1967.

Mills, Sean. *The Empire Within: Postcolonial Thought and Political Activism in Sixties Montreal*. Montreal; Kingston, ON: McGill-Queen's University Press, 2010.

Milroy, Sarah. "Art in Cuba: Freedom?" *Globe and Mail*, 8 April 2006.

Missionnaires Oblats de Marie Immaculée. "Canada's External Relations with Latin America." Brief submitted to the Canadian Government. Montreal, 1970.

Molinaro, Dennis. "Calculated Diplomacy: John Diefenbaker and the Origins of Canada's Cuba Policy." In *Our Place in the Sun: Canada and Cuba in the Castro Era*, edited by Robert Wright and Lana Wylie, 75–95. Toronto: University of Toronto Press, 2009.

Morley, Morris. "The United States and the Global Economic Blockade of Cuba: A Study in Political Pressures on America's Allies." *Canadian Journal of Political Science* 7, no. 1 (1984): 25–48.

Morris, Emily. "Unexpected Cuba." *New Left Review* 88 (July–August 2014): 5–45.

Munton, Don. "Intelligence Cooperation Meets International Studies Theory: Explaining Canadian Operations in Castro's Cuba." *Intelligence and National Security* 24, no. 1 (2009): 119–38.

Munton, Don. "Ottawa and the Great Missile Showdown." *Globe and Mail*, 22 October 1992.

Munton, Don. "Our Men in Havana: Canadian Foreign Intelligence Operations in Castro's Cuba." *International Journal* 70, no. 1 (2015): 23–39.

Munton, Don, and David Vogt. "Inside Castro's Cuba: The Revolution and Canada's Embassy in Havana." In *Our Place in the Sun: Canada and Cuba in the Castro Era*, edited by Robert Wright and Lana Wylie, 44–74. Toronto: University of Toronto Press, 2009.

Munton, Don, and David Welch. *The Cuban Missile Crisis: A Concise History*, 2nd ed. New York: Oxford University Press, 2012.

Murray, Stuart. "Consolidating the Gains Made in Diplomacy Studies: A Taxonomy 1." *International Studies Perspectives* 9, no. 1 (2008): 22–39.

Muse, Robert. "US Presidential Action on Cuba: The New Normalization?" *Americas Quarterly* (Fall 2014). Available online at http://www.americasquarterly.org/charticles/the-new-normalization/, accessed 13 August 2015.

Neborak, Jacklyn. "Family Reunification? A Critical Analysis of Citizenship and Immigration Canada's 2013 Reforms to the Family Class." RCIS Working Paper 2013/8. Toronto: Ryerson University, Ryerson Centre for Immigration and Settlement, 2013.

Newman, Peter C. *Renegade in Power: The Diefenbaker Years*. Toronto: McClelland & Stewart, 1963.

Nicol, Heather N. "Canada-Cuba Relations: An Ambivalent Media and Policy." *Canadian Foreign Policy Journal* 16, no. 1 (2010): 103–18.

Nicholson, Patrick. *Vision and Indecision*. Don Mills, ON: Longmans Canada, 1968.

Nossal, Kim Richard. *The Politics of Canadian Foreign Policy*. Scarborough, ON: Prentice-Hall, 1985.

Obama, Barack. "Barack Obama on the Cuban Embargo." *YouTube*, 20 January 2004. Available online at https://www.youtube.com/watch?v=I1FoZyRIDFE, accessed 14 July 2009.

Obama, Barack. "Our main goal: Freedom in Cuba," *Miami Herald*, 21 August 2007.

Obama, Barack. "President Obama Speech in Cuba." *C-SPAN*, 22 March 2016. Available online at https://www.youtube.com/watch?v=wEw3H0C-Lj8, accessed 1 June 2016.

Obama, Barack. "Statement by the president on Cuba policy changes." Press release, 17 December 2014. Washington, DC: White House, Office of the Press Secretary. Available online at https://www.whitehouse.gov/the-press-office/2014/12/17/statement-president-cuba-policy-changes, accessed 13 August 2015.

Ogelsby, J.C.M. *Gringos from the Far North: Essays in the History of Canadian-Latin American Relations, 1866–1968*. Toronto: Macmillan of Canada, 1976.

O'Malley, Martin. "Lurking guards, rats and revolution add Tracy touch to Cuban Pavilion." *Globe and Mail*, 10 May 1967.

Organization of American States. *International Migration of the Americas: Second Report of the Continuous Reporting System on International Migration in the Americas (SICREMI) 2012*. Washington, DC: OAS, 2012. Available online at http://www.oecd.org/els/mig/G48952_WB_SICREMI_2012_ENGLISH_REPORT_LR.pdf.

Oziewicz, Estanislao. "Brother expected to 'be there for some time.'" *Globe and Mail*, 2 August 2006.

Parent, Gilbert. "Canada and Cuba Mark 50 Years of Dialogue." *Canadian Speeches: Issues of the Day* 9, no. 7 (1995): 36–9.

Pelletier, Jean, and Claude Adams. *The Canadian Caper: The Inside Story of the Daring Rescue of Six American Diplomats Trapped in Tehran*. Toronto: Macmillan of Canada, 1981.

Pérez Jr, Louis A. *Cuba and the United States: Ties of Singular Intimacy*. Athens: University of Georgia Press, 2003.

Pérez Jr, Louis A. *Cuba in the American Imagination: Metaphor and the Imperial Ethos*. Chapel Hill: University of North Carolina Press, 2008.

Pérez Jr, Louis A. *On Becoming Cuban: Identity, Nationality, and Culture*. Chapel Hill: University of North Carolina Press, 1999.

Pérez Jr, Louis A. *The Structure of Cuban History: Meanings and Purpose of the Past*. Chapel Hill: University of North Carolina Press, 2013.

Pérez Jr, Louis A. "The United States Reengages Cuba: The Habit of Power." *AU-SSRC Implications of Normalization: Scholarly Perspectives on U.S.-Cuban Relations*. Washington, DC: American University, Center for Latin American

& Latino Studies, April 2015. Available online at http://www.american.
edu/clals/Implications-of-Normalization-with-SSRC-Perez.cfm, accessed
13 August 2015.

Pérez Jr, Louis A. *The War of 1898: The United States and Cuba in History and
Historiography*. Chapel Hill: University of North Carolina Press, 1998.

Pérez-López, Jorge, and Carmelo Mesa-Lago. "Cuban GDP Statistics under
the Special Period: Discontinuities, Obfuscation, and Puzzles." *Cuba in
Transition* 19 (2009): 153–67.

Pérez-Stable, Marifeli. *The United States and Cuba: Intimate Enemies*. New York:
Routledge, 2011.

Perreault, Luc. "Cuba va célébrer chaudement notre Expo et son
independence." *La Presse* (Montreal), 20 July 1967.

Péteri, György. "Sites of Convergence: The USSR and Communist Eastern
Europe at International Fairs Abroad and at Home." *Journal of Contemporary
History* 47, no. 1 (2012): 3–12.

Piazza, François. "Punta del Este: la farce est jouée." *Cité libre* 45 (March 1962):
18–19.

Pilon, Michael. "Expo 67 was the centre piece for me in 1967." Letter to the
editor, *Ottawa Citizen*, 5 June 2007.

Pinto, Sam. "Faded Red: The Rise and Fall of Radicalism at McGill." *McGill
Tribune*, 4 November 2014. Available online at http://mcgilltribune.com/
mcgill-marxism-faded-red/.

Plaza, Dwaine. "Migration caribéenne et intégration au Canada: à la poursuite
du rêve d'ascension sociale (1900–1998)." In *Dynamiques migratoires de la
Caraïbe*, Terres d'Amérique 6, 141–57. Paris: Karthala, 2007.

Plaza, Dwaine, and Frances Henry, eds. *Returning to the Source: The Final Stages
of the Caribbean Migration Circuit*. Kingston, Jamaica: University of the West
Indies Press, 2006.

Plokhii, Olesia, and James Munson. "Canada top target for Chinese foreign
investment last year." *iPolitics.ca*, 13 February 2013.

Plummer, Brenda Gayle. "Castro in Harlem: A Cold War Watershed." In
Rethinking the Cold War: Essays on Its Dynamics, Meaning, and Morality, edited
by Allen Hunter, 133–53. Philadelphia: Temple University Press, 1997.

Poisson, Jacques. "La difficile naissance de Presse-Québec." *Parti pris* 2, no. 2
(1964): 237–48.

Poznanska, Alice. "La contre-révolution cubaine végète en Floride." *Cité libre*
41 (November 1961): 11–13.

Princen, Thomas. "NGOs: Creating a Niche in Environmental Diplomacy." In
Environmental NGOs in World Politics: Linking the Local and the Global, edited
by Thomas Princen and Matthias Finger, 29–47. London: Routledge, 1994.

Pulfer, Rachel. "Castro's Favourite Capitalist." *Walrus*, 12 December 2009. Available online at https://thewalrus.ca/castros-favourite-capitalist/, accessed 7 April 2017.

Quigley, Neil C. "The Bank of Nova Scotia in the Caribbean." *Business History Review* 63 (1989): 797–838.

Rajotte, Pierre. "Introduction." In *Le voyage et ses récits au XXe siècle*, edited by Pierre Rajotte. Quebec City: Nota bene, 2005.

Ramachadran, Vijaya. "Is Haiti Doomed to Be the Republic of NGOs?" Washington, DC: Center for Global Development, 1 December 2012. Available online at http://www.cgdev.org/blog/haiti-doomed-be-republic-ngos, accessed 22 July 2014.

Reyes Trejo, Alfredo. "Dos crónicas." *Verde Olivo*, 7 May 1967.

Richler, Mordecai. "Notes on Expo." *New York Review of Books*, 14 September 1967.

Rifaat, Cherif. *Immigrants Adapt, Countries Adopt ... Or Not: Fitting into the Cultural Mosaic*. Montreal: New Canadian Press, 2004.

Ritter, Archibald R.M. "Canadian-Cuban Economic Relations: Past, Present and Prospective." In *Our Place in the Sun: Canada and Cuba in the Castro Era*, edited by Robert Wright and Lana Wylie, 246–81. Toronto: University of Toronto Press, 2009.

Ritter, Archibald R.M. "Shifting Realities in Special Period Cuba." *Latin American Research Review* 45, no. 3 (2010): 229–38.

Robinson, H. Basil. *Diefenbaker's World*. Toronto: University of Toronto Press, 1989.

Rochlin, James. *Discovering the Americas: The Evolution of Canadian Foreign Policy towards Latin America*. Vancouver: UBC Press, 1994.

Rochon, Lise. "Exposé: la réforme agraire à Cuba." *Parti pris* 4, nos 5–6 (1967): 63–70.

Rodríguez García, Rolando. *Cuba: las máscaras y las sombras: la primera ocupación*. Havana: Editorial Ciencias Sociales, 2007.

Rodríguez Rodríguez, Raúl. "Canada, Cuba, and the United States as Seen in Cuban Diplomatic History, 1959–1962." Cambridge, MA: Harvard University, David Rockefeller Center for Latin American Studies, 2010.

Roig-Franzia, Manuel. "Cuba repeals ban on its citizens staying in hotels on island." *Washington Post*, 31 March 2008. Available online at http://www.washingtonpost.com/wp-dyn/content/article/2008/03/31/AR2008033100703.html, accessed 13 August 2015.

Romero, Angel. "Interview with José Ortega of Lula Lounge Records in Toronto." *World Music Central*, 26 February 2013. Available online at http://worldmusiccentral.org/2013/02/26/interview-with-jose-ortega-of-lula-lounge-records-in-toronto/.

Sagebien, Julia. *Canadians in Cuba: Getting to Know Each Other Better*. Halifax: Dalhousie University, Centre for International Business Studies, 1998.

Said, Edward. *Culture and Imperialism*. New York: Vintage Books, 1993.

Sallot, Jeff. "U.S. sees strategic advantage in Ottawa's Cuban ties." *Globe and Mail*, 19 December 2006.

Sanschagrin, Albert, et al. *Lutte pour l'Amérique latine: journée d'étude organisée par les Ligues du Sacré-Cœur, avec le concours de vingt associations, sous la présidence de S.E. Mgr Albert Sanschagrin et de S.E. Mgr Agustín Adolfo Herrera*. Montreal: Le Gésu, 1961.

Saunders, Doug. "How Fidel missed his Mandela moment." *Globe and Mail*, 23 February 2008.

Schoultz, Lars. *Beneath the United States: A History of US Policy toward Latin America*. Cambridge, MA: Harvard University Press, 1998.

Schoultz, Lars. *That Infernal Little Cuban Republic*. Chapel Hill: University of North Carolina Press, 2011.

Shamsie, Yasmine, and Ricardo Grinspun. "Missed Opportunity: Canada's Re-engagement with Latin America and the Caribbean." *Canadian Journal of Latin American and Caribbean Studies* 35, no. 69 (2010): 177–99.

Sher, Julian. "Canadian entrepreneur who blew whistle on Cuban corruption faces 12-year term," *Toronto Star*, 16 May 2013.

Sher, Julian. "Toronto man sentenced to 9 years in Cuba on corruption charge." *Toronto Star*, 20 June 2013.

Sher, Julian, and Juan O. Tamayo. "Canada's ambassador to Cuba to attend Toronto man's corruption trial in Havana." *Toronto Star*, 23 May 2013.

Sherritt International Corporation. *2012 Annual Report*. Toronto, 2013.

Shulsky, Abram N., and Gary James Schmitt. *Silent Warfare: Understanding the World of Intelligence*, 3rd ed. Dulles, VA: Potomac Books, 2002.

Simmons, Alan B. "Latin American Migration to Canada: New Linkages in the Hemispheric Migration and Refugee Flow System." *International Journal* 48, no. 2 (1993): 282–309.

Smith, Wayne, and Esteban Morales Domínguez. *Subject to Solution: Problems in Cuban-U.S. Relations*. Boulder, CO: Lynne Rienner, 1988.

Soderlund, Walter C., Ronald H. Wagenberg, and Stuart H. Surlin. "The Impact of the End of the Cold War on Canadian and American TV News Coverage of Cuba: Image Consistency or Image Change?" *Canadian Journal of Communication* 23, no. 2 (1998): 217–31.

Soublière, Roger. "Hasta la victoria siempre!" *Parti pris* 5, no. 7 (1968): 27–37.

Spain. Instituto Nacional de Estadística. *Foreign Population by Nationality and Country of Birth*. Madrid, 2013.

Spencer, Rochelle. *Development Tourism: Lessons from Cuba*. Farnham, UK: Ashgate, 2010.

Spizzirri, Francesca. "Cuba's Tourism Minister Says Canada Remains Cuba's 'Top Priority.'" *Travel Week*, 10 May 2016. Available online at http://www.travelweek.ca/news/cubas-tourism-minister-says-canada-remains-cubas-top-priority/, accessed 13 May 2017.

Stankiewicz, Audrey. "The Last Word." *Canadian Architect* 12 (July–December 1967): 50.

Statistics Canada. "Figure 1: Number of Canadians whose mother tongue is one of the 22 immigrant languages reported by more than 100,000 persons, Canada, 2011." Ottawa, 2015. Available online at https://www12.statcan.gc.ca/census-recensement/2011/as-sa/98-314-x/2011003/fig/fig3_2-1-eng.cfm.

Statistics Canada. "Figure 1: Population growth (in percent) in number of persons who reported speaking one of the top 25 immigrant languages most often at home, Canada, 2006 to 2011." Ottawa, 2015. Available online at http://www12.statcan.ca/census-recensement/2011/as-sa/98-314-x/2011001/fig/fig1-eng.cfm.

Statistics Canada. *2011 National Household Survey: Data Tables*. Ottawa, 2011. Available online at http://www12.statcan.gc.ca/nhs-enm/2011/dp-pd/dt-td/Rp-eng.cfm?LANG=E&APATH=3&DETAIL=0&DIM=0&FL=A&FREE=0&GC=0&GID=0&GK=0&GRP=0&PID=105396&PRID=0&PTYPE=105277&S=0&SHOWALL=0&SUB=0&Temporal=2013&THEME=95&VID=0&VNAMEE=&VNAMEF=.

Statistics Canada. *2011 National Household Survey: Immigration and Ethnocultural Diversity*. Ottawa, 2013.

Sterling, Harry. "Stephen Harper out of step with Latin America over Cuba!" *Toronto Star*, 20 April 2012.

Stubbs, Jean. "Transnationalism and the Havana Cigar: Commodity Chains, Networks, and Knowledge Circulation." In *Cuba in Global Context: International Relations, Internationalism and Transnationalism*, edited by Catherine Krull, 227–42. Gainesville: University Press of Florida, 2014.

Taitt, Ria, "Canada: Embargo up to U.S., Cuba." *Miami Herald Online*, 19 April 2009.

Tamkin, Nicholas. *Britain, Turkey and the Soviet Union, 1940-45: Strategy, Diplomacy and Intelligence in the Eastern Mediterranean*. Basingstoke, UK: Palgrave Macmillan, 2009.

Teigrob, Robert. *Warming Up to the Cold War: Canada and the United States' Coalition of the Willing, from Hiroshima to Korea*. Toronto: University of Toronto Press, 2009.

Threinen, Norman J. *A Religious-Cultural Mosaic: A History of Lutherans in Canada*. Vulcan, AB: Today's Reformation Press, 2006.

Tiessen, Rebecca, and Robert Huish. "International Experiential Learning and Global Citizenship." In *Globetrotting or Global Citizenship: Perils and Potential of International Experiential Learning*, edited by Rebecca Tiessen and Robert Huish, 3–20. Toronto: University of Toronto Press, 2014.

Tolvaisas, Tomas. "Cold War 'Bridge-Building': U.S. Exchange Exhibits and Their Reception in the Soviet Union, 1959–1967." *Journal of Cold War Studies* 12, no. 4 (2010): 3–31.

Torreira Crespo, Ramón, and José Buajasán Marrawi. *Operación Peter Pan: un caso de guerra psicológica contra Cuba*. Havana: Editoria Politica, 2000.

Trent, Bill. "They Fight Castro from Afar." *Ottawa Citizen Weekend Magazine*, 9 November 1966.

Trotta, Daniel. "CEO's gifts to Cubans led to 15-year sentence." *Globe and Mail*, 4 October 2014.

Trudeau, Justin. "Statement by the Prime Minister of Canada on the death of former Cuban President Fidel Castro." Press release, Ottawa, 26 November 2016. Available online at http://pm.gc.ca/eng/news/2016/11/26/statement-prime-minister-canada-death-former-cuban-president-fidel-castro, accessed 9 December 2016.

Truslow, Francis. *Report on Cuba*. Washington, DC: International Bank for Reconstruction and Development, 1951.

Tulchin, Joseph, Andrés Serbín, and Rafael Hernández, eds. *Cuba and the Caribbean: Regional Issues and Trends in the Post-Cold War Era*. Lanham, MD: Rowman & Littlefield, 1997.

United Nations. General Assembly. "Election of the Human Rights Council." New York, 2012. Available online at http://www.un.org/en/ga/67/meetings/elections/hrc.shtml, accessed 13 August 2015.

United Nations. General Assembly. "General Assembly elects 47 members of new Human Rights Council; marks 'new beginning' for human rights promotion, protection." Press release, New York, 9 May 2006. Available online at http://www.un.org/press/en/2006/ga10459.doc.htm, accessed 13 August 2015.

United Nations Development Programme. "Summary Human Development Report 2013." New York: UNDP, 2013. Available online at http://hdr.undp.org/sites/default/files/hdr2013_en_summary.pdf, accessed 29 July 2015.

United States. Department of Commerce. "Foreign Trade: Trade in Goods with Cuba." Washington, DC, 2013. Available online at http://www.census.gov/foreign-trade/balance/c2390.html, accessed 29 June 2013.

United States. Library of Congress. Hispanic Division. "Teller and Platt Amendments." Washington, DC, n.d. Available online at http://www.loc.gov/rr/hispanic/1898/teller.html, accessed 29 July 2015.

United States Census Bureau. "Census Bureau releases 2011 American Community Survey estimates." Washington, DC, 19 September 2012. Available online at https://www.census.gov/newsroom/releases/archives/american_community_survey_acs/cb12-175.html.

US-Cuba Trade and Economic Council. "Foreign Investment and Cuba." New York, 2001.

Vadeboncœur, Pierre. "Les salauds contre Cuba." *Socialisme*, no. 3–4 (1964): 79–88.

Valdes, Rosa Tania. "Prices, not politics slow Cuba tourism; Tourists finding better value elsewhere." *Globe and Mail*, 7 March 2007.

Vallières, Pierre. "Cuba révolutionnaire" [Revolutionary Cuba]. *Parti pris* 5, no. 1 (1967): 19–25.

Vallières, Pierre. *White Niggers of America: The Precocious Autobiography of a Quebec "Terrorist."* Toronto: McClelland & Stewart, 1971.

Vatz Laaroussi, M. "L'intergénérationnel dans les réseaux transnationaux des familles immigrantes: mobilité et continuité." In *L'intergénérationnel: regards pluridisciplinaires*, edited by R. Hurtubise and A. Quéniart, 267–93. Rennes, France: Presses de l'École des hautes études en santé publique, 2009.

Verma, Sonia. "Cuba's challenge: Open up economy, but stay communist; Historic gathering of top-ranking officials debate a secret document aimed at lifting country out of stagnation." *Globe and Mail*, 21 April 2011.

Virdee, Harjit, and Don Munton. "Missing Links: An Organizational Archaeology of Intelligence Structures in Canada's Foreign Ministry." Unpublished.

Walkom, Thomas. "Justin Trudeau loses his nerve, skips Fidel Castro's funeral: Walkom," *Toronto Star*, 30 November 2016. Available online at https://www.thestar.com/opinion/commentary/2016/11/30/justin-trudeau-loses-his-nerve-skips-fidel-castros-funeral-walkom.html, accessed 15 December 2016.

Warren, Cristina. "Canada's Policy of Constructive Engagement with Cuba: Past, Present and Future." Background Briefing. Ottawa: Canadian Foundation for the Americas, 2003.

Wasem, Ruth Ellen. "Cuban Migration to the United States: Policy and Trends." Washington, DC: Congressional Research Service, 2 June 2009. Available online at https://fas.org/sgp/crs/row/R40566.pdf, accessed 13 August 2015.

Wells, Paul. "What about the whole communist thing?" *Maclean's Online*, 22 July 2011.

Werner, Michel, and Michel Espagne, eds. *Transferts: les relations interculturelles dans l'espace franco-allemand*. Paris: Éditions Recherche sur les civilisations, 1985.

Whittington, Les, and Bruce Campion-Smith. "Canada 'facilitated' Cuba-U.S. talks, Stephen Harper says." *Toronto Star*, 17 December 2014. Available online at http://www.thestar.com/news/canada/2014/12/17/canada_facilitated_cubaus_talks_stephen_harper_says.html, accessed 13 August 2015.

Wight, Martin. *Power Politics*. Harmondsworth, UK: Penguin, 1978.

Wilkinson, Stephen. "Just How Special Is 'Special': Britain, Cuba, and US Relations 1958–2008, an Overview." *Diplomacy and Statecraft* 20, no. 2 (2009): 291–308.

Winter, James W. "Fidel Castro, Jimmy Carter and George W. Bush in the Canadian News Media: A Critical Analysis." Windsor, ON: University of Windsor, 2006.

Woo, Yuen Pau. "Chinese Lessons: State-owned Enterprises and the Regulation of Foreign Investment in Canada." *China Economic Journal* 7, no. 1 (2014): 21–38.

World Health Organization. "Cuba." Geneva, 2015. Available online at http://www.who.int/countries/cub/en/, accessed 13 August 2015.

World Integrated Trade Solution. "Product Exports by Canada to Cuba 2013." Washington, DC: World Bank, 2014. Available online at http://wits.worldbank.org/CountryProfile/Country/CAN/Year/2013/TradeFlow/Export/Partner/CUB/Product/all-groups, accessed 31 July 2015.

Wright, Cynthia. "Between Nation and Empire: The Fair Play for Cuba Committees and the Making of Canada-Cuba Solidarity in the Early 1960s." In *Our Place in the Sun: Canada and Cuba in the Castro Era*, edited by Robert Wright and Lana Wylie, 96–120. Toronto: University of Toronto Press, 2009.

Wright, Robert. "'Northern Ice': Jean Chrétien and the Failure of Constructive Engagement in Cuba." In *Our Place in the Sun: Canada and Cuba in the Castro Era*, edited by Robert Wright and Lana Wylie, 195–222. Toronto: University of Toronto Press, 2009.

Wright, Robert. *Our Man in Tehran: Ken Taylor, the CIA and the Iran Hostage Crisis*. Toronto: HarperCollins Canada, 2010.

Wright, Robert. *Three Nights in Havana: Pierre Trudeau, Fidel Castro and the Cold War World*. Toronto: HarperCollins Canada, 2007.

Wright, Robert, and Lana Wylie, eds. *Our Place in the Sun: Canada and Cuba in the Castro Era*. Toronto: University of Toronto Press, 2009.

Wylie, Lana. "Ambassador MD: The Role of Health and Biotechnology in Cuban Foreign Policy." In *Our Place in the Sun: Canada and Cuba in the Castro Era*, edited by Robert Wright and Lana Wylie, 223–45. Toronto: University of Toronto Press, 2009.

Wylie, Lana. *Perceptions of Cuba: Canadian and American Policies in Comparative Perspective*. Toronto: University of Toronto Press, 2010.

Young, Mary, and Susan Henders. "'Other Diplomacies' and the Making of Canada-Asia Relations." *Canadian Foreign Policy Journal* 18, no. 3 (2012): 375–88.

Zolov, Eric. "Discovering a Land 'Mysterious and Obvious': The Renarrativizing of Postrevolutionary Mexico." In *Fragments of a Golden Age: The Political Culture in Mexico since 1940*, edited by Gilbert Joseph, Anne Rubenstein, and Eric Zolov, 234–72. Durham, NC: Duke University Press, 2001.

Contributors

Keith Bolender is the author of *Voices from the Other Side: An Oral History of Terrorism against Cuba* and of *Cuba Under Siege: American Policy, the Revolution and its People*.

Maurice Demers teaches history at the Université de Sherbrooke, and is the author of *Connected Struggles: Catholics, Nationalists, and Transnational Relations between Mexico and Quebec, 1917–1945*.

Karen Dubinsky is a professor in the Department of History and the Department of Global Development Studies at Queen's University, Kingston. She is the author or co-editor of numerous books, including *My Havana: The Musical City of Carlos Varela* and *Cuba Beyond the Beach: Stories of Life in Havana*.

Luis René Fernández Tabío is an economist and professor at the Centro de Estudios Hemisféricos y sobre Estados Unidos at the University of Havana. He has published widely including on Cuba-US relations and on Cuba and the Canadian and US economies.

Olga Rosa González Martin is a specialist in communications and professor at the Centro de Estudios Hemisféricos y sobre Estados Unidos at the University of Havana. She has been a visiting scholar at the David Rockefeller Center of Latin American Studies, Harvard University.

John M. Kirk is a professor in the Department of Spanish and Latin American Studies at Dalhousie University. He is the author or co-editor of over a dozen books on Cuba, including, most recently, *Healthcare without Borders: Understanding Cuban Medical Internationalism.*

Catherine Krull is a professor of Sociology and currently Dean of the Faculty of Social Sciences at the University of Victoria. She was formerly editor-in-chief of the *Canadian Journal of Latin American and Caribbean Studies,* and is the co-editor of the volume *Cuba in a Global Context: International Relations, Internationalism, and Transnationalism.* With Jean Stubbs, she is part of a major research project on Cuban diasporas in Canada and western Europe.

Rosa López-Oceguera is a specialist in US foreign policy and global issues at the Centro de Estudios Hemisféricos y sobre Estados Unidos at the University of Havana.

Peter McKenna is a professor in the Department of Political Studies at the University of Prince Edward Island in Charlottetown. He has published widely on Cuba, and is the editor, most recently, of *Canada Looks South: In Search of an Americas Policy.*

Asa McKercher is currently Assistant Professor of History, Royal Military College of Canada. He has published widely in Canadian international history and international relations. His book, *Camelot and Canada: Canadian-American Relations in the Kennedy Era,* was nominated for the John W. Dafoe Book Prize, recognizing the best non-fiction book on Canada.

Calum McNeil is a doctoral student in political science at McMaster University, Hamilton. His publications include "To Engage or Not to Engage: An (A)ffective Argument in Favour of a Policy of Engagement with Cuba," in *Canadian Foreign Policy Journal.*

Don Munton was the founding chair of the International Studies program at the University of Northern British Columbia. He has been a Fulbright Fellow, a NATO Fellow, and more recently a visiting professor at Kwansei Gakuin University, Japan, and Arthur M. Schlesinger Fellow at the John F. Kennedy Presidential Library. He conducts research and writes in the areas of intelligence, security, and environmental policy. He is co-author of *The Cuban Missile Crisis: A Concise History,* co-editor of *Canadian Foreign Policy: Selected Cases* and of *Rethinking*

National Security: The Public Dimension, editor of *Hazardous Waste Siting and Democratic Choice*, and author of numerous articles and book chapters. He is currently writing a book to be entitled *Canadian Spies in Castro's Cuba*.

Michel Nareau teaches literary studies at the Université du Quebec à Montréal.

Raúl Rodríguez Rodríguez is a specialist in twentieth-century history and international relations at the Centro de Estudios Hemisféricos y sobre Estados Unidos at the University of Havana. His publications focus on Cuban, US, and Canadian relations and on Cuban foreign policy.

Jean Stubbs is Professor Emerita at the London Metropolitan University, where she directed the Caribbean Studies Centre (2002–9). She has published widely on Cuba and the Caribbean on themes connected to race, gender, labour, and migration. With Catherine Krull, she is part of a major research project on Cuban diasporas in Canada and western Europe.

Cynthia Wright is Assistant Professor in the School of Gender, Sexuality, and Women's Studies at York University, Toronto. She has published widely on themes connected to migration and migrant politics, as well as on Cuba and Canada, and was a contributor to *Our Place in the Sun: Canada and Cuba in the Castro Era*.

Lana Wylie is Associate Professor of Political Science at McMaster University, Hamilton. Her publications include *Our Place in the Sun: Canada and Cuba in the Castro Era* (with Robert Wright) and *Perceptions of Cuba: Canadian and American Policies in Comparative Perspective*.

Index